Constitutional Statecraft in Asian Courts

Constitutional Statecraft in Asian Courts

YVONNE TEW

OXFORD
UNIVERSITY PRESS

OXFORD
UNIVERSITY PRESS

Great Clarendon Street, Oxford, OX2 6DP,
United Kingdom

Oxford University Press is a department of the University of Oxford.
It furthers the University's objective of excellence in research, scholarship,
and education by publishing worldwide. Oxford is a registered trade mark of
Oxford University Press in the UK and in certain other countries

First Edition published in 2020
Impression: 1

Published in the United States of America by Oxford University Press
198 Madison Avenue, New York, NY 10016, United States of America

British Library Cataloguing in Publication Data
Data available

Library of Congress Control Number: 2020934582

ISBN 978–0–19–871683–9

Printed and bound by
CPI Group (UK) Ltd, Croydon, CR0 4YY

Author's Note

Gajah sama gajah berjuang, pelanduk mati di tengah-tengah.

Malay proverb

There's an old Malay saying, "When elephants fight, it is the mouse deer between them that perishes." In February 2020, the Malaysian government, led by the democratically elected, multi-ethnic Pakatan Harapan coalition, the Alliance of Hope, collapsed. While the Malaysian public watched, largely from the sidelines, political giants battled for power in a high-stakes drama.

As this book goes to press, Malaysia has a new prime minister and government. By the end of February, Mahathir Mohamad was replaced as premier after the country's king appointed Muhyiddin Yassin as the head of government. Muhyiddin came into power at the helm of a predominantly mono-ethnic Malay-Muslim coalition, which includes member parties of the Barisan Nasional alliance that had ruled Malaysia since independence before being voted out in 2018 in the wake of corruption scandals. Amid threats that a vote of no confidence would be brought at the next parliamentary sitting, the newly appointed prime minister delayed the start of the next parliamentary session by more than two months.

Malaysia's change of government, triggered by political defections and followed by a dizzying leadership battle among allies-turned-rivals as well as unprecedented royal intervention, stands in stark contrast to the country's democratic transition two years earlier. In 2018, Pakatan Harapan scored a stunning electoral victory over the Barisan Nasional coalition that had ruled the country for six decades. Malaysia's democratic breakthrough had stood out as an outlier to the global rise of illiberal nationalism. Now that tale of democratic triumph appears to have faltered.

Ultimately, though, this volatility underscores a central theme of this book: political fates are fickle, and narratives focused on political heroes are fraught. It is thus imperative, as this book argues, to focus on the institutions that can help build and strengthen an enduring constitutional democracy. Courts and constitutional statecraft are crucial to that endeavor.

Political landscapes are ever-changing, after all, and Malaysia's remains in flux. As of March 2020, Prime Minister Muhyiddin announced an expansive Cabinet lineup that further consolidates his new administration. Still, ever since it ascended to power, the Perikatan Nasional coalition has been beset by charges that it lacks any electoral mandate. Even if this governing coalition manages to cling to power, it will be far more fragile than the Barisan Nasional ruling regime that enjoyed decades-long dominance. And it is in fragile democracies that the role of courts in constitutional state-building is all the more important.

As contemporary political crises only underscore, the crafting and strengthening of institutions that can help a constitutional democracy endure is ever more urgent.

Yvonne Tew
March 12, 2020

Acknowledgements

This book reveals the intersection of my intellectual passions and personal experiences. The seeds of this project were sown years ago; growing up in Malaysia's richly pluralistic yet fractured society, I became aware of the challenges of negotiating race, religion, and rights in an emerging constitutional democracy. The ideas that developed into this work have travelled with me across three continents and various institutional homes—from Malaysia to the Cambridge in England as well as the one in Massachusetts, and from New York to Washington, D.C. Along the journey I have been blessed by many mentors, colleagues, friends, and family.

At the University of Cambridge, where I began my first foray into the law, I am grateful to David Feldman for his encouraging confidence in a tentative first-year undergraduate and his steadfast support since that first supervision, which sparked an enduring interest in constitutional law. Fond thanks to Nicky Padfield at Fitzwilliam College for subtly but firmly nudging me toward academia, with her inimitable style, and for her infectious enthusiasm. At Harvard Law School, Noah Feldman and Jeannie Suk encouraged my pursuits while I was there and continued to guide me in the years after, providing indispensable counsel.

When I returned to the University of Cambridge to pursue my doctorate, Christopher Forsyth was outstanding in his supervision of my doctoral dissertation. His thoughtful direction, intellectual enthusiasm, and ability to combine good sense and good humor helped shape my project and ambitions. I also thank David Feldman and H.P. Lee for their deeply reflective and engaging examination of my Ph.D. dissertation, which took place in the same room in which I had had that first constitutional law supervision as an undergraduate. My doctoral research was made possible by the generous support of the Gates Cambridge Scholarship established by the Bill and Melinda Gates Foundation. The Tunku Abdul Rahman Graduate Scholarship Fund at St Catharine's College, Cambridge, and its capable graduate administrator, Heather Green, also helped support me in various ways. My fellow counterparts at the Faculty of Law and at St. Catharine's College were a marvelous part of my time at Cambridge and I am so glad that they remain lifelong friends.

Columbia Law School and New York University School of Law provided intellectually rich environments in which I carried out my post-doctoral fellowships. At Columbia Law School, during my time as Associate-in-Law, I benefited from the tremendous generosity of several faculty, especially Jamal Greene, Philip Genty, Kent Greenawalt, Sudhir Krishnaswamy, Benjamin Liebman, Henry Monaghan, Anthea Roberts, and Tim Wu, and also gained from engaging with the other fellows I met there. New York University Law School offered a stimulating global law school environment: my thanks to Sam Issacharoff, in particular, and the immensely supportive community of global scholars and program administrators, like Un Kyung Park, all of whom made memorable my experience as a Hauser Global Law Fellow.

At Georgetown University Law Center, I found a welcoming academic home and wonderful community of colleagues. I am grateful for friends and colleagues who have read drafts, offered comments, and talked through the ideas in this book project with me, especially Bill Buzbee, Peter Byrne, Lily Faulhaber, Jim Feinerman, Wally Mlyniec, Eloise Pasachoff, Alvaro Santos, Brad Snyder, Larry Solum, Madhavi Sunder, William Treanor, Franz Werro, and Robin West, as well as for many others who have encouraged and advised me as I navigated my scholarly trajectory. I am grateful to Dean William Treanor for generous institutional and financial support, including writing grants and a semester of research leave, as well as to Associate Deans John Mikhail and Josh Teitelbaum for their accommodating counsel on all matters research related. My thanks also to Raphael Calel, my colleague and friend at the McCourt School, with whom I have had many conversations about this book and its minutiae, for patiently reading several drafts and offering incisive suggestions on each one. Betsy Kuhn deserves special mention for her outstanding copyediting, thoughtful comments, and exceedingly careful reading of the entire manuscript. The librarians and staff at the Georgetown Law Library, in particular Marylin Raisch, Yelena Rodriguez, Erie Taniuchi, and Tammy Tran, provided consistent and prompt help with research materials. For great faculty assistance, I thank Victoire Saperstein, Alina Schmidt, and Sarah Naiman. I have also been aided by many excellent research assistants over the past several years at Georgetown Law: Ana Halsey, Anna Brennan, Kendall Edell, Keir Elmonairy, Danielle Flanagan, Caleb Graves, Ron Havas, Caitlin Hynes, Brock Jacobi, John Lapin, and Panida Pollawit. In particular, I thank Julie Bessler and Memmi Rasmussen who provided superb assistance in the final stages of putting together this book manuscript, with good cheer.

I benefited greatly from presenting parts of this book at many venues. I am grateful to the organizers and participants at workshops and colloquia at the Georgetown University Law Center, the University of Texas Law School, Tulane Law School, the University of Melbourne, the University of Minnesota, the University of Washington School of Law, the University of Victoria, and the University of Cambridge. I also presented draft chapters at the annual conferences of the International Society of Public Law in Santiago and Hong Kong; the annual meeting of the American Society of Comparative Law in Columbia, Missouri; the Annual Law and Religion Roundtable at the University of Toronto Law School; the International Association of Constitutional Law World Congress in Seoul; the annual meetings of the Law and Society Association; and the Asian Constitutional Law Forum in Bangkok. And I was delighted to deliver the 2020 Transitional

Justice Annual Lecture based on this work at the Center for Transnational Legal Studies in London.

At Oxford University Press, I thank Jamie Berezin and the editorial team for their assistance throughout the process of producing this book. I also appreciate the peer reviewers who provided constructive feedback on an earlier version of this manuscript.

Over the years that I have been engaged in this project, I have interacted with many lawyers, activists, academics, and friends who have provided illuminating perspectives. For perceptive insights into developments on the ground in Malaysia, I am especially grateful to K. Shanmuga, Si Ying Kong, Keith Leong, and Ganesan Nethi, and also thank Surendra Ananth, Choong Yeow Choy, Firdaus Husni, Johan Shamsuddin Sabaruddin, Khoo Boo Teong, Lim Wei Jiet, and Malik Imtiaz Sarwar. I have benefited, too, from many conversations about constitutional law and politics with scholars in Singapore, particularly Jaclyn Neo, Dian Shah, Andrew Harding, and Kevin Tan. Friends in D.C., and those who visited, provided welcome camaraderie and conversations while I was in the process of completing this book. Since our time as Cambridge undergraduates, Harsh Sancheti and I have had numerous talks that have helped provoke many ideas, not least on this book.

I feel privileged, and excited, to be part of a wider community of scholars in the field of comparative constitutional law, many of whom I regard as mentors and friends. For their intellectual generosity and enthusiasm, I thank Rosalind Dixon, Tom Ginsburg, Vicki Jackson, Heinz Klug, H.P. Lee, David Landau, David Law, Russell Miller, Yaniv Roznai, Kim Lane Scheppele, Mark Tushnet, Mila Versteeg, and Po Jen Yap. Sam Issacharoff has been a distinctive influence ever since our first meeting on the Upper West Side. With his signature mix of iconoclasm and enthusiasm, he has never failed to challenge me to expand my horizons in the law and beyond. Jamal Greene has been an extraordinary source of inspiration, wisdom, and friendship. His exceptional intellectual guidance has been foundational to my development as a scholar, even as his friendship has deeply enriched my life.

Finally, abiding thanks to my friends and family who have enhanced my life with joy in countless ways. Friends across four continents have added sparkle and color, warmth and meaning, and continue to do so from near and far. My aunts, uncles, and grandmother have watched over me through the years with unstinting affection and affirmation. My sister, Michelle, is the source of unwavering support, pragmatic wisdom, and consummate sisterly care. I am thankful for her and Grant, for their love, humor, and confidence. My parents have been unfailing in their love and support for as long as I can remember. I am profoundly grateful for their enduring faith, unconditional sacrifice, and steadfast love. This work is due in part to the influence and memory of my granny, Nonie: her *joie de vivre* and ability to transcend racial and religious boundaries through her friendship and generosity remain an inspiration. To her, my family, and all Malaysians who continue to hope, I dedicate this book.

Table of Contents

Table of Cases xv
Table of Legislation xix

Introduction: Building Constitutionalism in Fragile Democracies 1
I. Courts, Constitutional Politics, and Statecraft 4
II. Situating Constitutions and Courts in Context 6
III. Book Schema 13

PART I SETTING THE SCENE

1. Rights Rhetoric 21
I. Introduction 21
II. False Dichotomies 22
A. Universalism and Relativism 22
B. Individualism and Communitarianism 24
C. Civil-Political Rights and Economic Development 25
III. Rights Rhetoric and Practice 27
A. "Asian Values" and Rights Discourse 27
B. Emerging Rights Consciousness 28
IV. Constitutionalism in Context 31
V. Conclusion 33

2. Constitutional Adjudication and Constitutional Politics 34
I. Introduction 34
II. Setting the Stage 35
A. Malaysia: The Birth of a Nation and the Independence Constitution 35
1. Historical Background 35
2. Malaysia's Constitutional System 37
B. Singapore: Separation and Statehood 39
1. Historical Background 39
2. Singapore's Constitutional System 40
III. Constitutional Adjudication and Judicial Review 41
A. Constitutional Adjudication 41
B. Judicial Review 44
IV. Interpreting the Constitution in Malaysia and Singapore 46
A. The "Four Walls" of the Constitution 46
B. Strict Formalism and Literalism 49
C. The Basic Structure Doctrine: Unconstitutional Constitutional Amendments? 53

V. Courts and Constitutional Politics 57
A. Judicial Review in Political Context 57
B. The Judiciary's Uneven Journey So Far 62
VI. Conclusion 65

PART II A FRAMEWORK FOR CONSTITUTIONAL ADJUDICATION

3. Constitutional History 69
I. Introduction 69
II. Constitutional Foundings 70
A. The Making of Malaysia's *Merdeka* Constitution 70
B. The Singapore Constitution's Pragmatic Origins 75
III. Constitutional History and the Original Constitutional Framework 78
A. The Constitution's Original Framework 78
B. Constitutional History and Constitutional Change 80
IV. Constitutional History in Practice 81
A. Malaysia's Article 3(1) Constitutional Religion Clause 81
B. Singapore's Originalist Case Study: *Yong Vui Kong v. Public Prosecutor* 86
V. Conclusion 91

4. The Separation of Powers 92
I. Introduction 92
II. Conceptualizing the Separation of Powers 93
III. Separation of Powers in Context 95
A. Malaysia's 1988 Constitutional Amendment 95
B. The Judiciary's Response to the 1988 Constitutional Amendment 96
IV. Restoring the Separation of Powers 98
A. The Malaysian Judiciary's Constitutional Moment: *Semenyih Jaya* 98
B. Singapore's Emerging Jurisprudence on the Separation of Powers 105
V. Conclusion 106

5. The Rule of Law 107
I. Introduction 107
II. Contextualizing the Rule of Law 108
A. Conceptualizing the Rule of Law 108
B. Rule of Law Rhetoric in Practice 109
C. Locating a Basis for the Rule of Law 112
III. Developing the Rule of Law 113
A. *Indira Gandhi*: Entrenching the Basic Structure Doctrine in Malaysia 113
B. Singapore: "All Power has Legal Limits" 117
IV. Judicial Power and Judicial Strategy 119
V. Conclusion 122

6. Courts in Transition 123
I. Introduction 123
II. Courts and Judicial Review in Evolving Democracies 125
A. In Judges or Legislatures We Trust? 125
B. Deconstructing Dialogue 127
C. Judicial Empowerment and Judicial Role 131
III. Strategic Assertions of Judicial Power 133
A. *Semenyih Jaya:* Malaysia's *Marbury* Moment? 133
B. Judicial Entrenchment of Power: *Indira Gandhi* 137
IV. Forward: A Framework for Constitutional Adjudication 140
A. The Basic Structure of the Constitution 140
B. Purposive Interpretation of Constitutional Rights 147
C. Proportionality Analysis 149
V. Conclusion 153

PART III APPLYING CONSTITUTIONAL ADJUDICATION IN PRACTICE

7. Judicializing Religion 157
I. Introduction 157
II. Constitutionalizing Religion 159
III. Politicizing Religion 163
IV. Judicializing Religion 165
A. Jurisdictional Deference and Religious Authority 167
1. Apostasy Cases: Individuals Seeking to Leave Islam 167
2. Child Conversion and Custody Cases 171
B. Judicial Islamization of the Article 3(1) Constitutional Clause 173
V. Application: Adjudicating Religion and Rights 179
A. Judicial Power of the Civil Courts Inherent to Constitution's Basic Structure 180
B. Interpreting Religion and Rights Purposively 184
C. Operationalizing Proportionality 187
VI. Conclusion 187

8. Balancing Security and Liberty 189
I. Introduction 189
II. Emergency Powers and Security Laws 190
A. Constitutional Emergency Powers 190
B. Preventive Detention 192
C. National Security and Public Order Laws 194
III. Judicial Review and State Power 197
A. Confrontation 197
B. Retreat 200
C. Resurgence 200

IV. Application: Judicial Balancing of Security and Liberty 204
A. From Deference to Proportionality 205
B. Protecting the Constitution's Basic Structure 210
V. Conclusion 212

Conclusion: Beyond Sisyphus and Hercules 214

Bibliography 221
Books and Articles 221
Government Publications 231
Reports 232
Index 233

Table of Cases

NATIONAL COURTS

Canada

Reference re Secession of Quebec [1998] 2 SCR 217(Canada) 85–86
Reference re Senate Reform [2014] 1 SCR 704 (Canada). 148, 186

India

Kesavananda Bharati v. State of Kerala, A.I.R. 1973 S.C. 1461 (India) 53, 55, 80–81, 101, 103–4, 105, 133, 135, 138, 140–41, 143, 144, 180, 216
Minerva Mills Ltd. v. India, 1981 1 S.C.R. 206 (India) 138, 140–41
Mithu v. State of Punjab A.I.R. 1983 S.C. 473 (India). 90

Malaysia

A Child & Ors. v. Jabatan Pendaftaran Negara [2017] 4 Malayan L.J. 440 (C.A.) 183
Ah Thian v. Government of Malaysia [1976] 2 Malayan L.J. 112 (F.C.) 44–45
Alma Nudo v. Public Prosecutor [2019] 5 Current L.J. 780 (F.C.). 64, 66, 121, 151–52, 207, 216–17
Attorney General v. Arthur Lee Meng Kuang [1987] 1 Malayan L.J. 207 (S.C.) 46–47
Azmi Mohamad Azam v. Director of Jabatan Agama Islam Sarawak & Others [2016] 6 Current L.J. 562 (H.C.) 170–71
Berthelsen v. Director-General of Immigration [1987] 1 Malayan L.J. 134 (S.C.) 57, 95
Che Omar bin Che Soh v. Public Prosecutor [1988] 2 Malayan L.J. 55 (S.C). 166
Danaharta Urus v. Kekatong [2004] 2 Malayan L.J. 257 (F.C.) 50, 92, 109–10, 112–13
Dato' Menteri Othman v. Dato' Ombi Syed Alwi [1981] 1 Malayan L.J. 29 (F.C.). 43
Datuk Seri Anwar Ibrahim v. Kerajaan Malaysia & Anor [2017] M.L.J.U. 338 (H.C.) 212
Datuk Seri Anwar Ibrahim v. Kerajaan Malaysia & Anor [2018] M.L.J.U. 289 (C.A.) 212
Datuk Seri Khalid Abu Bakar & Ors. v. N. Indra P Nallathamby & Anor Appeal [2014] 9 Current L.J. 15 (C.A.) 148
Daud Mamat v. Majlis Agama Islam [2001] 2 Current L.J. 161 (H.C.) 176
Government of Malaysia v. Mat Shuhaimi [2018] 2 Malayan L.J. 133 (F.C.) 50–51, 202, 207–8
Government of the State of Kelantan v. Government of the Federation of Malaya & Tunku Abdul Rahman Putra Al-Haj [1963] 29 Malayan L.J. 355 (H.C.) 46–47, 53–54
Haris Fatillah Mohd Ibrahim v. Suruhanjaya Pilihan Raya Malaysia [2017] 3 Malayan L.J. 543 (C.A.). 47
Indira Gandhi a/p Mutho v. Pengarah Jabatan Agama Islam Perak & Ors. [2018] 1 Malayan L.J. 545 (F.C.) 3–4, 9, 10–11, 15, 16, 30, 47, 55, 56–57, 63, 66, 85–86, 107–8, 113–17, 119–20, 121, 122, 124, 137–40, 141, 142–44, 145, 146, 148–49, 158–59, 172–73, 179, 180, 182, 183, 184, 185–86, 188, 211, 215, 217
Indira Gandhi a/p Mutho v. Pengarah Jabatan Agama Islam Perak [2013] 5 Malayan L.J. 552 (H.C.) 47, 157, 168–69, 172
Indira Gandhi v. Patmanathan a/l Krishnan [2015] 7 Malayan L.J. 153 (H.C.). 172

Inspector-General of Police v. Tan Sri Raja Khalid Bin Raja Harun [1988] 1 Malayan L.J. 182 (S.C.) 57, 95, 198, 199
Jenny bt Peter @ Nur Muzdhalifah Abdullah v. Director of Jabatan Agama Islam Sarawak & Ors [2017] 1 Malayan L.J. 340 (C.A.) 171
JRI Resources Sdn Bhd v. Kuwait Finance House (Malaysia) Berhad [2019] 5 Current L.J. 569 (F.C.) 94, 184
Karam Singh v. Menteri Hal Ehwal Dalam Negeri [1969] 2 Malayan L.J. 129 (F.C.) 197–98
Karpal Singh v. Minister for Home Affairs [1988] 1 Malayan L.J. 468 (H.C.) 57, 95, 199
Karpal Singh v. Public Prosecutor [2016] M.L.J.U. 1675 (F.C.) 10–11
Kekatong v. Danaharta Urus [2003] 3 Malayan L.J. 1 (C.A.) 112–13
Kok Wah Kuan v. Public Prosecutor [2007] 5 Malayan L.J. 174 (C.A.) 96–97
Latifah bte Mat Zin v. Rosmawati bte Sharibun & Anor. [2007] 5 Malayan L.J. 101 (F.C.) 117
Lee Mau Seng v. Minister for Home Affairs [1971] 2 Malayan L.J. 137 (H.C.) 110–11, 197–98, 199
Lee Swee Fei v. Menteri Hal Ehwal Dalam Negeri Malaysia [1994] 2 Malayan L.J. 468 (H.C.) 200
Lim Kit Siang v. Dr. Mahathir Mohamed [1987] 1 Malayan L.J. 383 (S.C.) 10–11, 199
Lina Joy v. Majlis Agama Islam Wilayah Persekutuan [2004] 2 Malayan L.J. 119 (H.C.) 28, 169, 170–71, 175, 177–78, 184–85
Lina Joy v. Majlis Agama Islam Wilayah Persekutuan [2005] 6 Malayan L.J. 193 (C.A.) 25, 169, 171, 177–78
Lina Joy v. Majlis Agama Islam Wilayah Persekutuan [2007] 4 Malayan L.J. 585 (F.C.) 10–11, 25, 114, 167–68, 169–70, 171, 172–73, 176, 177–78, 179, 181, 182–83, 217–18
Loh Kooi Choon v. Government of Malaysia [1977] 2 Malayan L.J. 187 (F.C.) 46–47, 53–54, 81, 141, 143
Mamat bin Daud v. Government of Malaysia [1988] 1 Malayan L.J. 119 (S.C.) 7–8, 41
Marathaei Sangulullai v. Syarikat JG Containers Sdn Bhd [2003] 2 Malayan L.J. 337 (C.A.) 112
Maria Chin Abdullah v. Pendakwa Raya [2016] M.L.J.U. 249 (H.C.) 10–11, 62–63
Mat Shuhaimi v. Government of Malaysia [2017] 1 Malayan L.J. 436 (C.A.) 151, 202, 207–8
Menteri Dalam Negeri & Ors. v. Titular Roman Catholic Archbishop of Kuala Lumpur [2013] Malayan L.J. 468 (C.A.) 25, 173–74, 185, 186, 187
Meor Atiqulrahman bin Ishak v. Fatimah bte Sihi [2000] 5 Malayan L.J. 375 (H.C.) 175
Mohamad Ezam Noor v. Ketua Polis Negara [2002] 4 Malayan L.J. 449 (F.C.) 200–1
Mohamed Noor bin Othman v. Mohamed Yusoff Jaafar [1988] 2 Malayan L.J. 129 (H.C.) ... 57
Muhammad Hilman v. Kerajaan Malaysia [2011] 6 Malayan L.J. 507 (C.A.) 54, 62
Nik Nazmi bin Nik Ahmad v. Public Prosecutor [2014] 4 Malaysan L.J. 157 (C.A.) 10–11, 62–63, 98, 201, 206–7
Pathmanathan a/l Krishnan v. Indira Gandhi a/p Mutho [2016] 4 Malayan L.J. 455 (C.A.) 47, 137–38, 148–49, 172, 177
Persatuan Aliran Kesedaran Negara v. Minister of Home Affairs [1988] 1 Malayan L.J. 440 (H.C.) 57, 95
Phang Chin Hock v. Public Prosecutor [1980] 1 Malayan L.J. 70 (F.C.) 53–54, 141
Public Prosecutor v. Azmi Sharom [2015] M.L.J.U. 594 (F.C.) 10–11, 50, 52–53, 62–63, 151, 202, 206–7
Public Prosecutor v. Dato' Yap Peng [1987] 2 Malayan L.J. 311 (S.C.) 7–8, 41, 57, 60–61, 95, 99
Public Prosecutor v. Kok Wah Kuan [2008] 1 Malayan L.J. 1 (F.C.) 14, 46–47, 49–50, 92, 96–97, 98, 99, 100, 102–3, 109–10, 134–35, 217–18

Public Prosecutor v. Yuneswaran Ramaraj [2015] 9 Current
L.J. 873 (C.A.) 10–11, 62–63, 98, 201, 206–7
Raja Petra Kamaruddin v. Menteri Hal Ehwal Dalam Negeri [2008]
M.L.J.U. 1095 (H.C.) 200–1
Semenyih Jaya v. Pentadbir Tanah Daerah Hulu Langat [2017] 3 Malayan
L.J. 561 (F.C.) 3–4, 7–8, 9, 14, 15, 41, 54, 56–57, 63, 66, 85, 92–93, 98–104, 106, 108, 115–16, 117, 121, 124, 133–40, 141, 142, 143–44, 147, 180, 211, 215, 217
Shamala Sathiyaseelan v. Jeyaganesh Mogarajah & Anor [2011] 2 Malayan
L.J. 281 (F.C.) 171
Shamala Sathiyaseelan v. Jeyaganesh Mogarajah [2004] 2 Malayan L.J. 241 (H.C.) 176
Sisters in Islam Forum & Ors. v. Jawatankuasa Fatwa Negeri Selangor & Ors.
[2018] 3 Malayan L.J. 706 (C.A.) 10–11
Sivarasa Rasiah v. Badan Peguam Malaysia & Anor [2010] 2 Malayan
L.J. 333 (F.C.) 50, 54, 62, 141, 143–44, 147–48, 150–51, 206–7
Soon Singh Soon Singh a/l Bikar Singh v. Pertubuhan Kebajikan Islam
Malaysia (Perkim) [1999] 1 Malayan L.J. 489 (F.C.) 114, 169–70, 172–73
Subashini Rajasingam v. Saravanan Thangathoray [2008] 2 Malayan
L.J. 147 (F.C.) 171, 177
Sugumar Balakrishnan v. Pengarah Imigresen Negeri Sabah [1998] 3 Malayan.
L.J. 289 (C.A.) 96
Tan Boon Wah v. Datuk Seri Ahmad Said Hamdan [2010] 2 Malayan L.J. 411 (F.C.) 112
Tenaga Nasional Berhad v. Bukit Lenang Development Sdn Bhd [2018] M.Y.F.C. 26 148
Teoh Eng Huat v. Kadhi Pasir Mas (Susie Teoh) [1990] 2 Malayan L.J. 300 (S.C.) 166–67
Titular Roman Catholic Archbishop of Kuala Lumpur v. Menteri Dalam Negeri &
Anor [2010] 2 Malayan L.J. 78 (H.C.) 174
Titular Roman Catholic Archbishop of Kuala Lumpur v. Menteri Dalam Negeri &
Ors. [2014] 4 Malayan L.J. 765 (F.C.) 174
Yang Dipertua Dewan Rakyat & Ors v. Gobind Singh Deo [2014] 6 Malayan
L.J. 812 (F.C.) 98
ZI Publications Sdn Bhd & Anor v. Kerajaan Negeri Selangor [2016] 1 Malayan
L.J. 153 (F.C.) 178

Singapore

Chan Hiang Leng Colin v. Public Prosecutor [1994] 3 Sing. L. Rep. 662 (SGHC) 48
Chee Siok Chin v. Minister for Home Affairs [2006] 1 Sing. L. Rep. (R.)
582 (SGHC) 48, 51, 52–53, 152, 203
Chng Suan Tze v. Minister of Home Affairs [1988] 2 Sing. L. Rep. (R.)
525 (SGCA) 8, 9, 59–60, 61, 64–65, 107–8, 110, 111, 117, 118–19, 198–99, 200, 203, 204, 208–9
Jabar bin Kadermastan v. Public Prosecutor [1995] 1 Sing. L. Rep. 617 (SGCA) 51
Law Society of Singapore v. Tan Guat Neo Phyllis [2008] 2 Sing. L.
Rep. (R.) 239 (SGHC) 119
Lim Meng Suang v. Attorney-General [2015] 1 Sing. L. Rep. 26 (SGCA) 48, 203
Mohammad Faizal bin Sabtu v. Public Prosecutor [2012] 4 Sing. L.
Rep. 947 (SGHC) 44–45, 55, 105, 106, 145–46
Nappali Peter Williams v. Institute of Technical Education [1998] 2 Sing.
L. Rep. (R.) 529 (SGCA) 48
Public Prosecutor v. Ong Kian Cheong [2009] SGDC 163 196–97
Rajeevan Edakalavan v. Public Prosecutor [1998] 1 Sing. L. Rep. (R.) 10 (SGHC) 51
Ramalingam Ravinthran v. Attorney-General [2012] 2 Sing. L. Rep. 49 (SGCA) 119
Ravi s/o Madasamy v. Attorney-General [2017] 5 Sing. L. Rep. 489 (SGHC) 56, 105–6
Sun Hongyu v. Public Prosecutor [2005] 2 Sing. L. Rep. 750 (SGHC) 51

Tan Seet Eng v. Attorney-General [2016] 1 Sing. L. Rep. 779 (SGCA) 9, 15, 64, 105, 107–8, 118–20, 203, 204, 208–9
Taw Cheng Kong v. Public Prosecutor [1998] 1 Sing. L. Rep. (R.) 78 (SGHC) . . . 7–8, 41, 48, 105, 130
Taw Cheng Kong v. Public Prosecutor [1998] 1 Sing. L. Rep. (R.) 78 (SGHC), overruled by Public Prosecutor v. Taw Cheng Kong [1998] 2 Sing. L. Rep. (R.) 410 (SGCA). 7–8, 41, 130
Teo Soh Lung v. Minister of Home Affairs [1989] 1 Sing. L. Rep. (R) 461 (SGHC) 55, 60, 105, 111, 118, 200
Teo Soh Lung v. Minister of Home Affairs [1990] 1 Sing. L. Rep. (R.) 347 (SGCA) 111, 118, 200
Vellama d/o Marie Muthu v. Attorney-General [2013] 4 Sing. L. Rep. 1 (SGCA) 9, 64–65, 119
Vincent Cheng v. Minister of Home Affairs [1990] 1 Malayan L.J. 449 (SGHC). 55
Yong Vui Kong v. Attorney-General [2011] 2 Sing. L. Rep. 1189 (SGCA) 88, 89, 118
Yong Vui Kong v. Public Prosecutor [2010] 3 Sing. L. Rep. 489 (SGCA) 14, 51–52, 70, 86–91
Yong Vui Kong v. Public Prosecutor [2012] 2 Sing. L. Rep. 872 (SGCA) 119
Yong Vui Kong v. Public Prosecutor [2015] 2 Sing. L. Rep. 1129 (SGCA) 10–11, 48–49, 55–56, 88–89, 93, 105–6, 145–46

South Africa

Bato Star Fishing v. Ministry of Environmental Affairs and Tourism 2004(4) SA 490 (C.C.) (S. Afr.) 113
Nyambirai v. National Social Security Authority [1996] 1 L.R.C. 64 62

United Kingdom

Adegbenro v. Akintola (1963) 3 All E. R. 544 (P.C.) 46–47
A-G of St. Christopher, Nevis and Anguilla v. Reynolds [1980] A.C. 637 (P.C) 198
Associated Provincial Picture Houses Ltd. v. Wednesbury Corp., [1948] 1 K.B. 223 (C.A.). 187
de Freitas v. Permanent Secretary of Ministry of Agriculture, Fisheries, Lands and Housing [1998] UKPC 30 (P.C.) 150, 202, 206–7
Edwards v. Attorney-General for Canada [1930] A.C. 124 (P.C.). 43
Liversidge v. Anderson [1942] A.C. 206 (H.L.). 197–98
Minister of Home Affairs & Another v. Collins MacDonald Fisher & Another [1980] A.C. 319 (P.C.) 42–43, 53
Nakkuda Ali v. Jayaratne [1951] A.C. 66 (P.C.). 198
Ong Ah Chuan v. Public Prosecutor [1980] UKPCC 32 (P.C.). 43
R. v. IRC ex parte Rossminster [1980] A.C. 952, 1011 (H.L.) 198

United States

Brown v. Board of Education of Topeka, 347 U.S. 483 (1954) 137
Cooper v. Aaron, 358 U.S. 1 (1958). 139
Marbury v. Madison, 5 U.S. 137 (1803) 44–45, 103, 104, 120, 123–24, 133–37, 139

Table of Legislation

STATUTES

Canada Act 1982, c11
 s 33 127
 Sch B. 127
Human Rights Act 1998, c. 42
 s 4(1). 45, 127

OTHER LEGISLATION

Canada

Canadian Charter of Rights and Freedoms 24, 127
 s 1 23
Constitution Act 1982
 Pt I 127

Egypt

Constitution 2014
 Art 2. 84

Iraq

Constitution 2005
 Art 2, s 1. 84

Malaysia

Administration of the Religion of Islam and the Malay Custom of Pahang Enactment 1982
 § 185. 168–69
Administration of the Religion of Islam (Negeri Sembilan) Enactment 2003
 § 119(4)(b). 168–69
Anti-Fake News Act 2018 197
 § 4(1) 195–96
Births and Deaths Registration Act 1957
 § 13A(2). 183
Child Protection Act 2001 (Act 611)
 § 97(2) 96–97
Constitution (Amendment) Act 1960 (Act 10). 210
Constitution (Amendment) Act 1981 (Act 514). 210
Constitution (Amendment) Act 1984. . . 210–11
Constitutional (Amendment) Act 1988 . . . . . 60–61, 95–96, 99, 100, 109–10
Criminal Procedure Code
 s 418A. 41
Federal Constitution 1957. . . . . 6, 8, 14, 47, 58, 59, 74, 76, 77, 79, 85–86, 87, 91, 97, 158
 Pt I 113
 Pt II. 37–38, 113
 Pt VI
  Ch 1 37
  Ch 3 37
  Ch 4 37
 Pt IX. 37
 Art 3 . . . . . 83, 84–85, 162, 164–65, 166, 178, 185
 Art 3(1) 7, 25, 44, 70, 81, 82, 83–85, 86, 91, 158, 159, 161, 162, 164–65, 167, 173, 174, 175, 176, 178, 179, 184–86
 Art 3(2) 83–84
 Art 3(3)–(5). 37
 Art 3(3) 83–84
 Art 3(4) 84, 162, 185
 Art 3(5) 83–84
 Art 4. 113
 Art 4(1) 37–38, 42, 44–45, 99, 113, 135, 143–44
 Arts 5–13. . . . . 37–38, 42, 147
 Art 5(1) 121, 147–48, 151, 206, 207
 Art 8. 162–63
 Art 8(1) 44, 151–52, 207
 Art 8(2) 162–63
 Art 8(5) 162–63
 Art 10(1) 205–6, 207
 Art 10(2) 52–53, 202
 Art 10(2)(a). 206
 Art 11. . . . . 169, 176
 Art 11(1) 81, 84, 158, 162–63, 173–74, 175, 176
 Art 11(3) 173–74

Art 11(4) 77–78, 162–63
Art 11(5) 162–63
Art 12 162–63
Art 12(1)–(2). 162–63
Art 12(3) 162–63
Art 12(4) 138, 148, 162–63, 172
Art 32(1) 44
Art 32(3) 44
Art 38 37
Art 39 37
Art 43(2)(a) 37
Art 43(2)(b) 37
Art 44 37
Art 45 37
Art 66 210–11
Art 66(4B) .210–11
Art 74 41
Art 74(2) 84, 163
Art 77 41
Art 121 . . . . .95, 134, 199
Art 121(1) 8, 41, 49–50, 54, 57, 60–61, 63, 92, 95–97, 99, 100, 101–2, 103–4, 109–10, 112, 114–15, 134–36, 137, 138–39, 141, 199, 211
Art 121(1A) . . . 63, 114–15, 116–17, 138–39, 163, 167, 169–70, 172–73, 179
Art 121(2) 38
Art 121(3) 38
Art 121(1B) 38
Art 125(3) 58
Art 125(4) 58
Art 128(1) 38
Art 130 38
Art 149 . . . . 61, 190, 191, 192, 212–13
Art 149(2) 210
Art 150 . . . . 61, 190–91, 210, 212–13
Art 150(1) 61, 191, 210–11
Art 150(2) 210
Art 150(2B)–(2C). 191
Art 150(3) 210
Art 150(6) 61, 191
Art 150(8) 210, 211
Art 150(8)(b). 191
Art 159 34
Art 159(1) 38
Art 159(3) 80–81, 128–29
Art 159(4) 38
Art 160 . . . . .77–78, 169
Art 160(2) 163, 177–78
Art 161E(2) 38
Sch 2 163
Sch 9, List II, art. 1 . . . . 38, 84, 163
Internal Security Act 1960 . . . . . 61, 193–94, 195, 200–1
§ 8(1) .192, 197–98
§ 8B(1) 199
Islamic Family Law (Federal Territories) Act 1984
§ 10(2) 167–68
Land Acquisition Act 1960 . . . . 98–99, 133–34
§ 40D 41
§ 40D(1). 98–99
§ 40D(3). 98–99, 101
Law Reform (Marriage and Divorce) Act 1976. . . . . 114, 157, 167–68
Malacca Administration of Islamic Law Enactment 1991
§ 209 168–69
Malaysia (Singapore Amendment) Act 1965. 76
Melaka Sharia Offences Enactment 1991
§ 66 168–69
National Security Council Act 2016 (Act 776) 129–30, 203, 211–12
§ 18 195
§ 25 195
§ 26 195
§ 38 211–12
Peaceful Assembly Act 2012 (Act 736) 62, 206–7, 208
§§ 9–15. 195
§ 9(1) 201
§ 9(5) 62–63, 201
Penal Code (Act 574)
§ 124B-N 194
§ 298A 41
Perak Islamic Criminal Law Enactment 1992
§ 13 168–69
Prevention of Terrorism Act 2015. . . . . .129–30, 196
§ 3(1) 194–95
§ 8(1) 194–95
§ 13(1) 194–95
§ 17(1) 194–95
§ 19(1) 211–12
Printing Presses and Publications Act 1984 (Act 301)
§ 7(1) 178–79
Security Offences (Special Measures) Act 2012 (Act 747) 196, 208
§ 4(1) 194
§ 4(5) 194

Sedition Act 1948 (Act 15). 50, 196, 202, 206–7
§ 3(1)(e) 195
§ 3(1)(ea) 195
§ 4 195
§ 4(1)(a) 195
§ 10(a) 195
Sedition (Amendment) Act 2015
§ 3(a)(iv)–(v). 195
§ 4(a) 195
§ 4(b) 195
§ 9 195
Syariah Criminal Offences (Selangor) Enactment 1995
§ 16 178
Terengganu Administration of Islamic Law Enactment 1996
§ 29 168–69

India

Indian Constitution 55, 80–81
Pt III 42
Art 21 90
Indian Penal Code 90

Kenya

Constitution 2010
Ch 4 42

New Zealand

New Zealand Bill of Rights Act 1990
§ 7 127

Singapore

Colony Order-in-Council, Feb. 24, 1948 (SI 341/1948). 39
Constitution 1948 . . . 7, 8, 48, 51–52, 53–54, 55, 60, 64, 78, 79, 87–88, 90, 105–6, 111, 145–46
Art 4 . . . . .41, 42, 44–45, 77, 106
Art 5(2) 41, 80–81, 128–29
Art 8(1) 41
Arts 9–16 . . . . 41, 42, 147
Art 9(1) . . . 51–52, 86, 87, 88–89, 90, 206
Art 12(1) 44
Art 13 88
Art 14 51
Art 14(1) 206
Art 14(2) .51, 52–53
Art 20(1) 89
Art 21(2) 40
Art 22(1) 40
Art 22E. 40
Art 22I 40
Arts 23–25. 40
Art 25(1) 40
Art 38 40
Art 49 64–65
Art 93 . . . . .41, 60
Art 93(1) 106
Art 94(1) 41
Art 149 . . . . 61, 192
Art 149(1) 192
Art 149(3) 60, 111, 192
Art 150(1) 61, 191
Art 150(2) 191
Art 150(5) 61, 191
Art 151(4) 40
Art 152(1) 77–78
Art 153(2) 77–78
Constitution of Singapore (Amendment) Act 1965. 76
Constitution of the Republic of Singapore (Amendment) Act 2016 41
Constitution (Amendment) Act 1979 (Act 10)
Art 155(1) 78
Constitution (Amendment) Act 1981 (Act A514)
§ 15(d) 191
Criminal Law (Temporary Provisions) Act, Cap. 67, 2000 Rev. Ed. Sing . . . 64, 118–19, 196, 203, 208, 209
§ 30 196
Independence Act of 1965. . . . . 40, 76
Internal Security Act, Cap. 143, 1985 Rev. Ed. Sing. 40, 61, 64, 110–11, 112, 117–19, 146–47, 189–90, 196, 197–98, 199, 204, 209, 211–12
§ 8(1) 59–60, 110, 192, 197–98
§ 8B(1) 60, 110–11, 199
§ 8B(2) .60, 211–12
Judicial Committee (Repeal) Act, No. 2 of 1994 41
Misuse of Drugs Act 2008 88–89
Ch 185 . . . . .51–52, 86
Protection from Online Falsehoods and Manipulation Bill 2019, No. 10/2019
§ 7(1) 197
Singapore (Constitution) Order in Council 1958. 75

South Africa

Constitution 1996
 Ch 2 42
 § 36 23

United States

Constitution 80–81, 93–94, 95

TREATIES & CONVENTIONS

African Charter on Human and Peoples' Rights
 Art 27(2) 23

Convention for the Protection of Human Rights and Fundamental Freedoms
 Art 9(2) 23

Convention on Rights of the Child 47, 148–49

Convention on the Elimination of All Forms of Discrimination Against Women 47, 148–49

European Convention on Human Rights. 23, 24, 45, 87, 151–52

Universal Declaration of Human Rights 1948 . . . . 22, 47, 148–49

Introduction

Building Constitutionalism in Fragile Democracies

I.	Courts, Constitutional Politics, and Statecraft	4
II.	Situating Constitutions and Courts in Context	6
III.	Book Schema	13

On May 9, 2018, history reached a tipping point in Malaysia. For the first time since it gained independence more than half a century ago, Malaysia experienced a democratic change of government. In an unprecedented national election outcome, the Barisan Nasional ruling coalition lost its six-decade-long grasp on power.[1]

Kuala Lumpur erupted. Crowds reveled in the streets of the capital, cheers breaking out across the city. Forty-nine years earlier, on May 13, 1969, in the aftermath of another general election, the city had also exploded—but in violence. Communal race riots broke out, leaving hundreds dead, after the governing coalition managed to hold onto power but suffered large losses to ethnic minority-dominated opposition parties.[2] Now, half a century later, almost to the day, the city burst into celebration that the Malaysian electorate had just overturned the only government the country had ever known. The Barisan Nasional coalition, which had controlled the federal government since 1957 and survived the 1969 tumult, was finally, peacefully, removed from power.

The drama did not end with the election. The Pakatan Harapan coalition—the Alliance of Hope—that had swept to victory in the 2018 elections formed the new government under the leadership of Mahathir Mohamad. Opposition leader Anwar Ibrahim, freshly released from prison as part of Pakatan Harapan's pledge

[1] *See After Six Decades in Power, BN Falls to "Malaysian Tsunami"*, Malaysiakini (May 10, 2018), https://perma.cc/YY6E-TQG7; Richard Paddock, *Malaysia Opposition, Led by 92-Year-Old, Wins Upset Victory*, N.Y. Times (May 9, 2018), https://perma.cc/F3CY-Q8YS.

[2] *See Race War in Malaysia*, TIME (May 23, 1969), https://perma.cc/KS45-QNLN.

Constitutional Statecraft in Asian Courts. Yvonne Tew, Oxford University Press (2020). © Yvonne Tew.
DOI:10.1093/oso/9780198716839.001.0001

that he would eventually succeed Mahathir, finally appeared set to become the next prime minister.[3] Meanwhile, Najib Razak, the ousted premier who had been at the helm of Barisan Nasional, was stopped trying to leave the country on a private jet; authorities later arrested and charged him in connection with one of the world's largest corruption scandals, which involved the siphoning of billions of dollars from the government fund 1Malaysia Development Berhad.[4]

The story of Malaysia's 2018 regime transformation was held up as a triumph of democracy. With the rupture of the ruling party's power, democracy and constitutionalism appeared ascendant. "What we want to do is restore the rule of law," declared Mahathir minutes after Pakatan Harapan announced its electoral victory.[5] Malaysia's disruption of dominant party rule has been described as a "miracle," and an outlier to the global trend of rising illiberal nationalism.[6] Many in Asia and in the West hailed what happened in Malaysia as a democratic breakthrough,[7] and in many ways it was.

But there is a darker portrait of Malaysia's transition story. Mahathir, the ninety-two-year-old former prime minister lauded as a hero for returning to politics to lead Pakatan Harapan to victory, first imprisoned Anwar—his then protégé and deputy prime minister—two decades earlier on what was widely regarded to be politically trumped-up charges of corruption and sodomy. And during his tenure as prime minister and head of Barisan Nasional, it was Mahathir who weakened the government's system of checks and balances, creating the centralized executive power that Najib's administration would later enjoy. Embedded within the narrative of Malaysia's 2018 political turnover is thus a deep irony: the leader celebrated as democracy's savior was also responsible for dismantling many of the democratic institutions that enabled the ruling coalition to maintain dominance for so long.[8]

These contrasting portraits of the Malaysian transition underscore that regimes change, political destinies are uncertain, and popular narratives are fickle. As history has shown us, heroes can turn out to be villains, and return to be redeemed as saviors, all within a generation. Narratives that revolve around the appeal of

[3] *See* Simon Denyer, *Malaysian Reformist Anwar Ibrahim Released from Prison, Granted Royal Pardon*, Wash. Post (May 16, 2018), https://perma.cc/439NXK5R.

[4] *See* Hannah Ellis-Petersen, *Ousted Malaysian Leader Najib Prevented from Leaving Country*, Guardian (May 12, 2018), https://perma.cc/2CL33KVV; Yantoultra Ngui, *Former Malaysian Leader Najib Arrested, Faces New Charges in 1MDB Scandal*, Wall St. J. (Sept. 19, 2018), https://perma.cc/LGE8-E62H.

[5] *See* Alyaa Alhadjri, *Harapan Gov't Will Not Seek "Revenge" on Najib, Says Dr M*, Malaysiakini (May 9, 2018), https://perma.cc/P977-B4BU.

[6] *See* Marvin Ott, *Malaysian Miracle*, Asia Dispatches (May 24, 2018), https://perma.cc/H8KW-5T5G; Anwar Ibrahim, *How Malaysia's Democratic Disruption Stands Apart in a Year of Populist Nationalism*, S. China Morning Post (Dec. 13, 2018), https://perma.cc/HU3B-J4XS.

[7] *See* Larry Diamond, *Malaysia's Democratic Breakthrough*, Am. Interest (May 15, 2018), https://perma.cc/ZQ2E-E9S6; Tsu Chong Chan, *Democratic Breakthrough in Malaysia—Political Opportunities and the Role of Bersih*, 37 J. Current Se. Asian Aff. 109 (2018).

[8] *See* Laignee Barron, *Malaysia's Longest-Serving Prime Minister Returns to Power Promising a Tide of Change*, Time (May 11, 2018), https://perma.cc/69VJ-FWAB.

individuals and leaders are vulnerable to the capricious political winds of the time. For constitutional democracy to thrive, in Malaysia or elsewhere, requires a shift away from preoccupation with particular personalities or political parties.[9] This book focuses on the constitutional institutions and legal mechanisms that can help build an enduring framework for a developing democracy.[10]

Central to the project of state-building are courts and constitutionalism. Courts in developing democracies have both a protective role and a constructive role.[11] In their protective capacity, courts serve to defend fundamental elements of the constitutional order from being altered or destroyed. This judicial role as a constraint on consolidated political power is all the more important in states accustomed to control by a dominant political party.[12] In such contexts with a history of authoritarian rule, characteristic of many fragile Asian democracies, strong judicial review reinforces democratic governance by safeguarding core structures of democracy from being eroded by political actors.[13] One powerful judicial strategy that courts can use to preserve this constitutional core is to assert the power to review amendments that undermine the basic structure of the present constitution. Declaring the authority to nullify a constitutional amendment is an assertive, even audacious, judicial move, but it can be achieved—as the Malaysian apex court illustrated when it carefully built the framework to declare certain constitutional

[9] *See* Bridget Welsh, *"Saviour" Politics and Malaysia's 2018 Electoral Democratic Breakthrough: Rethinking Explanatory Narratives and Implications*, 37 J. CURRENT SE. ASIAN AFF. 85, 86 (2018) (observing that "[t]he analytical focus has ... been primarily on the role of individuals and leaders, in keeping with what is arguably the dominant paradigm for understanding Malaysian politics as a whole").

[10] Indeed, as this book goes to press, Malaysia has a new governing coalition and prime minister after a government crisis in early 2020. Malaysia's 2020 political crisis was triggered by political defections and followed by a battle for the country's premiership among political elites as well as unprecedented royal intervention. At the end of February 2020, two years after its victory in the 2018 national elections, the Pakatan Harapan government, the Alliance of Hope, collapsed. On March 1, 2020, Muhyiddin Yassin was sworn in as prime minister at the helm of the new Perikatan Nasional governing coalition, which includes parties from the Barisan Nasional alliance that had been voted out in 2018.

Malaysia's change of government in March 2020 was sudden and unexpected. Yet, ultimately, political crises such as these underscore this book's central argument: political narratives are fragile, and it is thus all the more important to strengthen constitutional institutions, like the courts, that can help construct an enduring constitutional democracy.

See Hannah Beech, *Malaysia's Premier, Mahathir Mohamad, Is Ousted in a Surprising Turn*, N.Y. TIMES (Feb. 29, 2020), https://perma.cc/98KE-6YSH; *see also* Yvonne Tew, *Malaysia's 2020 Government Crisis: Revealing the New Emperor's Clothes*, INT'L J. CONST. L. BLOG (Apr. 15, 2020), https://perma.cc/7NZR-ZMP7.

[11] *See* David S. Law & Hsiang-Yang Hsieh, *Judicial Review of Constitutional Amendments: Taiwan*, *in* CONSTITUTIONALISM IN CONTEXT 1, 21–22 (David S. Law ed., forthcoming) (manuscript on file with author) (describing the judiciary's "rear-guard or protective use of amendment-review" to "defend key elements of the existing order" and "vanguard actions" to "facilitate regime transformation" specifically in the context of judicial review of constitutional amendment).

[12] *See* SAMUEL ISSACHAROFF, FRAGILE DEMOCRACIES: CONTESTED POWER IN THE ERA OF CONSTITUTIONAL COURTS 13 (2015).

[13] *See* JOHN HART ELY, DEMOCRACY AND DISTRUST: A THEORY OF JUDICIAL REVIEW (1980) (arguing for a "representation-reinforcing" approach to judicial review that focuses on protecting democratic processes).

fundamentals, including judicial power and the separation of powers, as beyond the reach of the political institutions.[14]

There is also a constructive role for courts to build and develop the foundational principles of an emerging constitutional order. In aspiring democracies, like Asian states transitioning from dominant party regimes, judiciaries have the potential to build a culture of constitutionalism. While its protective role focuses on the existing structures of constitutional governance, this facilitative role is explicitly forward-looking: it calls on courts to be conscious about crafting principles of constitutionalism and rights protection. In reaching for judicial tools to employ in practice, courts can use an interpretive approach informed by the constitution's overarching purposes and a proportionality analysis in constitutional rights adjudication. Purposive interpretation and proportionality review offer adjudicative mechanisms that can be applied robustly yet flexibly, which courts can develop incrementally over time to enhance effective constitutional review.

This book explores the role of judicial review and constitutionalism in safeguarding democracy and facilitating constitutional governance. It considers how the judiciary can negotiate institutional power to consolidate its position vis-à-vis the dominant political branches of government. It also examines the facilitative role courts can play in crafting the foundational principles of a fragile constitutional order. The strategies evident in Malaysia and Singapore suit the challenges of many other emerging Asian democracies, providing both guidance and caution as these states negotiate their evolving constitutionalism. At the heart of this book is an account of how judicial strategies of constitutionalism can sculpt the contours of state-building. It is, in brief, about how courts engage in constitutional statecraft.

I. Courts, Constitutional Politics, and Statecraft

A hallmark of the global rise of modern constitutions created in the twentieth and twenty-first centuries has been the proliferation of constitutional courts and judicial review.[15] Different visions have emerged of the judicial role. One pictures courts in a heroic frame: as constitutional guardians and protectors of rights. The judge as Hercules, famously articulated by Ronald Dworkin, is engaged in seeking to interpret the constitution in its best light to reach a right decision that achieves justice, fairness, and integrity.[16]

[14] *See* Semenyih Jaya v. Pentadbir Tanah Daerah Hulu Langat [2017] 3 Malayan L.J. 561 [hereinafter *Semenyih Jaya*]; Indira Gandhi a/p Mutho v. Pengarah Jabatan Agama Islam Perak & Ors. [2018] 1 Malayan L.J. 545 (F.C.) [hereinafter *Indira Gandhi* (F.C.)].

[15] *See, e.g.*, Ran Hirschl, Towards Juristocracy (2004); Martin Shapiro & Alec Stone Sweet, On Law, Politics and Judicialization (2002).

[16] *See* Ronald Dworkin, *Hard Cases*, 88 Harv. L. Rev. 1057 (1975); Ronald Dworkin, Law's Empire (1986).

A contrasting vision portrays courts as ineffectual and the promise of judicial constitutionalism as largely illusory. In Asian democracies controlled by a dominant political party, for example, courts are considered to be on the fringes of constitutional politics.[17] Judicially enforced constitutionalism has been dismissed as "inapt" for non-liberal polities in Asia.[18] Others have characterized courts as serving the instrumental goals of authoritarian regimes.[19] For courts to act as a constraint on consolidated political power appears to be a hopeless undertaking. The task confronting these courts does not appear Herculean, but Sisyphean.[20]

This book sees the judicial role as neither heroic nor futile. Rather, it recognizes that courts both possess the capacity to intervene in the political environment and are themselves impacted by the forces and constraints of the broader context within which they operate. The question I seek to explore is not simply about the judicial role in an emerging democratic order but how courts in these aspiring democracies can and should carry out their constitutional task. My central concern is what strategies courts can use to strengthen their own institutional position and engage in constitutional state-building.

Constitutional statecraft involves special challenges, of course, for courts in fragile political orders. A key part of this book's account focuses on how courts interact with their system's particular configuration of political power.

Singapore and Malaysia have long been considered exemplars of dominant party democracies. Both states have been controlled for decades by a single party or coalition, which has dominated political power since each country gained independence. Singapore's People's Action Party has governed continuously since the country became a unitary sovereign state in 1965. The ruling party has never lost a single election, controlling an overwhelming majority of more than 90 percent of all elected parliamentary seats post-independence. With a ruling party that dominates politics and policymaking, the Singaporean state practices what has been described as authoritarian constitutionalism.[21]

Malaysia's story, too, begins under the long shadow of dominant coalition rule. The Barisan Nasional alliance, which held a dominant political position even before the country gained independence from the British in 1957, maintained its grip on governing power for more than six decades.[22] Yet, even a seemingly impervious

[17] *See* Po Jen Yap, Courts and Democracies in Asia 2 (2017).

[18] *See* Li-ann Thio, *Soft Constitutional Law in Nonliberal Asian Constitutional Democracies*, 8 Int'l J. Const. L. 766, 767 (2010).

[19] *See* Tamir Moustafa & Tom Ginsburg, *Introduction: The Functions of Courts in Authoritarian Politics*, *in* Rule by Law: The Politics of Courts in Authoritarian Regimes (Tom Ginsburg & Tamir Moustafa eds., 2008).

[20] *See* H.P. Lee & Richard Foo, *The Malaysian Judiciary: A Sisyphean Quest for Redemption?*, *in* Asia-Pacific Judiciaries: Independence, Impartiality and Integrity 231 (H.P. Lee & Marilyn Pittard eds., 2018).

[21] *See* Mark Tushnet, *Authoritarian Constitutionalism*, 100 Cornell L. Rev. 391 (2015).

[22] The Alliance, Barisan Nasional's predecessor, won the first general elections held in 1955 before Malaya's independence by a landslide.

regime can slip from power. Contemporary Malaysia presents a striking example of a fragile democracy after the rupture of the only ruling government it had ever experienced in 2018, and then the new governing coalition's collapse in 2020. Following the regime changes of 2018 and 2020, post-transition Malaysia is in the process of renegotiating the dynamics of power for its nascent constitutional democracy.

II. Situating Constitutions and Courts in Context

On August 31, 1957, at the stroke of midnight, the *Merdeka*—or Independence—Constitution came into force when Malaya gained independence from the British. Six years later, Singapore, together with the Borneo states of Sabah and Sarawak, joined Malaya to form the new Federation of Malaysia, with a new Constitution of Malaysia. The union was unhappy and brief. On August 9, 1965, after hastily cobbling together a makeshift constitution, Singapore separated from the federation to become its own sovereign state.

Malaysia and Singapore are situated at the heart of Asia between China and India, described as places where the East meets the West. Labeled the Golden Peninsula by ancient Greek and Roman geographers,[23] the Malay Peninsula rose to prominence in the fifteenth century, with ports in Malacca, Penang, and Singapore becoming key hubs of trade routes for ships carrying spices, silks, and tea between the Indian and Pacific Oceans. Upon arriving in Malacca in 1854, Alfred Russel Wallace, a British naturalist and geographer, marveled: "This place is the market of all India, of China . . . and of other islands around about—from all which places, as well as from Banda, Java, Sumatra, Siam, Pegu, Bengal, Coromandel, and India—arrive ships which come and go incessantly, charged with an infinity of merchandises."[24] The countries that would emerge from this archipelago of gold are a heady mix of cultures and communities, made up of different ethnicities, religions, and languages. Their stories take place amidst a long history of colonialism, as these lands changed hands from the Portuguese to the Dutch, and then to the British.

The Southeast Asian democracies of Malaysia and Singapore are richly illustrative examples for this book's exploration of constitutional adjudication and politics. Malaysia and Singapore present a unique dual case study. They share a common constitutional origin: both post-colonial states were part of the same country—the Federation of Malaysia—after gaining independence from the British, before

[23] W. Linehan, *The Identifications of Some of Ptolemy's Place Names in the Golden Khersonese*, 24 J. Malayan Branch of Royal Asiatic Soc'y, pt. 3, at 86–98 (1951), https://perma.cc/F9JA-L6PQ.

[24] Alfred Russel Wallace, The Malay Archipelago 26 (London, 1872).

splitting apart and developing as two separate sovereign nations. Both countries have common law systems based on British legal traditions and parliamentary systems modeled on Westminster.

Crucially, though, unlike Britain, Malaysia and Singapore possess codified constitutions with bills of rights and judiciaries constitutionally empowered with judicial review. Their written constitutions share many similarities, unsurprisingly, since Singapore's Constitution is heavily based on the Constitution of Malaysia of which it was once part. Still, there are significant differences. Religion is one prominent example: Singapore's Constitution does not establish an official religion, while Malaysia constitutionalized Islam as the religion of the federation[25]—a constitutional design arrangement that would have serious, if unintended, implications.

Constitutions capture a nation's imagination in different ways. Some nations may celebrate their constitution as indissolubly linked to their independence and founding—a marker of a break from the past. Such a narrative resonates in Malaysia, where local political leaders negotiated independence from the British colonial power. Other narratives of the constitution are more skeptical. Postcolonial constitutions have been described as maps that legitimate and reproduce power in governance,[26] and, indeed, the Malaysian and Singaporean constitutions authorize broad emergency powers and security regimes. Another strand born of skepticism toward Western liberal traditions advances instead an inward-looking constitutionalism based on purported Asian values. Still other narratives perpetuate an illiberal, even authoritarian, constitutionalism rooted in divisions of race and religion.

The struggles between these different constitutional narratives were evident at the founding of Malaysia and Singapore, reflected in battles over citizenship, language, identity, and religion. And these battles would be fought again in the decades to come, in recurring conflicts over race and religion, and over state power and individual rights.

Courts in these Asian democracies are expressly empowered to invalidate legislation and executive actions that violate constitutional guarantees. Yet, in practice these judiciaries have been highly passive, deferring extensively to the political branches. Tellingly, Singapore's highest court has never once struck down a

[25] FED. CONST. (MALAY.), art. 3(1) ("Islam is the religion of the Federation; but other religions may be practised in peace and harmony in any part of the Federation.").

[26] *See generally* H.W.O. Okoth-Ogendo, *Constitutions Without Constitutionalism: Reflections on an African Political Paradox*, *in* CONSTITUTIONALISM AND DEMOCRACY: TRANSITIONS IN THE CONTEMPORARY WORLD 67 (Douglas Greenberg et al. eds., 1993) (arguing that "*all law*, and *constitutional law* in particular, is concerned, not with abstract norms, but with the creation, distribution, exercise, legitimation, effects, and reproduction of *power*").

legislative provision as unconstitutional.[27] And, until recently, its Malaysian counterpart had done so only a handful of times.[28]

The constitution has itself been the site of struggle between the courts and the political branches of government. Most provisions in the Malaysian and Singaporean constitutions can be amended by a simple two-thirds majority of parliament—an easy task for a government controlled by a dominant party.[29] In both countries, the government has amended the constitution frequently in the past. The Singapore Constitution has been amended more than forty times,[30] while the Malaysian government has passed upwards of fifty constitutional amendment bills.[31] Some of these amendments have been expressly aimed at curtailing judicial power. In 1988, the Malaysian Constitution was altered to subordinate the courts' powers to the legislature's control.[32] The same year, Singapore's government swiftly amended its constitution to reverse the impact of a Singapore apex court decision and restrict judicial review.[33]

In light of this political environment, it is especially challenging for courts to seek an empowered role. Indeed, courts have been thought to play little more than a "marginal role" in the constitutional governance of these fragile or dominant party states.[34] Following such aggressive political efforts to curtail judicial review through amendments, many commentators assumed that the state had effectively suppressed judicial power.[35] And some argue that these courts should avoid strong-form review, viewing political confrontation under such conditions as imprudent.[36] Attempting to achieve judicial empowerment appeared futile.

[27] The Singapore High Court has declared a statutory provision unconstitutional in only one case, and even this decision was later overturned by the Court of Appeal. *See* Taw Cheng Kong v. Public Prosecutor [1998] 1 Sing. L. Rep. 943 (H.C.), *overruled by* Public Prosecutor v. Taw Cheng Kong [1998] 2 Sing. L. Rep. 410 (C.A.).

[28] Prior to *Semenyih Jaya v. Pentadbir Tanah Daerah Hulu Langat* [2017] 3 Malayan L.J. 561, the Malaysian Federal Court had not declared a statute unconstitutional in twenty years. *See* Mamat bin Daud v. Gov't of Malaysia [1988] 1 Malayan L.J. 119; Public Prosecutor v. Dato' Yap Peng [1987] 2 Malayan L.J. 311.

[29] Singapore's People's Action Party has always controlled far more than two-thirds of the parliamentary seats. The Barisan Nasional coalition maintained a two-thirds legislative majority for decades until the 2008 national elections, when it obtained only a simple majority.

[30] *See* Li-ann Thio, A Treatise on Singapore Constitutional Law ¶ 04.052 (2012).

[31] *See* Cindy Tham, *Major Changes to the Constitution*, The Sun (July 17, 2007), https://perma.cc/5LU7-LRQ9 (noting that there have been more than fifty constitutional amendment acts totaling about 700 individual textual amendments to Malaysia's Constitution since 1957).

[32] The Malaysian government amended the Federal Constitution to remove the reference in Article 121(1) to "judicial power being vested in a Supreme Court and such inferior courts as may be provided by federal law." The amended Article 121(1) now stipulates that "courts shall have such jurisdiction and powers as may be conferred by or under federal law." *See* Chapter 4, The Separation of Powers, section III.

[33] When the Court of Appeal ruled against the government on constitutional grounds in *Chng Suan Tze v. Minister of Home Aff.* [1988] 2 Sing. L. Rep. (R.) 525, the Singapore government responded by quickly passing constitutional and statutory amendments to reverse the Court's decision and limit judicial review. For more detailed discussion, see Chapter 5, The Rule of Law, section III(B).

[34] Thio, *Soft Constitutional Law, supra* note 18, at 767; *see also* Yap, Courts and Democracies in Asia, *supra* note 17, at 2–4.

[35] *See, e.g.*, Richard Foo, *Malaysia—The Death of a Separate Constitutional Judicial Power*, 2010 Sing. J. Legal Stud. 227 (2010) ; Ratna Rueban Balasubramaniam, *Has Rule by Law Killed the Rule of Law in Malaysia?*, 8 Oxford Uni. Commonwealth L.J. 211 (2008).

[36] *See* Po Jen Yap, Constitutional Dialogue in Common Law Asia 77–78 (2015).

Still, it can be accomplished. In 2017, the Malaysian Federal Court unanimously invalidated a federal statute as unconstitutional—for the first time in twenty years—for infringing judicial power and the separation of powers.[37] Even more striking is that the Malaysian court repudiated the 1988 constitutional amendment, declaring that Parliament does not have the power to amend the Constitution to the effect of undermining the separation of powers and judicial power, which it called "critical" and "sacrosanct" to the Constitution's framework.[38] A year later, in another remarkable assertion of power, the Federal Court expressly affirmed that the civil courts' power of judicial review and constitutional interpretation are part of the Constitution's basic structure—beyond even constitutional amendment.[39]

While the Singaporean courts have taken a more incremental approach toward asserting constitutional review compared to their Malaysian counterparts, they have nevertheless begun to reveal a subtle but perceptible shift.[40] In several recent decisions,[41] the Singapore Court of Appeal expressly affirmed the notion that "all power has legal limits," recovering the significance of this principle of legality from earlier jurisprudence that had declared that the courts are able to examine any exercise of governing power.[42]

A pliant court can transform itself into an assertive one, but it must do so strategically. Political forces matter, of course, and so some accounts counsel judicial restraint in the interest of self-preservation when faced with consolidated political power.[43] But it is not enough to wait for an opportunity to arise. Courts must also be capable of seizing the opportunity.[44] By exercising strategic assertions of power, a court can lay the groundwork for judicial tools that it can later employ to reinforce its position, whether or not the political space opens up. These legal tools can expand the court's capacity to fulfill its protective role or to capitalize on the opportunity, if it presents itself, to exercise more transformative judicial review in constructing constitutionalism for a new political order. This book considers how.

[37] *Semenyih Jaya*, [2017] 3 MALAYAN L.J. 561.

[38] *Id.* at [90].

[39] *Indira Gandhi* (F.C.), [2018] 1 MALAYAN L.J. 545.

[40] *See* Jaclyn Neo, *Introduction* to CONSTITUTIONAL INTERPRETATION IN SINGAPORE: THEORY AND PRACTICE 8 (Jaclyn Neo ed., 2016) (noting "a discernible shift from strong judicial deference to Parliament and the executive towards an increasing openness to creating a real conversation about the proper scope and limits of their constitutional powers").

[41] *See* Tan Seet Eng v. Att'y Gen. [2016] 1 SING. L. REP. 779; Vellama d/o Marie Muthu v. Att'y Gen. [2013] 4 SING. L. REP. 1.

[42] Chng Suan Tze v. Minister of Home Aff. [1988] 2 SING. L. REP. (R.) 525, at [86].

[43] *See* YAP, CONSTITUTIONAL DIALOGUE IN COMMON LAW ASIA, *supra* note 36.

[44] *See* Law & Hsieh, *Judicial Review of Constitutional Amendments: Taiwan*, *supra* note 11, at 24 (arguing that "for a docile court to transform into a robust and assertive agent of transformation . . . there are two basic requirements: an opportunity must present itself, and the court must be capable of capitalizing on the opportunity"); *see also* Wen-Chen Chang, *Strategic Judicial Responses in Politically Charged Cases: East Asian Experiences*, 8 INT. J. CONST. L. 885 (2010).

The book charts a path forward for courts to protect and build constitutionalism in aspiring but fragile democracies in Asia. On a contextual level, the account offered here is embedded within a detailed study of the Asian democracies of Malaysia and Singapore.[45] The foundational constitutional principles it draws on are located in the framework of these post-colonial Southeast Asian constitutional orders, not from what are perceived as Western universal traditions. I aim to develop a contextually attentive approach to constitutional adjudication that draws legitimacy from within the Malaysian and Singaporean constitutions. At the same time, the analysis of these two contexts has resonance for other fledgling democracies in Asia that have not yet developed a robust constitutional culture and grapple with similar challenges from colonial legacies and authoritarian rule to societies divided by race, religion, and identity.

There is another aspect in which this book's focus on courts is deeply contextual, one of more individual potency: courtrooms are theaters for the stories of people whose battles are part of broader constitutional contestations. My account seeks to make visible the individuals who approach the courts as fora for their disputes and, in the process, show how their legal conflicts constitute wider social and political struggles.[46] Many of the cases in the following chapters involve people whose lives are intimately bound up with the conflict before the courts: from Lina Joy, the Malay-Muslim woman seeking to leave Islam and marry her non-Muslim fiancé, and Yong Vui Kong, the nineteen-year old drug courier sentenced to death for trafficking, to Indira Gandhi, the Hindu mother who has not seen her youngest child in a decade after her ex-husband converted their children to Islam.[47] These cases are not merely legal disputes but also focal points for larger clashes over the country's constitutional identity. Religion cases, for example, engage issues that go to the very core of the Malaysian state's character as secular or religious. Often, they involve people who have pushed, pulled, and struggled to advance their constitutional vision within the constraints of a hegemonic state.[48] Unlike doctrine-driven

[45] The Southeast Asian states of Malaysia and Singapore are relatively underexplored in the comparative constitutional law literature. *See* RAN HIRSCHL, COMPARATIVE MATTERS: THE RENAISSANCE OF COMPARATIVE CONSTITUTIONAL LAW 207 (2014) (critiquing comparative constitutional law for its selection bias toward the "global north" countries, which typically include North America, Europe, Australia, New Zealand, and East Asia, and the lack of comparative studies on "global south" polities, which includes much of Asia).

[46] *See* TAMIR MOUSTAFA, CONSTITUTING RELIGION: ISLAM, LIBERAL RIGHTS, AND THE MALAYSIAN STATE 3 (2018) (arguing that courts constitute ideological conflicts over religion in Malaysia).

[47] Lina Joy v. Majlis Agama Islam Wilayah Persekutuan [2007] 4 MALAYAN L.J. 585 (F.C.); Yong Vui Kong v. Public Prosecutor [2015] 2 SING. L. REP. 1129; *Indira Gandhi* (F.C.), [2018] 1 MALAYAN L.J. 545.

[48] In Malaysia, the litany of case names that include lawyers, politicians, academics, activists, and civil society organizations show a growing culture of rights constitutionalism and the rise of strategic rights litigation over the last decade. *See, e.g.*, Public Prosecutor v. Azmi Sharom [2015] M.L.J.U. 594; Public Prosecutor v. Yuneswaran [2015] 9 CURRENT L.J. 873; Nik Nazmi v. Public Prosecutor [2014] 4 MALAYAN L.J. 157; Karpal Singh v. Public Prosecutor [2016] M.L.J.U. 1675; Lim Kit Siang v. Dr. Mahathir Mohamad [1987] 1 MALAYAN L.J. 383; Maria Chin Abdullah v. Pendakwa Raya [2016] M.L.R.H. 260; Sisters in Islam Forum & Ors. v. Jawatankuasa Fatwa Negeri Selangor & Ors. [2018] 3

scholarship, the narrative told here focuses not only on the legal implications of judicial decisions; it also considers how these cases and the litigants that bring them interact with historical, political, and social dynamics, and tell us something about a particular constitutional culture.

Looking outward, this book contributes to broader comparative constitutional studies. It participates in a global discourse on the role of courts in a constitutional democracy. Much of the debate on the place of judicial review has developed from the standpoint of mature liberal democracies in North America and Europe,[49] with premises that do not apply to younger, fragile democracies.[50] In terms of courts in new democracies, scholars have focused on the wave of democratization at the end of the twentieth century.[51] But the experience of post-colonial Asian democracies is different from the constitutional transitions in Eastern Europe, South Africa, and Latin America, where strong constitutional courts played highly interventionist roles in facilitating the democratization process. Nor does it reflect the ethnically homogenous and economically stable East Asian democracies of South Korea, Taiwan, and Japan, which have developed into fully thriving constitutional democracies.[52] For nascent democracies in Southeast Asia, which have yet to develop robust constitutional cultures, scholars have generally advocated for courts to avoid exercising strong judicial review.[53]

MALAYAN L.J. 706. And in Singapore, rising public law litigation has been noted as a recent trend. *See* V.K. Rajah, Attorney-General, Speech at the Opening of the Legal Year 2015, The Rule of Law (Jan. 5, 2015), at [16], https://perma.cc/HQ7Q-D2QE ("Another cultural change in recent years is the increase in civil litigation between the public and the state in administrative and constitutional law issues . . . due to the rise of an educated class with more awareness of their civil and constitutional rights.").

[49] *See, e.g.*, ALEXANDER BICKEL, THE LEAST DANGEROUS BRANCH 16–17 (1962); ELY, *supra* note 13; Barry Friedman, *The Birth of an Academic Obsession: The History of the Counter-Majoritarian Difficulty*, 112 YALE L.J. 153 (2002); Jeremy Waldron, *The Core of the Case Against Judicial Review*, 115 YALE L.J. 1341, 1346 (2006); RICHARD BELLAMY, POLITICAL CONSTITUTIONALISM: A REPUBLICAN DEFENCE OF THE CONSTITUTIONALITY OF DEMOCRACY 261 (2007).

[50] *See* David Landau, *A Dynamic Theory of Judicial Role*, 55 B.C. L. REV. 1501 (2014); Samuel Issacharoff, *Judicial Review in Troubled Times: Stabilizing Democracy in a Second-Best World*, 98 N.C. L. REV. 1 (2019).

[51] *See, e.g.*, ISSACHAROFF, FRAGILE DEMOCRACIES, *supra* note 12; Samuel Issacharoff, *Constitutional Courts and Consolidated Power*, 62 AM. J. COMP. L. 585 (2014); TOM DALY, THE ALCHEMISTS: QUESTIONING OUR FAITH IN COURTS AS DEMOCRACY-BUILDERS (2017); WOJCIECH SADURSKI, RIGHTS BEFORE COURTS: A STUDY OF CONSTITUTIONAL COURTS IN POSTCOMMUNIST STATES OF CENTRAL AND EASTERN EUROPE (2008); Kim Lane Scheppele, *Guardians of the Constitution: Constitutional Court Presidents and the Struggle for the Rule of Law in Post-Soviet Europe*, 154 U. PA. L. REV. 1757 (2006); THEUNIS ROUX, THE POLITICS OF PRINCIPLE: THE FIRST SOUTH AFRICAN CONSTITUTIONAL COURT, 1995–2005 (2013).

[52] Jiunn-rong Yeh & Wen-Chen Chang, *The Emergence of East Asian Constitutionalism: Features in Comparison*, 59 AM. J. COMP. L. 805, 839 (2011); *see also* Jiunn-rong Yeh & Wen-Chen Chang, ASIAN COURTS IN CONTEXT (Jiunn-rong Yeh & Wen-Chen Chang eds., 2015); ANDREW HARDING & PENELOPE NICHOLSON, NEW COURTS IN ASIA (2010); TOM GINSBURG, JUDICIAL REVIEW IN NEW DEMOCRACIES: CONSTITUTIONAL COURTS IN ASIA (2003).

[53] *See, e.g.*, Thio, *Soft Constitutional Law*, *supra* note 18; YAP, COURTS AND DEMOCRACIES IN ASIA, *supra* note 17; YAP, CONSTITUTIONAL DIALOGUE IN COMMON LAW ASIA, *supra* note 36.

The account in this book integrates the Malaysian and Singaporean examples into the comparative scholarship on courts and constitutionalism in evolving democracies. These Asian case studies show how courts negotiate their institutional dynamics of power and also pluralize constitutional accounts beyond familiar notions of liberal constitutionalism.[54] These two polities illustrate different stages of an evolving democracy: Singapore's dominant party state remains a model of authoritarian constitutionalism,[55] while Malaysia offers the experience of an aspiring, yet fragile, democracy. Further, the Malaysian experience adds the complicated, but deeply salient, dimension of religion.[56] Malaysia's constitutional arrangements on religion contribute to comparative scholarship on the constitution-making and design of religion clauses,[57] particularly in societies riven by religious and ethnic cleavages. The politicization and judicialization of Islam's position as the state religion—fueled by a febrile combination of religion and ethno-nationalism—is a case study in how religion, courts, and constitutional identity are central to the story of many pluralistic constitutional orders.[58]

Finally, this book's project faces forward. For courts to play a more vibrant role in constitutional governance requires developing jurisprudence that enables them to protect and construct constitutionalism. In what follows, I am concerned not only with the judicial role but also with how courts can develop specific mechanisms to shape constitutional adjudication. The chapters that follow outline a framework of core constitutional elements—such as constitutional supremacy grounded in the original framework, the separation of powers, and the rule of law—that courts can use to chart a path forward in constitutional adjudication.[59] Courts building on this constitutional framework can develop specific legal interventions in the form of a basic structure doctrine to safeguard the constitution's core, a purposive interpretive approach that draws on overarching constitutional principles, and proportionality review in rights adjudication.

[54] *See* Mark Tushnet, Editorial, *Varieties of Constitutionalism*, 14 INT'L J. CONST. L., https://perma.cc/J7TZ-B4QV.

[55] Singapore's governance regime has often been referred to as a model for other authoritarian Asian states, most notably China. *See* Audrey Jiajia Li, *Is Singapore Still the Model Authoritarian State for China?*, S. CHINA MORNING POST (Dec. 13, 2016), https://perma.cc/TL2W-T3SK.

[56] As Ran Hirschl has observed, "Malaysia . . . features what is arguably one of the most fascinating and complex settings for studying the dynamic intersection of constitutional and religious law." RAN HIRSCHL, CONSTITUTIONAL THEOCRACY 127 (2010).

[57] *See, e.g.*, CONSTITUTION WRITING, RELIGION AND DEMOCRACY (Aslı Ü Bâli & Hanna Lerner eds., 2017); TAMIR MOUSTAFA, CONSTITUTING RELIGION: ISLAM, LIBERAL RIGHTS, AND THE MALAYSIAN STATE (2018); DIAN SHAH, CONSTITUTIONS, RELIGION AND POLITICS IN ASIA: INDONESIA, MALAYSIA AND SRI LANKA (2017); Kristen Stilt, *Contextualizing Constitutional Islam: The Malayan Experience*, 13 INT'L J. CONST. L. 407 (2015).

[58] *See* Yvonne Tew, *Stealth Theocracy*, 58 VA. J. INT'L L. 31 (2018); *see also* HIRSCHL, CONSTITUTIONAL THEOCRACY, *supra* note 56.

[59] *See* Chapter 3, Constitutional History; Chapter 4, The Separation of Powers; Chapter 5, The Rule of Law; Chapter 6, Courts in Transition.

III. Book Schema

Part I sets the scene for the book by describing the constitutional rights discourse and the role of courts in the Asian democracies that it explores. Chapter 1, *Rights Rhetoric*, begins with the competing narratives of rights constitutionalism that have emerged in the rights discourse in Asia. One account has been characterized as a universalist approach toward individual rights, driven by Western notions of liberalism and focused on civil and political liberties. In contrast, some Asian states have asserted a relativist approach toward rights, prioritizing communitarian interests and economic development over individual freedoms of expression, assembly, and personal liberty. Pitted against each other, these two frames have produced dichotomies perceived as in tension with each other: between universalism and relativism, between individualism and communitarianism, and between civil-political rights and economic development. These constructed dichotomies perpetuated during the "Asian values" debate have continued even in the aftermath of that discourse to shape rights rhetoric and practice in the states that had been its strongest proponents. This broader discourse on constitutionalism and rights sets the backdrop for understanding the ineffectual approach toward rights protection in these Asian states.

Chapter 2, *Constitutional Adjudication and Constitutional Politics*, turns to the role of courts and how judicial review operates in practice within the wider constitutional politics of these Asian democracies. Judiciaries in Malaysia and Singapore are empowered by their written constitutions to invalidate legislation and executive actions for rights violations. Yet these Asian courts have long adopted an insular, rigidly formalistic approach toward constitutional review, marked by extensive deference to the political branches. This chapter considers why. Constitutional adjudication in practice is inextricably bound to constitutional politics. Courts facing a dominant political party operate within a challenging environment for exercising strong judicial review. In the 1980s, for example, the government's aggressive backlash to judicial decisions with which it disagreed resulted in constitutional crises in Malaysia and Singapore. Chastened, the courts retreated to an exceedingly subdued position toward constitutional review. Over the next twenty years, the Malaysian apex court would refrain from invalidating any federal statute, while its Singaporean counterpart has not once struck down any law. Occasional displays of judicial assertiveness, particularly in Malaysia, hinted that judicial power had not been completely extinguished, but for decades the courts' path to reinvigoration appeared uneven.

Part II develops a framework of the foundational elements that comprise these Asian constitutions, aimed at constructing an account of constitutionalism in theory to guide constitutional adjudication in practice. Chapters 3 to 5 explore the fundamental principles at the core of these constitutions: I use constitutional history to illuminate the constitution's original framework and then examine the foundational principles of the separation of powers and the rule of law. Chapter 6 draws these strands together to articulate a conception of the judicial role based on the constitutional core and how courts use particular mechanisms to structure adjudication.

Chapter 3, *Constitutional History*, begins at the founding. It examines the constitution-making process and road to independence in the post-colonial states of Malaysia and Singapore. This chapter provides the historical context for understanding the constitution's text and the foundations of the constitutional framework. Understanding the broader purposes that motivated the constitutional project provides us with the context necessary to interpret the constitutional text. For example, Malaysia's constitutionalization of Islam as the state religion was part of a social contract memorialized in a constitutional bargain that also sought to protect minorities and individuals. This historical context is vital for understanding the role that religion would play in the new constitutional order. More generally, the constitutions of Malaysia and Singapore set in place an overarching framework for governance that envisaged continuing constitutional construction in these independent democracies. Rather than mandating a narrow focus on the framers' specific expectations,[60] constitutional history helps reveal the foundational elements of a polity that can guide a contemporary adjudication approach. Faithfulness to the constitution calls for a deeper understanding of the foundational principles that underlie its structure and rights guarantees.

Chapter 4, *The Separation of Powers*, explores the judiciary's institutional role in maintaining balance among the branches of government. To contextualize the judiciary's fraught position, the chapter recounts how Malaysia's dominant party government infamously amended the Constitution in 1988 to remove the provision vesting judicial power in the courts. The Malaysian judiciary's response was initially anemic, with the Federal Court appearing to concede that the courts' powers were now at the mercy of the federal legislature.[61] This chapter uses as its central case study the landmark decision of the Malaysian Federal Court in the 2017 case of *Semenyih Jaya v. Pentadbir Tanah Daerah Hulu Langat*.[62] For the first time in decades, the Court struck down a federal statute, declaring that constitutional judicial power is vested solely in the courts; to wit, nullifying the 1988 constitutional amendment. *Semenyih Jaya* represents a constitutional inflection point: it recognized judicial power and the separation of powers as features so central to the constitutional framework that they cannot be altered by the legislature, effectively establishing that a basic structure doctrine applied to the Malaysian Constitution. By affirming judicial power as fundamental to the constitution, the Malaysian Federal Court reinvigorated the separation of powers.

[60] *Cf.* Yong Vui Kong v. Public Prosecutor [2010] 3 Sing. L. Rep. 489.
[61] *See* Public Prosecutor v. Kok Wah Kuan [2008] 1 Malayan L.J. 1 (F.C.).
[62] [2017] 5 Malayan L.J. 561.

Chapter 5, *The Rule of Law*, turns to another foundational element of the constitution's framework. Accounts of the rule of law in some Asian states have typically been portrayed in highly formalistic terms. Singapore, for example, has long been characterized as having a stable, efficient legal system that perpetuates a "thin" rule of law in service of the state's objectives.[63] This chapter constructs a more robust conception of the rule of law, which is fundamentally connected to the courts' power of judicial review. The 2018 Malaysian case of *Indira Gandhi v. Pengarah Jabatan Agama Islam*[64] reveals a notion of the judicial power of the courts as a necessary corollary of the rule of law. What's more, the Federal Court expressly declared the civil courts' judicial review power and constitutional interpretation as basic features of the Constitution that cannot be altered by formal amendment. This rule of law conception reflects the principle of legality, premised on the notion that all power has legal limits, articulated by the Singapore Court of Appeal in the 2016 case of *Tan Seet Eng v. Attorney General.*[65] The emerging account of the rule of law is inextricably linked to judicial review as integral to the constitution's core framework.

Chapter 6, *Courts in Transition*, draws together the strands in Part II to make the case for a more empowered judicial role in the constitutional governance of the aspiring democracies of Malaysia and Singapore. Courts play a significant role in both checking political power in dominant party states and building foundational principles of constitutionalism in fragile democracies. In the face of concentrated political power, the judiciary can strengthen its institutional role through strategic assertiveness, as the Malaysian apex court illustrates in its two seminal decisions in 2017 and 2018.[66] This chapter takes on the question of how courts can develop the constitutional jurisprudence necessary to support a more robust judicial role. It argues that the constitution's foundational elements—the constitution's original framework, the separation of powers, and the rule of law—provide a core basis for courts to safeguard and draw on in structuring constitutional adjudication. It then explores specific legal mechanisms that courts can invoke in practice: a constitutional basic structure doctrine, purposive interpretation, and proportionality analysis in constitutional adjudication. Taken together, these judicial interventions equip courts in developing democracies to defend the constitution's core structure and to further construct principles of constitutionalism.

Part III turns from theory to practice. It explores how to apply the theoretical framework outlined in Part II in constitutional practice. Chapters 7 and 8 each

[63] *See* Gordon Silverstein, *Singapore: The Exception That Proves Rules Matter*, *in* Rule by Law: The Politics of Courts in Authoritarian Regimes 73 (Tom Ginsburg & Tamir Moustafa eds., 2008); Jothie Rajah, Authoritarian Rule of Law: Legislation, Discourse and Legitimacy in Singapore (2012).

[64] [2018] 1 Malayan L.J. 545 (F.C.).

[65] [2016] 1 Sing. L. Rep. 779.

[66] *Semenyih Jaya*, [2017] 5 Malayan L.J. 561; *Indira Gandhi* (F.C.), [2018] 1 Malayan L.J. 545.

examine one of the two fault lines that epitomize the deep tensions between individual liberty and state power in these Asian democracies: religion and security powers.

Chapter 7, *Judicializing Religion*, focuses on a highly fraught area in the Malaysian public order: the role of religion within the state and religious freedom. As historical evidence shows, the constitutional arrangements on religion were meant to establish a generally secular state. Politicization of religion over the last two decades, however, has led to an expansion of Islam's role, fueling polarizing debate over the Malaysian state's identity as secular or Islamic. Courts have contributed to elevating Islam's position by deferring jurisdiction to the Sharia courts and expansively interpreting Islam's constitutional position. This chapter shows that the constitution's original framework is crucial for understanding religion's place in the public order. It also examines how the power of the civil courts is fundamental to the constitution's basic principles of the separation of powers, the rule of law, and the protection of minorities. Judicial review and constitutional interpretation are solely the province of the civil courts, as affirmed in 2018 by the Malaysian Federal Court in *Indira Gandhi*.[67] Drawing on the constitution's basic structure to restore the federal civil courts to their proper role vis-à-vis the religious Sharia courts, this chapter argues, would enable courts to reclaim jurisdiction over areas implicating fundamental rights, such as apostasy. Judges could also use a purposive approach toward interpreting religious liberty and equality rights to reverse the trend of prioritizing Islamic norms over constitutional principles. Finally, a robustly applied proportionality analysis would enable courts to enforce constitutional rights against government regulations on religion that restrict religious freedom or freedom of expression.

Chapter 8, *Balancing Security and Liberty*, considers the emergency powers and national security laws wielded by a powerful state. In addition to extensive emergency powers, security laws have long been features of the authoritarian regimes in Malaysia and Singapore, from preventive detention to public order statutes restricting the freedom of expression and assembly. Courts traditionally have been passive in scrutinizing government actions taken in the name of national security or public order, refusing to assess whether the vast powers wielded by the executive were reasonable. This chapter makes the case for greater judicial scrutiny over whether government restrictions on individual liberties are justified. Proportionality analysis offers a rigorous, yet flexible, framework that the court can use to engage directly with the government's justifications of national security and public order. On some occasions the court may have to rely on a constitutional basic structure doctrine to strike down legislative efforts, through constitutional amendment or statutes, to remove judicial review or erode institutional safeguards.

[67] *Indira Gandhi* (F.C.), [2018] 1 Malayan L.J. 545.

These doctrinal tools would aid courts in the critical, but sensitive, endeavor of balancing security and liberty.

* * *

The story of Malaysia's political transition unfolds like a Greek drama, along themes of power, glory, betrayal, reconciliation, and irony. Sometimes such dramas end in redemption, but they can also end in tragedy. The forces that drive democratic movements focused on particular political leaders or parties can equally fuel the rise of an illiberal populism—as trends the world over illustrate, from Asia and the Middle East to Europe and Latin America.[68]

Whether a constitutional narrative ends in redemption or tragedy ultimately depends on the strength of the polity's institutions. Many democratic institutions—like the legislature, the media, the electoral commission, and civil society organizations—are important for a project of constitutional governance like Malaysia's to succeed. Constitutions and legal institutions on their own are not enough, but they can and should play a critical role. This book focuses on how courts can chart a path forward in developing constitutionalism.

Moving the constitutional story forward calls for a judicial role that goes beyond Sisyphus and Hercules. To reclaim their constitutional position as a co-equal branch of government, these Asian courts must break out of their old Sisyphean mold of reflexive deference to the political branches. At the same time, enduring institutions can no more be built on judicial heroes than on political ones, and this book does not seek to place uncritical faith in the wisdom of Herculean judges.[69] My account of courts is located in their institutional capacity to serve as a protective check on political power and as agents that can facilitate constitutional construction. Fulfilling this task of crafting the principles that form the foundation of a constitutional order calls for courts to use strategies of state-building. Building an enduring institution that is capable of maintaining a constitutional balance of power in a democracy beats the efforts of a spasmodic Hercules.[70]

The future of constitutional statecraft in Malaysia, Singapore, and other developing constitutional democracies in Asia has not yet been scripted. It is time for courts to shape their own destiny, and the ending of that constitutional narrative.

[68] *See* Tom Ginsburg & Aziz Z. Huq, How to Save a Constitutional Democracy 49–119 (2018) (describing the democratic collapse and erosion of constitutional democracies globally).

[69] *See* Issacharoff, Fragile Democracies, *supra* note 12, at 241.

[70] To paraphrase Anthony Trollope, *see* Anthony Trollope, An Autobiography (Vol. 1) 161 (1883) ("A small daily task . . . will beat the labours of a spasmodic Hercules.").

PART I
SETTING THE SCENE

1

Rights Rhetoric

I. Introduction

Two competing accounts, broadly speaking, have emerged in the rights discourse in Asian democracies. The first account is often characterized as a universalist approach toward rights grounded in a liberal, individualistic ethos. Another account adopts a relativist position, which views the definition and application of rights as contingent on the cultural context. Proponents of "Asian values," for example, assert that there are distinct Asian values that prioritize communitarian interests over individualism and economic development over civil and political liberties. Asian states seeking to distance themselves from "Western" traditions have tended to be skeptical of perceived universalist notions of individual rights. And so, over the past decades, political actors and courts have perpetuated variants of a communitarian, cultural relativist position on rights constitutionalism.

Viewing rights engagement through these two frames has resulted in the construction of flawed dichotomies. This chapter argues that these polarizing accounts have distorted perspectives on constitutionalism and led to an impoverished approach toward rights adjudication in these Southeast Asian contexts. I begin by identifying three dichotomies that exemplify the supposed divide between the two approaches: universalism and relativism, individualism and communitarianism, and civil-political liberties and economic development. Framing these positions as antithetical to each other presents false tensions.

These dichotomies were largely constructed and reinforced during the so-called Asian values debate. As this chapter describes, although political rhetoric on Asian values largely diminished after the 1990s, remnants of this ideology remain. Particularly in the states that had been among its chief proponents—Malaysia and Singapore—these tensions have continued to influence rights rhetoric and practice in the region. Over many decades, the dominant political parties that controlled these states continued to assert the necessity of prioritizing social stability and economic development over protecting individual rights. Meanwhile, courts facing the consolidated power of the political branches have traditionally shied away from assuming a robust role in developing constitutional principles or protecting rights.

Yet the established political and constitutional paradigm has begun to shift. The changing political and popular landscape has been due in part to sustained

Constitutional Statecraft in Asian Courts. Yvonne Tew, Oxford University Press (2020). © Yvonne Tew.
DOI:10.1093/oso/9780198716839.001.0001

political participation and growing rights consciousness since the turn of the twenty-first century in modern Malaysia and Singapore. This emerging culture of constitutionalism sets the backdrop for developing constitutional adjudication in these aspiring Asian democracies.

II. False Dichotomies

A. Universalism and Relativism

The global diffusion of rights in the twentieth century has been associated with a notion of these rights as universal, inalienable, and generally applicable to all individuals.[1] This perspective aligns with a view which ascribes rights priority, whereby "rights are prima facie trumps,"[2] and has been accompanied by the language of universalist standards applicable across societies and governments.[3] Universalists emphasize the political consensus worldwide on the content of rights;[4] as the preamble to the 1948 Universal Declaration of Human Rights articulates: "All human beings are born free and equal in dignity and rights."

Cultural relativism emerged as a reaction to the universal rights model.[5] Relativists argued for understanding rights as contingent on local norms and cultural context. The Asian values approach is a variant of cultural relativism.[6] Its proponents rejected universal rights as Western constructs incompatible with Asian contexts. Among the most influential advocates of Asian values in the 1990s were Prime Ministers Lee Kuan Yew of Singapore and Mahathir Mohamad of Malaysia who staunchly claimed that distinct "Asian" values offered an alternative to the universalist "Western" liberal agenda.[7] Member states of the Association of Southeast Asian Nations (ASEAN) soon lent their support to the "Asian values" position, releasing the 1993 Bangkok Declaration emphasizing that rights must be considered

[1] *See* Jack Donnelly, Universal Human Rights in Theory and Practice 10 (2013) (stating that human rights are "the rights that one has simply because one is a human being").

[2] *Id.* at 7; *see generally* Ronald Dworkin, Taking Rights Seriously xi (1977).

[3] *See* Tom Campbell, Rights: A Critical Introduction 4–5 (2006); Michael Ignatieff, Human Rights as Politics and Idolatry 3–12 (2003).

[4] Donnelly, *supra* note 1, at 24.

[5] *See, e.g.*, Executive Board, Am. Anthropological Ass'n, Statement on Human Rights, 49 Am. Anthropologist 539, 542 (1947) ("Standards and values are relative to the culture from which they derive so that any attempt to formulate postulates that grow out of the beliefs or moral codes of one culture must to that extent detract from the applicability of any Declaration of Human Rights to mankind as a whole.").

[6] *See generally* Randall Peerenboom, *Beyond Universalism and Relativism: The Evolving Debates about Values in Asia*, 14 Ind. Int'l & Comp. L. Rev. 1 (2003); Karen Engle, *Culture and Human Rights: The Asian Values Debate in Context*, 32 N.Y.U. Int'l L. & Pol. 291 (2000).

[7] *See* Philip J. Eldridge, Politics of Human Rights in Southeast Asia 33 (2001).

"bearing in mind the significance of national and regional particularities and various historical, cultural, and religious backgrounds."[8]

The relativist position based on Asian values is deeply problematic. For a start, it is neither accurate nor meaningful to speak about an overarching concept of Asian values for a region as vast and diverse as Asia. Religious, historical, political, and economic variations exist between and also within each Asian society. Culture is not homogenous even within a particular state; an individual or group's perception of rights will vary depending on their social and economic class.[9] As Günter Frankenberg points out, in regions like Asia, which are anything but homogenous, it makes more sense to speak of a diversity of types of constitutionalism rather than a "secretly essentialized" Asian constitutionalism.[10]

Another difficulty is that the difference between Asian and Western rights perspectives appears to be a matter of degree rather than of kind. The Asian values ideology differs from "Western" ideas of constitutionalism "only in the degree" to which standard limitations on individual rights are used to justify government policies.[11] Limitations on rights are hardly unique to the Asian states. The European Convention of Human Rights, for example, expressly recognizes limits on religious freedom that are deemed "necessary in a democratic society in the interests of public safety, for the protection of public order, health or morals, or for the protection of the rights and freedoms of others."[12] Claiming that Asian constitutionalism prioritizes certain values over others is simply an exercise in balancing competing values. Many jurisdictions globally carry out this same weighing act in rights adjudication, most commonly through the use of a proportionality analysis.[13]

What is more troubling is that the notion of cultural values is highly vulnerable to being employed as an ideological tool. Culture is, after all, a multifaceted notion connected to religion, history, language, and values. As Yash Ghai observes, the question of which of these aspects is "privileged at a particular moment, as the crucial manifestation of 'culture' is more a matter of political choice than inherent value to the identity of a community."[14] Many critics of "Asian values," unsurprisingly, have viewed it as a form of political ideology perpetuated by authoritarian

[8] *See* World Conference on Human Rights, Mar. 29–Apr. 2, 1993, *Report of the Regional Meeting for Asia of the World Conference on Human Rights*, U.N. Doc. A/Conf.157/ASRM/8 (Apr. 7, 1993), art. I, para. 8 [hereinafter Bangkok Declaration].

[9] Yash Ghai, *Yash Ghai*, *in* Human Rights, Southern Voices 113–14 (William Twining ed., 2009).

[10] *See* Günter Frankenberg, Comparative Constitutional Studies: Between Magic and Deceit 106 (2018).

[11] Mark Tushnet, *Authoritarian Constitutionalism*, 100 Cornell L. Rev. 391, 451–52 (2015).

[12] *See* European Convention on Human Rights, Convention for the Protection of Human Rights and Fundamental Freedoms, art. 9(2); *see also* African Charter on Human and Peoples' Rights, art. 27(2); Canadian Charter of Rights and Freedoms, § 1; S. Afr. Const., 1996 § 36.

[13] Alec Stone Sweet & Jud Mathews, *Proportionality Balancing and Global Constitutionalism*, 47 Colum. J. Transnat'l L. 72, 73–75 (2008).

[14] Ghai, *supra* note 9, at 113.

governments to justify their dominance.[15] The malleability of the idea of cultural values allows particular aspects to be invoked to shape a state's rights discourse or, more troublingly, to fuel tendencies of illiberal nationalism.

B. Individualism and Communitarianism

Another purported dichotomy focuses on the "individualistic ethos" of Western liberalism as being in tension with the "communitarian traditions of Asia,"[16] which prioritize public order and social harmony.[17] In a much-cited interview with journalist Fareed Zakaria in 1994, Lee Kuan Yew insisted: "In the East, the main object is to have a well-ordered society so that everybody can have maximum enjoyment of his 'freedoms' ";[18] the individual is "not pristine and separate," but "exists in the context of the family," which is part of "friends and wider society."[19] And tellingly, Malaysia's Mahathir Mohamad identified the Asian values he believed most important as societal order, social harmony, accountability of public officials, and respect for authority.[20]

Critics of individualism often appear to caricature individual rights.[21] Lee Kuan Yew, for example, excoriated "[t]he expansion of the right of the individual to behave or misbehave as he pleases" which "has come at the expense of an orderly society."[22] But this characterization of rights as a license for individuals to act antisocially with unrestricted freedom is simply a "straw man" version of individualism. As noted earlier, limitation clauses on rights—including the freedom of expression, assembly, and association—are common in liberal constitutionalist documents like the European Convention on Human Rights and the Canadian Charter of Rights and Freedoms.

Moreover, it is artificial to ascribe individual-oriented and community-related values, respectively, as distinctly "Western" and "Asian." Values oriented toward the family and societal order are hardly uniquely Asian, just as commitments to individual liberty do not have antecedents only in Western cultures.[23] The relative

[15] *See, e.g.*, Stephanie Lawson, *Culture, Relativism and Democracy: Political Myths about "Asia" and the "West" in* PATHWAYS TO ASIA: THE POLITICS OF ENGAGEMENT (Richard Robison ed., 1995).

[16] Bilahari Kausikan, *Asia's Different Standard*, 92 FOREIGN POL'Y 24, 35 (1993).

[17] Li-ann Thio, *Implementing Human Rights in ASEAN Countries: "Promises to Keep and Miles to Go Before I Sleep,"* 2 YALE HUM. RTS. AND DEV. L.J. 1, 15 (1999).

[18] Fareed Zakaria, *Culture is Destiny: A Conversation with Lee Kuan Yew*, FOREIGN AFF., March/April 1994, at 109, 111.

[19] *Id.* at 113.

[20] *See* Michael Freeman, *Human Rights, Democracy and "Asian Values"*, 9 PAC. REV. 352, 354–55 (1996) (citing Mahathir Mohamad, *Let's Have Mutual Cultural Enrichment*, NEW STRAITS TIMES (Malay.), May 20, 1995, at 14).

[21] Damien Kingsbury, *Universalism and Exceptionalism in "Asia", in* HUMAN RIGHTS IN ASIA: A REASSESSMENT OF THE ASIAN VALUES DEBATE 33 (Leena Avonius & Damien Kingsbury eds., 2008).

[22] Zakaria, *supra* note 18, at 111.

[23] *See* Amartya Sen, *Human Rights and Asian Values*, SIXTEENTH MORGENTHAU MEMORIAL LECTURE ON ETHICS & FOREIGN POL'Y 14–31 (1997), https://perma.cc/M2RV-QMRU.

priority placed on the importance of community vis-à-vis the individual is also a matter of debate, not least between liberals and conservatives in the political discourse of many Western states. Seen in this light, "Asian values are not much more than conservative western values."[24]

Despite the problems with this dichotomy, the framing of individualism as in tension with a communitarian view of constitutionalism has long had a hold on the legal as well as the political discourse of these Asian states. As an illustrative example, consider the Malaysian Court of Appeal's 2014 decision upholding a government ban on the use of the word "Allah" by a non-Muslim publication against a religious freedom challenge.[25] In justifying its restrictive approach to the right to religious freedom, the Court of Appeal interpreted the phrase "other religions may be practised in peace and harmony" in Article 3(1) of the Malaysian Constitution as having to conform to the notion that "the welfare of the individual or group must yield to that of the community."[26]

Rhetoric like this belies the claim that prioritizing communitarian values is conducive to societal stability, especially in societies polarized along religious and ethnic lines. In pluralistic societies with a history of social cleavages among ethnic or religious groups, an approach that bestows priority to one community's interests may lead to greater polarization among the various groups. In Malaysia, for example, judicial invocation of communitarian rhetoric apparently directed at protecting the interests of a particular community—in this case, the Malay-Muslim majority group—is likely to deepen inter-communal tensions.[27]

C. Civil-Political Rights and Economic Development

For many East and Southeast Asian developing economies, the 1990s was a period of rapid development. During this heady time, political elites often pointed to the economic success of these states in asserting Asian communitarian values as important determinants of development.[28] Western preoccupation with civil and political liberties was frequently framed as being in tension with the economic priorities of Asian developmentalist states.[29]

[24] Surain Subramaniam, *The Asian Values Debate: Implications for the Spread of Liberal Democracy*, 27 Asian Aff. 19, 24 (2000).

[25] Menteri Dalam Negeri & Ors. v. Titular Roman Catholic Archbishop of Kuala Lumpur [2013] Malayan L.J. 468 (C.A.).

[26] *Id.* at [48].

[27] *See* Lina Joy v. Majlis Agama Islam Wilayah Persekutuan [2007] 4 Malayan L.J. 585 (F.C.); Lina Joy v. Majlis Agama Islam Wilayah Persekutuan [2005] 6 Malayan L.J. 193 (C.A.).

[28] *See* Kausikan, *supra* note 16, at 35.

[29] *See, e.g., id.*; Anwar Ibrahim, Speech from The International Conference on Rethinking Human Rights (Dec. 7, 1994), https://perma.cc/E843-42LF.

Critics assailed this narrow understanding of "development" for being focused on a nation's economic output with little regard for the state of its citizens' liberties. Economist Amartya Sen advanced a more expansive understanding of development that included "substantive freedoms" as "constituent components of development."[30] Still, dominant governments continued to invoke Asian values to justify a strong centralized state and extensive state intervention as necessary for their states to thrive economically. This position gained momentum when China published a White Paper on Human Rights in 1991 and the ASEAN published the 1993 Bangkok Declaration. By all appearances, the "Asian values" approach, linked to economic development, was on a march of ascendency.

Until, that is, the Asian financial crisis of 1997. The crisis dealt a crippling blow to Asian states that had previously argued "from a position of economic and social success."[31] Although Malaysia and Singapore eventually recovered from the economic setback, the fallout saw many proponents of Asian values recalibrating their previous assertions.[32] In 2001, Lee Kuan Yew admitted that certain values like familial cronyism had "led to excesses," although he maintained that an Asian values approach could work if "tempered" by the global system.[33] Mahathir Mohamad, however, showed no hint of recantation, blaming the Asian economic crisis on the "abuse of the free market by a few capitalists in the developed countries."[34] Nevertheless, the Asian values debate appeared to be over, with most commentators dismissing the approach as an internationally discredited regime ideology.[35]

Yet although explicit invocations of Asian exceptionalism faded from official discourse, its underlying ideas about prioritizing economic development over civil and political rights remain potent in these Asian states.[36] Economic priority continued to propel claims of "Singapore exceptionalism," which "fulfils the same ideological functions" as the "Asian values" argument.[37] Even after the financial crisis of the 1990s, the claim that protecting individual liberties would hinder economic development remained a familiar strand of the government's discourse in Singapore and Malaysia.[38]

[30] AMARTYA SEN, DEVELOPMENT AS FREEDOM 5 (1999).

[31] *Competitive Order*, ECONOMIST, Feb. 15, 1992, at 58–59.

[32] *See* Mark Thompson, *Whatever Happened to "Asian Values"?*, 12 J. DEMOCRACY 154 (2001).

[33] Michael Hirsch, *Rethinking Confucius: Lee Kuan Yew Recants*, NEWSWEEK, Jan. 28, 2001.

[34] Mahathir Mohamad, Prime Minister of Malaysia, Speech on Management of an Economy in Crisis, 6th Prime Ministerial Lecture of the Harvard Club (Oct. 5, 1998).

[35] *See, e.g.*, Francis Fukuyama, *Asian Values in the Wake of the Asian Crisis*, *in* DEMOCRACY, MARKET ECONOMICS & DEVELOPMENT: AN ASIAN PERSPECTIVE 151 (Farrukh Iqbal & Jong-Il You eds., 2001) (observing that "[s]ince few people today seem to be interested in making the case for Asian values . . . criticizing the concept may seem a bit like beating a dead horse").

[36] Thio, *supra* note 17, at 21–22.

[37] *See* Laurence Wai-Teng Leong, *From "Asian Values" to Singapore Exceptionalism*, *in* HUMAN RIGHTS IN ASIA: A REASSESSMENT OF THE ASIAN VALUES DEBATE 121, 133 (Damien Kingsbury & Leena Avonius eds., 2008).

[38] Kingsbury, *supra* note 21, at 29.

III. Rights Rhetoric and Practice

A. "Asian Values" and Rights Discourse

In a speech delivered in 2009 to the New York State Bar Association, Singapore's Law Minister, K. Shanmugam, expressed little patience for the "prescriptions from some in developed countries" to "take the Western Liberal model of government and apply it without regard to the state of the society."[39] The result, the Law Minister concluded, "is like putting a lipstick on a pig."

Although the term "Asian values" faded from the political rhetoric after the turn of the twenty-first century, the remnants of the ideology it perpetuated remained powerful in the rights discourse of Malaysia and Singapore. As Surain Subramaniam observes, "many critics are too quick to dismiss the legitimate role played by Asian values in shaping the political institutions in the region."[40] Well after the Asian values debate was thought to be over, ruling party governments continued to assert "the necessity of curbing civil-political liberties to maintain the sociopolitical stability integral to attracting foreign investment" to justify "stymieing the emergence of a rights culture."[41]

Those skeptical of Western liberal constitutionalism routinely continued to invoke claims echoing a relativist perspective. In 2016, Singapore Chief Justice Sundaresh Menon, speaking to members of the American Law Institute, maintained that Singapore's "fidelity to the rule of law has co-existed comfortably with a prominent feature of our cultural substratum, which is an emphasis on communitarian over individualist values"; these include "notions such as dialogue, tolerance, compromise and placing the community above self."[42] The People's Action Party government has maintained that a Singapore-style bureaucratic rule of law ensures societal stability in service of economic development and efficient governance.[43] The Singapore government has been "unapologetic" about its limited protection of fundamental liberties, dismissing its liberal critics as having "a lack of knowledge and sensitivity to the local culture and situation."[44]

In Malaysia, various leaders of the Barisan Nasional ruling coalition claimed that social stability and economic development must take precedence over individual liberties. During Najib Razak's tenure as Prime Minister from 2009 to 2018,

[39] K. Shanmugam, Minister for Law, Speech at the New York State Bar Association (NYSBA) Rule of Law Plenary Session (Oct. 27, 2009), at [52], https://perma.cc/V2VG-JXBQ.

[40] Subramaniam, *supra* note 24, at 22.

[41] Li-Ann Thio, *Soft Constitutional Law in Nonliberal Asian Constitutional Democracies*, 8 Int'l J. Const. L. 766, 782 (2010).

[42] Sundaresh Menon, Lecture, *The Rule of Law: The Path to Exceptionalism*, 28 Sing. Acad. L.J. 413, 420 (2016).

[43] Shanmugam, *supra* note 39, at [25], [35].

[44] Jack Tsen-Ta Lee, *Shall the Twain Never Meet? Competing Narratives and Discourses of the Rule of Law in Singapore*, 2012 Sing. J. Legal Stud. 298, 299 (2012).

his administration promoted a "1Malaysia" agenda that pushed familiar strands of the Asian values ideology, espousing principles like unity, mutual respect, piety, moderation in conduct and speech, and prudence in decisions and actions.[45] Najib also condemned expressions of individual liberty, like the *Bersih* rallies for electoral reform, as not "part of Malaysian culture."[46]

Courts in Malaysia and Singapore, meanwhile, rejected robust judicial review and protection of individual rights as alien to their constitutional system. While many constitutional courts created in the post-war period claimed universal rights as a source of legitimacy for asserting rights-protective judicial review,[47] these Asian courts spurned such universalist traditions and avoided exercising strong judicial review. Faced with concentrated political power within their domestic constitutional orders, these courts extensively deferred to the political branches.

For years, prioritizing community interests over individual rights became a familiar strand in the judicial rhetoric of many constitutional cases.[48] Such judicial deference to the government, especially in relation to civil and political liberties, "resonates" with Singapore's "purported communitarian ideology" that "emphasises the community's interest in social cohesion and stability above individual rights and liberties."[49] As we will see in Chapter 2, constitutional adjudication in Singapore and Malaysia has featured narrow, formalistic approaches to rights interpretation along with an insular focus on domestic practice.[50]

B. Emerging Rights Consciousness

The turn of the twenty-first century has witnessed a shift in rights consciousness and rising public engagement in the civil societies of the aspiring democracies of Malaysia and Singapore. In recent years, sustained popular and legal mobilization has risen along with public awareness of constitutional governance issues, most notably in Malaysia.

[45] *See* Najib Razak, *The 1Malaysia Concept Part 1*, NAJIB RAZAK BLOG (June 15, 2009), https://perma.cc/6HBL-364R.

[46] *PM: "Please Don't Make Demonstrations Part of Malaysian Culture"*, STAR ONLINE (July 10, 2011), https://perma.cc/7N92-Y668.

[47] *See* Samuel Issacharoff, *Comparative Constitutional Law as a Window on Democratic Institutions*, *in* COMPARATIVE JUDICIAL REVIEW 60 (Erin F. Delany & Rosalind Dixon eds., 2018).

[48] *See, e.g.*, Lina Joy v. Majlis Agama Islam Wilayah Persekutuan [2004] 2 MALAYAN L.J. 119 (H.C.), at [10] (stating that "allowing Muslims to convert out of Islam without approval from the religious courts would 'create chaos and confusion' with the religious authority as well as 'the Muslim community and the non-Muslim community as a whole' ").

[49] David Tan, *Whither the Autochthonous Narrative of Freedom of Speech in Singapore?: A Guide to Defaming Politicians and Scandalising Judges*, *in* CONSTITUTIONAL INTERPRETATION IN SINGAPORE: THEORY AND PRACTICE 210, 214 (Jaclyn Neo ed., 2016).

[50] *See* Chapter 2, Constitutional Adjudication and Constitutional Politics, section IV.

Malaysia's increased political participation and the growth of rights consciousness has been the result of several developments. To begin, greater access to information as a result of the expansion of the Internet and online media sources created a sea change in Malaysia,[51] where the government has traditionally tightly regulated the mainstream print and broadcast media.[52] Online news sources able to operate free of government regulation—like *Malaysiakini*,[53] which was launched in 1999—have provided independent sources of news. Blogs and social media proliferated as platforms for political discussion and have become a powerful medium for activists and non-government organizations to mobilize the citizenry.[54] The increased access to information and the rise of new media have facilitated greater rights awareness among Malaysians as well as their broader participation in the democratic process.[55]

Relatedly, a politically mobilized citizenry has increased political and civil society participation. Several political developments led to the Malaysian public, particularly a mobilized middle class, becoming increasingly skeptical of the Barisan Nasional government. Events that helped spur public mobilization include the controversial sacking and imprisonment in 1998 of Anwar Ibrahim, deputy prime minister at the time, on what appeared to be politically trumped-up charges of corruption and sodomy; these developments would transform Anwar into an opposition leader and icon. More recently, a massive corruption scandal that involved billions of dollars channeled from Malaysian government fund 1Malaysia Development Berhad (1MDB), in which then prime minister Najib Razak was allegedly implicated, stoked widespread frustration with the Barisan Nasional government. In recent years, Malaysians have participated in large-scale protests against electoral fraud and corruption, calling for government and legal reform.

Political engagement in Malaysia has also been aided by a growing number of civil society groups and a robust legal bar. Rights revolutions, as Charles Epps argues, tend to be driven by the deliberate organization of rights advocates and the strengthening of support structures for legal mobilization.[56] Several Malaysian non-governmental organizations and civil society groups have launched a sustained constitutional reform agenda over the past several years. An example is

[51] *See generally* Meredith L. Weiss, *Parsing the Power of "New Media" in Malaysia*, 43 J. Contemp. Asia 591 (2013); Pauline Leong, *Political Communication in Malaysia: A Study on the Use of New Media in Politics*, 7 JeDEM 46 (2015).

[52] The Printing Presses and Publications Act of 1984 makes the renewal of all print media permits subject to the absolute discretion of the Home Affairs Minister. Parties in the Barisan Nasional political coalition also held significant corporate control of the main newspapers and television channels.

[53] *About Malaysiakini*, Malaysiakini, https://perma.cc/J72D-X9G7.

[54] *See* Tamir Moustafa, Constituting Religion: Islam, Liberal Rights, and the Malaysian State 94 (2018).

[55] *See* Human Rights Resource Center, Keeping the Faith: A Study of Freedom of Thought, Conscience, and Religion in ASEAN 294 (2015).

[56] *See* Charles R. Epp, The Rights Revolution: Lawyers, Activists, and Supreme Courts in Comparative Perspective (1st ed. 1998).

the *Bersih* movement for electoral reform—*Bersih* is the Malay word for clean—which led to mass rallies from 2011 to 2017 calling for free and fair elections.[57] The Malaysian Bar Association, widely regarded as a "custodian of civil liberties,"[58] has also played a key role by mobilizing lawyers in defense of rights and raising public awareness of constitutional issues through various initiatives.[59]

In addition, strategic rights litigation has played a key part in shaping the rights discourse over the last decade. Volunteer lawyers and activists carrying out public interest litigation—like the Malaysian Centre for Constitutionalism and Human Rights known as LoyarBurok[60]—have pushed constitutional rights issues to the foreground. Such litigation has brought constitutional religious freedom and equality issues to the public's attention.[61] A prominent example is the *Indira Gandhi* litigation over the religious conversion of children to Islam by one parent in custody disputes, which garnered immense public attention over the course of the non-Muslim mother's almost decade-long legal battle.[62]

All these developments contributed to a political tsunami during the 2018 Malaysian national elections, which resulted in the incumbent Barisan Nasional government being voted out for the first time since the country's independence in 1957. The Pakatan Harapan government came into power with an agenda of governance reform.[63] Two years later, however, it lost governing power following a political crisis. But in sharp contrast to the 2018 government changeover, the 2020 regime change was not brought about by an electoral outcome or popular mobilization; rather, it was generated by leading political contenders competing for ascendency after a crisis sparked by several politicians switching allegiances between coalitions.

In Singapore, changes to the constitutional culture have been more incremental. Public interest litigation traditionally has not featured in Singapore's legal landscape, not least because rights advocates operate "in the context of a specific social memory" of lawyers who have been punished for challenging the hegemonic

[57] *See Malaysia's Masses Protest against Corruption*, ECONOMIST (Aug. 30, 2015), https://perma.cc/P547-VTY3; *Growing Public Support for Bersih Rally Despite Police Warnings*, STRAITS TIMES (Aug. 27, 2015), https://perma.cc/6RR4-F6U9.

[58] *See* Andrew Harding & Amanda Whiting, *Custodian of Civil Liberties and Justice in Malaysia: The Malaysian Bar and the Moderate State*, *in* FORTUNES AND MISFORTUNES OF POLITICAL LIBERALISM: THE LEGAL COMPLEX IN THE BRITISH POST-COLONY (T.C. Halliday et al. eds., 2011).

[59] *See, e.g., MyConstitution Campaign: How the Constitution Affects Us*, MALAYSIAN BAR, https://perma.cc/4KR6-JYCR.

[60] *See* Shanmuga Kanesalingam, *Monkey in a Wig: Loyarburok, Undimsia!, Public Interest Litigation and Beyond*, 31 WIS. INT'L L.J. 586 (2013).

[61] *See* MOUSTAFA, *supra* note 54, at 96–123.

[62] For greater detail on this case, see Chapter 7, Judicializing Religion, and Chapter 5, The Rule of Law; *see also* Khairah N. Karim, *Indira Ghandi Wins 9-Year Legal Battle to Nullify Children's Conversion to Islam by Ex-Husband*, NEW STRAITS TIMES (Jan. 29, 2018), https://perma.cc/93TS-XFX6.

[63] *See* Andrew Harding, *Malaysian Reform Dynamics*, E. ASIA FORUM (Dec. 6, 2018), https://perma.cc/ZDK2-4G3H.

state.[64] Even so, in 2015, the Singapore Attorney-General noted that a "cultural change" in recent years has been "the increase in civil litigation between the public and the state in administrative and constitutional law issues," which he attributed to "the rise of an educated class with more awareness of their civil and constitutional rights."[65]

And although Singapore has never experienced a change of government, it is notable that the People's Action Party has shown some degree of self-awareness of late that it should not take its dominance for granted. After the ruling party experienced an electoral setback in the 2011 national elections, Prime Minister Lee Hsien Loong acknowledged that the People's Action Party would have to engage in some "soul-searching" to better serve the electorate.[66] Over the past decade, as Jaclyn Neo observes, Singapore has experienced "significant expansion in political space for debate and opposition" in line with the current administration's "emphasis on a more consultative and responsive style of government."[67]

Growing constitutional rights consciousness has become increasingly perceptible over the first two decades of the twenty-first century, whether in the context of a significant political shift, like Malaysia experienced in 2018, or Singapore's more evolutionary change. Contemporary public discourse and increasing political participation in these societies stand in marked contrast to a previously passive citizenry, reflecting an aspiring culture of constitutionalism.

IV. Constitutionalism in Context

Stories about the constitution can be told in different ways. These narratives are often associated with different ideas of constitutionalism.[68]

One story is a celebratory narrative of the constitution linked to the rise of modern constitutionalism. On this telling, the constitution's triumph is inextricably connected to the nation's founding. In post-colonial contexts, like Malaysia, where the constitution's origin is tied to the country achieving independence from a departing colonial power, the idea of the constitution marking a break from the past and the start of a new sovereign democracy is particularly resonant. This triumphant story of the constitution's achievement fits with an account of the wave of constitutions created across the world after the Second World War.

[64] Jothie Rajah & Arun Thiruvengadam, *Of Masks, Absences and Exceptions: Cause Lawyering in Singapore*, 30 WIS. INT'L L.J. 646, 649 (2013).

[65] *See* V.K. Rajah, Attorney General, Speech at the Opening of the Legal Year 2015, The Rule of Law (Jan. 5, 2015), at [16], https://perma.cc/HQ7Q-D2QE.

[66] *See* Shamim Adam, *Lee Kuan Yew Ends Five-Decade Role in Singapore Cabinet After Poll Setback*, BLOOMBERG (May 15, 2011), https://perma.cc/D93A-VTBB.

[67] Jaclyn Neo, *Introduction* to CONSTITUTIONAL INTERPRETATION IN SINGAPORE: THEORY AND PRACTICE 1, 4 (Jaclyn Neo ed., 2016).

[68] Mark Tushnet, Editorial, *Varieties of Constitutionalism*, 14 INT'L J. CONST. L. 1 (2016).

Liberal constitutionalism is perhaps the account of constitutionalism most commonly associated with the global rise of modern constitutions. This form of constitutionalism is typically understood to comprise a democratic electoral system with free and fair elections, adherence to the rule of law, and reasonable protection for liberal rights, including freedom of speech and association.[69]

Other portraits of the constitution are more skeptical. Constitutions in postcolonial systems have been described as maps that create, distribute, exercise, legitimate, and reproduce power in governance.[70] Another skeptical strand, as discussed earlier in this chapter, reflects suspicion of Western liberal traditions, resulting in an inward-looking constitutionalism based on asserted Asian values. Some others portray constitutions in authoritarian states as being employed instrumentally by the regime. Tom Ginsburg and Alberto Simpser argue that constitutions in authoritarian states function to facilitate coordination by the ruling government, to signal the regime's intentions to domestic and international audiences, or simply as window dressing to obscure actual political practice.[71]

Singapore and Malaysia have typically been held up as examples of illiberal or authoritarian constitutions.[72] Indeed, the term "illiberal democracy" was articulated by Fareed Zakaria a few years after his well-known interview with Singapore's Lee Kuan Yew.[73] Li-ann Thio observes that Asian developmentalist states, like Singapore, Malaysia, and China, exemplify non-liberal constitutional orders that emphasize communitarian values over individual liberties and collective interest to justify a strong centralized state that can facilitate effective government.[74] Mark Tushnet characterizes Singapore's system as "authoritarian constitutionalism,"[75] a form of constitutionalism in between "mere rule-of-law" and liberal constitutionalism. In such a system, elections are reasonably free and fair and there is some protection for liberal freedoms and adherence to a thin rule of law, but a dominant party makes all relevant policy decisions.[76]

[69] *Id.* at 2; *see also* Tom GINSBURG & AZIZ Z. HUQ, HOW TO SAVE A CONSTITUTIONAL DEMOCRACY 10–15 (2018).

[70] *See* H.W.O. Okoth-Ogendo, *Constitutions Without Constitutionalism: Reflections on an African Political Paradox*, *in* CONSTITUTIONALISM AND DEMOCRACY: TRANSITIONS IN THE CONTEMPORARY WORLD 67 (Douglas Greenberg et al. eds., 1993).

[71] *See* Tom Ginsburg & Alberto Simpser, *Introduction* to CONSTITUTIONS IN AUTHORITARIAN REGIMES 1, 6–8 (Tom Ginsburg & Alberto Simpser eds., 2015); *see also* STEVEN LEVITSKY & LUCAN A. WAY, COMPETITIVE AUTHORITARIANISM: HYBRID REGIMES AFTER THE COLD WAR 3 (2010); Terry Lynn Karl, *The Hybrid Regimes of Central America*, 6 J. DEMOCRACY 72, 73 (1995).

[72] *See, e.g.*, JOTHIE RAJAH, AUTHORITARIAN RULE OF LAW: LEGISLATION, DISCOURSE AND LEGITIMACY IN SINGAPORE (2012); *see also* Thomas Kellogg, *Rule of Law in Asia: The Case of China*, *in* HANDBOOK ON THE RULE OF LAW 490, 490 (Christopher May & Adam Winchester eds., 2018) (describing Singapore and Malaysia as "committed to the strange and contradictory mixture of law and authoritarianism that is often referred to as 'authoritarian legality'").

[73] Fareed Zakaria, *The Rise of Illiberal Democracy*, 76 FOREIGN AFF. 22 (1997).

[74] Li-ann Thio, *Constitutionalism in Illiberal Polities*, *in* THE OXFORD HANDBOOK OF COMPARATIVE CONSTITUTIONAL LAW 133, 143–44 (Michel Rosenfeld & András Sajó eds., 1st ed. 2012).

[75] Tushnet, *supra* note 11.

[76] *Id.* at 396, 448–50.

For the past few decades, Singapore and Malaysia operated as dominant party states, with formal democratic institutions controlled in practice by a single political party or coalition. The People's Action Party has governed continuously since Singapore became a sovereign state in 1965, while the Barisan Nasional coalition maintained its grip on political power in Malaysia for more than six decades.[77] While relatively robust constitutional cultures have emerged in the East Asian states of South Korea, Taiwan, and Japan,[78] the Southeast Asian states of Singapore and Malaysia have generally been thought to lack a culture of rights constitutionalism.

Yet even a dominant regime may lose its seemingly unassailable grip on power. Malaysia's regime upset after the 2018 national elections ruptured the polity's dominant party dynamics. And while the Perikatan Nasional coalition replaced the Pakatan Harapan government in March 2020, the new governing coalition does not enjoy the same dominance that the Barisan Nasional ruling regime had enjoyed unbroken for decades; it is far more fragile. Modern Malaysia illustrates the experience of a deeply fragile democracy adjusting to uncertain political dynamics.

V. Conclusion

Rights discourse in Malaysia and Singapore should move definitively beyond the false dichotomies that framed the earlier rhetoric that perpetuated purported Asian values. Constitutionalism in these Southeast Asian states is not necessarily illiberal; nor should it simply be regarded as a Western transplant. Rather, an account of constitutionalism should be contextually attentive to the constitutional framework of the Asian democracies within which it operates. In these democracies, increased political participation and constitutional awareness among the public in recent years reflect the people's aspiration toward developing a more robust constitutional democracy. The aspiring democracies of Malaysia and Singapore call for a more nuanced and developed culture of constitutionalism.

[77] Barisan Nasional's predecessor, the Alliance, was dominant even before independence, winning the first general elections pre-independence in 1955.

[78] Jiunn-rong Yeh & Wen-Chen Chang, *The Emergence of East Asian Constitutionalism: Features in Comparison*, 59 Am. J. Comp. L. 805 (2011) (advancing a model of East Asian constitutionalism characterized by an instrumental approach to state building, institutional continuity, cautious judicial review, and a wide range of rights responsive to social and political progress). *But see* Albert Chen, *Pathways of Western Liberal Constitutional Development in Asia: A Comparative Study of Five Major Nations*, 8 Int'l J. Const. L. 849, 884 (2010) (disagreeing with the idea of a regional notion of Asian constitutionalism and arguing that strands of Western liberal constitutionalism have "universal appeal" to many modern societies in Asia).

2
Constitutional Adjudication and Constitutional Politics

I. Introduction

For decades, the Asian courts of Malaysia and Singapore have adhered to rigidly formalistic judicial review and extensively deferred to the political branches of government. Although these courts are empowered by their constitutions with the power to strike down laws and executive actions for rights infringements, they have traditionally avoided exercising robust constitutional review against the legislature and executive.

Constitutional adjudication in these contexts is inextricably connected to constitutional politics. For more than half a century, the Malaysian and Singaporean political systems have been controlled by a single dominant political party or coalition. The Barisan Nasional coalition in Malaysia and the People's Action Party in Singapore held unbroken rule for decades following their country's independence. These ruling parties have also typically commanded more than a two-thirds legislative majority, enabling the government to pass constitutional amendments with ease. Judicial attempts to constrain the state's power in the past have been rebuffed by powerful political branches. At core, this chapter explores the challenging role that the courts must undertake in the face of consolidated political power.

This chapter situates constitutional adjudication within the broader historical context of Malaysia and Singapore and sketches the parameters of judicial review in these constitutional democracies. It then takes a deep dive into the prevailing judicial approach to describe how courts have traditionally adopted an inward-looking and highly formalistic attitude toward constitutional adjudication, stridently rejecting notions of implied constitutional principles or basic structures. Finally, it draws the lens back to consider the practice of judicial review within the wider political context of states historically dominated by consolidated political power. It tells the story of the rise and fall of these Asian judiciaries, and their uneven journey toward constitutional redemption.

Constitutional Statecraft in Asian Courts. Yvonne Tew, Oxford University Press (2020). © Yvonne Tew.
DOI:10.1093/oso/9780198716839.001.0001

II. Setting the Stage

A. Malaysia: The Birth of a Nation and the Independence Constitution

1. Historical Background

Ancient Greek geographer Claudius Ptolemy called it the Golden Peninsula.[1] The Malay Peninsula lies at the heart of Southeast Asia, connecting its mainland with the islands in the region, and situated between the Bay of Bengal and the South China Sea. During the fifteenth century, the Malayan Archipelago rose to prominence, with the development of the port city of Malacca, as the epicenter of a network of trade routes between the Indian and Pacific Oceans.[2] The Sultanate of Malacca was first captured by the Portuguese in 1511, before coming under Dutch control in 1641.

And then the British arrived. In 1786, the British established dominion on the island of Penang through the British East India Company. By 1819 they had acquired Singapore, followed by Malacca in 1824. With Penang, Malacca, and Singapore, the British controlled three major port hubs central to trading routes between India and China. Collectively known as the Straits Settlement, these port cities came under the direct governance of the British Colonial Office and became a base for the British to expand their influence over the rest of the Malay Peninsula.[3]

Over the decades to come, the British established a system of indirect rule in nine Malay States between 1874 and 1930 through treaties with individual state sultans. Under the terms of these treaties, the state rulers were made to accept a British Resident and act according to the Resident's advice, except in matters relating to Malay religion and custom. By 1898, the states of Perak, Selangor, Pahang, and Negeri Sembilan came to be known as the Federated Malay States. The Unfederated Malay Sates were made up of Kedah, Kelantan, Perlis, Terengganu, and Johor. By the end of the nineteenth century, the British had also acquired the Northern Borneo sultanates of Brunei, Sabah, and Sarawak as British protectorates. Over the early twentieth century, under British colonial rule, tin and rubber became major industries, prompting an influx of Chinese and Indian immigrants to meet the growing labor needs of the Malay Peninsula and Borneo.

[1] W. Linehan, *The Identifications of Some of Ptolemy's Place Names in the Golden Khersonese*, 24 J. Malayan Branch of Royal Asiatic Soc'y, pt. 3, at 86–98 (1951), https://perma.cc/Y7VH-R89H.

[2] *See* U.N. Educ., Sci. and Cultural Org., UNESCO Silk Road Online Platform, Ancient Ports in Malaysia, https://perma.cc/E5RR-SJ5F. To this day, the Strait of Malacca remains one of the world's busiest shipping channels for trade.

[3] Several British geographers, naturalists, and writers—including Isabella Bird, William Somerset Maugham, and Alfred Russel Wallace—visited Penang, Malacca, and Singapore during this period of British colonialism. Rudyard Kipling, visiting briefly in 1889, extolled the "curries of the rarest" he had eaten at the Oriental Hotel in Penang, although he regretted "the turtle steaks of Raffles' at Singapur." Rudyard Kipling, From Sea to Sea: Letters of Travel 308 (1913).

The Second World War brought Japanese armed forces, who occupied Malaya, Northern Borneo, and Singapore from 1942 to 1945. After the Japanese were defeated, the Allied forces regained control of Malaya in 1945. The British subsequently attempted to unify Penang, Malacca, and the nine Malay States into a unitary Malayan Union. The Malays were outraged at the proposed formation of the Malayan Union, incensed that it would require the Malay rulers of individual states to surrender their sovereignty and grant citizenship to all residents, including the immigrant Chinese and Indians. In 1946, the United Malays' National Organisation (UMNO) was formed to oppose the Union. Soon after, the Malayan Indian Congress (MIC) and the Malayan Chinese Association (MCA) were created, setting the foundation for a political party system rooted in race and communal identity.

In 1948, as a result of negotiations between the local political parties and the British, the Malayan Union was eventually replaced with a federal entity called the Federation of Malaya. UMNO, MCA, and MIC formed a coalition known as the "Alliance," which swept to victory in the Kuala Lumpur municipal elections of 1952. The Alliance coalition achieved even more impressive results in Malaya's first national legislative elections in 1955, winning by a landslide of fifty-one out of fifty-two seats. Following its overwhelming success, the Alliance Party assumed control of the Federal Legislative Council, with Tunku Abdul Rahman, the leader of UMNO, becoming the first Chief Minister of Malaya.

Momentum rapidly began to build toward achieving full independence for the Federation of Malaya. In 1956, Tunku Abdul Rahman led a delegation to London to negotiate with the British. Finally, at the London constitutional conference, representatives of the Malayan government, the Malay rulers, and the British government agreed to Malaya's independence. They also agreed that an independent constitutional commission would be created to draft Malaya's new constitution.

Five legal experts from the United Kingdom, Australia, India, and Pakistan were appointed to form a constitutional commission chaired by Lord Reid, a justice of Britain's Appellate Committee of the House of Lords. As Chapter 3 describes in detail, the Reid Commission's task was to draft a constitution for the soon-to-be independent nation. For guidance, the Commission was given specific terms of reference, which had been discussed and agreed upon during the constitutional conference in London.[4] After gathering evidence and meeting with various stakeholders in Malaya, the Reid Commission submitted a draft constitution and working report in February 1957. Next, a working party, established to examine

[4] *See* FEDERATION OF MALAY CONSTITUTIONAL COMMISSION, REPORT OF 1956–57 § COLONIAL NO. 330, at [3] [hereinafter REID REPORT].

the commission's recommendations, suggested several changes to constitutional provisions relating to the special position of the Malays, citizenship, religion, and language. The resulting draft constitution was submitted to the Malayan Federal Legislative Council, where it was unanimously approved.

On August 31, 1957, the Merdeka Constitution went into effect as the Federation of Malaya became an independent nation.[5] Six years later, on September 16, 1963, Singapore, Sabah, and Sarawak merged with Malaya to create the new Federation of Malaysia, with the 1957 Constitution as the basis for the Federal Constitution of Malaysia.[6]

2. Malaysia's Constitutional System

The Federal Constitution of Malaysia established a federal system of government,[7] with a legislative, executive, and judicial branch,[8] and a constitutional monarch. Under the Westminster parliamentary system, it has a bicameral Parliament with a lower house and upper house: the *Dewan Rakyat* (House of Representatives) and the *Dewan Negara* (Senate).[9] The Prime Minister, who is appointed by the *Yang di-Pertuan Agong*, is constitutionally required to be a member of the House of Representatives who, in the King's judgment, is likely to command the confidence of the majority of the members of that House.[10] The Cabinet is appointed by King on the advice of the Prime Minister.[11]

The constitutional monarch and head of state is the *Yang di-Pertuan Agong*, the King of Malaysia.[12] The Conference of Rulers, which comprises the rulers of the nine Malay states and the governors of the other four states, has the power to elect and remove the King.[13] The *Yang di-Pertuan Agong* is the head of the religion of Islam in his own state, as well as in the states of Penang, Malacca, Sabah, Sarawak, and the three federal territories.[14]

The Malaysian Constitution has a supremacy clause, Article 4(1), which declares that the "Constitution is the supreme law of the Federation and any law … shall, to the extent of the inconsistency, be void." The fundamental liberties guaranteed

[5] *Merdeka* in Malay means "independence." For more detailed discussion of Malaysia's constitutional history, see JOSEPH M. FERNANDO, THE MAKING OF THE MALAYAN CONSTITUTION (2002); ANDREW HARDING, THE CONSTITUTION OF MALAYSIA: A CONTEXTUAL ANALYSIS (2012); Rais Yatim, *The Road to Merdeka*, *in* CONSTITUTIONAL LANDMARKS IN MALAYSIA: THE FIRST 50 YEARS, 1957–2007 1 (Andrew Harding & H.P. Lee eds., 2007).

[6] Modern Malaysia is a federation of thirteen states—eleven states in Peninsular Malaysia and the East Malaysian states of Sabah and Sarawak—and three federal territories of Kuala Lumpur, Labuan, and Putrajaya.

[7] FED. CONST. (MALAY.), pt.VI, ch. 1.

[8] *Id.* pt. IV, chs. 3, 4; *id.* pt. IX.

[9] *Id.* arts. 44–45.

[10] *Id.* art. 43(2)(a).

[11] *Id.* art. 43(2)(b).

[12] *Id.* art. 39.

[13] *Id.* art. 38.

[14] *Id.* art. 3(3)–(5).

under Part II of the Constitution include the right to life and personal liberty, freedom from slavery and forced labor, the right to equality, freedom of speech and assembly, freedom of religion, and the right to property.[15]

Courts in Malaysia have the power of judicial review to invalidate unconstitutional legislation and executive actions as a corollary of the Constitution's supremacy clause.[16] The highest appellate court is the Federal Court of Malaysia, which was known as the Supreme Court from 1985 to 1994.[17] Prior to 1985, the court of last resort was the Judicial Committee of the Privy Council, the court of final appeal for some British overseas territories and Commonwealth countries. The possibility of final appeal to the Privy Council was abolished in 1985, leaving the Federal Court as Malaysia's court of final resort. The Federal Court has original and advisory jurisdiction over certain matters,[18] and it also hears appeals from the Court of Appeal.[19] The other appellate courts consist of the Court of Appeal and two High Courts of coordinate standing, one in Malaya and the other in Sabah and Sarawak.[20] In addition to the civil superior courts and subordinate courts, Malaysia has a system of state Sharia courts, which have jurisdiction over "persons professing the religion of Islam" in respect of matters governed by state Islamic law such as personal and family law.[21]

Constitutional amendment rules in Malaysia vary based on the constitutional provision involved.[22] Most commonly, an amendment must have the support of at least two-thirds of the total membership of each House of Parliament,[23] though there are some exceptions to this general requirement. Amendments to provisions dealing with citizenship, the Conference of Rulers, the Malay national language, and the special position of the Malays and the natives of Sabah and Sarawak require the consent of the Conference of Rulers in addition to a two-thirds parliamentary majority.[24] Likewise, alterations to provisions concerning the safeguards for the constitutional position of Sabah and Sarawak require the consent of the respective state governments.[25] Some amendments—like those concerning supplementary citizenship provisions or admitting a new state into the Federation—may be passed with a simple parliamentary majority.[26]

[15] *Id.* arts. 5–13.
[16] *Id.* art. 4(1).
[17] *Id.* art. 121(2).
[18] *Id.* arts. 128(1), 130.
[19] *Id.* art. 128(3).
[20] *Id.* arts. 121(1), 121(1B).
[21] *Id.* Ninth Schedule, List II, art. 1.
[22] *Id.* art. 159.
[23] *Id.* art. 159(3).
[24] *Id.* art. 159(5). The Conference of Rulers is constituted of the Malay rulers and governors of individual states in Malaysia. Its primary function is to elect or remove the *Yang di-Pertuan Agong*.
[25] *Id.* art. 161E(2).
[26] *Id.* art. 159(1), (4).

B. Singapore: Separation and Statehood

1. Historical Background

Sitting at the southern tip of the Malay Peninsula, Singapore held a prime strategic location amidst the trade routes that passed through the Straits of Malacca. In 1819, Sir Stamford Raffles, tasked with leading an expedition to seek a new British base in the region, arrived in Singapore. Raffles secured a British foothold on the island by forging an agreement with the Sultan of Johor that allowed the East India Company to establish a trading post in Singapore.[27] During the nineteenth century, Singapore became a principal port in the Malay Archipelago. In 1826, it was united with Penang and Malacca as part of the Straits Settlements, which became a Crown Colony under direct British rule in 1867.

After a period of Japanese occupation during the Second World War, Britain regained control of Singapore in 1945. The Straits Settlements were soon disbanded; Penang and Malacca were constituted into the Malayan Union while Singapore became a separate Crown Colony with its own constitution in 1948.[28] In the period after the war, Singapore gained increasing self-governance and was granted full internal self-government following an act of the British Parliament in 1958. A year later, in the first general elections for a new legislative assembly, the People's Action Party won forty-three out of fifty-one seats and Lee Kuan Yew became Singapore's first prime minister. The People's Action Party began to campaign for Singapore to merge with Malaya to gain full political independence.

On September 16, 1963, Singapore became fully independent from the British when it signed an agreement to join Malaya, Sabah, and Sarawak to form the Federation of Malaysia. The union turned out to be an unhappy one, riven with tensions fueled by racial politics and exacerbated by communist insurgency threats.[29] Relations between the central government in Kuala Lumpur and the Singapore state government became increasingly strained, and eventually culminated in Singapore separating from the Malayan Federation. On August 9, 1965, the island state left the federation to become the sovereign, and unitary, Republic of Singapore.

The new country's abrupt separation from the Federation of Malaysia meant that Singapore's Constitution "did not have a storied birth."[30] Instead of drafting

[27] *See generally* A HISTORY OF SINGAPORE (Ernest C.T. Chew & Edwin Lee eds., 1991); Kevin Tan, *A Short Legal and Constitutional History of Singapore*, *in* THE SINGAPORE LEGAL SYSTEM 1 (Walter Woon ed., 1989).

[28] Singapore Colony Order-in-Council, Feb. 24, 1948 (SI 341/1948); Order in Council, Feb. 24, 1948, Statutory Instruments, 1948, No. 341.

[29] Kevin Tan, *Foundational Moments: The "Singapore Constitution"*, *in* CONSTITUTIONAL FOUNDING IN SOUTHEAST ASIA 189 (Kevin Tan & Bui Ngoc Sun eds., 2017).

[30] V.K. Rajah, *Interpreting the Singapore Constitution*, *in* CONSTITUTIONAL INTERPRETATION IN SINGAPORE: THEORY AND PRACTICE 23, 23 (Jaclyn Neo ed., 2016) [hereinafter CONSTITUTIONAL INTERPRETATION IN SINGAPORE].

a new constitution at the time of the separation, the Singapore government cobbled together a working constitution. It drew from Singapore's state constitution and certain provisions of Malaysia's Federal Constitution, such as the fundamental liberties chapter, which had been incorporated by the Republic of Singapore Independence Act of 1965.[31] The constitution would remain in this form until the various parts were codified into the 1980 Reprint of the Constitution of the Republic of Singapore.

2. Singapore's Constitutional System

Like Malaysia, Singapore has a tripartite system of government modeled after the Westminster parliamentary system. Singapore has a unicameral Parliament comprising only one House,[32] and its executive branch consists of the President, the Prime Minister, and the Cabinet.[33] The President has the authority to appoint as Prime Minister the person who he judges likely to command the confidence of the majority of the Members of Parliament.[34]

Singapore's head of state is the President. At the time of the country's separation from Malaysia, the Presidency was a largely ceremonial position. In 1991, the Parliament passed a constitutional amendment to change the office of the President from a nominated office to an elected position.[35] In addition to the traditional discretionary powers of the Presidency—such as appointing the Prime Minister and withholding consent to a request to dissolve Parliament[36]—the constitutional changes granted the elected President personal discretion to withhold his assent to borrowings that draw on the nation's financial reserves,[37] the appointments of key civil servants,[38] and detentions under Singapore's Internal Security Act and prohibition orders under the Maintenance of Religious Harmony Act.[39] In 2016, another constitutional amendment instituted a "reserved election scheme," designed to ensure minority representation by reserving certain elections for presidential candidates from a specified ethnic group if no-one from that community had been President for five continuous terms.[40]

[31] *See* Kevin Tan, *The Evolution of Singapore's Modern Constitution: Developments from 1945 to the Present Day*, 1 SING. ACAD. L.J. 1, 16–17 (1989).
[32] CONST. OF THE REP. OF SING., art. 38.
[33] *Id.* arts. 23–25.
[34] *Id.* art. 25(1).
[35] *See* KEVIN TAN, THE CONSTITUTION OF SINGAPORE: A CONTEXTUAL ANALYSIS 123–45 (2015).
[36] CONST. OF THE REP. OF SING., art. 21(2).
[37] *Id.* art. 22E.
[38] *Id.* art. 22(1).
[39] *Id.* arts. 22I, 151(4).
[40] *See* Jaclyn Neo, *Constitutional Change in Singapore's Elected Presidency: Navigating Questions of Ethnic Identity and Representation*, IACL-AIDC BLOG (Dec. 1, 2017), https://perma.cc/DWB7-TEUC. In 2017, the Singapore presidential election was reserved for Malay candidates and a Malay woman was elected President for the first time.

Singapore's judiciary is composed of the Supreme Court—which consists of the Singapore Court of Appeal and High Court—and the lower state courts.[41] Prior to 1994, the Judicial Committee of the Privy Council was the court of final appeal. The Singapore Court of Appeal is now the final appellate court after the possibility of appeal to the Judicial Committee of the Privy Council was abolished.[42]

Article 4 of the Singapore Constitution declares the Constitution as "the supreme law of the Republic of Singapore and any law enacted by the Legislature ... which is inconsistent with this Constitution shall, to the extent of the inconsistency, be void."[43] In addition, a bill of rights, enshrined in Part IV, includes the right to life and liberty, freedom from slavery or forced labor, protection against retrospective criminal laws, equality, freedom of religion and freedom of speech and assembly.[44]

The Singapore Constitution can mostly be amended by a simple two-thirds majority of parliament.[45] Changes to provisions regarding the surrender of Singapore's sovereignty, however, additionally require the support of two-thirds of the total number of voters in a national referendum.[46]

III. Constitutional Adjudication and Judicial Review

A. Constitutional Adjudication

Judicially enforceable constitutionalism is commonly perceived to be "inapt" in Asian democracies like Malaysia and Singapore where courts are assumed to play a "marginal role" in constitutional governance.[47] Courts have long tended to exercise extensive judicial deference to the political branches. Singapore's apex court has never declared a law to be unconstitutional in its history.[48] And in Malaysia, prior to 2017, the Malaysian Federal Court had not struck down a federal law in twenty years.[49]

41 CONST. OF THE REP. OF SING., arts. 93, 94(1).

42 Judicial Committee (Repeal) Act, No. 2 of 1994.

43 CONST. OF THE REP. OF SING., art. 4.

44 *Id.* arts. 9–16.

45 *Id.* art. 5(2).

46 *Id.* art. 8(1). Two new constitutional amendment procedures were introduced in the 1990s, though these provisions have been subsequently repealed. These amendments allowed the President to veto any amendments that curtail the President's discretionary powers and the discretion to refuse to concur with any bill that would amend certain parts of the Constitution, including the fundamental liberties provisions. Both of the referenced provisions were repealed by Act 28 of 2016 effective April 2017.

47 *See, e.g.*, Li-ann Thio, *Soft Constitutional Law in Nonliberal Asian Constitutional Democracies*, 8 INT'L J. CONST. L. 766, 767 (2010) ("[R]ights-oriented, judicially enforceable constitutionalism is inapt in jurisdictions where the apex court plays a relatively marginal role in constitutional politics.").

48 Singapore's High Court (the lower appellate court) has only once declared a statutory provision unconstitutional, and that decision was later overturned by the Court of Appeal. Taw Cheng Kong v. Public Prosecutor [1998] 1 SING. L. REP. 943 (H.C.), *overruled by* Public Prosecutor v. Taw Cheng Kong [1998] 2 SING. L. REP. 410 (C.A.).

49 *See* Semenyih Jaya v. Pentadbir Tanah Daerah Hulu Langat [2017] 3 MALAYAN L.J. 561 [hereinafter *Semenyih Jaya*] (striking down section 40D of the Land Acquisition Act for infringing on the judicial

The reluctance of these Asian courts to exercise strong constitutional review stems in part from legal traditions inherited from the United Kingdom, where a Diceyan notion of parliamentary sovereignty traditionally has been axiomatic.[50] Moreover, as we saw in Chapter 1, these courts were also influenced by the notion that Western-style individual rights protection are antithetical to "Asian values."

For courts in Malaysia and Singapore to approach constitutional adjudication under a frame of *de facto* legislative supremacy, however, is fundamentally misguided. The constitutional architecture of these post-colonial democracies differs from the British legal system in crucial ways. Chief among these is that these Asian democracies possess written constitutions that are acknowledged to be the supreme law. In brief, these polities operate under a framework of *constitutional* supremacy, rather than parliamentary sovereignty. Unlike in the United Kingdom, which does not possess a codified constitution, these Asian courts are empowered by their constitutions to invalidate legislative and executive actions that violate fundamental rights. Like many other post-Second World War constitutions,[51] the constitutions of these Asian states declare the constitution to be the highest law of the land,[52] and also contain judicially enforceable bills of rights.[53]

Interpreting the constitution in these new democracies is an inherently different task from the British legal system where the Parliament is acknowledged as supreme.[54] The need for a different approach to interpreting constitutions modeled on the Westminster system was recognized by the Judicial Committee of the Privy Council. In its 1980 decision in *Minister of Home Affairs v. Fisher*,[55] a case originating from a British territory, the Privy Council called for "a generous interpretation avoiding what has been called 'the austerity of tabulated legalism,' suitable to give to individuals the full measure of fundamental rights and freedoms."[56]

power contained in Article 121(1) of Malaysia's Federal Constitution). For earlier decisions, see Mamat bin Daud v. Gov't of Malaysia [1988] 1 MALAYAN L.J. 119 (invalidating section 298A of the Penal Code which prohibited actions that prejudice unity among those professing the Islamic faith for violating articles 74 and 77 of the Malaysian Constitution which reserve the power to legislate on religious matters to the states); Public Prosecutor v. Dato' Yap Peng [1987] 2 MALAYAN L.J. 311 (striking down section 418A of the Criminal Procedure Code for infringing the judicial power Article 121(1) of the Malaysian Constitution).

50 *See* Jaclyn Neo & Yvonne Lee, *Constitutional Supremacy: Still a Little Dicey?*, *in* EVOLUTION OF A REVOLUTION: FORTY YEARS OF THE SINGAPORE CONSTITUTION 153 (Li-ann Thio & Kevin Tan eds., 2009); *see also* ALBERT VENN DICEY, INTRODUCTION TO THE STUDY OF THE LAW OF THE CONSTITUTION 3–4 (1959). *But see* VERNON BOGDANOR, THE NEW BRITISH CONSTITUTION 284 (2009) (arguing that the notion that Parliament has "the right to make or unmake any law whatever" no longer accurately describes the modern British constitutional system)..

51 *See, e.g.*, INDIA CONST., pt. III; CONSTITUTION ch. 4 (2010) (Kenya); S. AFR. CONST., 1996, ch. 2.

52 FED. CONST. (MALAY.), art. 4(1); CONST. OF THE REP. OF SING., art. 4.

53 FED. CONST. (MALAY.), arts. 5–13; CONST. OF THE REP. OF SING., arts. 9–16.

54 *See generally* Kevin Tan, *Into the Matrix: Interpreting the Westminster Model Constitution*, *in* CONSTITUTIONAL INTERPRETATION IN SINGAPORE: THEORY AND PRACTICE 50 (Jaclyn Neo ed., 2016); Andrew Harding, *The "Westminster Model" Constitution Overseas: Transplantation, Adaptation and Development in Commonwealth States*, 4 OXFORD U. COMMW. L.J. 143 (2004).

55 [1980] A.C. 319 (P.C.) (appeal taken from Bermuda).

56 *Id.* at 328.

Written constitutions like this "should be treated as *sui generis*, calling for principles for interpretation of its own, suitable to its character already described."[57] As Lord Wilberforce recognized:

> A constitution is a legal instrument given rise, amongst other things, to individual rights capable of enforcement in a court of law... It is quite consistent with this, and with the recognition that rules of interpretation may apply, to take as a point of departure for the process of interpretation recognition of the character and origin of the instrument, and to be guided by the principle of giving full recognition and effect to those fundamental rights and freedoms.[58]

The Privy Council expressed a similar view in the Canadian case known as the *Persons Case*,[59] where it famously analogized constitutional interpretation to "a living tree capable of growth and expansion."[60] Lord Sankey expressed the view that "like all written constitutions" Canada's constitution "has been subjected to development through usage and convention," and should be given "a large and liberal interpretation" so that the post-colonial dominion "may be a mistress in her own house."

Such a progressive approach to constitutional interpretation applies to Singapore and Malaysia's constitutional jurisprudence. In construing Singapore's Constitution in 1980,[61] the Privy Council, referring to Lord Wilberforce's approach in *Fisher*, affirmed that a Westminster model constitution should be interpreted in a manner that would give to individuals the full measure of the fundamental liberties contained in the constitution.[62] Likewise, in a 1981 Malaysian Federal Court case,[63] Justice Raja Azlan Shah declared the constitution "a living piece of legislation," the provisions of which "must be construed broadly and not in a pedantic way."[64]

On these accounts, the nature of the constitution is a framework for governance, rather than a mere collection of categorical rules. The process of constitutional interpretation inevitably involves a certain amount of construction to implement and apply the constitution's provisions in practice.[65] When constitutional provisions are unambiguous, interpretation is a fairly straightforward process of ascertaining the text's ordinary meaning. For instance, it is clear, as the Malaysian Constitution

[57] *Id.* at 329.
[58] *Id.*
[59] Edwards v. Att'y Gen. for Canada [1930] A.C. 124 (P.C.) (appeal taken from Canada).
[60] *Id.* at 136.
[61] Ong Ah Chuan v. Public Prosecutor [1980] UKPCC 32.
[62] *Id.* at 39.
[63] Dato' Menteri Othman v. Dato' Ombi Syed Alwi [1981] 1 MALAYAN L.J. 29.
[64] *Id.* at 30.
[65] *See, e.g.*, JACK BALKIN, LIVING ORIGINALISM 4–5 (2011).

specifies, that the *Yang di-Pertuan Agong* is elected "for a term of not more than five years."[66]

Other constitutional provisions, though, are more general or abstract. Take, for example, "Islam is the religion of the Federation; but other religions may be practised in peace and harmony,"[67] or "equal protection of the law."[68] These types of provisions call for constitutional construction to determine how to apply the general principles to particular circumstances.[69]

Understanding that the process of constitutional interpretation encompasses some degree of construction fits with adjudication within a framework of constitutional supremacy. While there may be some fairly determinate constitutional rules that the courts can interpret easily, constitutional adjudication also involves the broader endeavor of constructing legal norms in the form of standards or principles. Constitutional interpretation and construction are part of the legitimate role of the courts.

B. Judicial Review

Courts in Malaysia and Singapore are empowered to strike down legislation and executive action as unconstitutional. The power of the courts to review the constitutionality of legislation is accepted as a necessary corollary of the constitution's supremacy clause, which declares any law inconsistent with the constitution to be void.[70] Judicial review in the strong-form style of *Marbury v. Madison* is viewed as part of the judiciary's power under a written constitution.[71] As Malaysian Lord President Tun Mohamed Suffian observed in a 1976 case:[72] "The doctrine of the supremacy of Parliament does not apply in Malaysia. Here we have a written constitution. The power of Parliament and of State legislatures in Malaysia is limited

[66] FED. CONST. (MALAY.), art. 32(1) ("There shall be a Supreme Head of the Federation, to be called the Yang di-Pertuan Agong[.]"); *id.* art. 32(3) ("The Yang di-Pertuan Agong shall be elected by the Conference of Rulers for a term of five years[.]").

[67] *Id.* art. 3(1).

[68] FED. CONST. (MALAY.), art. 8(1) ("All persons are equal before the law and entitled to the equal protection of the law."); CONST. OF THE REP. OF SING., art. 12(1) ("All persons are equal before the law and entitled to the equal protection of the law.").

[69] *See* RANDY E. BARNETT, RESTORING THE LOST CONSTITUTION: THE PRESUMPTION OF LIBERTY 100 (2004) (arguing that "[c]onstitutional construction fills the inevitable gaps created by the vagueness of ... words when applied to particular circumstances"); *see also* KEITH E. WHITTINGTON, CONSTITUTIONAL INTERPRETATION: TEXTUAL MEANING, ORIGINAL INTENT, AND JUDICIAL REVIEW 5 (1999).

[70] FED. CONST. (MALAY.), art. 4(1) ("This Constitution is the supreme law of the Federation and any law passed ... which is inconsistent with this Constitution shall, to the extent of the inconsistency, be void."); CONST. OF THE REP. OF SING., art. 4 ("This Constitution is the supreme law of the Republic of Singapore and any law enacted ... which is inconsistent with this Constitution shall, to the extent of the inconsistency, be void.").

[71] 5 U.S. 137 (1803).

[72] Ah Thian v. Gov't of Malaysia [1976] 2 MALAYAN L.J. 112.

by the Constitution."[73] The Singapore Court of Appeal likewise affirmed that its system is "based on the supremacy of the Singapore Constitution, with the result that the Singapore courts may declare an Act of the Singapore parliament invalid for inconsistency with the Singapore Constitution and, hence, null and void."[74]

The written constitutions of Malaysia and Singapore guarantee fundamental liberties. Unlike in the United Kingdom, where the judiciary has no power to invalidate statutes,[75] in Malaysia and Singapore, their constitutions contain a justiciable bill of rights that the courts are meant to protect against infringement.[76] Like many of the constitutional systems of the twentieth century,[77] Malaysia and Singapore empower courts to ensure that the actions of the legislature and executive are in line with the constitution.

Before we proceed, a few points about the parameters of this book are in order. First, my primary focus is on courts and their approach to constitutional adjudication. The attention on courts is not to deny the importance of other institutional actors and their impact on the judiciary in Malaysia and Singapore. Indeed, throughout this book, I locate the courts' approach to constitutional adjudication within the broader political context of these emerging Asian states. An awareness of the political dynamics within which the courts operate is crucial to understand the judiciary's perception of its role. Institutional design and judicial selection, too, undoubtedly has an important impact on judicial behavior, although I do not focus in detail on issues of judicial selection and appointment. Still, institutional design alone cannot fully account for how courts discharge their judicial task. Judicial independence must be accompanied by a shift in judicial attitude and reasoning for courts to play an important role in constitutional governance.

Second, I begin from the starting point that these courts are empowered to exercise judicial review to strike down laws that violate constitutional guarantees. Much has been written defending and critiquing the role of judicial review in a democracy.[78] My argument in this book is not primarily about that debate. Judicial review is acknowledged as part of the constitutional system in Malaysia and Singapore; courts are authorized by their constitutions to invalidate legislation and

73 *Id.* at 112.

74 Mohammad Faizal bin Sabtu v. Public Prosecutor [2012] 4 SING. L. REP. 947, at [14].

75 Under the Human Rights Act 1998, courts may issue a "declaration of incompatibility" if the court finds the provision inconsistent with the European Convention of Human Rights, but such a declaration does not invalidate the statute. *See* Human Rights Act 1998, c. 42, § 4(1) (Gr. Brit.).

76 *See* William John Kenneth Diplock, *Judicial Control of the Government*, MALAYAN L.J. cxl, cxlvi (1979) (emphasizing that judicial control in systems like Malaysia extends over the legislature, which "imposes upon the judiciary in Malaysia an even greater responsibility than that borne by the judiciary of England in the field of public law").

77 *See* TOM GINSBURG, JUDICIAL REVIEW IN NEW DEMOCRACIES: CONSTITUTIONAL COURTS IN ASIA 3 (2003).

78 *See, e.g.*, RONALD DWORKIN, FREEDOM'S LAW: THE MORAL READING OF THE AMERICAN CONSTITUTION (1996). *Cf.* MARK TUSHNET, TAKING THE CONSTITUTION AWAY FROM THE COURTS (2000); Jeremy Waldron, *The Core of the Case Against Judicial Review*, 115 YALE L.J. 1346, 1354–57 (2006).

executive actions that violate the fundamental rights. My focus is on how courts in these democracies can exercise constitutional review effectively in practice.

A third, and related, clarification is that this book's argument is not about judicial supremacy.[79] It does not advocate judicial supremacy in the political sense of courts viewing themselves "as not merely being the supreme *court* but the supreme *institution* of government as far as constitutional issues are concerned."[80] The judiciary is one constitutional institution among others in a pluralist democracy; other actors, too, have a role to play in interpreting the constitution. There is sometimes, of course, room for courts to defer to the positions taken by other constitutional actors and for a degree of dialogue between courts and the political branches of government.[81] Nevertheless, as I argue in Chapter 6, courts must be prepared to use assertive review when needed to decide constitutional questions in the face of governmental intrusions on judicial power or fundamental rights guarantees.[82]

IV. Interpreting the Constitution in Malaysia and Singapore

A. The "Four Walls" of the Constitution

Courts in Malaysia and Singapore have traditionally adopted an inward-looking approach to constitutional adjudication, dismissing comparative sources or international law as irrelevant to interpreting their domestic constitutions.

More than half a century ago, the Malaysian Supreme Court articulated what became known as the "four walls" approach in *Government of Kelantan v. Government of Malaya*.[83] According to the Chief Justice: "The Constitution is primarily to be interpreted within its own four walls and not in the light of analogies drawn from other countries such as Great Britain, the United States of America or Australia."[84] Likewise, in the 1977 case of *Loh Kooi Choon v. Government of*

[79] *See* Waldron, *supra* note 78, at 1354 n.22 ("The distinction between strong and weak judicial review is separate from the question of judicial supremacy. Judicial supremacy refers to a situation in which (1) the courts settle important issues for the whole political system, (2) those settlements are treated as absolutely binding on all other actors in the political system, and (3) the courts do not defer to the positions taken on these matters in other branches[.]").

[80] *See* Stephen Gardbaum, *What is Judicial Supremacy?*, *in* COMPARATIVE CONSTITUTIONAL THEORY 21, 34 (Gary Jacobsohn & Miguel Schor eds., 2018).

[81] *See* PO JEN YAP, CONSTITUTIONAL DIALOGUE IN COMMON LAW ASIA (2015).

[82] *See* Gardbaum, *supra* note 80, at 22–29 (describing this sort of judicial authority as "interpretive supremacy" and "decisional supremacy" as distinguished from "political supremacy").

[83] Gov't of the State of Kelantan v. Gov't of the Federation of Malaya & Tunku Abdul Rahman Putra Al-Haj [1963] 29 MALAYAN L.J. 355.

[84] *Id.* at 369; *see also, e.g.*, Li-ann Thio, *Beyond the Four Walls in an Age of Transnational Judicial Conversations Civil Liberties, Rights Theories, and Constitutional Adjudication in Malaysia and Singapore*, 19 COLUM. J. ASIAN L. 428 (2006); Arun Thiruvengadam, *The Continuing Resistance to Foreign Law in Constitutional Adjudication in Singapore*, *in* CONSTITUTIONAL INTERPRETATION IN SINGAPORE: THEORY AND PRACTICE 318 (Jaclyn Neo ed., 2016).

Malaysia,[85] Justice Raja Azlan Shah declared that "our Constitution now stands in its own right" and its wording "cannot be overridden by the extraneous principles of other Constitutions."[86] For decades, the "four walls" doctrine captured the approach of many Malaysian judges. In 2007, the Federal Court in *Public Prosecutor v. Kok Wah Kuan* affirmed that "[t]he ultimate touchstone of constitutionality is the Constitution itself and not any general principle outside it."[87]

The *Indira Gandhi* litigation illustrates the conflicting positions among Malaysian courts over the relevance of transnational and international legal sources. In this high-profile case, Indira Gandhi's ex-husband had obtained certificates converting their three children to Islam and custody from a Sharia court without her knowledge. Citing various international conventions that Malaysia had ratified, the High Court quashed the children's conversion by the Sharia Court, ruling that each parent had a constitutionally guaranteed equal right to determine their child's religion.[88] "As a member of the international community, Malaysia cannot ignore our commitment to various conventions that we have adopted," observed the High Court judge.[89]

In a decision emblematic of the "four walls" approach, the Court of Appeal overruled the High Court. Rebuking the lower court for using international norms as a guide to interpreting Malaysia's Federal Constitution, the Court of Appeal declared that the approach taken by the High Court of "sticking very closely to the standard of international norms in interpreting the Federal Constitution is not in tandem with the accepted principles of constitutional interpretation."[90] In a remarkable decision in 2018, however, the Federal Court overturned the Court of Appeal's decision, instead endorsing the High Court's approach as "consistent with international norms and conventions vesting equal rights in both parents."[91]

[85] [1977] 2 Malayan L.J. 187.

[86] *Id.* at 188–89 (quoting Adegbenro v. Akintola (1963) 3 All E. R. 544, 551). Likewise, the Supreme Court in *Att'y General v. Arthur Lee Meng Kuang* [1987] 1 Malayan L.J. 207, observed that "criticisms which are considered as within the limit of reasonable courtesy elsewhere are not necessarily so here." *Id.* at 209.

[87] [2008] 1 Malayan L.J. 1, 17 (F.C.) [hereinafter *Kok Wah Kuan* (F.C.)].

[88] Indira Gandhi a/p Mutho v. Pengarah Jabatan Agama Islam Perak [2013] 5 Malayan L.J. 552 (H.C.), at [85]–[111] [hereinafter *Indira Gandhi* (H.C.)].

[89] *Id.* at [85]. According to the High Court, this interpretation would be in line with Malaysia's commitments under the Universal Declaration of Human Rights, the Convention on Rights of the Child, and the Convention on the Elimination of All Forms of Discrimination Against Women. *See id.* at [86]–[111].

[90] Pathmanathan a/l Krishnan v. Indira Gandhi a/p Mutho [2016] 4 Malayan L.J. 455 (C.A.), at [71] [hereinafter *Indira Gandhi* (C.A.)]; *see also* Haris Fatillah Mohd Ibrahim v. Suruhanjaya Pilihan Raya Malaysia [2017] 3 Malayan L.J. 543 (C.A.), at [46] (declaring its strong adherence to "homegrown interpretive constitutional principles" and that "what we take pride of and observe is our Constitution which stands in its own right").

[91] Indira Gandhi a/p Mutho v. Pengarah Jabatan Agama Islam Perak & Ors. [2018] 1 Malayan L.J. 545 (F.C.), at [144] [hereinafter *Indira Gandhi* (F.C.)]. The *Indira Gandhi* case, especially the Federal Court decision, is discussed in greater detail in Chapters 5 and 6.

Courts in Singapore, too, have resisted looking beyond the "four walls" of domestic constitutional practice. In the 1994 case of *Colin Chan v. Public Prosecutor*,[92] Chief Justice Yong rejected references to American constitutional jurisprudence on religious liberty, observing that "[t]he social conditions in Singapore are, of course, markedly different from those in the United States."[93] The Singapore Constitution "must be read within its four walls and reference to the constitutional documents of other countries are of little assistance in matters of interpretation."[94] Particularly in light of Singapore's common law tradition, Arun Thiruvengadam observes that "judges and courts in Singapore continue to resist the use of foreign and comparative law to an extent that is quite remarkable."[95] While some have noted that contemporary Singaporean courts are less absolutist against engaging with transnational and international sources,[96] Thiruvengadam describes these changes as "more superficial than substantial."[97]

The Singapore Court of Appeal's 2014 decision in *Lim Meng Suang v. Public Prosecutor* offers an example.[98] Upholding a statute criminalizing same-sex sexual relations between men, the Court of Appeal cautioned that "foreign cases that have conferred an expansive constitutional right to life and liberty should be approached with circumspection" because such cases had been decided "in the context of their unique social, political and legal circumstances."[99] It summarily dismissed the argument that Singapore should align its domestic law with international obligations, observing that "international and domestic law are regarded in Singapore as separate systems of law, and the former does not form part of the latter."[100]

The following year, in *Yong Vui Kong v. Public Prosecutor*, the Singapore Court of Appeal rejected a constitutional challenge to corporal punishment. A court "operating within a domestic legal system," declared the Court, "is obliged to apply domestic law in the event of any inconsistency with international law norms."[101] After

92 Chan Hiang Leng Colin v. Public Prosecutor [1994] 3 SING. L. REP. 662.

93 *Id.* at [53].

94 *Taw Cheng Kong*, [1998] 1 SING. L. REP. 943 (H.C.), at [78]; *see also* Nappali Peter Williams v. Inst. of Tech. Educ. [1998] 2 SING. L. REP. (R.) 529, at [19]; Chee Siok Chin v. Minister for Home Aff. [2006] 1 SING. L. REP. (R.) 582, at [132].

95 Thiruvengadam, *supra* note 84.

96 *See, e.g.*, Li-ann Thio & David Chong, *The Chan Court and Constitutional Adjudication: "A Sea Change into Something Rich and Strange?"*, *in* THE LAW IN HIS HANDS: A TRIBUTE TO CHIEF JUSTICE CHAN SEK KEONG 87, 118 (Chao Hick Tin et al., 2012) (observing that "the judicial trajectory under the Chan Court has been oriented towards greater and more nuanced engagement with academic ideas, foreign cases and international law"); Eugene Tan, *Much Ado About Nothing? The Enigma of Engagement of Foreign Constitutional Law in Singapore*, *in* CONSTITUTIONAL INTERPRETATION IN SINGAPORE: THEORY AND PRACTICE 289 (Jaclyn Neo ed., 2016).

97 Thiruvengadam, *supra* note 84, at 319.

98 [2015] 1 SING. L. REP. 26.

99 *Id.* at [48].

100 *Id.* at [188].

101 [2015] SING. L. REP. 1129, at [121] (despite the Court's acceptance that "the use of judicial corporal punishment is on the wane internationally, and there is a growing body of international opinion that it amounts to a form of inhuman punishment that is cruel and degrading").

all, the Court wrote, "it is not the role of the courts to pass judgment on whether a particular type of sentence prescribed by Parliament is justified as a matter of deterrence or otherwise."[102]

The "four walls" doctrine relied on by these Asian courts reflects what Cheryl Saunders describes as "a comparative methodology that favors particularism," informed by the debate on "Asian values" and an inclination toward a more autochthonous constitutional system.[103] But such rigid judicial refusal to engage beyond the "four walls" of the domestic constitution is unduly insular, particularly for the modern constitutional jurisprudence of these twenty-first-century courts. As Vicki Jackson describes, judges can adopt a model of engaging with transnational sources as "a way of testing understanding of one's own traditions and possibilities by examining them in the reflection of others."[104] Foreign or international law need not be treated as presumptively binding, but neither should courts "put on blinders" to comparative or international sources.[105]

B. Strict Formalism and Literalism

Malaysian and Singaporean constitutional jurisprudence has long been marked by a highly formalist and literalist approach toward interpreting constitutional guarantees. Judges have tended to interpret constitutional rights narrowly in service of deferring extensively to the political branches.

Consider, for example, the Malaysian Federal Court's 2008 decision in *Public Prosecutor v. Kok Wah Kuan*.[106] At issue in this case was the Article 121(1) constitutional provision, which the government had amended in 1988 to curtail judicial power. Article 121(1), which originally provided that judicial power shall be vested in the courts, was amended to specify that the courts "shall have such jurisdiction and powers as may be conferred by or under federal law."[107] Interpreting the amended Article 121(1) in a highly literalist fashion, the Malaysian Federal Court held that the amended provision meant that the courts' powers and jurisdiction were indeed subject to federal law. In a decision remarkable for its extensive deference to the legislature, the majority simply accepted that the extent to which judicial powers are vested in the courts "depend on what federal law provides, not on the interpretation of the term 'judicial power' as prior to the amendment."[108] The majority took a rigidly textualist approach, rejecting norms like the separation of

102 *Id.* at [100]–[101].

103 Cheryl Saunders, *Judicial Engagement*, *in* COMPARATIVE CONSTITUTIONAL LAW IN ASIA 80, 89–90 (Rosalind Dixon & Tom Ginsburg, eds., 2014).

104 VICKI JACKSON, CONSTITUTIONAL ENGAGEMENT IN A TRANSNATIONAL ERA 9 (2010).

105 *Id.*

106 [2008] 1 MALAYAN L.J. 1 (F.C.).

107 FED. CONST. (MALAY.), art. 121(1).

108 *Kok Wah Kuan* (F.C.), [2008] 1 MALAYAN L.J. 1, at [11].

powers and limited government as "political theory," which it did not regard as part of the constitution because they had not been specifically incorporated into the text.[109]

Likewise, in *Danaharta Urus v. Kekatong*, the Malaysian Federal Court held that access to justice does not form part of the constitutional right to equal protection.[110] In upholding a statutory provision that prohibited any judicial order to restrain actions by a government-run asset management company, the Court held that "the manner and the extent of the exercise of the right to access to justice is subject to and circumscribed by the jurisdiction and powers of the court as provided by federal law."[111]

Indications of a more generous and purposive approach in Malaysian constitutional interpretation emerged in the 2010 case of *Sivarasa Rasiah v. Badan Peguam Malaysia & Anor.*[112] The plaintiffs challenged a statute that prohibited a member of the Bar Council from holding office in a political party arguing that it violated constitutional rights to freedom of association and personal liberty. Although the Federal Court upheld the statute, it emphasized that "the provisions of the Constitution, in particular the fundamental liberties guaranteed under Part II, must be generously interpreted," endorsing what it called "a prismatic approach to interpretation."[113] Drawing on transnational sources from the United Kingdom, Canada, and South Africa, the Court also stated that restrictions on constitutional freedoms must be reasonable and proportionate.[114]

Later decisions, however, demonstrated a judicial return to a rigidly formalist approach. In the 2015 case of *Public Prosecutor v. Azmi Sharom*, the Malaysian Federal Court upheld the Sedition Act against a freedom of expression challenge.[115] Since the drafters had omitted the word "reasonable" from Article 10, it said, it was "not for the Court to determine" whether the restriction imposed by the legislature "is reasonable or otherwise."[116] To do so would amount to "rewriting" the constitutional provision on freedom of expression.[117]

In a 2018 decision, the Federal Court reinstated a part of the sedition law that criminalized sedition on strict liability that Court of Appeal had declared unconstitutional.[118] Ruling the matter *res judicata* because it had been raised in the appellant's earlier criminal proceedings, the Federal Court revived the sedition law

[109] *Id.* at [18]; *see also* Jaclyn Neo, *Beyond Mortals? Constitutional Identity, Judicial Power, and the Evolution of the Basic Structure Doctrine in Malaysia*, *in* CPG PUBLICATION: "IDENTITY AND CHANGE—THE BASIC STRUCTURE IN ASIAN CONSTITUTIONAL ORDERS" 19 (2016).

[110] [2004] 2 MALAYAN L.J. 257.

[111] *Id.* at [27].

[112] [2010] 2 MALAYAN L.J. 333.

[113] *Id.* at [3].

[114] *Id.* at [5], [29].

[115] [2015] M.L.J.U. 594.

[116] *Id.* at [36]–[37].

[117] *Id.* at [40].

[118] Gov't of Malaysia v. Mat Shuhaimi [2018] 2 MALAYAN L.J. 133 (F.C.), at [19] –[41].

provision, demonstrating the Court's unwillingness "to look beyond unnecessary formalisms in order to administer justice."[119]

Singapore courts have also been heavily literalist in using textualist or originalist methods to interpret constitutional provisions.[120] For instance, in *Jabar bin Kadermastan v. Public Prosecutor*,[121] which involved a challenge to capital punishment, the Singapore Court of Appeal declared: "Any law which provides for the deprivation of a person's life or personal liberty is valid and binding so long as it is validly passed by Parliament."[122] And in *Rajeevan Edakalavan v. Public Prosecutor*,[123] the Court of Appeal refused to find that a defendant had a right to be informed that he could consult a lawyer as part of the constitutional right to legal counsel. To imply such a right, said the Court, would be "tantamount to judicial legislation."[124]

The 2006 case of *Chee Siok Chin v. Minister of Home Affairs* is another example of the Singapore courts' textualist approach.[125] The applicants, who had been dispersed by the police while staging a peaceful protest, challenged the public order statute arguing that it violated their right to freedom of assembly under Article 14 of the Singapore Constitution. The Singapore High Court reasoned that because Article 14(2) qualified this right by allowing the legislature to impose "such restrictions as it considers necessary or expedient in the interest of ... security and public order," this clause "confers on Parliament an extremely wide discretionary power" that permits the legislature to use "a multifarious and multifaceted approach" toward achieving any of security or public order interests.[126] By concluding that "there can be no questioning of whether the legislation is 'reasonable,'" the Singapore court's approach insulates laws restricting freedom of expression and assembly from challenge.

Originalist arguments have also been used in a formalistic manner to interpret the Singapore Constitution. A prominent illustration is the Singapore Court of Appeal's decision in the 2010 case of *Yong Vui Kong v. Public Prosecutor*.[127] Yong argued that the mandatory death penalty for drug trafficking was an inhuman

[119] Shukri Ahmad Shahizam, *One Step Forward, Two Steps Back? Constructive Res Judicata in Malaysian Constitutional Cases*, INT'L J. CONST. L. BLOG (Feb. 3, 2018), https://perma.cc/5R9D-XU9Y.

[120] *See* Po Jen Yap, *Uncovering Originalism and Textualism in Singapore*, *in* CONSTITUTIONAL INTERPRETATION IN SINGAPORE: THEORY AND PRACTICE 117 (Jaclyn Neo ed., 2016); *see also* Jack Tsen-Ta Lee, *According to the Spirit and not to the Letter: Proportionality and the Singapore Constitution*, 8 VIENNA J. INT'L CONST. L. 276, 280 (2014).

[121] [1995] 1 SING. L. REP. 617.

[122] *Id.* at [53].

[123] [1998] 1 SING. L. REP. 10. This was affirmed in Sun Hongyu v. Public Prosecutor [2005] 2 SING. L. REP. 750.

[124] *Id.* at [17]–[18].

[125] [2006] 1 SING. L. REP. (R.) 582.

[126] *Id.* at [49].

[127] [2010] 3 SING. L. REP. 489. This case is discussed in detail in Chapter 3, Constitutional History, section IV(B).

form of punishment that infringed the constitutional right to life and liberty.[128] The Singapore Court of Appeal unanimously dismissed his appeal, reasoning that the framers had deliberately omitted to include any prohibition against inhuman punishment.[129] Since a provision against inhuman treatment had already existed in the European Convention on Human Rights at the time of the Malayan Constitution was drafted in 1957, which was the basis of Singapore's constitution, the Court concluded that the omission was not due to ignorance or oversight on the part of the constitutional drafters.[130] Rather, the Singapore Constitution's lack of any explicit textual prohibition of inhuman punishment was evidence of the Reid Constitutional Commission's original understanding of Article 9(1). The Singapore Court's use of originalism is consistent with its general interpretive approach of strict legalism, which it employs in service of judicial constraint and deference toward the legislature.

The rigid literalism exhibited by the courts in Malaysia and Singapore often goes beyond standard textualist interpretive approaches. Even U.S. Supreme Court Justice Antonin Scalia, an avowed textualist, explained that textualism—a method of construing the text "reasonably" in order "to constrain all that it fairly means"—should not be confused with strict constructionism, a literalist interpretive method he called "a degraded form of textualism that brings the whole philosophy into disrepute."[131] The methods adopted by the Malaysian and Singaporean courts fall much closer to the strict constructionist end of the interpretive spectrum.

Narrow constructions like these distort the constitutional text. Recall the Malaysian Federal Court's opinion in *Azmi Sharom*[132] and the Singapore Court of Appeal's decision in *Chee Siok Chin*,[133] which considered the constitutional guarantees on freedom of expression and assembly that allow the legislature to impose "such restrictions as it considers necessary or expedient."[134] The constitutional text can fairly be construed as meant to allow restrictions that are *reasonably* "necessary or expedient." Or, as Po Jen Yap notes, it would have been "perfectly plausible, even as a textualist" for the *Chee Siok Chin* court to "hold that the Singapore Constitution only authorizes Parliament to pass such legislative restrictions that are necessary *and* expedient in the interest of public order."[135] Otherwise, virtually

[128] The Misuse of Drugs Act, 2008 Rev. Ed. Sing., ch. 185 (mandating the death penalty for trafficking fifteen grams or more of heroin); *see also* Const. of the Rep. of Sing., art. 9(1) ("No person shall be deprived of his life or personal liberty save in accordance with law.").

[129] *Yong Vui Kong*, [2010] 3 Sing. L. Rep. 489, at [60]–[75].

[130] *Id.* at [62].

[131] Antonin Scalia, A Matter of Interpretation: Federal Courts and the Law 23 (1997).

[132] Public Prosecutor v. Azmi Sharom [2015] M.L.J.U. 594.

[133] Chee Siok Chin v. Minister for Home Aff. [2006] 1 Sing. L. Rep. (R.) 582

[134] *See* Const. of the Rep. of Sing., art. 14(2) ("Parliament may by law impose ... such restrictions [on speech] as it considers necessary or expedient in the interest or security of Singapore[.]"); *see also* Fed. Const. (Malay.), art. 10(2) (providing that Parliament may impose "such restrictions as it deems necessary or expedient in the interest of the security of the Federation").

[135] *See* Po Jen Yap, *Constitutional Fig Leaves in Asia*, 24 Wash. Int. L.J. 421, 436–37 (2016).

any law restricting constitutional rights that the legislature regards as "expedient" would be insulated from challenge.

Judicial adherence to stringent literalism in constitutional interpretation is emblematic of what the Privy Council denounced in *Fisher* as the "austerity of tabulated legalism."[136] Courts in Westminster model democracies would do well to heed the call to generously interpret their written constitutions to ensure the "full measure" of fundamental rights and freedoms.[137]

C. The Basic Structure Doctrine: Unconstitutional Constitutional Amendments?

The basic structure doctrine emerged as a means to protect the "basic structure" of the constitution from any amendment that seeks to alter or destroy the constitution's essential core.[138] This doctrine of implicit unamendability, famously articulated by the Indian Supreme Court in *Kesavananda v. State of Kerala*,[139] has migrated to many constitutional systems globally.[140]

For decades, judges in Malaysia and Singapore have been skeptical of the notion that there are implied substantive limits on the legislature's ability to amend the constitution. The basic structure doctrine's applicability to Malaysia's Constitution was first considered and dismissed by the Supreme Court in the 1963 case of *Government of the State of Kelantan v. Government of the Federation of Malaya and Another*,[141] a position it affirmed in two subsequent decisions. In the 1977 case of *Loh Kooi Choon*, Justice Raja Azlan Shah called "a doctrine of implied restrictions on the power of constitutional amendment" a "fallacy" because "it concedes to the court a more potent power of constitutional amendment through judicial legislation than the organ formally and clearly chosen by the Constitution for the exercise of the amending power."[142] Likewise, in *Phang Chin Hock v. Public Prosecutor*,[143] the Supreme Court reiterated that "it is enough for us merely to say that Parliament may amend the Constitution in the way they think fit, provided they comply with all the conditions precedent and subsequent regarding manner and form prescribed by the Constitution itself."[144] It is worth noting, though, that although the Court declined to apply the basic structure doctrine in these cases, it

[136] Minister of Home Aff. v. Fisher [1980] A.C. 319, 328.

[137] *Id.* at 328.

[138] *See generally* YANIV ROZNAI, UNCONSTITUTIONAL CONSTITUTIONAL AMENDMENTS: THE LIMITS OF AMENDMENT POWERS (2017).

[139] AIR 1973 SC 1461 (India); *see also* ROZNAI, UNCONSTITUTIONAL CONSTITUTIONAL AMENDMENTS, *supra* note 138.

[140] *See id.* at 212.

[141] [1963] MALAYAN. L.J. 355.

[142] Loh Kooi Choon v. Gov't of Malaysia [1977] 2 MALAYAN L.J. 187, at 189.

[143] [1980] 1 MALAYAN L.J. 70.

[144] *See id.* at 70, 73.

left unresolved the question of whether the doctrine could be invoked in a future context.[145]

Yet a judicial turn has occurred in Malaysia. Initial signs emerged in *Sivarasa Rasiah v. Badan Peguam Malaysia*,[146] where the Malaysian Federal Court declared in *obiter* that "Parliament cannot enact laws (including Acts amending the Constitution) that violate the basic structure."[147] Calling the Supreme Court's view in *Loh Kooi Choon* "misplaced," Justice Gopal Sri Ram emphasized that unlike "a country whose Parliament is supreme," the doctrine of parliamentary supremacy does not apply to Malaysia's written constitution.[148] Fundamental rights guarantees, he declared, are "part of the basic structure of the Constitution." Shortly after, when the Court of Appeal invalidated a statutory provision in *Muhammad Hilman bin Idham*,[149] it underscored that the Federal Court in *Sivarasa* had given "recognition for the first time, albeit in a limited fashion, to the doctrine of basic structure of the Constitution."[150]

Significantly, in 2017, the Federal Court endorsed the basic structure doctrine in *Semenyih Jaya v. Pentadbir Tanah Daerah Hulu Langat*.[151] In invalidating part of a statute, the Court held that "the judicial power of the court resides in the judiciary and no other."[152] Significantly, the Federal Court went on to declare that "Parliament does not have the power to amend the Federal Constitution to the effect of undermining the features [of the separation of powers and the independence of the judiciary]," which it declared basic features of the Malaysian Constitution.[153] In doing so, the apex court negated the controversial 1988 amendment in which the government removed a textual provision vesting judicial power in the courts.[154] The Federal Court rejected the idea that the 1988 amendment subjected the courts' power to Parliament: "the judicial power of the court resides in the Judiciary and no other as is explicit in [Article] 121(1) of the Constitution."[155] The Federal Court's acceptance of the basic structure doctrine has been viewed as "the most surprising, and most radical aspect of the decision in *Semenyih*," not least because "it departed from long-held Malaysian jurisprudence."[156]

145 Andrew Harding, *The Death of a Doctrine? Phang Chin Hock v. Public Prosecutor*, 21 Malayan L.J. 365 (1979).
146 [2010] 2 Malayan L.J. 333.
147 *Id.* at [7].
148 *Id.*
149 Muhammad Hilman v. Kerajaan Malaysia [2011] 6 Malayan L.J. 507.
150 *Id.* at [44].
151 [2017] 3 Malayan L.J. 561. This case is discussed extensively in Chapter 4, Separation of Powers.
152 *Id.* at [54].
153 *Id.* at [74]–[76].
154 *See infra* section V(A) (describing the 1988 Malaysian judicial crisis).
155 *Semenyih Jaya*, [2017] 3 Malayan L.J. 561, at [86].
156 H.P. Lee et al., *Constitutional Change in Malaysia*, *in* Constitutional Amendment in Southeast Asia, 14 J. Comp. L. 119, 135 (2019).

The following year, in the 2018 case of *Indira Gandhi*, the Federal Court cemented the basic structure doctrine in Malaysian constitutional jurisprudence.[157] In this case involving the judicial authority of the civil courts vis-à-vis the Sharia courts, the Court expressly declared that the principles of "the separation of powers, the rule of law and the protection of minorities" are "part of the basic structure of the Constitution" that "cannot be abrogated or removed."[158]

Singapore's approach to the basic structure doctrine resembles the Malaysian story.[159] In the 1989 case of *Teo Soh Lung v. Minister of Home Affairs*,[160] the High Court rejected the *Kesavananda* doctrine's applicability to Singapore's constitution, emphasizing "the differences in the making of the Indian and Singapore Constitutions."[161] "If the framers of the Singapore Constitution had intended limitations on the power of amendment, they would have expressly provided for such limitations," Justice Chua wrote for the majority, expressing concerns that applying the basic structure doctrine would usurp Parliament's legislative function.[162]

Still, signs of greater judicial openness toward the idea of a constitutional basic structure in Singapore have emerged. At a lecture given in 2012, Chief Justice Chan declared "judicial power as part of the basic structure" of the Singapore Constitution, calling "its exercise through judicial review [as] the cornerstone of the 'rule of law.'"[163] Intriguingly, the Chief Justice noted that the Court of Appeal in *Teo Soh Lung* had left open the issue of whether the *Kesavananda* doctrine was applicable to "constitutional amendments of any nature," observing that "academics may well have to revisit their analysis on this issue."[164] And several months later, in a Singapore High Court decision in *Mohammad Faizal bin Sabtu v. Public Prosecutor*,[165] Chief Justice Chan declared that "[t]he principle of separation of powers, whether conceived as a sharing or division of sovereign power between these three organs of state" is "a part of the basic structure of the Singapore Constitution."[166]

In the 2015 case of *Yong Vui Kong v. Public Prosecutor*,[167] the Singapore Court of Appeal acknowledged that some aspects of the Singapore Constitution that are "fundamental and essential to the political system that is established thereunder,"

[157] *Indira Gandhi* (F.C.), [2018] 1 MALAYAN L.J. 545.

[158] *Id.* at [90]

[159] Yaniv Roznai, *Constitutional Amendability and Unamendability in Southeast Asia*, *in* CONSTITUTIONAL AMENDMENT IN SOUTHEAST ASIA, 14 J. COMP. L. 188, 193 (2019).

[160] [1989] 2 SING. L. REP. 449.

[161] *Id.* at [3].

[162] *Id.* at [34]–[35]. The High Court affirmed this position in another case two years later. *See* Vincent Cheng v. Minister of Home Aff. [1990] 1 SING. L. REP. 449.

[163] Chan Sek Keong, *The Courts and the "Rule of Law" in Singapore*, SING. J. LEGAL STUD. 209, 223 (2012); *see also* Chan Sek Keong, *Basic Structure and Supremacy of the Singapore Constitution"*, 29 SING. ACAD. L. J. 619 (2017).

[164] Chan, *The Courts and the "Rule of Law" in Singapore*, *supra* note 163, at 224.

[165] [2012] 4 SING. L. REP. 947.

[166] *Id.* at [11].

[167] [2015] 2 SING. L. REP. 1129.

like the separation of powers and the right to vote, may be part of the basic structure.[168] But the Court avoided pronouncing decisively on whether the basic structure doctrine applied, finding it unnecessary in that case to determine the doctrine's extent and effect in Singapore.[169]

Likewise, in 2017, the Singapore High Court declined to recognize a basic structure doctrine in *Ravi s/o Madasamy v. Attorney-General*,[170] which dealt with an equal protection challenge to constitutional amendments that imposed stricter eligibility criteria for presidential candidates, noting that an expansive view of the basic structure doctrine "has not received explicit judicial recognition as being part of Singapore law."[171] The High Court observed that "any ostensible support of the basic structure doctrine was rather more minimalist and related to a 'thin' conception" of the basic structure; it was no more than a "a broad restatement" of the idea "that the Constitution rests on an overarching principled framework embracing the precepts of the rule of law and the separation of powers."[172]

Still, scholars have taken up the Chief Justice's provocation to "revisit" their analysis of the basic structure doctrine in Singapore.[173] Much analysis has centered on the extent of the doctrine's applicability. Jaclyn Neo notes that a "thin" conception of the basic structure could mean an interpretive principle for courts to strive to interpret any amendments in a manner that does not violate the constitution's structural framework.[174] And Kevin Tan has suggested that there are some "minimal constraints" on the legislature's power to amend the "structural matrix" of Singapore's Westminster model of government, such as provisions guaranteeing judicial power or fundamental liberties.[175]

What seems clear is that reception to the basic structure doctrine has evolved from outright skepticism to increasing acceptance of the idea that the Malaysian and Singaporean constitutions contain certain immutable features. The extent of judicially implied limits on constitutional amendments remains a live debate. With *Semenyih Jaya* and *Indira Gandhi*, Malaysia appears to have joined the

[168] *Id.* at [71].
[169] *Id.*
[170] [2017] SGHC 163.
[171] *Id.* at [56].
[172] *Id.* at [65]–[66].
[173] Chan, *The Courts and the "Rule of Law" in Singapore*, *supra* note 163, at 223. *See, e.g.*, Calvin Liang & Sarah Shi, *The Constitution of Our Constitution: A Vindication of the Basic Structure Doctrine*, Sing. L. Gazette 12 (Aug. 2014); Jaclyn Neo, *Should Constitutional Principles Be Eternal?*, Straits Times (Oct. 6, 2014), https://perma.cc/HX49-DZN7; Swati Jhaveri, *Recent Judicial Comments on the Basic Structure of the Constitution*, Sing. Pub. L. Blog (Apr. 20, 2016), https://perma.cc/L5Y8-8CLN; Andrew Harding, *Does the "Basic Structure" Doctrine Apply in Singapore's Constitution? An Inquiry into Some Fundamental Constitutional Premises*, *in* Constitutional Interpretation in Singapore 32 (Jaclyn Neo ed., 2016).
[174] Jaclyn Neo, *Towards a "Thin" Basic Structure Doctrine in Singapore*, Int'l J. Const. L. Blog (Jan. 17, 2018), https://perma.cc/FCK7-D2PL.
[175] Tan, *supra* note 54, at 70.

global judicial embrace of constitutional unamendability.[176] Malaysia's turn toward the basic structure doctrine may well influence other courts in the region, and Singapore appears already to be shifting in that direction.[177] Developing the basic structure doctrine would serve as a powerful judicial tool in protecting fundamental elements of the constitution's core in these Asian democracies.

V. Courts and Constitutional Politics

A. Judicial Review in Political Context

In much of constitutional law, constitutional politics matter. For almost all of their history, courts in Malaysia and Singapore have operated within a political environment controlled by a single political coalition or party. The Barisan Nasional coalition in Malaysia and the People's Action Party in Singapore both dominated politics in their respective countries for decades. Tensions between the judiciary and the political branches have reached several inflection points.

Authoritarian power has sometimes been displayed transparently through direct assails on the courts and judicial independence. One stark example is the 1988 Malaysian judicial crisis.[178] The 1980s were a turbulent period in Malaysia. Following a series of judicial decisions viewed as unfavorable to the ruling government,[179] relations between the judiciary and then prime minister Mahathir Mohamad became increasingly strained. In *Public Prosecutor v. Dato Yap Peng*,[180] the Supreme Court struck down a federal law that allowed the Attorney General to withdraw a criminal case to the High Court, holding that the statute infringed the judicial power vested in the courts.[181] Several other assertive decisions followed. What's more, the Court was set to hear a politically charged challenge to UMNO's internal party election results, which would implicate Mahathir's position as the president of UMNO and, hence, prime minister.[182]

[176] *See also* Andrew Harding et al., *Malaysia: The State of Liberal Democracy*, 16 INT'L J. CONST. L. 625, 629 (2018) (observing that *Semenyih Jaya* is "is a landmark development that departs significantly from previous rulings on the issue and brings Malaysia in line with some other Commonwealth jurisdiction").

[177] Roznai, *Constitutional Amendability and Unamendability in Southeast Asia*, *supra* note 159.

[178] *See generally* H.P. LEE, CONSTITUTIONAL CONFLICTS IN CONTEMPORARY MALAYSIA 77–110 (2017); Visu Sinnadurai, *The 1988 Judiciary Crisis and its Aftermath*, *in* CONSTITUTIONAL LANDMARKS IN MALAYSIA 173, 173–96 (Andrew Harding & H.P. Lee eds., 2007); A.J. Harding, *The 1988 Constitutional Crisis in Malaysia*, 39 INT. COMP. LAW Q. 57 (1990).

[179] *See, e.g.*, Berthelsen v. Dir. Gen. of Immigr. [1987] 1 MALAYAN L.J. 134; Persatuan Aliran Kesederan Negara v. Minister of Home Aff. [1988] 1 MALAYAN L.J. 440; Inspector-Gen. of Police v. Tan Sri Raja Khalid [1988] 1 MALAYAN L.J. 182; Karpal Singh v. Minister of Home Aff. [1988] 1 MALAYAN L.J. 468.

[180] [1987] 2 MALAYAN L.J. 311.

[181] FED. CONST. (MALAY.), art. 121(1).

[182] *See* Mohamed Noor bin Othman v. Mohamed Yusoff Jaafar [1988] 2 MALAYAN L.J. 129 (the "UMNO 11" case).

Prime Minister Mahathir Mohamad made no secret of his frustration with the judiciary, publicly excoriating the courts in several speeches and interviews.[183] Distressed by these public rebukes, the Lord President of the Supreme Court, Tun Salleh Abas, after meeting with several senior judges in Kuala Lumpur, sent a letter to the *Yang di-Pertuan Agong* expressing the judiciary's disappointment with the Prime Minister's comments. The King considered the letter to be a request for intervention; concerned that the issue would bring the Rulers into conflict with the executive, he consulted the Prime Minister about what action to take. The Prime Minister advised the *Yang di-Pertuan Agong* to remove the Lord President on grounds of misbehavior. Shortly after, Tun Salleh was summoned to the Prime Minister's office, where Mahathir informed the Lord President of the King's displeasure and requested that he resign.

Stunned, the Lord President refused to resign. In short shrift, he was suspended from his duties, and events began to unfold like a falling stack of dominos. A tribunal was hastily assembled to preside over the Lord President's removal. Not least among the many procedural problems with this tribunal was that it was chaired by the judge who would assume the office of Lord President if Tun Salleh were removed. Tun Salleh applied for an order to restrain the tribunal from submitting its report to the King. Five Supreme Court justices granted this order in a special sitting. They were then suspended themselves for misbehavior, and a second tribunal convened to deal with the removal of these five Supreme Court justices. The two tribunals released reports concluding that the chief judge and two of the five Supreme Court justices had been guilty of misbehavior.[184]

Soon after, the Lord President and two Supreme Court judges were officially removed from office. As Andrew Harding notes, "the events of 1988 were a shattering blow to the judiciary and the Constitution."[185] It would take two decades before a panel of eminent persons set up by the Malaysian Bar Council in 2008 cleared the Lord President and the two Supreme Court judges of any wrongdoing and declared the removal of all three judges unjustified.[186] The panel's conclusion only affirmed the widely held view that the 1988 judicial crisis was one of the lowest points in Malaysia's constitutional history.

[183] In an interview with *TIME Magazine*, Mahathir stated: "The Judiciary says [to us], 'Although you passed a law with a certain thing in mind, we think that your mind is wrong, and we want to give our interpretation.' " *"I Know How the People Feel": An Interview with Prime Minister Dr. Mahathir Mohamad*, TIME, Nov. 24, 1986, at 20; *see also* Harding, *The "Westminster Model" Constitution Overseas, supra* note 54, at 210.

[184] *See* Report of the Tribunal Established under Article 125(3) and (4) of the Federal Constitution, Re: YAA Tun Dato Haji Mohamed Salleh Abas, Lord President, Malaysia (Kuala Lumpur, Government Printer, 1988); Report of the Tribunal Established under Article 125(3) and (4) of the Federal Constitution, Re: YA Tan Sri Wan Suleiman bin Pawan Teh, Supreme Court Judge, etc., (Kuala Lumpur, Government Printer, 1988).

[185] Harding, *1988 Constitutional Crisis, supra* note 178, at 80.

[186] *See* Report of the Panel of Eminent Persons to Review the 1988 Judicial Crisis in Malaysia (Kuala Lumpur, Bar Council, 2008).

After 1988, several episodes compounded the erosion of public confidence in the Malaysian judiciary's independence. In 2007, a leaked videotape showed a lawyer speaking on the phone with someone who appeared to be a senior judge about fixing judicial appointments.[187] After an outcry by the Bar Council and civil society activists,[188] the government set up a Royal Commission of Inquiry, which found that the videotaped conversation did show inappropriate political involvement in judicial appointments.[189] The government eventually established a Judicial Appointments Commission in 2009 based on a commission's recommendations, but no action was ever taken against any of the individuals implicated in the videotape and concerns about the appointment and promotion of senior judges continued to be raised.[190]

Another mechanism that ruling party governments have used to consolidate power is to employ formal constitutional amendments to constrain judicial review. The dominance of a single party or coalition has meant that amending the constitution easy in practice. A simple two-thirds legislative majority is all that is required to amend the constitution in both Malaysia and Singapore. For most of its time in power, the Barisan Nasional ruling party controlled more than the parliamentary majority required to amend the constitution.[191] The Malaysian Constitution has been amended through more than fifty amendment acts, totaling around 700 individual textual amendments, since it was enacted in 1957.[192] In Singapore, the People's Action Party, which has always controlled well over the parliamentary two-thirds majority required to amend constitution, has passed more than forty constitutional amendment acts.[193] The use of formal amendment by dominant regimes is not uncommon globally, as David Landau has shown in his cross-regional study of regimes using "abusive" constitutional change to achieve anti-democratic ends.[194]

Consider, as an illustrative example, the Singapore government's response to the judiciary's 1988 decision in *Chng Suan Tze v. Minister of Home Affairs*.[195] Under

[187] *Special Report: The Lingam Tape*, MALAYSIAKINI (Sept. 24, 2007), https://perma.cc/2BVF-478P.

[188] *See* Jalil Hamad, *Malaysia Lawyers Hold Rare Demonstration for Reform*, REUTERS (Sept. 26, 2007), https://perma.cc/LR7H-SVQ4. *See generally* Andrew Harding & Amanda Whiting, *Custodian of Civil Liberties and Justice in Malaysia: The Malaysian Bar and the Moderate State*, *in* FORTUNES AND MISFORTUNES OF POLITICAL LIBERALISM: THE LEGAL COMPLEX IN THE BRITISH POST-COLONY (T.C. Halliday et al. eds., 2011).

[189] The Commission of Enquiry on the Video Clip Recording of Images of a Person Purported to be an Advocate and Solicitor Speaking on the Telephone on Matters Regarding the Appointment of Judges, *The Report* (May 9, 2008), at 76.

[190] *See, e.g.*, *Ex-appellate Judge Hishamudin Says Hit Glass Ceiling Because Didn't Get PM's Nod*, MALAY MAIL (Sept. 20, 2015), https://perma.cc/S333-ES3H.

[191] The Barisan Nasional government lost its two-thirds legislative majority in the 2008 Malaysian general elections.

[192] Cindy Tham, *Major Changes to the Constitution*, THE SUN (July 17, 2007), https://perma.cc/5LU7-LRQ9.

[193] LI-ANN THIO, A TREATISE ON SINGAPORE CONSTITUTIONAL LAW [04.052] (2012).

[194] David Landau, *Abusive Constitutionalism*, 47 U.C.D. L. REV. 189, 196 (2014); *see also* TOM GINSBURG & AZIZ Z. HUQ, HOW TO SAVE A CONSTITUTIONAL DEMOCRACY 91–95 (2018).

[195] [1988] 2 SING. L. REP. (R.) 525.

Singapore's Internal Security Act, an individual can be detained without trial if the executive is "satisfied" that the detention is necessary to prevent the person from acting in a manner prejudicial to national security.[196] In what is still considered perhaps the Singapore judiciary's most assertive decisions to date, the Singapore Court of Appeal unanimously held that there must be an objective basis for the executive's belief that a detainee poses a threat.[197] Declared the Chief Justice: "[T]he notion of a subjective or unfettered discretion is contrary to the rule of law. All power has legal limits and the rule of law demands that the courts should be able to examine the exercise of a discretionary power."[198]

The Singaporean government responded by reversing the judicial decision swiftly and forcefully. The legislature revised the preventive detention statute, reinstating a purely subjective test for the executive's decision and eliminating judicial review over all executive decisions except on procedural grounds.[199] It also amended the Singapore Constitution to curtail judicial review of any anti-subversion laws.[200] The detainees in *Chng Suan Tze* were released—and promptly rearrested.

Shortly thereafter, the Singapore judiciary again confronted new *habeas corpus* applications filed by the same detainees.[201] This time, though, the Singapore Court of Appeal's reaction was more cautious. The Court upheld the executive's decisions, ruling the applicants could not show on the facts that the government had not taken into account national security considerations when they were re-detained.[202] Although it left open the question of whether the constitutional amendments violated the basic structure of the Singapore Constitution,[203]the Singapore Court of Appeal's decision was widely regarded as a capitulation to legislative fiat.

The Malaysian government, too, has amended the Constitution to undermine judicial power. Most prominently, the Barisan Nasional government passed an amendment in 1988 to alter the Article 121(1) constitutional provision vesting judicial power in the courts.[204] This amendment followed the Malaysian Supreme Court's decision in *Public Prosecutor v. Dato' Yap Peng*, which invalidated a statute for infringing the courts' judicial power.[205] The Court declared the statute a

[196] *See* Internal Security Act, Cap. 143, 1985 Rev. Ed. Sing., § 8(1) [hereinafter ISA (Sing.)].

[197] *Chng Suan Tze*, [1988] 2 Sing. L. Rep. (R.) 525, at [55].

[198] *Id.* at [86].

[199] ISA (Sing.), §§ 8B(1), 8B(2).

[200] Const. of the Rep. of Sing., art. 149(3) (providing that "any question arises in any court as to the validity of any decision made or act done in pursuance of any power conferred upon the President or the Minister by any law referred to in this Article, such question shall be determined in accordance with the provisions of any law as may be enacted by Parliament for this purpose; and nothing in Article 93 shall invalidate any law enacted pursuant to this clause").

[201] Teo Soh Lung v. Minister of Home Aff. [1989] 1 Sing. L. Rep. 108.

[202] *Id.* at [28].

[203] *Id.* at [44].

[204] Prior to being amended, Article 121(1) of the Malaysian Constitution stated: "[T]he judicial power of the Federation shall be vested in two High Courts of coordinate jurisdiction and status . . . and in such inferior courts as may be provided for by federal law."

[205] [1987] 2 Malayan L.J. 311.

"legislative and executive intromission into the judicial power of the Federation," denouncing the idea that "judicial power amounted to 'doing what you are told to do.'"[206] The Malaysian government responded by simply removing the reference to judicial power being vested in the courts. In a move that left little doubt of the administration's position on judicial power, the amended provision now states that the courts "shall have such jurisdiction and powers as may be conferred by or under federal law."[207]

Sometimes, though, the tools that enable the state to consolidate political power are already built into the constitutional framework. Take, for example, the extensive emergency and security powers authorized by the constitutions of Malaysia and Singapore.[208] Under Article 150, the head of state can declare an emergency if satisfied of a threat to the security, economic life, or public order of the state.[209] During an emergency, Parliament can pass laws infringing constitutional rights that cannot be invalidated.[210] For more than four decades, Malaysia was continuously under a state of emergency, until the three proclamations still in force were finally revoked in 2011.[211]

In addition to the emergency powers provisions, Article 149 allows the legislature to pass laws against subversion. The legislature is given the power to prevent threats of organized violence against persons or property, to excite disaffection against the government, or to promote racial hostility likely to cause violence.[212] The Internal Security Acts in both Malaysia and Singapore were passed under Article 149, empowering each state to detain individuals without trial indefinitely.

For years, courts in Malaysia and Singapore have operated in a particularly challenging political environment. Until it was defeated in 2018, the Barisan Nasional coalition's rule was marked by direct attacks on judicial independence as well as the more subtle use of constitutional amendments designed to undermine the courts' judicial power. In Singapore, judicial assertiveness was met with aggressive legislative rebuffs, as the Singapore Court of Appeal discovered after its 1988 decision in *Chng Suan Tze*. The dominance of the ruling government has no doubt had a significant impact on the courts' exercise of judicial review.

But constitutional politics are not static, and neither is constitutional adjudication. As we shall see in the following section, the dynamic between the courts and political branches has begun to shift.

206 *Id.* at [318].

207 FED. CONST. (MALAY.), art. 121(1) ("There shall be two High Courts ... and such inferior courts as may be provided by federal law; and the High Courts and inferior courts shall have such jurisdiction and powers as may be conferred by or under federal law" (as amended by the Constitutional (Amendment) Act 1988)).

208 For more extensive discussion of emergency and security powers, see Chapter 8, Balancing Liberty and Security.

209 FED. CONST. (MALAY.), art. 150(1); CONST. OF THE REP. OF SING., art. 150(1).

210 FED. CONST. (MALAY.), art. 150(6); CONST. OF THE REP. OF SING., art. 150(5).

211 *Emergency Laws Lifted, EO Void*, MALAYSIA TODAY (Nov. 24, 2011), https://perma.cc/K27J-D85C.

212 FED. CONST. (MALAY.), art. 149.

B. The Judiciary's Uneven Journey So Far

Courts approaching constitutional adjudication in these Asian democracies have, so far, tread an uneven path. What is striking, though, is that the judiciary, particularly in Malaysia, has begun to take on a more assertive role in constitutional governance.

Begin with the Malaysian Federal Court's 2010 decision in *Sivarasa Rasiah*.[213] The apex court's decision was a significant marker in Malaysia's constitutional jurisprudence for several reasons. It marked a shift away from a "traditional and narrow" approach to rights adjudication toward what the Court called a "prismatic approach" to constitutional interpretation, in line with an exhortation that "the fundamental liberties guaranteed [by the Constitution] must be generously interpreted."[214] Second, the Court endorsed the use of a proportionality analysis to scrutinize government rights infringements, drawing on transnational sources from the United Kingdom, Canada, and South Africa.[215] Moreover, the Court in *dicta* laid the foundation for a basic structure doctrine by declaring that "Parliament cannot enact laws to amend the Constitution that violate its basic structure."[216]

In the wake of *Sivarasa*, the Malaysian courts took an unsteady approach to constitutional adjudication. The courts appeared initially emboldened. In the following years, the Malaysian Court of Appeal struck down two statutory provisions restricting freedom of expression and assembly.[217] In *Muhammad Hilman*, it invalidated a law preventing students from expressing support or opposition to any political party.[218] And in the 2014 case of *Nik Nazmi*, the court struck down a part of the Peaceful Assembly Act that imposed criminal sanctions on an organizer who failed to notify the police at least ten days before an assembly.[219]

Barely a year later in *Public Prosecutor v. Yuneswaran*,[220] in an about-face from its approach in *Nik Nazmi*, the Court of Appeal upheld as constitutional the same Peaceful Assembly Act provision it had invalidated in *Nik Nazmi*.[221] In a stark departure from its approach just the year before, the Court said it did "not consider it any part of its judicial function to paint any law as 'reasonable' or 'unreasonable' or 'harsh' or 'unjust'[.]"[222] Along similar lines, in *Azmi Sharom*, the Malaysian Federal Court unanimously upheld the constitutionality of the Sedition Act, finding the

[213] Sivarasa Rasiah v. Badan Peguam Malaysia & Anor [2010] 2 Malayan L.J. 333.

[214] *Id.* at [3], [19].

[215] *See* Nyambirai v. Nat'l Soc. Sec. Auth. [1996] 1 L.R.C. 64.

[216] *Id.* at [7].

[217] *See* Muhammad Hilman v. Kerajaan Malaysia [2011] 6 Malayan L.J. 507; Nik Nazmi v. Public Prosecutor [2014] 4 Malayan L.J. 157.

[218] *Muhammad Hilman*, [2011] 6 Malayan L.J. 507.

[219] *Nik Nazmi*, [2014] 4 Malayan L.J. 157, at [27].

[220] [2015] 9 Current L.J. 873.

[221] *Id.* at [84]-[86].

[222] *Id.* at [63]; *see also* Maria Chin Abdullah v. Pendakwa Raya [2016] M.L.J.U. 249 (H.C.) (holding section 9(5) of the Peaceful Assembly Act constitutional on freedom of expression grounds).

statute's strict liability basis for sedition to be a proportionate restriction of free expression.[223]

Yet in recent times, the Malaysian Federal Court has asserted a more empowered role. Several landmark decisions display a reinvigorated judiciary.

In 2017, in *Semenyih Jaya v. Pentadbir Tanah Daerah Hulu Langat*,[224] for the first time in twenty years, the Federal Court struck down a federal law as unconstitutional, ruling that the law infringed the courts' judicial power. Strikingly, the Court directly took on the 1988 constitutional amendment to Article 121(1), which had removed the reference to judicial power being vested in the courts, repudiating the amendment as "manifestly inconsistent with the supremacy of the Federal Constitution."[225] "[A]ny alterations made in the judicial functions would be tantamount to a grave and deliberate incursion in the judicial sphere,"[226] wrote the Court, explicitly declaring that judicial power is vested only in the courts and cannot be undermined by parliament.[227] It pronounced that "judicial power, judicial independence, and the separation of powers are as critical as they are sacrosanct" in Malaysia's constitutional framework.[228]

The Federal Court delivered another seminal decision in the 2018 case of *Indira Gandhi*.[229] This time, the Court addressed the other significant constitutional amendment implemented in 1988: the inclusion of a new clause, Article 121(1A), stating that the civil courts "shall have no jurisdiction in respect of any matter within the jurisdiction of the Syariah courts." Ruling that the civil courts retain jurisdiction over matters relating to Islamic law that involve constitutional questions, the Malaysian apex court explicitly established the hierarchy of civil courts over Sharia courts.[230] Judicial review and constitutional interpretation are "pivotal constituents of the civil courts' judicial power," the Court declared.[231] "As part of the basic structure of the constitution, it cannot be abrogated from the civil courts or conferred upon the Syariah Courts, whether by constitutional amendments, Act of Parliament or state legislation." It also rejected a "literal" reading of the Constitution in favor of a "purposive" approach in line with the equal rights of both parents.[232] In *Indira Gandhi*, the Court solidified the position it laid down in *Semenyih Jaya* that the judicial power of the courts is an unalterable part of the basic structure of the Malaysian Constitution.

223 Public Prosecutor v. Azmi Sharom [2015] M.L.J.U. 594.
224 [2017] 3 MALAYAN L.J. 561.
225 *Id.* at [75].
226 *Id.* at [84].
227 *Id.* at [67].
228 *Id.* at [90].
229 *Indira Gandhi* (F.C.), [2018] 1 MALAYAN L.J. 545; *see also* Jaclyn Neo, *Return of Judicial Power: Religious Freedom and the Tussle over Jurisdictional Boundaries in Malaysia*, INT'L J. CONST. L. BLOG (Mar. 15, 2018), https://perma.cc/6XUW-CWAK.
230 *Indira Gandhi* (F.C.), [2018] 1 MALAYAN L.J. 545, at [92]–[99].
231 *Id.* at [104].
232 *Id.* at [150]–[174].

Then, in the 2019 case of *Alma Nudo v. Public Prosecutor*, the Federal Court endorsed a robust proportionality analysis in a decision that invalidated a statutory provision that allowed a double presumption against accused drug traffickers.[233] A full bench of the Federal Court applied a three-stage proportionality analysis: first, whether there is a sufficiently important objective to justify the infringement of rights; second, whether the governmental means has a rational nexus with its intended objective; and, third, whether the rights restriction is proportionate to the importance of the right at stake.[234] In so doing, the Court expressly established the doctrine of proportionality as part of Malaysian law,[235] finding that the constitutional equal protection guarantee "imports the principle of substantive proportionality."[236]

The Singapore courts have been less assertive than their Malaysian counterparts, but there has nevertheless been a discernible shift in the court's judicial review approach over the last decade.[237] Although the Singapore courts have not yet overturned a law passed by Parliament,[238] they have become increasingly willing to exercise review over executive decisions.

In the 2016 case of *Tan Seet Eng v. Attorney-General*,[239] the Singapore Court of Appeal held that the Court had the power to examine the Home Affairs Minister's ability to authorize preventive detentions under the Criminal Law (Temporary Provisions) Act.[240] The Court declared that an objective standard of review should be applied to determine whether there is a reasonable basis for the Minister's decision. Significantly, this objective standard was similar to the one it had articulated in its earlier decision of *Chng Suan Tze*,[241] which the legislature had spectacularly snuffed out by amending the Internal Security Act and the Constitution. But in *Tan Seet Eng*, the Singapore court insisted that "the courts can inquire into whether the decisions are made within the scope of the relevant legal power or duty and arrived at in a legal manner," even for matters of "high policy."[242]

As another example, consider *Vellama d/o Marie Muthu v. Attorney-General*.[243] Singapore's Prime Minister has discretion to call for a by-election when the seat of an elected Member of Parliament falls vacant. Under the Constitution, such vacancies "shall be filled by election in the manner provided by or under any law relating to Parliamentary elections for the time in force."[244] The Singapore Court of Appeal

233 [2019] 5 Current L.J. 780.
234 *Id.* at [143]–[145].
235 *Id.* at [126].
236 *Id.* at [118].
237 Jaclyn Neo, *Introduction* to Constitutional Interpretation in Singapore 8 (Jaclyn Neo ed., 2016).
238 *See supra* note 48.
239 [2016] 1 Sing. L. Rep. 779.
240 *Id.* at [97].
241 Chng Suan Tze v. Minister of Home Aff. [1988] 2 Sing. L. Rep. (R.) 525.
242 *Tan Seet Eng*, [2016] 1 Sing. L. Rep. 779, at [106].
243 [2013] 4 Sing. L. Rep. 1.
244 Const. of the Rep. of Sing., art. 49.

held the Prime Minister did not have "unfettered discretion" to decide whether to call for an election; rather, the Prime Minister is constitutionally obliged to call for an election "within a reasonable time."[245] Although "the Prime Minister should be accorded a measure of latitude in deciding when to call for election to fill a vacancy," the Prime Minister could not indefinitely defer calling an election. The Court emphasized the principle of legality in *Chng Suan Tze* that it is "a basic proposition of law that all discretionary power is subject to legal limits."[246]

Unlike the assertive turn displayed by the Malaysian Federal Court, the Singaporean judiciary's constitutional engagement has been more incremental and evolutionary. Judicial review in Singapore has typically been described as "pragmatic" and "communitarian."[247] Even so, while the courts' general approach to constitutional review "remains persistently restrained and deferential," scholars observe that "there are tentative but real overtures towards more respectful engagement in constitutional law."[248]

VI. Conclusion

Constitutional politics matter for constitutional adjudication. Yet political landscapes can shift dramatically. May 9, 2018, marked the end of the governing Barisan Nasional coalition's six-decade-long dominance.[249] Then, two years after its stunning electoral victory, the Pakatan Harapan government collapsed following a political crisis in February 2020, resulting in the rise of the Perikatan Nasional governing coalition. What all these unprecedented political developments underscore is that all political alliances, including the new government in power, are fragile.[250]

Within contexts of political instability or government dominance, the role of courts is all the more important. Context and timing are often crucial. Recent cases reveal that the Malaysian Federal Court has already begun to develop a more critical jurisprudence that enables courts to assert a more empowered role. It's worth noting that the Malaysian Court delivered its landmark decisions in *Semenyih Jaya* and *Indira Gandhi* before the 2018 rupture of the ruling Barisan Nasional government, which speaks to a shift in judicial self-perception even amidst a challenging

[245] [2013] 4 SING. L. REP. 1., at [87].

[246] *Id.* at [85].

[247] *See* Li-ann Thio, *Principled Pragmatism and the "Third Wave" of Communitarian Judicial Review in Singapore*, *in* CONSTITUTIONAL INTERPRETATION IN SINGAPORE: THEORY AND PRACTICE 75 (Jaclyn Neo ed., 2016).

[248] Neo, *Introduction*, *supra* note 237, at 9.

[249] *See After Six Decades in Power, BN Falls to "Malaysian Tsunami"*, MALAYSIAKINI (May 10, 2018), https://perma.cc/YY6E-TQG7; *Malaysia Election: Opposition Scores Historic Victory*, BBC (May 10, 2018), https://perma.cc/2959-XJUM; Paul Shinkman, *After Vote, Malaysia's Real Test Approaches*, U.S. NEWS (May 22, 2018), https://perma.cc/MN9N-Y7E2.

[250] *See Beset at its Birth: Malaysia's New Government May Be Even More Unstable than the Old One*, ECONOMIST (Mar. 5, 2020), https://perma.cc/D4W6-LGVD.

political environment. Emerging from these cases is a jurisprudence that provides a concrete foundation for courts to protect and develop fundamental principles of the constitutional order. Courts have begun to equip themselves with powerful tools that can be used to negotiate various political contexts, whether to consolidate their position vis-à-vis dominant political actors or to craft constitutionalism for a fragile democracy.

Courts in Malaysia and Singapore are poised to assume a central role in constitutional governance as a co-equal branch of government in these Asian democracies. Developing a framework for constitutional adjudication that can safeguard the core fundamentals of these constitutions is a critical part of this endeavor. In the chapters that follow, this book seeks to chart the path forward.

PART II

A FRAMEWORK FOR CONSTITUTIONAL ADJUDICATION

3

Constitutional History

I. Introduction

"The infant periods of most nations are buried in silence, or veiled in fable," James Madison wrote in 1819.[1] Not so with many of the states born in the twentieth century. For many of these modern democracies, the nation's founding played out on the public stage of post-colonial constitutional history. Malaysia and Singapore are no exceptions. Their paths to independence and processes of constitution-making are captured in commission documents, draft constitutional texts, news reports, letters, speeches, and even on film.[2]

Constitutional history provides us with the broader context necessary to understand the constitutional text and the purposes motivating the new democratic order. Constitutions are not merely textual documents; they express a nation's foundational commitments and also reveal the competing interests and compromises reached at the time of drafting. As historian Joseph Fernando observes, writing about Malaysia, "the constitutional history which shaped the contours of the post-independent state" helps inform contemporary constitutional debates.[3] In this chapter, I explore how constitutional history illuminates the foundational elements of the constitution's core and serves as a significant resource for courts in constitutional interpretation.

This chapter outlines the historical background for understanding the constitution's textual provisions as well as the foundations of the constitutional framework. It begins with the constitution-making process leading to the creation of Malaysia as well as Singapore's later separation from the federation. In telling the story of the founding of Malaysia and Singapore, I describe the Malayan road to independence and process of constitution framing, and the contrasting story of Singapore's abrupt separation from the Federation of Malaysia and untidy constitutional origins. I then explore the original constitutional framework and the

[1] James Madison to William Eustis, July 6, 1819, *in* Letters and Other Writings of James Madison, Vol. III, 140 (Philadelphia, 1865).

[2] *See, e.g.*, Malaysians fill the Stadium Merdeka in Kuala Lumpur to declare and celebrate the independence of Malaya from Britain (Aug. 31, 1957) (video on file with Critical Past), https://perma.cc/96KP-GQYF.

[3] Joseph M. Fernando, *A Playmaker and Moderator: Lord Reid and the Framing of the Malayan Federal Constitution*, 50 J. Se. Asian Stud. 431, 432 (2019).

Constitutional Statecraft in Asian Courts. Yvonne Tew, Oxford University Press (2020). © Yvonne Tew.
DOI:10.1093/oso/9780198716839.001.0001

broader commitments that motivated the constitutional project. These constitutions set in place an overarching framework for governance and continuing constitutional construction in these newly independent democracies.

The chapter then turns to the use of constitutional history and originalist arguments in practice in Malaysia and Singapore. In Malaysia, arguments that reach back to the founding premises are often used to advance particular visions of the nation's identity. A prime example of this relates to the role of religion and the state. Situating the Article 3(1) clause—the declaration that "Islam is the religion of the Federation; but other religions may be practised in peace and harmony"[4]—within the constitution's original framework illuminates how the role of religion in the state does not detract from the protection of individuals and minorities. I also consider the Singapore Court of Appeal's prominent originalist decision in 2010, which upheld the constitutionality of the mandatory death penalty. The Singapore court's approach exhibits a narrow focus on the framers' specific expectations, resulting in a highly formalist interpretation in line with judicial deference to the political branches.[5]

Faithfulness to the constitution calls for a deeper understanding of its structural framework and the broad principles that underlie its rights guarantees. Understanding the constitution's founding purposes and its original framework illuminates the fundamental elements of the constitutional order, insights that can and should inform contemporary constitutional engagement.

II. Constitutional Foundings

A. The Making of Malaysia's *Merdeka* Constitution

The Malayan Constitution was conceived in the heady climate of a nation at the cusp of independence. As one scholar describes, "Malaysia stands out in British colonial constitutional history as one of the most complex and unique constitutional founding moments, let alone in Southeast Asia."[6] By the second half of the 1950s, Malayan political leaders negotiating with the British colonial power at a constitutional conference in London were close to the desired end: *merdeka*, that is, independence. With the Federation of Malaya's *merdeka* moment slated for August 1957,[7] the British and Malayan representatives turned to the "mass

[4] Fed. Const. (Malay.), art. 3(1).

[5] Yong Vui Kong v. Public Prosecutor [2010] 3 Sing. L. Rep. 489.

[6] H. Kumarasingham, *A Foreign Commission for Domestic Needs: The Constitutional Founding of Malaysia*, *in* Constitutional Founding in Southeast Asia 139, 140 (Kevin Tan & Bui Ngoc Sun eds., 2017).

[7] *Merdeka* is the Malay word for "independence."

of business to complete" before Malaya could be proclaimed independent.[8] Not least among these was the drawing up of a new constitution for the soon-to-be sovereign nation.

Completing that task would be no small feat. The challenge involved framing a constitution for a society divided along lines of race and religion, and dealing with a legacy of British colonialism as well as the threat of communist insurgency emerging after the Japanese occupancy during the Second World War. A range of players were key stakeholders in Malaya's independence: the British government; the Malay sultans, the hereditary rulers of the individual states of the federation; and the "Alliance," a political coalition made up of the United Malays National Organisation, the Malayan Indian Congress, and the Malayan Chinese Association.[9] It was evident, though, that the Alliance held the most sway: the coalition had swept fifty-one out of the fifty-two contested seats in Malaya's first legislative council elections in 1955, where it had run on an electoral platform focused on gaining independence.

The Alliance pushed for a constitutional drafting commission comprising non-Malayan members because they thought that such a body would avoid local biases and be able to work impartially.[10] Tunku Abdul Rahman—the Cambridge-educated Malay aristocrat and leader of the Alliance who had spearheaded the Malayan delegation to London—made clear to the British High Commissioner that the Alliance wanted the constitutional commission to include non-Malayan members who had expertise with other Commonwealth countries.[11]

"The caliber of the commission will have to be very high, since the problems will be unusual and of great complexity," wrote Sir Donald MacGillivray, the last British High Commissioner in Malaya.[12] Britain appointed James Reid, a Lord of Appeal on the British House of Lords, as the chair of the commission. The other British appointee was Sir Ivor Jennings, a constitutional scholar at the University of Cambridge—and, as it turns out, a friend of Tunku Abdul Rahman's from their time as students at St. Catharine's College, Cambridge,[13] where the young Tunku had, "scraping through," obtained his law degree.[14] The British High Commissioner in Australia nominated Sir William McKell, a former

[8] Kumarasingham, *supra* note 6, at 145 (quoting BRITISH DOCUMENTS ON THE END OF EMPIRE—MALAYA, PART I: THE MALAYAN UNION EXPERIMENT 1942–1948 lxxvii (A.J. Stockwell ed., London: Her Majesty's Stationery Office, 1995)).

[9] CHARLES PARKINSON, BILLS OF RIGHTS AND DECOLONIZATION: THE EMERGENCE OF DOMESTIC HUMAN RIGHTS INSTRUMENTS IN BRITAIN'S OVERSEAS TERRITORIES 78 (2007).

[10] JOSEPH M. FERNANDO, THE MAKING OF THE MALAYAN CONSTITUTION 103 (2002).

[11] *Id.*

[12] Kumarasingham, *supra* note 6, at 139 (quoting Letter from Sir D. MacGillivray to AM MacKintosh on the views of Tunku Abdul Rahman, January 5, 1956, CO 1030/132 no. 3, *in* BRITISH DOCUMENTS ON THE END OF EMPIRE—MALAYA, PART III: THE ALLIANCE ROUTE TO INDEPENDENCE 1953-1957 227(A.J. Stockwell ed., London: Her Majesty's Stationery Office, 1995)).

[13] PARKINSON, *supra* note 9, at 80.

[14] Chandran Jeshurun, *Tunku Abdul Rahman Putra and His Links with the Universities of Cambridge and Malaya, 1960–1962*, 82 J. MALAYSIAN BRANCH ROYAL ASIATIC SOC'Y 1, 4 (2009).

governor-general of Australia, while India proposed Bidhubhushan Malik, who had been Chief Justice of Allahabad. The fifth appointee was Abdul Hamid, a judge of the High Court of Western Pakistan who had served as an adviser on the Pakistan Constituent Assembly before becoming the chief draftsman (taking over the role from Jennings, no less).[15]

In the middle of 1956, the newly formed Reid Commission, as it was known, arrived in Malaya to prepare for the drafting of the independence constitution. The commission was tasked with following the specific terms of reference that the Alliance Party and the Malay rulers had agreed upon and discussed at the London Conference. As Andrew Harding notes, "the most persuasive reason" for having external experts draft the constitution was that "the main positions had already been negotiated amongst the key players" and the drafters were well aware that "departing from those positions might potentially have led to political disarray."[16] The constitutional commission's task was spelled out in the following terms:

> To make recommendations for a federal form of constitution for the whole country as a single, self-governing unit within the Commonwealth based on Parliamentary democracy with a bicameral legislature, which would include provision for: (i) the establishment of a strong central government with States and Settlements enjoying a measure of autonomy … ; (ii) the safeguarding of the position and prestige of Their Highnesses as constitutional rulers of their respective States; (iii) a constitutional Yang di-Pertuan Besar (Head of State) for the Federation to be chosen from among Their Highnesses the Rulers; (iv) a common nationality for the whole of the Federation; (v) the safeguarding of the special position of the Malays and the legitimate interests of other communities.[17]

After arriving in Malaya, the Reid Commission began conducting hearings and gathering evidence from various groups and individuals across the country. In total, the commission reported holding 118 meetings—which included "meetings at which we heard evidence, meetings at which Federal officers attended to give us information, conferences with State and Settlement officers, and meetings for private discussions"—and considered 131 memoranda from various organizations representing Chinese, Malays, Hindus, Singhalese, Sikhs, Indians, Tamils, and Pakistanis.[18] Submissions from these groups poured in at such a high rate that they filled five folders, each three inches thick.[19]

[15] *Id.* at 81.

[16] Andrew Harding, The Constitution of Malaysia: A Contextual Analysis 31–32 (2012).

[17] Federation of Malay Constitutional Commission, Report of 1956–57 § Colonial No. 330 [hereinafter Reid Report].

[18] *Id.* at [12].

[19] Parkinson, *supra* note 9, at 87.

On February 20, 1957, the Reid Commission published its report together with a draft of the constitution. Reaction to the commission's report was mixed. Contention between the Malays and non-Malays centered on issues relating to the Malays' special position, citizenship, language, and religion.[20] The United Malays National Organisation, the main constituent party of the Alliance, was concerned about ensuring that the ethnic Malays, who saw themselves as sons of the soil,[21] would not be overwhelmed post-independence by the Indian and Chinese population.[22] The Reid Commission's draft constitution did provide for the Malays' special position, but included a fifteen-year timeline for reviewing the special privileges given to the Malays. It also permitted the use of the Chinese and Tamil languages in the legislative council and did not include an establishment clause for a state religion.

A Working Party chaired by Sir Donald MacGillivray, composed of representatives of the Alliance, the Sultans, and the British government, was assembled to review the Reid Commission's recommendations. The Working Party eventually amended several provisions: it removed the fifteen-year Malay special privileges timeline as well as the Chinese and Tamil language provision. Significantly, it also agreed to include a constitutional clause declaring Islam as the official state religion.

In May 1957, after the Working Party completed its recommendations, Malayan and British delegates met in London for a final conference on the new constitution. Following the London Conference, the British Colonial Office published a White Paper in July explaining the Working Party's changes to the Reid Commission's draft constitution. Back in Kuala Lumpur, the Malayan Legislative Council debated the White Paper and the draft constitution. A member of the Malayan Chinese Association voiced objections to the changes in the protections afforded to the Chinese community, but the legislative council ultimately unanimously approved the draft constitution. With that, the final piece of the new federal constitution was put in place.

On August 31, 1957, at the stroke of midnight, the *Merdeka* Constitution came into force as the Federation of Malaya gained independence from the British to become a fully sovereign nation. Chants of "*Merdeka! Merdeka! Merdeka!*" filled the site that would come to be known as Merdeka Stadium, as Tunku Abdul Rahman—Malaya's first prime minister—read the Proclamation of Independence. The proclamation expressed the nation's founding ideal for the establishment of "a sovereign democratic and independent state founded upon the principles of

[20] FERNANDO, THE MAKING OF THE MALAYAN CONSTITUTION, *supra* note 10, at 144.

[21] The Malay term *bumiputera*, which is typically used to refer to the ethnically Malay and indigenous peoples, means "princes of the soil."

[22] Kristen Stilt, *Contextualizing Constitutional Islam: The Malayan Experience*, 13 INT'L J. CONST. L. 407, 410 (2015).

liberty and justice and ever seeking the welfare and happiness of its people and the maintenance of just peace among nations."[23]

* * *

It has often been remarked that the Malayan constitution-making process, with its appointment of a constitutional commission of Commonwealth drafters, took a somewhat unusual path compared to other British colonies.[24] Unlike India, whose constitution was founded a decade earlier, Malaya did not seek to convene a local constituent assembly to draft the constitution. Because the Reid constitutional commission comprised external legal experts, some have questioned the autochthony of Malaysia's Constitution.[25]

To characterize the independence constitution as lacking in local legitimacy or influence, however, is misleading. For one, the decision to appoint a commission to draft the constitution was very much a deliberate choice of the local Alliance coalition, which had tremendous electoral legitimacy at that point. The three-party Alliance—made up of the United Malays National Organisation, the Malaysian Chinese Association, and the Malaysian Indian Congress—represented the three major ethnic communities in Malayan society.[26] As Fernando notes, "the choice of an independent body made up of legal experts from the Commonwealth was a conscious choice of the ruling Alliance party and was intended to avoid local prejudices in the framing of the Constitution."[27] Moreover, the commission was constrained by the specific terms of reference; its task was viewed essentially as a technical one of translating into legal and practical terms that which had already been politically settled.[28] It is also worth reiterating that the framers did not "work in a vacuum": they consulted extensively with local groups and people throughout Malaya "from across the social and political spectrum" before drafting the constitution.[29] Further, the Reid Commission's draft was examined and amended by a constitutional working group made up of Malayan representatives from the Alliance Party and the Conference of Rulers.[30] Each stage of the constitution-making process reveals a measure of—often substantial—local influence.

23 Tunku Abdul Rahman, Proclamation of Independence (Malaysia) (Aug. 31, 1957), at [10].

24 Kumarasingham, *supra* note 6, at 148.

25 *See, e.g.*, HARDING, *supra* note 16, at 31 (noting that "the Malaysian Constitution ... has often been seen or presented as a foreign document rather than an indigenous one"); Tommy Thomas, *MySay: Evolution of the Federal Constitution—in Hindsight*, EDGE MKTS. (Jan. 16, 2018), https://perma.cc/Z6EX-JB2G (observing that the Reid Commission was made up of "foreigners with no previous links to Malaya" and "all legally trained," and did not include any politicians, economists, or political scientists).

26 *See* Kumarasingham, *supra* note 6, at 148.

27 JOSEPH M. FERNANDO, FEDERAL CONSTITUTIONS: A COMPARATIVE STUDY OF MALAYSIA AND THE UNITED STATES 12 (Univ. Malaya Press, 2007).

28 HARDING, *supra* note 16, at 32.

29 FERNANDO, FEDERAL CONSTITUTIONS, *supra* note 27, at 12–13.

30 PARKINSON, *supra* note 9, at 95.

More significantly, it is worth reflecting on the broader constitutional project. Crucially, the commission recognized that the constitutional text was meant to provide a framework for governance that the people of the new nation would continue to construct over time. In the Reid Report of 1957, the drafters emphasized that they "constantly had in mind" dual objectives: first, that the constitution should provide for "the fullest opportunity for the growth of a united, free and democratic nation" and, second, that there be "every facility for the development of the resources of the country and the maintenance and improvement of the standard of living of the people."[31] The framers realized, though, that the constitutional document could only provide the architecture; it could not itself provide the outcome. "These objectives can only be achieved by the action of the people themselves," declared the Reid Commission, "our task is to provide the framework most appropriate for their achievement."[32]

B. The Singapore Constitution's Pragmatic Origins

Unlike the *Merdeka* Constitution, which was born in the midst of the exciting period leading up to Malaya gaining independence from the British, the constitution of the accidental nation of Singapore had far more pragmatic origins.[33] The Singapore Constitution was not the product of a constituent assembly or successful negotiations with colonial powers; rather, it "emerged out of the ashes of a failed inter-communal experiment that was the Federation of [Malaysia]."[34]

A British colony since 1824, Singapore attained full internal self-government in 1958 under the Singapore (Constitution) Order in Council. Soon after, it sought to achieve full independence by merging with the Federation of Malaya. Singapore's People's Action Party government headed by Lee Kuan Yew—another Cambridge-educated lawyer, who graduated several years after the Tunku with flying colors—believed that a merger would enable Singapore to achieve full independence and guarantee its economic survival.[35] On September 16, 1963, Singapore, together with the North Borneo states of Sabah and Sarawak, joined Malaya to form the new Federation of Malaysia.

The union was unhappy and short-lived. Political relations between the central federal government and the Singapore state government, exacerbated by racial and

[31] Reid Report, *supra* note 17, at [14].

[32] *Id.*

[33] Sajjad Ashraf, *A Tale of Two Accidental Nations*, Straits Times (Aug. 3, 2015), https://perma.cc/HY48-L59V.

[34] Li-ann Thio, A Treatise on Singapore Constitutional Law ¶ 02.102 (2012).

[35] Kevin Tan, *Foundational Moments: The "Singapore Constitution"*, *in* Constitutional Founding in Southeast Asia 182 (Kevin Tan & Bui Ngoc Sun eds., 2017).

economic tensions, quickly deteriorated.[36] On August 9, 1965, Singapore separated from the Federation of Malaysia, becoming an independent, sovereign state.

As a result of this abrupt separation, the Singapore Constitution's origins were, in a word, messy. "Because of the way in which Singapore lurched and spluttered its way to independence between 1955 and 1965," Singapore scholar Kevin Tan notes, "it is impossible to identify a single document as its foundational constitution."[37] While part of the Malaysian Federation, Singapore had been governed by the Federal Constitution of Malaysia as well as its own individual state constitution. After separating from the federation, Singapore did not draft a new constitutional document. Instead, the origins of Singapore's Constitution are rooted in various legal documents created upon Singapore's separation from Malaysia.[38] The first of these was the Constitution and Malaysia (Singapore Amendment) Act in which the Malaysian Parliament transferred all legislative and executive powers from Malaysia's federal government to the new government of Singapore. Singapore's Parliament then passed the Constitution of Singapore (Amendment) Act 1965, which amended Singapore's State Constitution, and the Republic of Singapore Independence Act 1965, which applied certain provisions of the Malaysian Constitution to Singapore.

These documents provided Singapore with a working constitution, albeit a patchwork one. Singapore's "new" constitution was essentially a composite of three documents: its amended State Constitution, the Republic of Singapore Independence Act 1965, and provisions of the Federal Constitution of Malaysia that had been made applicable to Singapore.[39] Writing in 1965, Singapore's first Chief Minister David Marshall called it "the untidiest and most confusing constitution that any country has started life with."[40] He wasn't wrong.

In the immediate aftermath of its separation from Malaysia, the Singapore government announced that it would commission a team of legal experts to draft a new constitution,[41] but later abandoned these plans. Instead, the government eventually established a constitutional commission chaired by Chief Justice Wee Chong Jin to consider "how the rights of racial, linguistic and religious minorities can be adequately safeguarded in the Constitution."[42] Given the lack of a constitutional drafting moment, the Wee Chong Jin Commission has been described as "the next

[36] *See* Kevin Tan, *Singapore: In and Out of the Federation*, *in* CONSTITUTIONAL LANDMARKS IN MALAYSIA: THE FIRST 50 YEARS 1957–2007 55 (Andrew Harding & H.P. Lee eds., 2007).

[37] Tan, *supra* note 35, at 161.

[38] *See* Kevin Tan, *The Evolution of Singapore's Modern Constitution: Developments from 1945 to the Present Day*, 1 SING. ACAD. L.J. 17 (1989).

[39] *See* SUPREME COURT SINGAPORE, OUR CONSTITUTION, https://perma.cc/QZ9H-JTXT.

[40] *Id.* (citing Sir David Marshall, *Singapore's "Untidy Constitution"*, STRAITS TIMES, Dec. 21, 1965, at 12).

[41] *A Team of Experts to Draft S'pore Charter*, STRAITS TIMES, Sept. 11, 1965, at 20.

[42] CONSTITUTIONAL COMMISSION 1966, REPORT OF THE CONSTITUTIONAL COMMISSION 1966, at [1] (Singapore Government Printer, 1966) [hereinafter WEE REPORT].

best thing to convening a full-fledged constituent assembly to craft a constitution that would be consonant with Singapore's newly independent status."[43]

In its report published in 1966, the Wee Commission identified several broad principles to frame the modern Singapore Constitution: namely, "faith in the democratic system of government," "belief in the rule of law," and "tolerance and understanding among the many communities."[44] In line with these foundational principles, the Commission recommended including a clause establishing the constitution's status as supreme law, enshrined in Article 4 of the Singapore Constitution. It also proposed three methods of entrenching the constitution which would increase the difficulty of amending constitutional provisions in accordance with their importance.[45] And it suggested several institutional changes; these included creating a Council of State to offer Parliament advice on how proposed laws would effect minority groups,[46] creating a Parliamentary Ombudsman as an independent check on civil servants,[47] and entrenching the independence of the judiciary.[48]

With regards to fundamental rights, the Wee Commission recommended retaining many of the constitutional provisions from Malaysia's bill of rights, with some important modifications.[49] Significantly, it proposed including three new provisions not found in the Malaysian Constitution: a prohibition against torture,[50] the right to vote,[51] and the right to apply to the court for the enforcement of rights.[52]

The Singapore Constitution does not identify an official religion. The Wee Commission described Singapore as a "democratic secular state,"[53] although the Constitution does not have an explicit statement to this effect.[54] The Commission recommended against restricting religious propagation in the constitution's religious freedom guarantee and, unlike the Malaysian Constitution, rejected religious identity as a criterion for defining a "Malay" person.[55] The Singapore Constitution provides that the government shall "care for the interests of the

[43] Kevin Tan & Li-ann Thio, *Introduction* to EVOLUTION OF A REVOLUTION: FORTY YEARS OF THE SINGAPORE CONSTITUTION 2 (Kevin Tan & Li-ann Thio eds., 2009).

[44] WEE REPORT, *supra* note 42, at [74].

[45] *Id.* at [76]–[80]. For example, the Commission recommended that constitutional provisions relating to fundamental liberties, the judiciary, the legislature, general elections, minority rights, the special position of the Malays, and the amendment procedures be entrenched by requiring a two-thirds majority in Parliament and a two-thirds vote at a national referendum.

[46] *Id.* at [59].

[47] *Id.* at [66]–[69].

[48] *Id.* at [83].

[49] *Id.* at [29]–[44].

[50] *Id.* at [40].

[51] *Id.* at [43].

[52] *Id.* at [44].

[53] *Id.* at [38].

[54] *See* Jaclyn Neo, *Secularism without Liberalism: Religious Freedom in a non-Secular State*, 2017 MICH. ST. L. REV. 333, 352 (2017).

[55] WEE REPORT, *supra* note 42, at [38]. *Cf.* FED. CONST. (MALAY.), arts. 11(4), 160.

racial and religious minorities in Singapore"[56] and "recognise the special position of the Malays, who are the indigenous people of Singapore," which involves responsibility "to protect, safeguard, support, foster and promote their political, educational, religious, economic, social and cultural interests and the Malay language."[57]

After debating the Commission's recommendations, the Singapore Parliament eventually adopted some of the proposals. In 1969, Parliament established a Presidential Council to draw attention to any legislative bill that discriminated against the fundamental liberties of racial or religious minorities. But it rejected all of the commission's proposals regarding constitutional entrenchment (the Singapore Parliament adopted a two-thirds legislative majority in 1979 as the requirement for amending most constitutional provisions).

With regards to the commission's proposal to insert constitutional provisions prohibiting torture and guaranteeing the right to vote and the right to a judicial remedy, the government found that these clauses to be "acceptable in principle," promising that they "would be incorporated in some form in the new Constitution to be drawn up."[58] But since a new constitution never materialized, these articles never became part of the Singapore Constitution. Four decades later, the failure to incorporate these provisions would play a pivotal role in a major Singapore Court of Appeal's decision, as we will see later in this chapter.

The Singapore Constitution remained in its mish-mash form for years. In 1979, Parliament passed a constitutional amendment authorizing the Attorney-General to consolidate the various constitutional provisions applicable to Singapore "into a single composite document."[59] A decade and a half after Singapore became a sovereign nation, the Singapore Constitution issued in 1980 unified the various parts of the constitution for the first time into a single constitutional text.

III. Constitutional History and the Original Constitutional Framework

A. The Constitution's Original Framework

A constitution, according to Sir Ivor Jennings, a member of the Reid Commission, is "a framework, a skeleton."[60] As he explained, a constitution's content and

[56] CONST. OF THE REP. OF SING., art. 152(1).
[57] *Id.* art. 153(2).
[58] Li-ann Thio, *The Passage of a Generation: Revisiting the report of the 1966 Constitutional Commission, in* EVOLUTION OF A REVOLUTION: FORTY YEARS OF THE SINGAPORE CONSTITUTION 16 (Kevin Tan & Li-ann Thio eds., 2009) (citing E.W. Barker, 25 SPR Dec. 21, 1966, col 1053).
[59] Constitution (Amendment) Act, 1979, Act 10, art. 155(1).
[60] IVOR JENNINGS, THE LAW AND THE CONSTITUTION 34 (5th ed. 1967).

meaning must be interpreted and understood "according to the circumstances of the moment and the special problems being faced by the State while it is being drafted."

The constitutions of Malaysia and Singapore set in place a framework of governance for the newly independent states, establishing a system of government based on constitutional supremacy and parliamentary democracy. These written constitutions represented a break from the British tradition of parliamentary sovereignty. But "reliance on the formal legal text alone is not enough to aid our understanding on how constitutional provisions operate,"[61] as Dian Shah notes. Constitutional history provides the necessary context for understanding the written document.

These constitutions were created to provide a foundation for these states' democratic self-governance. As noted earlier, the drafters recognized that their task was to supply a framework for realizing objectives that "can only be achieved by the action of the people themselves."[62] They understood that institutions and actors—the legislature, the executive, the judiciary, and the people—are part of an ongoing process of constitutional construction within this larger constitutional framework.[63] Thus, they contemplated a vision of the constitution not as a static, finished product, but as an initial foundation on which construction could continue over time.

On this account, the constitution provides an overarching architecture for constitutional governance, with room for various branches of government and the people to engage in constitutional construction. At the same time, the constitution's original framework encapsulates a core of fundamental elements that lie at the heart of the constitutional project.

Understanding the broader purposes motivating the constitutional project is significant to the endeavor of constitutional interpretation. As Sanford Levinson observes, "one cannot begin to engage in constitutional interpretation without having in mind a model of the point of the entire constitutional enterprise."[64] In the case of Malaysia and Singapore, the constitution's framework must be understood in light of the underlying goals that motivated the constitutional endeavor. For example, the Malaysian Constitution is linked to the history of the nation's independence from its colonial past and built on a social contract negotiated among the communal groups in its pluralistic society. It is no wonder that debates in Malaysian legal and political discourse often refer back to the constitution's founding premises to advance a narrative of the nation's identity.

[61] Dian Shah, Constitutions, Religion and Politics in Asia: Indonesia, Malaysia and Sri Lanka 4 (2017).

[62] Reid Report, *supra* note 17, at [14].

[63] For an account of framework constitutionalism in the U.S. context, see Jack Balkin, Living Originalism 21–23 (2011); Jack Balkin, *Framework Originalism and the Living Constitution*, 103 Nw. U. L. Rev. 549 (2009).

[64] Sanford Levinson, Constitutional Faith 77 (2011).

Identifying the essential features of the constitution's original framework makes it possible to construct an account that can help inform constitutional adjudication. Indeed, the fundamental principles that make up the constitution's structure are part of a constitutional core that the courts should safeguard from erosion. Constitutional history is a significant source of guidance for the courts as they take on the task of identifying the basic features of the constitution in contemporary constitutional adjudication.[65]

B. Constitutional History and Constitutional Change

Originalist arguments in constitutional interpretation are frequently criticized for binding contemporary society to the dead hand of a past generation.[66] A few observations are relevant at this juncture about the use of constitutional history in newer democracies like Malaysia and Singapore.

Much of the concern with the dead hand problem is linked to the difficulty of constitutional amendment. Worries about future generations being unable to replace inherited constitutional provisions with norms of their own choosing is especially salient when a constitution is rigid, like the U.S. Constitution which is "practically unamendable."[67] In contrast, most constitutional provisions in Malaysia and Singapore can be amended with a two-thirds parliamentary majority,[68] and their ruling party governments have had little trouble amending the constitution in practice.[69] Historically, threats to democratic legitimacy have not stemmed from the inability to change a rigid inherited constitution but from the political branches being able to amend the constitution at will. The Indian Supreme Court recognized a similar danger when it developed a doctrine to protect the basic structure of the Indian Constitution from being altered by its Parliament.[70] Likewise, constitutional history in the Malaysian and Singaporean context is

[65] *See* Sudhir Krishnaswamy, Democracy and Constitutionalism in India: A Study of the Basic Structure Doctrine 154–57 (2009) (on the role that constitutional history plays in aiding courts in identifying the basic structure of Indian Constitution).

[66] *See, e.g.*, Akhil Reed Amar, *Philadelphia Revisited: Amending the Constitution Outside Article V*, 55 U. Chi. L. Rev. 1043, 1072 (1988); David A. Strauss, *Common Law, Common Ground, and Jefferson's Principle*, 112 Yale L.J. 1717, 1717–19 (2003).

[67] Henry Paul Monaghan, *Doing Originalism*, 104 Colum. L. Rev. 32, 35 (2004); *see also* U.S. Const. art. V (providing that an amendment may be proposed either by the Congress with a two-thirds majority vote in both the House of Representatives and the Senate or by a constitutional convention called for by two-thirds of the State legislatures).

[68] Fed. Const. (Malay.), art. 159(3); Const. of the Rep. of Sing., art. 5(2).

[69] Both parties have usually controlled more than two-thirds majority in Parliament. Following the 2008 Malaysian general elections, however, the National Front lost its two-thirds majority for the first time since 1969. It continues to hold a simple majority in Parliament, which it maintained after the 2012 general elections.

[70] *See* Kesavananda Bharati v. State of Kerala, AIR 1973 SC 1461 (India).

relevant for courts to identify the fundamental features of their constitutions in order to protect them from legislative intrusion.

The Lord President of the Malaysian Supreme Court, Raja Azlan Shah, once called the "vanity and presumption of governing beyond the grave ... the most ridiculous and insolent of all tyrannies," arguing that "[i]t is the living and not the dead, that are to be accommodated."[71] But this concern focuses on commitment to a group of people rather than faithfulness to a constitutional plan for governance.[72] The idea of the constitution as an initial project that continues over time reflects the constitutional founding of post-colonial Malaysia and Singapore. The use of constitutional history in practice, properly understood, does not detract from this objective. From the time of their founding, it was clear that the framers were aware the constitution's objectives could only be achieved through continuing constitutional construction.[73]

IV. Constitutional History in Practice

A. Malaysia's Article 3(1) Constitutional Religion Clause

Constitutional foundings affect the national imagination in different ways. In Malaysia, the founding of the constitution marks a break from its British colonial past and the expression of a new national identity for the independent nation. Its founding premises are thus often invoked in legal and political discourse to support a particular vision of the Malaysian state's identity.

Nowhere is this illustrated more vividly than in debates over the position of Islam in Malaysia's constitutional order.[74] Contemporary public discourse has become polarized over the identity of the Malaysian state as secular or Islamic. Much of this debate has revolved around the understanding of the Article 3(1) constitutional clause: "Islam is the religion of the Federation; but other religions may be practised in peace and harmony."[75] What does the Article 3(1) clause mean for the relationship between religion and the state? And what is the scope of protection for religious freedom guaranteed in Malaysia's bill of rights?[76]

Advocates of Islam's supremacy argue that the history of Islam in the Malay states supports an elevated position for Islam.[77] Secularists, on the other hand, argue

[71] Loh Kooi Choon v. Gov't of Malaysia [1977] 2 MALAYAN L.J. 187, 189.

[72] *See* BALKIN, *supra* note 63, at 56–57.

[73] *See* REID REPORT, *supra* note 17, at [14].

[74] For more detailed discussion, see Chapter 7, Judicializing Religion.

[75] FED. CONST. (MALAY.), art. 3(1).

[76] *Id.* art. 11(1).

[77] *See, e.g.*, Abdul Aziz Bari, *Islam in the Federal Constitution: A Commentary on the Decision of* Meor Atiqulrahman, 2 MALAYAN L.J. cxxix, cxxxv (2000) (arguing that "history and the essential character of the country" are the "most important" reasons supporting Islam's supremacy).

that the constitution set up a generally secular basis for governance. Strikingly, the use of constitutional history in Malaysia tends to be employed in service of a more rights-expansive constitutional approach. Unlike the rise of originalism in the United States, which has been closely associated with a conservative political movement and the promotion of judicial restraint,[78] originalist arguments in Malaysia have been the domain of secularists seeking to expand individual rights protection and judicial oversight of the political branches. Secularists routinely reach back to the founding premises of the Malaysian Constitution to argue for more robust protection of religious freedom and other constitutional rights.[79]

In this section, I explore the historical context for the Article 3(1) clause and the purposes motivating its drafting. I show how the text, history, and structure of the Malaysian Constitution reveal a role for religion in line with the protection of minorities and individual rights. The constitutional settlement reached at the founding serves as a significant source of guidance for interpreting the religion clauses in the Malaysian Constitution.

The framers of the Malayan Constitution did not originally intend to constitutionalize a state religion. Indeed, the Reid Commission's initial draft constitution contained no clause establishing any religion. And although the commission's report was accompanied by a separate dissenting note by Justice Abdul Hamid that advocated for a clause declaring Islam as the state religion, even Abdul Hamid thought that such an "innocuous" clause would not "impose any disability on non-Muslim citizens."[80] Negotiations between all the stakeholders involved in the constitution-making process—the Alliance leaders, the Malay rulers, and minority group representatives—eventually resulted in a constitutional scheme that represented a social contract between the various communities in Malaya's pluralistic society. Eventually, after the United Malay National Organisation conceded to expand citizenship for non-Muslims, the Malaysian Chinese Association and the Malaysian Indian Congress agreed to a provision for an official religion.[81]

The constitutional bargain was made on the understanding by all involved that such a state religion provision would not impose any disability on non-Muslims or imply that the state was not secular. This position was explicitly memorialized in the Alliance's memorandum to the constitutional commission.[82] What seems

[78] *See* Keith E. Whittington, *The New Originalism*, 2 GEO. J.L. & PUB. POL'Y 599, 601 (2004) (noting that "originalism was a reactive theory motivated by substantive disagreement with the recent and then-current actions of the Warren and Burger Courts"); Thomas B. Colby, *The Sacrifice of the New Originalism*, 99 GEO. L.J. 713, 716 (2011) (explaining that originalism "arose as a by-product of the conservative frustration with the broad, rights-expansive decisions of the Warren and Burger Courts").

[79] Malaysian originalist argument in constitutional practice is akin to what Sujit Choudhry has described in India as "a comparatively inflected living originalism in practice." *See* Sujit Choudhry, *Living Originalism in India: Our Law and Comparative Constitutional Law*, 25 YALE J.L. & HUMAN. 1, 3 (2013).

[80] REID REPORT, *supra* note 17, at [11], [12].

[81] Joseph Fernando, *The Position of Islam in the Constitution of Malaysia*, 37 J. SE. ASIAN STUD. 249, 253 (2006).

[82] *See* Alliance Memorandum to the Reid Constitutional Commission, Sept. 27, 1956, at 19.

clear is that the final constitution was meant to reflect what all the parties involved in the constitution-making process had affirmed. As Prime Minister Tunku Abdul Rahman declared, "the whole Constitution was framed on the basis that the Federation would be a secular state."[83] This constitutional history is crucial for understanding the role that religion and religious protection would play in the new constitutional order.

Article 3(1) of the Malaysian Constitution famously declares that "Islam is the religion of the Federation," but critically adds "other religions may be practised in peace and harmony in any part of the Federation."[84] Islam's role as the religion of the state is inseparable from the constitutional protection for religious minorities, which is contained in the same constitutional provision. The framers did not conceive of Article 3(1) constitutional clause as elevating Islam's position vis-à-vis other religions; rather, they contemplated an inter-religious communal agreement. Article 3 is not directed at establishing Islam's supremacy within the constitutional order; rather, it is about religious accommodation—for Islam and other religions—in a pluralistic society of various religious and ethnic communities.

Viewing the Article 3(1) constitutional declaration through this lens puts the two clauses that it contains into perspective. Begin with the first clause: "Islam is the religion of the Federation." The broader historical context illuminates the nature and extent of this clause and how it fits with the understanding that the constitution was setting up a generally "secular state."[85] Any apparent incompatibility between establishing an official state religion and a secular state falls away when we understand how Islam's position was conceived at the constitution's founding. The framers envisioned the declaration of an official state religion to function alongside constitutional protection for the rights of religious minorities. Such a set-up would not have appeared alien to anyone in the post-colonial era familiar with the British arrangement of an established Church of England headed by the monarch.[86] In Malaysia, the King—the *Yang di-Pertuan Agong*—is constitutionally designated as the head of the religion of Islam.[87] Islam's position as the state religion was intended to be symbolic, rather than practical.[88] As the Colonial Office's memorandum on the London constitutional conference noted, all those involved

[83] Fernando, *The Position of Islam in the Constitution of Malaysia*, *supra* note 81, at 259–60 (citing Minutes of the 19th Meeting of the Working Party, Apr. 17, 1957, CO 941/87).

[84] FED. CONST. (MALAY.), art. 3(1) ("Islam is the religion of the Federation; but other religions may be practised in peace and harmony in any part of the Federation.").

[85] Fernando, *The Position of Islam in the Constitution of Malaysia*, *supra* note 81, at 259–60 ("On the possibility of the provision on religion being misinterpreted, the Tunku assured the Working Party that 'the whole Constitution was framed on the basis that the Federation would be a secular State.' ").

[86] *See* SHAH, *supra* note 61, at 46.

[87] The *Yang di-Pertuan Agong* is the head of the religion of Islam in his state, states without a head of Islam, and in the federal territories. FED. CONST. (MALAY.), art. 3(2), (3), & (5).

[88] Fernando, *The Position of Islam in the Constitution of Malaysia*, *supra* note 81, at 258 (observing that United Malays National Organisation representatives were primarily concerned with the symbolic importance of Islam as the official religion for the Malay-Muslim community).

in the constitutional discussions agreed that the state religion provision "has more political significance than practical effect."[89]

Understanding Islam's position within the original constitutional framework helps illuminate the notion of a "secular state" in the Malaysian context. Secularism does not mean a complete separation of religion and the state in Malaysia. The Malaysian state engages with religion in various ways: for example, individual states can regulate Islamic personal law, and state Sharia courts have jurisdiction over "persons professing the religion of Islam."[90] Importantly, though, under the Constitution's framework, religious law does not form the basis of general legal or constitutional norms. In contrast to a constitution that enshrines religious principles as "a" or "the" source of legislation,[91] the Malaysian Constitution declares Islam as the official religion, but the formal clause is not a basis for the general laws of the land. The constitutional drafters did not aim to set up a theocratic state or achieve a particular vision of Islam; the religion clause was part of a broader debate about ethnic privileges and federalism.[92] Indeed, the Alliance leaders emphasized that "they had no intention of creating a Muslim theocracy and that Malaya would be a secular State."[93] In line with that, the Constitution establishes a generally secular framework that explicitly protects all religious communities and individuals.

Related, and crucially, the second part of the Article 3(1) constitutional clause declares that "other religions may be practised in peace and harmony in any part of the Federation."[94] This second clause is constitutive of the constitutional compromise embodied in the text. The provision that "other religions may be practised in peace and harmony" is designed to guarantee the protection of religious minorities. And that's not all. Article 3(4)—another provision in the same Article—states explicitly: "Nothing in this Article derogates from any other provision of the Constitution." That includes the Constitution's chapter on fundamental liberties, which guarantees individual rights like the right to religious freedom.[95] Taken together, Article 3(1) and 3(4) reveal a constitutional framework that guarantees the protection of minority groups and the rights of individuals.

The constitutional text and history illuminate that the Article 3 constitutional clause, properly understood, establishes a framework that guarantees Islam's

[89] *Id.* at 260 (citing Memorandum by Jackson, May 23, 1957, CO 1030/494 (20)).

[90] FED. CONST. (MALAY.), art. 74(2), sched. 9, list II, item 1.

[91] *See, e.g.*, CONSTITUTION OF THE ARAB REPUBLIC OF EGYPT, 18 Jan. 2014, art. 2 ("Islam is the religion of the state. . . . The principles of Islamic Sharia are the principle source of legislation."); Article 2, Section 1, The Constitution of the Republic of Iraq of 2005 ("Islam is the official religion of the State and is a foundation source of legislation.").

[92] Stilt, *supra* note at 22, at 408.

[93] Fernando, *The Position of Islam in the Constitution of Malaysia, supra* note 81, at 260 (citing Memorandum by Jackson, May 23, 1957, CO 1030/494 (20)).

[94] FED. CONST. (MALAY.), art. 3(1) ("Islam is the religion of the Federation; but other religions may be practised in peace and harmony in any part of the Federation.").

[95] *Id.* art 11(1).

position as the religion of the state alongside the protection of other religions. The two elements of Article 3(1) are fundamentally intertwined. In Article 3, the framers of the Malaysian Constitution envisaged a constitutional scheme that simultaneously endorses Islam's official position along with guaranteed protection for religious minorities and individuals. Article 3(1) reflects the constitutional compromise reached at the founding in Malaysia's multi-religious and multi-racial society. The new polity's pluralistic identity is baked into Malaysia's constitutional arrangements.

Viewing the protection of minorities as a part of the constitution's foundational core has concrete implications for constitutional adjudication. Consider the Malaysian Federal Court's 2018 decision in *Indira Gandhi v. Pengarah Jabatan Agama Islam Perak*.[96] The Federal Court declared that the principles of "the separation of powers, the rule of law and the *protection of minorities*" are "part of the basic structure of the Constitution" that "cannot be abrogated or removed."[97] Remarkably, in this case involving the religious authority of the civil courts vis-à-vis the Sharia courts, the Court expressly recognized "the protection of minorities" as part of the Malaysian Constitution's basic structure. While the separation of powers and judicial independence have been identified as fundamental features in earlier decisions,[98] *Indira Gandhi* was the first time that the Court specifically declared the minority protection as a foundational principle of the Malaysian Constitution's core structure.

In *Indira Gandhi*, the Malaysian Federal Court underscored this landmark declaration by referring to the Canadian Supreme Court's 1998 decision concerning the secession of Quebec, in which the Canadian court recognized that "the protection of minority rights is itself an independent principle" underlying the Canadian constitutional order.[99] Citing the Canadian opinion with approval, the Malaysian Court emphasized that "a constitution may seek to ensure that vulnerable minority groups are endowed with the institutions and rights necessary to maintain and promote their identities against the assimilative pressures of the majority."[100] Even as respect for minority rights is regarded as fundamental to the multicultural nature of Canada's constitutional identity, so too the Malaysian Court appeared to recognize that the pluralistic character of its multi-religious society is likewise integral to the Malaysian Constitution. Malaya's constitution-making process involved protracted negotiation among the various ethnic and religious groups and reflected inter-communal compromise. The social contract struck at the founding

[96] [2018] 1 Malayan L.J. 545 (F.C.) [hereinafter *Indira Gandhi* (F.C.)]. For further discussion of this case, see Chapter 5, The Rule of Law, section III(A), and Chapter 7, Judicializing Religion.

[97] *Id.* at [90] (emphasis added).

[98] *See, e.g.*, Semenyih Jaya v. Pentadbir Tanah Daerah Hulu Langat [2017] 3 Malayan L.J. 561, at [74].

[99] *Indira Gandhi* (F.C.), [2018] 1 Malayan L.J. 545, at [31].

[100] *Id.* at [30] (quoting Reference re Secession of Quebec [1998] 2 SCR 217, at [73]–[74]).

underscores that a degree of religious and ethnic pluralism is essential to the Malaysian Constitution's core.

The lens of constitutional history brings into focus that the protection of minorities is embedded in the constitution's basic framework. The Malaysian Federal Court in *Indira Gandhi* emphasized: "A constitution must be interpreted in light of its historical and philosophical context, as well as its fundamental underlying principles."[101] Properly understood, Article 3(1) is constitutive of both Islam's role as the state religion *and* the religious freedom of individuals and groups. The protection of minority rights has now been recognized as part of a domain of fundamental values so central to the constitution that it cannot be altered. The Malaysian Constitution's basic framework encompasses not only structural principles, like judicial power and the separation of powers, but also expressly compels the protection of the fundamental rights of minorities and individuals.

B. Singapore's Originalist Case Study: *Yong Vui Kong v. Public Prosecutor*

The Singaporean courts have generally taken an interpretive approach characterized by strict legalism and a highly deferential stance toward the legislature and executive. Unsurprisingly, in light of the Singapore Constitution's lack of a momentous founding moment, arguments based on constitutional history did not feature prominently in its constitutional jurisprudence for decades—that is, until the Singapore apex court delivered a heavily originalist decision in the 2010 case of *Yong Vui Kong v. Public Prosecutor*.[102]

Yong Vui Kong, a nineteen-year old Malaysian drug runner, was arrested carrying packages that contained more than forty grams of heroin and convicted of drug trafficking. Under Singapore law, drug trafficking offenses carry a mandatory death penalty.[103] Yong appealed his death sentence, arguing that the mandatory death penalty violated Article 9(1) of the Singapore Constitution, which provides that "[n]o person shall be deprived of his life or personal liberty save in accordance with law."[104] Yong argued that the mandatory death penalty is an inhuman punishment not "in accordance with law" under Article 9(1).

The Singapore Court of Appeal unanimously rejected Yong's argument. The Court's decision is self-consciously originalist, focused on the constitutional text and framers' intent.[105] It refused to find an implied prohibition against inhuman

[101] *Id.* at [29].
[102] [2010] 3 SING. L. REP. 489.
[103] *See* Misuse of Drugs Act, ch. 185, 2008 Rev. Ed. Sing. (mandating the death penalty for trafficking fifteen grams or more of heroin).
[104] CONST. OF THE REP. OF SING., art. 9(1).
[105] *Yong Vui Kong*, [2010] 3 SING. L. REP. 489, at [60]–[75].

punishment in the Singapore Constitution, reasoning that the lack of any explicit textual prohibition at the time of drafting was evidence that the framers had deliberately chosen to omit such a prohibition.[106]

The Singapore court's focus on the framers' original intent is striking, especially given that the Singapore Constitution is based on the 1957 Malayan Constitution drafted by Reid Commission.[107] Despite the oddity of relying on the original intent of another nation's constitutional framers,[108] Chief Justice Chan Sek Keong emphasized that the Reid Commission had not recommended a prohibition against inhuman treatment in the Malayan Constitution even though such a provision existed in the European Convention on Human Rights at the time of the constitution's drafting.[109] Thus, the Court insisted that the framers' omitting of the prohibition "was clearly not due to ignorance or oversight on the part of the Reid Commission."[110] For the Court to find such an implied prohibition against inhuman punishment, declared the Court of Appeal, would be "to legislate new rights into the Singapore Constitution under the guise of interpreting existing constitutional provisions."[111]

The Court also pointed out that the Wee Chong Jin Constitutional Commission convened in Singapore in 1966 had proposed adding an express prohibition against inhuman punishment, "but that proposal was ultimately rejected by the Government."[112] The Singapore government's "unambiguous" rejection of the Constitutional Commission's proposal meant that it was "not legitimate" for the court to read into Article 9(1) "a constitutional right which was decisively rejected by the Government in 1969."[113] The Court concluded that it could not find an implied prohibition against inhuman punishment "because of our constitutional history, in particular, the Government's conscious decision not to incorporate such a prohibition into the Singapore Constitution notwithstanding the recommendation of the Wee Commission."[114]

Putting aside the evidence that the Singapore government's rejection of a prohibition against torture and inhuman treatment was not as unequivocal as the Court made it out to be,[115] for the Court to find that Parliament's failure to incorporate the Wee Commission's proposal is evidence of an "original" intent not to prohibit inhuman treatment is bizarre. For one thing, the 1966 Wee Commission's report

106 *Id.* at [61].
107 *Id.* at [62].
108 Po Jen Yap, *Constitutionalising Capital Crimes: Judicial Virtue or 'Originalism' Sin?*, SING. J. LEGAL STUD. 281, 284 (2011).
109 *Yong Vui Kong*, [2010] 3 SING. L. REP. 489, at [62].
110 *Id.*
111 *Id.* at [59].
112 *Id.* at [64].
113 *Id.* at [72].
114 *Id.* at [120]
115 *See* Jack Tsen-Ta Lee, *The Mandatory Death Penalty and A Sparsely Worded Constitution*, 127 LAW Q. REV. 192, 193 (2011).

was released four years after the Singapore Constitution came into force; none of the commission's members participated in the original drafting of the Singapore Constitution.

Moreover, taking the Court's reasoning to its logical conclusion, any Wee Commission recommendation not adopted by the Singapore government (in 1966) cannot be deemed a constitutional right.[116] The Wee Commission had in fact recommended adding three new provisions into the Singapore Constitution. In addition to prohibiting torture and inhuman treatment, it had also proposed including a constitutional guarantee of the right to vote and the right to a judicial remedy[117]—all recommendations that the Singapore government at the time found "acceptable in principle."[118] Although the Wee Commission's recommendation against torture had also not been incorporated into the Singapore Constitution, the Chief Justice in *Yong Vui Kong* dismissed the notion that the Singapore Constitution could be said to permit torture.[119] Attempting to find an exit strategy for its distinction between a prohibition against torture and inhuman treatment, the Court observed that the Singapore government had "explicitly recognized that torture is wrong" by relying on a statement by the Minister of Home Affairs during parliamentary debates in 1987.[120] The link here is tenuous, at best. Whether one considers the constitution's framing to be at the time of Singapore's independence in 1963 or associated with the 1966 Constitutional Commission's review, a ministerial statement two decades after the Commission's report is not remotely connected to any original intent of the framers.[121]

The Singapore Court of Appeal maintained its narrow focus on constitutional history in two subsequent cases involving the same appellant. In 2011, the Court rejected Yong's argument that the President had discretion in clemency decisions.[122] To conclude that the Singapore Constitution "excludes any role for the President's personal discretion in the exercise of the clemency power," the Court drew on the "legislative history of the clemency power in this jurisdiction," which included a speech given by Prime Minister Lee Kuan Yew in 1965.[123]

The Singapore legislature eventually amended the statute mandating the death penalty for drug trafficking. Yong was then re-sentenced to a mandatory life sentence and fifteen strokes of the cane. In 2015, Yong challenged his corporal punishment sentence arguing that it constituted a form of torture that violated the right

116 *See* Yap, *Constitutionalising Capital Crimes*, *supra* note 108, at 284.

117 Wee Report, *supra* note 42, at [14].

118 Thio, *The Passage of a Generation*, *supra* note 58.

119 *Yong Vui Kong*, [2010] 3 Sing. L. Rep. 489, at [75] (noting that "[t]his conclusion does not mean that, because the proposed Art 13 included a prohibition against torture, an Act of Parliament that permits torture can form part of 'law' for the purposes of Art 9(1)").

120 *Id.*

121 *See* Po Jen Yap, *Uncovering Originalism and Textualism in Singapore*, *in* Constitutional Interpretation in Singapore: Theory and Practice 117 (Jaclyn Neo ed., 2017).

122 Yong Vui Kong v. Att'y Gen. [2011] 2 Sing. L. Rep. 1189.

123 *Id.* at [173]–[174].

to life and liberty in Article 9(1).[124] Reiterating the originalist stance exhibited in its 2010 decision, the Court held that Article 9(1) did not prohibit the caning sentence as there was "no evidence in the historical record to indicate that this understanding of 'life' had been altered by the time Article 9(1) was adopted into the Singapore Constitution."[125] Notably, though, the Court accepted that certain aspects of the Singapore Constitution that are "fundamental and essential to the political system," like the separation of powers or the right to vote, may be part of its "basic structure,"[126] although the basic structure doctrine did not help Yong in this case as the Court did not find it to encompass any prohibition against torture.[127]

The originalist approach employed by the Singapore Court of Appeal bears little resemblance to the popular appeals to constitutional history displayed across the border in Malaysia. Constitutional interpretation in Singapore is heavily formalist, and its originalist jurisprudence is no exception. The Singapore Court's originalist understanding is narrowly fixated on the text and in service of judicial deference to the political branches.

One fundamental difficulty with how the Court used constitutional history is its rigid focus on the framers' specific expected applications. In considering the Reid Commission's drafting of the Malayan Constitution and the Wee Commission's recommendations for Singapore's Constitution, the Court placed dispositive weight on the commission members' expected applications, even relying on what the framers omitted from the text as determinative of their expectations. According to the Court, the scope of Article 9(1) is limited by how the framers expected the provision to be applied. So, the right to "life and personal liberty" cannot be interpreted to prohibit the death penalty[128]—or corporal punishment[129]—because the framers could not have expected the constitutional text to prohibit these sentences.

Faithfulness to the constitution, however, doesn't require applying a constitutional provision according to the framers' specific expectations. Constitutional history can be used by courts in many ways.[130] Different types of constitutional provisions lend themselves differently to historical analysis.[131] Rules and standards are distinct. Rules that prescribe government structures and procedural details are often intended to be applied specifically; for example, "the President of Singapore shall hold office for a term of six years."[132] Constitutional rules that limit discretion are more suited to being interpreted according to what the framers expected.

[124] Yong's death penalty sentence had been reduced to life imprisonment and fifteen strokes of caning following Singapore's amendments to the Misuse of Drugs Act.

[125] Yong Vui Kong v. Public Prosecutor [2015] 2 SING. L. REP. 1129, at [23].

[126] *Id.* at [71].

[127] *See* Swati Jhaveri, *Recent Judicial Comments on the Basic Structure of the Constitution*, SING. PUB. L. BLOG (Apr. 20, 2016), https://perma.cc/L5Y8-8CLN.

[128] *See Yong Vui Kong*, [2011] 2 SING. L. REP. 1189.

[129] *See Yong Vui Kong*, [2015] 2 SING. L. REP. 1129.

[130] *See* Jamal Greene & Yvonne Tew, *Comparative Approaches to Constitutional History*, *in* COMPARATIVE JUDICIAL REVIEW 379, 380–83 (Erin Delaney & Rosalind Dixon eds., 2018).

[131] *See* Jamal Greene, *Rule Originalism*, 116 COLUM. L. REV. 1639 (2016).

[132] CONST. OF THE REP. OF SING., art. 20(1).

By contrast, constitutional provisions that declare broad standards or general principles call for ongoing constitutional construction.[133] Principles and standards setting out fundamental liberties, for example, by their nature suggest progressive application by future interpreters.[134] The framers of the Singapore Constitution deliberately chose open-ended language, such as "life or personal liberty" and "in accordance with law," fully contemplating that such broad constitutional provisions would be open to future development.[135]

Consider, for example, the Indian Supreme Court's more expansive approach to Article 21 of the Indian Constitution, which is worded similarly to Singapore's Article 9(1),[136] in a challenge to a mandatory death penalty provision of the Indian Penal Code. Article 21 likewise requires that any deprivation of life or liberty must be in accordance to "law." The Indian Supreme Court interpreted this provision to mean that any such deprivation has to be "fair, just, and reasonable" and invalidated the statute.[137]

In its 2010 decision in *Yong Vui Kong*, however, the Singapore Court explicitly rejected a similar test of reasonableness for Article 9(1) of the Singapore Constitution. It tried to distinguish the Singapore case from the Indian one, stating that the "expansive interpretation" of the right to life and liberty made sense in India in light of the "pro-active approach of the Indian Supreme Court in matters relating to the social and economic conditions of the people of India."[138] Because the mandatory death penalty had existed in Singapore at the time of its constitutional drafting, the Court concluded that the framers could not possibly have expected to prohibit it.

The Singapore Court of Appeal's reasoning shackles Article 9(1) to the framers' original expected applications, instead of viewing the article as embodying a principle protecting the right to life and liberty. A more expansive understanding of Article 9(1), on the other hand, would be compatible with requiring that rights restrictions be reasonable and would also avoid the inconsistent reasoning exhibited in the *Yong Vui Kong* decisions. For instance, it would make sense of the Court's recognition of an implied constitutional prohibition against torture, which the Court struggled to reconcile with its reasoning in *Yong*. It's worth noting the Court relied on a minister's parliamentary statement to conclude that the Singapore Constitution had evolved to recognize an implied prohibition against torture—a move that itself illustrates constitutional construction in practice.[139]

[133] *See* Balkin, *supra* note 63, at 6–7 (arguing that constitutional adopters "use standards or principles because they want to channel politics through certain key concepts but delegate the details to future generations").

[134] Greene & Tew, *supra* note 130, at 383.

[135] *Id.*; *see also* Yap, *Uncovering Originalism and Textualism in Singapore*, *supra* note 121.

[136] India Const. art. 21 ("No person shall be deprived of his life or personal liberty except according to procedure established by law.").

[137] Mithu v. State of Punjab A.I.R. 1983 S.C. 473.

[138] Yong Vui Kong v. Public Prosecutor [2010] 3 Sing. L. Rep 489, at [83]–[84].

[139] *Id.* at [75].

The originalist approach employed by the Singapore Court of Appeal appears in service of judicial restraint,[140] and reflects the Singapore courts' highly deferential position toward the political branches. To avoid interfering with laws enacted by the Singapore government, the Court uses originalist arguments as a "constitutional fig leaf."[141] Indeed, the Court's original intent analysis in the 2010 *Yong* decision is strained precisely because it is concerned with the intent of the Singapore legislature, not the actual constitutional framers.[142] Historical arguments are employed in this manner in light of Singapore's legal culture within a dominant party system, which tends to reflect "a predominant constitutional pragmatism."[143]

V. Conclusion

Sir Ivor Jennings, one of the framers of the Malaysian Constitution, once described the nature of a constitution as "a framework... which has to be filled out with detailed rules and practices."[144] The purposes motivating a constitution's founding and the point of the constitutional project are fundamental to the endeavor of understanding and interpreting a constitution.[145] A constitution is not merely a document, but, most significantly, as Felix Frankfurter put it, "a stream of history."[146]

Constitutional history helps to reveal the fundamental principles at the constitution's core and the deeper values underlying the larger constitutional project. Understood thus within its historical context, Article 3(1) of the Malaysian Constitution creates a constitutional framework that establishes a state religion alongside protection for minorities and individuals. Faithfulness to the constitution, ultimately, calls for commitment to its foundational elements and overarching principles. Unlike the practice displayed by the Singapore Court of Appeal, it does not mandate a narrow originalist approach tied to the specific applications expected by the framers. Constitutional history can serve broader, and nobler, purposes.

[140] *See* Li-ann Thio, *"It Is A Little Known Legal Fact": Originalism, Customary Human Rights Law, and Constitutional Interpretation*, SING. J. LEGAL STUD. 558, 570 (2010) (observing of the Singapore Court of Appeal's decision in *Yong* that "[o]riginalism here acts to restrain judicial discretion. This avoids the spectre of juristocracy, where activist judges advance a political agenda through applying their subjective values in interpretation").

[141] *See* Yap, *Uncovering Originalism and Textualism in Singapore, supra* note 121.

[142] *Yong Vui Kong*, [2010] 3 SING. L. REP. 489, at [64]–[74].

[143] THIO, A TREATISE ON SINGAPORE CONSTITUTIONAL LAW, *supra* note 34, ¶ 02.060.

[144] IVOR JENNINGS, THE LAW AND THE CONSTITUTION 34 (5th ed. 1967).

[145] Kim Lane Scheppele, *Jack Balkin Is an American*, 25 YALE J.L. & HUMAN. 23, 24 (2013).

[146] *See* FELIX FRANKFURTER, THE COMMERCE CLAUSE UNDER MARSHALL, TANEY, AND WAITE 2 (1937).

4

The Separation of Powers

I. Introduction

From Montesquieu to Mahathir, political thinkers have persistently invoked—and persistently contested—the principle of separation of powers to justify particular forms of allocating government power. How does the separation of powers operate in practice in a fragile democracy historically dominated by consolidated political power? In this chapter, I explore this dynamic using as a central case study the Malaysian Federal Court's decision in the 2017 case of *Semenyih Jaya v. Pentadbir Tanah Daerah Hulu Langat*.[1]

This chapter explores the separation of powers—in theory and practice—in Asian democracies like Malaysia and Singapore. It starts by situating various approaches to the separation of powers within a conceptual framework. But theory can only take us so far. Moving beyond the theoretical foundations of the separation of powers, I examine how the separation of powers operates in the constitutional practice of these democracies. In 1988, the Malaysian legislature aggressively amended Article 121(1) of the Federal Constitution to remove the provision vesting judicial power in the courts.[2] The political branches' strike at judicial power was met with an anemic response from the Malaysian Federal Court, which appeared to accept that the amended provision meant that the courts' powers were indeed subject to federal law.[3] In light of the courts' narrow, blinkered approach to the separation of powers, which effectively subsumed the judiciary under the control of the legislature, many commentators thought that judicial power in Malaysia had been effectually smothered.[4]

Stifled, but not destroyed. In a unanimous decision in 2017, the Malaysian apex court in *Semenyih Jaya* struck down a statutory provision that restricted the courts' jurisdiction as unconstitutional for violating the separation of powers.[5] Declaring judicial power, judicial independence, and the separation of powers as "critical"

[1] [2017] 3 Malayan L.J. 561 [hereinafter *Semenyih Jaya*].

[2] Fed. Const. (Malay.), art. 121(1).

[3] Public Prosecutor v. Kok Wah Kuan [2008] 1 Malayan L.J. 1 (F.C.) [hereinafter *Kok Wah Kuan* (F.C.)]; *see also* Danaharta Urus v. Kekatong [2004] 2 Malayan L.J. 257 (F.C.).

[4] *See, e.g.*, Richard S.K. Foo, *Malaysia—The Death of a Separate Constitutional Judicial Power*, Sing. J. Legal Stud. 227 (2010); Ratna Rueban Balasubramaniam, *Has Rule by Law Killed the Rule of Law in Malaysia?*, 8 Oxford Uni. Commonwealth L.J. 211 (2008).

[5] *Semenyih Jaya*, [2017] 3 Malayan L.J. 561.

Constitutional Statecraft in Asian Courts. Yvonne Tew, Oxford University Press (2020). © Yvonne Tew.
DOI:10.1093/oso/9780198716839.001.0001

and "sacrosanct" in the Malaysian constitutional framework,[6] the Federal Court ruled that, despite the amended constitutional provision, judicial power continues to vest in the *courts*.[7] Significantly, the Court declared that Parliament does not have the power to amend the Constitution to the effect of undermining basic features like the separation of powers and the independence of the judiciary.[8]

Semenyih Jaya represents a landmark in Malaysia's constitutional jurisprudence. It breathes new life into the separation of powers as a foundational feature of the Constitution, revealing a more robust jurisprudence that enables courts to assume a protective role over the Constitution's core structure. Singapore's constitutional jurisprudence has developed more incrementally; still, the Singapore Court of Appeal has identified the separation of powers as fundamental and essential to the democratic order established by the Constitution.[9] In Malaysia, the judiciary is well-poised to build on the foundation it has laid in *Semenyih Jaya* to consolidate its constitutional position vis-à-vis the political branches. Establishing an empowered institutional role for courts would rebalance the distribution of government power, which thus far has been concentrated in the political branches, reanimating the separation of powers as an effective principle of checks and balances.

II. Conceptualizing the Separation of Powers

Long considered a central principle in the political arrangements of a modern state, the separation of powers recognizes the functional independence of the three branches of government. Drawing on John Locke's argument for dividing state power to prevent government tyranny, Montesquieu argued for a tripartite model of government—with the legislature enacting laws, the executive implementing these laws, and the judiciary adjudicating legal disputes—to prevent the abuse of power.[10]

Of course, the separation of powers operates differently in the particular constitutional order in which it takes root. For example, in addition to separating the exercise of the different powers of government, the framers of the U.S. Constitution emphasized the importance of a system of checks and balances as "essential to the preservation of liberty."[11] As James Madison wrote in the Federalist No. 51, "the great security against a gradual concentration of the several powers in the same department, consists in giving to those who administer each department the

[6] *Id.* at [90].
[7] *Id.* at [86].
[8] *Id.* at [74], [76].
[9] *See* Yong Vui Kong v. Public Prosecutor [2015] 2 SING. L. REP. 1129.
[10] CHARLES LOUIS DE SECONDAT, BARON DE MONTESQUIEU, THE SPIRIT OF THE LAWS (Book XI, ch. IV) (1748), *in* THE COMPLETE WORKS OF M. DE MONTESQUIEU (1777).
[11] THE FEDERALIST No. 51 (James Madison).

necessary constitutional means and personal motives to resist encroachments of the others."[12]

While the American model of limited government is a familiar articulation of the separation of powers as a system of checks and balances, the British legal system's commitment to parliamentary supremacy is premised on a very different approach to the separation of powers.[13] In the United Kingdom, the close connection between the legislature and executive reflects the lack of a "pure" separation between the branches of government at Westminster.[14] Indeed, under Britain's parliamentary model, members of the executive are drawn from Parliament.

Like many former British colonies, Malaysia and Singapore are modeled on a Westminster parliamentary system. Political branches of government have a great degree of overlap. The Prime Minister and his Cabinet members are typically also Members of Parliament; as the Malaysian Federal Court put it, "the Executive is, therefore, present at the heart of Parliament."[15] What's more, these states are usually controlled by a dominant political party or coalition, resulting in even more power being concentrated in the political branches. Singapore's People's Action Party continues to control more than 90 percent of the seats in Parliament and, until 2018, Malaysia's Barisan Nasional coalition had not lost its legislative majority for over half a century.

The fusion of power between the executive and legislative branch is particularly concerning in systems where a ruling party facing no significant political competition controls most institutions of government.[16] "Such a system places obvious pressures on the separation of powers," as David Bilchitz and David Landau observe, because the other institutional branches of government "may all be unwilling or unable to check an executive at the head of a dominant-party system."[17] These contexts risk entrenching an "elective dictatorship."[18] Given the inordinate pressure that courts operating in dominant party systems face in carving out space for judicial power,[19] it is unsurprising that much of the earlier jurisprudence in Malaysia and Singapore has not led to a robust conception of the separation of powers.

[12] *Id.*

[13] *See* David Feldman, *'Which in Your Case You Have Not Got': Constitutionalism at Home and Abroad*, 64 Current Legal Probs. 117, 120 (2011).

[14] *See* E. Barendt, *Separation of Powers and Constitutional Government*, Pub. L. 599 (1995); *see also* M.J.C. Vile, Constitutionalism and the Separation of Powers (Liberty Fund, Inc., 2d ed. 1998) (distinguishing between a "pure" and "partial" version of the separation of powers).

[15] JRI Resources Sdn. Bhd v. Kuwait Fin. House Bhd [2019] 5 Current L.J. 569, at [96].

[16] *See* Samuel Issacharoff, Fragile Democracies: Contested Power in the Era of Constitutional Courts 254–55 (2015).

[17] David Bilchitz & David Landau, *Introduction* to The Evolution of the Separation of Powers: Between the Global North and the Global South 13 (David Bilchitz & David Landau eds., 2018).

[18] Lord Hailsham of St. Marylebone, Richard Dimbleby Lecture, *Elective Dictatorship*, 96 The Listener 496 (1976).

[19] Issacharoff, *supra* note 16, at 254.

III. Separation of Powers in Context

A. Malaysia's 1988 Constitutional Amendment

In an interview published in *Time* Magazine in 1986, Mahathir Mohamad, then the fourth prime minister of Malaysia, made clear his frustration with the Malaysian judiciary:[20]

> The judiciary says, "Although you passed a law with a certain thing in mind, we think that your mind is wrong, and we want to give our interpretation." If we disagree, the courts say, "We will interpret your disagreement." If we go along, we are going to lose our power of legislation. We know exactly what we want to do, but once we do it, it is interpreted in a different way, and we have no means to interpret it our way. If we find that a court always throws us out on its own interpretation, if it interprets contrary to why we made the law, then we will have to find a way of producing a law that will have to be interpreted according to our wish.

Tensions between Mahathir's administration and the judiciary continued to build as the courts issued a series of decisions striking down a number of legislative and executive actions.[21] In one of the few occasions in which the Malaysian apex court declared a federal law unconstitutional, the Supreme Court in *Public Prosecutor v. Dato' Yap Peng* struck down a Criminal Procedure Code provision that allowed the Attorney General to remove any criminal case pending before an inferior court to the High Court.[22]

Central to the Malaysian court's decision in *Dato' Yap Peng* was the Article 121(1) constitutional clause that vested the judicial power of the federation in the courts. The Court held that the statutory provision empowering the Attorney General was "both a legislative and executive intromission into the judicial power of the Federation."[23] "[A]ny other view," wrote Supreme Court Justice Eusoffe Abdoolcader, would relegate the Article 121 judicial power provision "to no more than a teasing illusion, like a munificent bequest in a pauper's will."[24] Those words would prove ominously prescient.

In March 1988, the Malaysian government amended the constitutional judicial power clause. Article 121(1) of the Federal Constitution originally provided that

[20] *'I Know How the People Feel': An Interview with Prime Minister Dr. Mahathir Mohamad*, TIME, Nov. 24, 1986, at 20.

[21] *See, e.g.*, Berthelsen v. Director-Gen. of Immigr. [1987] 1 MALAYAN L.J. 134; Persatuan Aliran Kesedaran Negara v. Minister of Home Aff. [1988] 1 MALAYAN L.J. 440; Inspector-Gen. of Police v. Tan Sri Raja Khalid [1988] 1 MALAYAN L.J. 182; Karpal Singh v. Menteri Hal Ehwal Dalam Negeri [1988] 1 MALAYAN L.J. 468.

[22] Public Prosecutor v. Dato' Yap Peng [1987] 2 MALAYAN L.J. 311.

[23] *Id.* at 318.

[24] *Id.* at 319.

"the judicial power of the Federation shall be vested in two High Courts of co-ordinate jurisdiction and status[.]" The amended provision specified: "There shall be two High Courts of co-ordinate jurisdiction... and the High Courts and inferior courts shall have such jurisdiction and powers as may be conferred by or under federal law."[25] If there had been any doubt about how the government thought the separation of powers ought to operate, Prime Minister Mahathir Mohamad clarified the executive's position during discussions in the House of Representatives:

> The amendment is necessary to clarify further the position of the courts. At this time, with the [original] provision vesting judicial power of the Federation, the boundary between the judiciary and the executive or the legislature is vague. With this amendment, the Government hopes to demarcate that boundary clearly. This is important so that the executive, legislature, and judiciary can fulfil their respective responsibilities without disturbing or being disturbed by the other institutions.[26]

B. The Judiciary's Response to the 1988 Constitutional Amendment

In the aftermath of the 1988 amendment, the Malaysian courts' response to the legislature's removal of their judicial power was tepid. A decade after the government passed the amendments, the Court of Appeal addressed the effect of the modified Article 121(1) in *Sugumar Balakrishnan v. Pengarah Imigresen Negeri Sabah*.[27] In a decision regarding a statutory ouster clause that prevented judicial review of an administrator's decisions, the court declared that "the deletion [of the judicial vesting provision] did not have the effect of taking away judicial power" from the courts.[28] The Court of Appeal's decision, however, was later set aside by the Federal Court.

The low watermark of the Malaysian judiciary's approach toward the amended Article 121(1) provision occurred in *Public Prosecutor v. Kok Wah Kuan*.[29] The case involved the Child Act 2001 which provides for a juvenile offender convicted of murder to be detained "during the pleasure of *Yang di-Pertuan Agong*."[30] Since the King must act on ministerial advice, the Court of Appeal held the provision to be unconstitutional because it gives the executive the power to determine the length

[25] FED. CONST. (MALAY.), art. 121(1) (as amended by the Constitutional (Amendment) Act 1988).

[26] House of Representatives Malaysia, Parliamentary Debates, Seventh Parliament, Session 2, Vol. 2 (Mar. 17, 1988), at 1353 (translated from Malay by the author).

[27] [1998] 3 MALAYAN. L.J. 289.

[28] *Id.* at [37].

[29] [2008] 1 MALAYAN L.J. 1. (F.C.) [hereinafter *Kok Wah Kuan* (F.C.)].

[30] Child Protection Act (Act 611), 2001, § 97(2) (Malay.).

of a sentence. Such authority violated the separation of powers, which the Court of Appeal declared "an integral part" of the Constitution.[31]

The Federal Court overturned the Court of Appeal's decision. In a stunningly narrow interpretation of Article 121(1), the majority simply deferred to the legislature, ruling that the amended provision meant that the courts' powers and jurisdiction were indeed subject to federal law.[32] According to Justice Abdul Hamid, writing for the majority:

> If we want to know the jurisdiction and powers of the two High Courts we will have to look at the federal law… [T]o what extent such "judicial powers" are vested in the two High Courts depend on what federal law provides, not on the interpretation of the term "judicial power" as prior to the amendment.

Malaysia has its "own" constitutional model,[33] declared Justice Abdul Hamid, observing that Malaysia has a written constitution, like the United States, which specifies the functions of the three branches, yet also follows the Westminster model—and "has its own peculiarities."[34]

According to the majority, although the doctrine had undoubtedly "influenced the framers of the Malaysian Constitution," it emphasized that the separation of powers "is not a provision of the Malaysian Constitution."[35] Judicial power "depends on what the Constitution provides, not what some political thinkers think 'judicial power' is."[36]

The *Kok Wah Kuan* majority's approach to the separation of powers is highly literalist and insular and runs contrary to the idea of constitutional supremacy. For the majority, the extent—indeed, the existence—of the doctrine of separation of powers has no constitutional basis because it is not explicitly mentioned in the text. On this view, judicial power and the separation of powers is limited to whatever the legislature bestows.

Justice Richard Malanjum delivered a powerful solo dissent in *Kok Wah Kuan* where he made clear that he was "unable to accede to the proposition that with the amendment of Article 121(1) of the Federal Constitution … the courts in Malaysia can only function in accordance with what [has] been assigned to them by federal law."[37] The amendment, Justice Malanjum declared, "should by no means be read to mean that the doctrines of the separation of powers and independence of the judiciary are now no more the basic features of our Federal Constitution."[38]

[31] Kok Wah Kuan v. Public Prosecutor [2007] 5 Malayan L.J. 174 (C.A.), at [8].
[32] *Kok Wah Kuan* (F.C.), [2008] 1 Malayan L.J. 1, at [11].
[33] *Id.* at [16]
[34] *Id.* at [17].
[35] *Id.*
[36] *Id.* at [22].
[37] *Id.* at [37].
[38] *Id.* at [38].

In sharp contrast to the majority, Justice Malanjum advanced a notion of the separation of powers as a constitutional fundamental beyond the reach of Parliament. The function of the separation of powers is "to ensure that there is 'check and balance' in the system," he emphasized, highlighting the courts' crucial role as the third branch of government.[39] The courts' judicial review power is a necessary corollary of "a country with a supreme Constitution and with [a] provision for judicial review to prevent the courts from examining constitutional provisions."[40] Justice Malanjum explicitly disavowed the majority's position on judicial power: "I do not think that as a result of the amendment our courts have now become servile agents of a federal Act of Parliament and that the courts are now only to perform mechanically any command or bidding of a federal law."[41]

Judicial decisions following the Federal Court's decision in *Kok Wah Kuan* reflected a faltering jurisprudence.[42] In the 2014 case of *Nik Nazmi bin Nik Ahmad v. Public Prosecutor*,[43] the Court of Appeal defended judicial power along the same vein as the dissent in *Kok Wah Kuan*, distinguishing Malaysia's framework of constitutional supremacy from Britain's tradition of parliamentary sovereignty.[44] But the year later, the Court of Appeal in *Public Prosecutor v. Yuneswaran* differed from the *Nik Nazmi* decision, emphasizing that the "correct approach" is to pay heed to the "legislative competency of Parliament."[45]

IV. Restoring the Separation of Powers

A. The Malaysian Judiciary's Constitutional Moment: *Semenyih Jaya*

The *Semenyih Jaya v. Pentadbir Tanah Daerah Hulu Langat* case started with a dispute over land acquisition compensation.[46] Developers of land that had been compulsorily acquired by the state of Selangor for a highway project were unhappy with how much they had been compensated. Two lay assessors sitting with a High Court judge had determined the value of the acquired land in accordance with the Land

[39] *Id.* at [37].
[40] *Id.* at [39].
[41] *Id.* at [38].
[42] *See* Chapter 2, Constitutional Adjudication and Constitutional Politics, section V(B).
[43] [2014] 4 Malayan L.J. 157.
[44] *Id.* at [8].
[45] [2015] 9 Current L.J. 873, at [56]; *see also* Yang di-Pertua Dewan Rakyat v. Gobind Singh Deo [2014] 6 Malayan L.J. 812, at 826 (citing the *Kok Wah Kuan* (F.C.) majority that "the extent to which the doctrine [of separation of powers] applies depends on the provision of the Constitution").
[46] [2017] 3 Malayan L.J. 561.

Acquisition Act 1960, which also provided that such a decision was final with no possibility of further appeal to a higher court.[47]

The landowners argued that the Land Acquisition Act provision infringed their rights to property and the Article 121(1) judicial power clause because it allowed lay assessors to conclusively determine the amount of compensation.[48] They argued that, under Article 121(1), judicial power to decide a dispute should be exercised only by a judge. Thus the stage was set for the Federal Court to address the meaning of Article 121(1) in light of the 1988 constitutional amendment that had removed the provision vesting "the judicial power of the Federation" in the courts.[49]

The Malaysian Federal Court in *Semenyih Jaya* unanimously struck down the statutory provision as unconstitutional for violating the Article 121(1) judicial power clause—the first time in twenty years that the Malaysian apex court had declared a federal law invalid.[50] Because the Land Acquisition Act provision allowed lay assessors deciding on the land acquisition compensation to "in effect take over the judicial power of the court enshrined under Article 121(1),"[51] judicial power had been "whittled away from the High Court Judge to the lay assessors" in breach of Article 121(1).[52]

Categorically rejecting the "narrow interpretation" of Article 121(1) taken by the *Kok Wah Kuan* majority, the Federal Court aligned itself instead with Justice Malanjum's dissent.[53] It affirmed that courts are required by the Constitution "to ensure that there is a 'check and balance' in the system, including the crucial duty to dispense justice according to law for those who come before them."

The Court then directly took on the government's 1988 amendment to Article 121(1), repudiating the amendment for "undermining the judicial power" of the courts as well as the separation of powers.[54]

> With the removal of judicial power from the inherent jurisdiction of the Judiciary, that institution was effectively suborned to Parliament, with the implication that Parliament became sovereign. This result was manifestly inconsistent with the supremacy of the Federal Constitution enshrined in Article 4(1).[55]

[47] Land Acquisition Act 1960 § 40D(1) ("In a case before the Court as to the amount of compensation or as to the amount of any of its items the amount of compensation to be awarded shall be the amount decided upon by the two assessors."); *id.* § 40D(3) ("Any decision made under this section is final and there shall be no further appeal to a higher Court on the matter.").

[48] *Semenyih Jaya*, [2017] 3 MALAYAN L.J. 561, at [6].

[49] *See supra* note 25 and accompanying text.

[50] For earlier decisions, see Mamat bin Daud v. Gov't of Malaysia [1988] 1 MALAYAN L.J. 119; Public Prosecutor v. Dato' Yap Peng [1987] 2 MALAYAN L.J. 311.

[51] *Semenyih Jaya*, [2017] 3 MALAYAN L.J. 561, at [95].

[52] *Id.* at [96].

[53] *Id.* [70].

[54] *Id.* at [74].

[55] *Id.* at [75].

> …
>
> It is worthwhile reiterating that Parliament does not have power to amend the Federal Constitution to the effect of undermining the features [of separation of powers and the independence of the Judiciary].[56]

This passage reveals a remarkable assertion of judicial power. In effect, the Federal Court interpreted Article 121(1) to mean that the amended provision continued to enshrine the separation of powers and the independence of the judiciary. Moreover, it entrenched these principles by expressly declaring that these basic features of the Malaysian Constitution cannot be amended by the legislature.

The Federal Court's robust conception of the separation of powers is inextricably tied to the courts' judicial power. Concluding that "the judicial power of the court resides in the Judiciary and no other" as explicit in Article 121(1),[57] the Court insisted that any alterations to judicial functions would be "tantamount to a grave and deliberate incursion in the judicial sphere."[58] In an extraordinary passage on the separation of powers, the Federal Court declared:

> The Judiciary is thus entrusted with keeping every organ and institution of the State within its legal boundary. Concomitantly the concept of the independence of the Judiciary is the foundation of the principle of the separation of powers. This is essentially the basis upon which rests the edifice of judicial power. The important concepts of judicial power, judicial independence and the separation of powers are as critical as they are sacrosanct in our constitutional framework.[59]

Semenyih Jaya is an immensely important landmark in Malaysian constitutional jurisprudence for at least three reasons. First, the Malaysian Federal Court held that the 1988 amendment, which altered the text referring to judicial power being vested in the courts, had no effect. Although the Malaysian court did not expressly invalidate the amendment, it made clear that Article 121(1) is "explicit" that judicial power resides in the courts "and no other."[60] By interpreting Article 121(1) in this way, the Court nullified the impact of the 1988 amendment and restored the provision to the position it had before being amended. The Court's approach to Article 121(1) marks a significant departure from the uncritical, formalistic approach it adopted in earlier decisions like *Kok Wah Kuan*, where it had simply accepted that the legislature could determine the courts' judicial power.[61]

56 *Id.* at [76].
57 *Id.* at [86].
58 *Id.* at [84].
59 *Id.* at [88]–[90].
60 *Id.* at [86].
61 *See, e.g., Kok Wah Kuan* (F.C.) [2008] 1 Malayan L.J. 1, at [11] (holding that the "extent such 'judicial powers' are vested in the [courts] depend on what federal law provides").

Second, and of immense significance, Malaysia's apex court in *Semenyih Jaya* endorsed a doctrine protecting the constitution's basic structure. In a marked departure from previous precedent, the Malaysian Federal Court held that Parliament does not have the power to pass amendments that would undermine the Malaysian Constitution's "basic features" of the separation of powers and the independence of the judiciary.[62] It explicitly referred to *Kesavananda Bharati v. State of Kerala*, the case in which the Indian Supreme Court articulated the idea that certain core constitutional features are beyond the reach of even the constitutional amendment process.[63] What the Court did in the *Semenyih Jaya* opinion was establish that the Malaysian Constitution consists of immutable basic features—including the courts' power—that cannot be undermined by the legislature.

A third implication of *Semenyih Jaya* is the Federal Court articulated a broad conception of the separation of powers that focuses on the judiciary's role in maintaining a system of check and balances. Judicial power and the separation of powers, noted the Court, are "as critical as they are sacrosanct" in Malaysia's constitutional framework.[64] To function as an "effective check and balance mechanism" in a system of constitutional governance, it is important for the court to ensure that the executive and legislature "act within their constitutional limits and ... uphold the rule of law."[65] On this account of the separation of powers, the judiciary plays a key role as a "bulwark of the Constitution in ensuring that powers of the Executive and the Legislature are to be kept within their intended limit."[66]

Specifically with respect to this case, the Court held that the statute's ouster clause, which attempted to oust the court from hearing any appeal regarding the compensation determination, "ought to be narrowly and strictly construed."[67] This enabled the Federal Court to justify its own jurisdiction to hear the appeal in *Semenyih Jaya*, and it also lays a foundation for courts to take a generally restrictive approach toward any other legislative attempts to remove judicial review. As some have noted, the Court's declaration has potentially far-reaching implications for the many statutory clauses removing the jurisdiction of the courts over specific matters, which now appear open to challenge.[68]

The significance of the Federal Court's decision in *Semenyih Jaya* is difficult to overstate. Over the course of its sweeping opinion, the Malaysian Federal Court

62 *Semenyih Jaya*, [2017] 3 Malayan L.J. 561, at [76].

63 Kesavananda Bharati v. State of Kerala, AIR 1973 SC 1461. The basic structure doctrine has since migrated to other contexts globally. *See* Yaniv Roznai, *Unconstitutional Constitutional Amendments—The Migration and Success of a Constitutional Idea*, 61 Am. J. Comp. L. 657 (2013); Yaniv Roznai, Unconstitutional Constitutional Amendments: The Limits of Amendment Powers (2017).

64 *Semenyih Jaya*, [2017] 3 Malayan L.J. 561, at [90].

65 *Id.* at [91].

66 *Id.*

67 *Id.* at [148]; Land Acquisition Act 1960, § 40D(3) (providing that "[a]ny decision made under this section is final and there shall be no further appeal to a higher Court on the matter").

68 *See* Press Release, George Varughese, President, Malaysian Bar, An Independent Judiciary is Indispensable to the Rule of Law (May 8, 2017), https://perma.cc/YM76-87EN.

reversed the interpretive understanding of Article 121(1), endorsed a doctrine to protect basic features of the constitution against alteration, and articulated a robust separation of powers basis for protecting the courts' power of judicial review.

* * *

The *Semenyih Jaya* decision garnered much attention from various quarters. Many lauded the decision as a "momentous decision" which had "reasserted the notion of separation of powers and judicial independence as central to the Constitution."[69] Retired Justice Gopal Sri Ram colorfully observed that "*Semenyih Jaya* has correctly consigned the majority decision in *Kok Wah Kuan* to the judicial waste bin, where it rightfully belongs."[70]

Others have been more circumspect about the Federal Court's move in *Semenyih Jaya*. For those who saw the case as an opportunity for the Malaysian judiciary to strike down the 1988 amendment as unconstitutional, the Federal Court's interpretive approach did not go far enough, leaving as it did the amended text of Article 121(1) intact.[71] Wilson Tay argues that the Court's reluctance to definitively declare the 1988 amendment unconstitutional left the status of the amended provision unclear.[72] Should future courts decide not to adhere to the specific interpretation of Article 121(1) adopted by the Federal Court, cautions Tay, "the approach in *Semenyih Jaya* could collapse like a house of cards."

Such criticisms, I argue, fail to appreciate the true significance of the Malaysian Court's careful assertion of power and judicial maneuvering. The *Semenyih Jaya* decision is best viewed as a strategic maneuver in which the Court laid the groundwork for developing judicial tools directed at strengthening its institutional power. While the Court did not expressly strike down the 1988 constitutional amendment, its interpretative approach amounted to a *de facto* overruling of the amendment that had emasculated the power of the courts.[73] That the Court refrained from declaring outright that the amendment was unconstitutional appears to reveal a strategic move that allowed the Court to avoid provoking immediate backlash while consolidating judicial power.

Nor was such political backlash to *Semenyih Jaya* an unrealistic reaction. The Court's decision has been criticized already by those who argue that the Court

[69] Shad Saleem Faruqi, *Restoring Judicial Clout*, STAR ONLINE (June 8, 2017), https://perma.cc/55KK-TZ5V; *see also* Surendra Ananth, *Bravo! Judicial Power Restored after Almost 30 Years*, FREE MALAYSIA TODAY (Apr. 27, 2017), https://perma.cc/9DXU-MXZC.

[70] Gopal Sri Ram, *The Dynamics of Constitutional Interpretation*, 4 MALAYAN L.J. i, xxvi (2017).

[71] *Sri Ram Blames Mahathir, Ex-AG For Removing Judicial Power*, MALAYSIA TODAY (July 22, 2017), https://perma.cc/T88A-JWZP (observing that while *Semenyih Jaya* was a courageous decision the judgment fell short of striking down Article 121(1) as unconstitutional, likening it to a "football team who dribble the ball beautifully but gives it to the goalkeeper").

[72] *See* Wilson Tay, *Basic Structure Revisited: The Case of* Semenyih Jaya *and the Defence of Fundamental Constitutional Principles in Malaysia*, 14 ASIAN J. COMP. L. 113, 136 (2019).

[73] Faruqi, *supra* note 69.

overstepped its boundaries. Retired Justice Abdul Hamid Mohamad, who authored the *Kok Wah Kuan* majority opinion, stridently criticized the *Semenyih Jaya* judges for distorting the doctrines of the independence of the judiciary and the separation of powers "to give themselves the power to encroach into the jurisdiction of the Legislature," decrying the "unchecked expansion of the grounds for intervention by judges."[74] Striking down the 1988 constitutional amendment outright may well have drawn greater political attention that could have set the courts on course for a frontal confrontation with the political branches.

Another striking feature of the *Semenyih Jaya* decision is the remedy used by the Federal Court. After striking down the Land Acquisition Act provision, the Federal Court laid out, in unprecedented detail, a full set of procedural guidelines to replace the invalidated portion of the statute, which would leave the final determination to the judge.[75] Yet the Court declared that its decision would only have prospective effect, which ensured that previous awards made under this law would be unaffected.[76] As Samuel Issacharoff and Rosalind Dixon explain, courts often use doctrines like prospective overruling as a judicial deferral mechanism to avoid provoking direct political confrontation.[77] Read in this way, the Malaysian Court's effort to mitigate the effects of its immediate decision through prospective overruling appears to be aimed at insulating the judiciary from immediate backlash.

The Federal Court articulated a broad and forceful ambit for judicial power in its *Semenyih Jaya* opinion, but it did not strike down the constitutional amendment outright, instead nullifying the amendment's effect interpretively. In many ways, the *Semenyih Jaya* opinion is reminiscent of the judicial strategy shown in the U.S. case of *Marbury v. Madison*, in which Chief Justice Marshall embedded a wide assertion of judicial authority in a decision that ultimately denied any remedy against the government.

The Federal Court's ruling in *Semenyih Jaya* has been called "decidedly anticlimactic" by those disappointed that the Court did not definitively pronounce on the constitutionality of the amendment to Article 121(1).[78] Tay concludes that "*Semenyih Jaya* was by no means a *Kesavananda* moment for the Malaysian judiciary."[79] But it's worth remembering that even *Kesavananda* laid out the doctrine of unconstitutional constitutional amendments tentatively.[80] In that case, a sharply divided Indian Supreme Court held that the amendment power could not be used

[74] Tun Abdul Hamid Mohamad, *No Judge is a Parliament*, New Straits Times (June 15, 2017), https://perma.cc/RU2X-82HJ.

[75] *Semenyih Jaya*, [2017] 3 Malayan L.J. 561, at [116]–[125].

[76] *Id.* at [126].

[77] Rosalind Dixon & Samuel Issacharoff, *Living to Fight Another Day: Judicial Deferral in Defense of Democracy*, 2016 Wis. L. Rev. 683, 685 (2016).

[78] Tay, *supra* note 72, at 143.

[79] *Id.*

[80] Dixon & Issacharoff, *supra* note 77, at 712.

to alter the constitution's basic structure. But it would be only after the Indian Supreme Court had established a line of case law that built support for the idea of an unalterable constitutional basic structure that the Court wielded the doctrine with full force.[81] The Malaysian experience exhibits a similar judicial approach; in a unanimous decision issued by a full five-member bench, the Federal Court in *Semenyih Jaya* set the stage to build support for future assertions of the court's power to safeguard the constitution's basic structure against amendment.

The Federal Court's decision in *Semenyih Jaya* is strategically aimed at empowering the courts vis-à-vis the political branches. The *Marbury* strategy employed by the Malaysian court is not "dialogic" in its approach or aims. Unlike dialogic review, which is purportedly focused on promoting a democracy-enhancing "dialogue" between courts and political institutions, the Federal Court's decision in *Semenyih Jaya* is primarily directed at strengthening judicial power. Tay argues that the Court "appears to have chosen to contribute more incrementally to the 'constitutional dialogue' between itself and the political branches" by using a deliberate approach that "permits a range of responses from the political branches, thereby allowing 'dialogue' to progress."[82] But the judiciary's move here is about strengthening the *court's* authority for future assertions of power against the political institutions. Establishing a doctrine of implied limits on parliament's power to amend the Constitution is an immensely powerful judicial tool, often viewed as the ultimate counter-majoritarian doctrine. Such an assertion of judicial power is not "dialogic" in that it is not concerned with contributing "a continuing constitutional colloquy with the political institutions and the society at large."[83] Rather, it is a clear signal of the Court's willingness to assert power vis-à-vis the legislature. Put simply, the Malaysian court's approach is aimed at enhancing—not restraining—judicial power.

The *Semenyih Jaya* judicial move was bold, but it was also prudent. The Malaysian Federal Court asserted strong judicial review in this case—striking down a federal law for the first time in decades. And although the Court avoided invalidating the constitutional amendment outright, it established a clear mandate for doing so by expressly laying the foundation for a doctrine that guards against altering the constitution's basic structure. The *Semenyih Jaya* Court exhibited judicial strategy in rebalancing the distribution of governmental power, which had been traditionally concentrated in the political branches, by laying a formidable judicial tool on the constitutional table.

[81] *Id.* at 715–16; Aman Ullah & Samee Uzair, *Basic Structure of Constitution: Impact of* Kesavananda Bharati *on Constitutional Status of Fundamental Rights*, 26 S. Asian Stud. 299, 305 (2011).

[82] Tay, *supra* note 72, at 141–42.

[83] *See, e.g.*, Po Jen Yap, Constitutional Dialogue in Common Law Asia 30 (2015) (arguing that courts, including those in Malaysia and other Asian states, should employ "dialogic review" to participate in "a continuing constitutional colloquy" with political actors).

B. Singapore's Emerging Jurisprudence on the Separation of Powers

The Singapore story resembles the Malaysian one,[84] albeit in its earlier stages. While there has not been a *Semenyih Jaya* equivalent in Singapore's constitutional jurisprudence,[85] consistent judicial statements affirming the separation of powers as a foundational feature of the constitution indicate a developing notion of the Singapore Constitution's basic structure.[86]

In the 1989 case of *Teo Soh Lung v. Minister of Home Affairs*,[87] the Singapore High Court rejected the idea of implied limits on constitutional amendments, dismissing the *Kesavananda* doctrine as "not applicable to the Singapore Constitution."[88] It declared that if the framers had wished to impose limitations on the amendment power, they would have done so explicitly.[89]

In 2012, though, Chief Justice Chan Sek Keong in *Mohammad Faizal bin Sabtu v. Public Prosecutor* called "the principle of separation of powers, whether conceived as a sharing or a division of sovereign power" between the legislative, executive, and judicial branches, "part of the basic structure of the Singapore Constitution."[90] In this High Court decision, the Chief Justice emphasized: "All Constitutions based on the Westminster model incorporate the principle of separation of powers as part of their constitutional structure in order to diffuse state power among different organs of state."[91]

Later, in the 2015 case of *Yong Vui Kong v. Public Prosecutor*,[92] the Singapore Court of Appeal acknowledged that certain features of the Singapore Constitution that are "fundamental and essential to the political system" may be considered part of the constitution's basic structure.[93] It said that "these might include the right to vote and the separation of powers. Still, since the Court refused to declare any aspect of the constitution unamendable in that case, it avoided pronouncing definitively on the extent of a basic structure doctrine in Singapore. In 2017, the Singapore High Court in *Ravi s/o Madasamy v. Attorney General* dismissed any

84 *See* Yaniv Roznai, *Constitutional Amendability and Unamendability in South-East Asia*, *in* Constitutional Amendment in Southeast Asia, 14 J. Comp. L. 188 (2019).

85 So far, with the exception of one High Court case, which was later overturned by the Court of Appeal, the Singapore courts have never declared any law unconstitutional. *See* Taw Cheng Kong v. Public Prosecutor [1998] 1 Sing. L. Rep. 943 (H.C.), *overruled by* Public Prosecutor v. Taw Cheng Kong [1998] 2 Sing. L. Rep. 410 (C.A.).

86 *See* Mohammad Faizal bin Sabtu v. Public Prosecutor [2012] 4 Sing. L. Rep. 947, at [11]–[15]; Tan Seet Eng v. Att'y Gen. [2016] 1 Sing. L. Rep. 779, 784; *see also* Chan Sek Keong, *Basic Structure and Supremacy of the Singapore Constitution*, 29 Sing. Acad. L.J. 619, 624 (2017).

87 [1989] 2 Sing. L. Rep. 449.

88 *Id.* at [47].

89 *Id.* at [34].

90 [2012] 4 Sing. L. Rep. 947, at [11].

91 *Id.* at [12].

92 [2015] 2 Sing. L. Rep. 1129.

93 *Id.* at [71].

support for the basic structure doctrine as "no more than a broad restatement of the truism that the Constitution rests on an overarching principled framework embracing the precepts of the rule of law and the separation of powers."[94]

Debate continues on the scope of the basic structure doctrine in the Singaporean context,[95] particularly in light of the Malaysian Federal Court's jurisprudence in *Semenyih Jaya*. After all, many of the principles articulated in *Semenyih Jaya* are equally applicable to the Singaporean context.[96] Like Malaysia, Singapore's Constitution also has a supremacy clause and a provision guaranteeing judicial power. Indeed, Chief Justice Chan referred to both these constitutional provisions in *Mohamad Faisal bin Sabtu* when he declared constitutional supremacy and the separation of powers to be fundamental aspects of Singapore's system.[97] The Singaporean courts can draw on these principles in developing their own jurisprudence on the separation of powers to evolve in the direction of recognizing a constitutional basic structure.

V. Conclusion

With *Semenyih Jaya*, the Malaysian Federal Court powerfully recommitted to the judicial task of enforcing constitutional limits on political power. It carved out a role for the courts to protect an immutable core of the constitution's fundamental features including judicial independence and the separation of powers. The Malaysian apex court's strategic move laid the foundation for developing a contextual model of the basic structure doctrine that safeguards judicial power. The Malaysian Federal Court's constitutional vision sets an example for other emerging Asian democracies, not least Singapore, whose jurisprudence appears to be evolving toward developing a role for the courts as a meaningful institutional check and balance.

[94] [2017] 5 SING. L. REP. 489, at [66].

[95] *See* Jaclyn Neo, *Towards a "Thin" Basic Structure Doctrine in Singapore*, INT'L J. CONST. L. BLOG (Jan. 17, 2018), https://perma.cc/BQL3-YXSP; Swati Jhaveri, *Recent Judicial Comments on the Basic Structure of the Constitution*, SING. PUB. L. BLOG (Apr. 20, 2016), https://perma.cc/U8YZ-TXN2.

[96] *See* CONST. OF THE REP. OF SING., art. 4 ("This Constitution is the supreme law of the Republic of Singapore and any law enacted by the Legislature after the commencement of this Constitution which is inconsistent with this Constitution shall, to the extent of the inconsistency, be void."); *id.* art. 93(1) ("The judicial power of Singapore shall be vested in a Supreme Court and in such subordinate courts as may be provided by any written law for the time being in force.").

[97] *Mohamad Faisal bin Sabtu*, [2012] 4 SING. L. REP. 947, at [14]–[17].

5
The Rule of Law

I. Introduction

In a keynote address at a symposium on the rule of law in 2012, Singapore's Minister for Foreign Affairs and Minister for Law, K. Shanmugam, declared: "Singapore accepts the Rule of Law as a universal value. It is the foundation on which our nation was built, and provides the framework for its proper functioning."[1] Yet Singapore has been described as a "regime that has systematically undercut 'rule of law' freedoms,"[2] and practices a model of "authoritarian constitutionalism."[3]

This paradox foregrounds the question of how to understand the rule of law within states like Singapore and Malaysia. Many Asian democracies have advanced a "thin," even "authoritarian," model of the rule of law as a means of facilitating the agenda of a developmentalist state.[4] This chapter begins by contextualizing how discourse on the rule of law has developed in these states. These exceedingly formalistic notions of the rule of law stem in part from lack of clarity regarding its basis. Ultimately, I argue that a legitimate account of the rule of law must be explicitly located in the constitution.

The chapter develops an account of the rule of law as a fundamental feature of the constitution's core structure. It takes a deep dive into the Malaysian Federal Court's 2018 decision in *Indira Gandhi v. Pengarah Jabatan Agama Islam*.[5] In this seminal decision, the Federal Court entrenched the doctrine of a constitutional basic structure in Malaysian jurisprudence, establishing the power of judicial review and constitutional interpretation as inherent to the role of the civil courts.[6] And in the 2016 Singaporean case of *Tan Seet Eng v. Attorney-General*,[7] the country's highest court affirmed the principle of legality articulated in its earlier jurisprudence: "All power has legal limits and the rule of law demands that the courts should be able

[1] K. Shanmugam, *The Rule of Law in Singapore*, Sing. J. Legal Stud. 357, 357 (2012).
[2] Jothie Rajah, Authoritarian Rule of Law: Legislation, Discourse and Legitimacy in Singapore 3 (2012).
[3] Mark Tushnet, *Authoritarian Constitutionalism*, 100 Cornell L. Rev. 391 (2015).
[4] *See* Rajah, *supra* note 2; Tushnet, *supra* note 3; Gordon Silverstein, *Singapore: The Exception That Proves Rules Matter*, *in* Rule by Law: The Politics of Courts in Authoritarian Regimes 73, 78–79 (Tom Ginsburg & Tamir Moustafa eds., 2008); Thomas Kellogg, *Rule of Law in Asia: The Case of China*, *in* Handbook on the Rule of Law 490, 490 (Christopher May & Adam Winchester eds., 2018).
[5] [2018] 1 Malayan L.J. 545 (F.C.) [hereinafter *Indira Gandhi* (F.C.)].
[6] *Id.* at [48].
[7] [2016] 1 Sing. L. Rep. 779.

Constitutional Statecraft in Asian Courts. Yvonne Tew, Oxford University Press (2020). © Yvonne Tew.
DOI:10.1093/oso/9780198716839.001.0001

to examine the exercise of discretionary power."[8] These recent Malaysian and Singaporean decisions reveal a significant turn toward understanding judicial review as "a natural and necessary corollary of the rule of law."[9]

Indira Gandhi is especially remarkable for what the decision shows us about judicial role and judicial strategy. In terms of judicial power, the Malaysian Federal Court declared that the judicial review power of the courts is part of the rule of law and the constitutional basic structure. But articulating a rule of law conception is one thing; how a judiciary manages to entrench its authority is another. By building on the foundation it had strategically laid down in a case decided the year before,[10] the Malaysian apex court placed the rule of law and judicial power beyond the reach of the legislature and cemented these features as part of the constitution's unalterable core.

II. Contextualizing the Rule of Law

A. Conceptualizing the Rule of Law

Despite being lauded as an important ideal of modern governance, the conception of the rule of law has long been contested. Lon Fuller's well-known principles of legality specify that laws be general, clear, public, prospective, stable, coherent, and practicable.[11] As Joseph Raz puts it, the "basic intuition" underlying these accounts of the rule of law is that "the law must be capable of guiding the behaviour of its subjects."[12] Jeremy Waldron argues that procedural principles connected with administering these norms of legality—like the right to a fair hearing and an independent judiciary—are indispensable elements of the rule of law.[13]

Proponents of more substantive accounts of the rule of law seek to include elements like liberty, [14] democracy,[15] and fundamental rights. For example, the late

[8] Chng Suan Tze v. Minister of Home Aff. [1988] 2 SING. L. REP. (R.) 525, at [86] [hereinafter *Chng Suan Tze*].

[9] *Indira Gandhi* (F.C.), [2018] 1 MALAYAN L.J. 545, at [33].

[10] *See* Semenyih Jaya v. Pentadbir Tanah Daerah Hulu Langat [2017] 3 MALAYAN L.J. 561 [hereinafter *Semenyih Jaya*]; *see also* Chapter 4, The Separation of Powers.

[11] LON L. FULLER, THE MORALITY OF LAW 38–39 (1964).

[12] Joseph Raz, *The Rule of Law and its Virtue*, 93 LAW Q. REV. 195 (1977).

[13] *See* Jeremy Waldron, *The Rule of Law and the Importance of Procedure*, *in* GETTING TO THE RULE OF LAW 3 (James E. Fleming ed., 2011); *see also* A. Wallace Tashima, *The War on Terror and the Rule of Law*, 15 ASIAN AM. L.J. 245, 264 (2008).

[14] T.R.S. ALLAN, LAW, LIBERTY, AND JUSTICE: THE LEGAL FOUNDATIONS OF BRITISH CONSTITUTIONALISM 21 (1993) (arguing that "[t]he rule of law . . . encompasses traditional ideas about individual liberty and natural justice, and, more generally, ideas about the requirements of justice and fairness in the relations between government and governed").

[15] Document of the Copenhagen Meeting of the Conference on the Human Dimension of the CSCE, June 5-29, 1990, ¶ I(3) (stating that "democracy is an inherent element of the rule of law"), https://perma.cc/E2VC-GU4J.

British judge Lord Bingham rejected Raz's formalistic conception of the rule of law "in favour of a 'thick' definition, embracing the protection of human rights within its scope."[16]

In general, though, the rule of law is distinguished from rule *by* law.[17] Rule by law is typically associated with political power using the law instrumentally.[18] Jothie Rajah, writing about Singapore, observes that rule by law "signifies 'law,' which in context and execution, is susceptible to power such that the rights content of 'law,' and restraints on and scrutiny of state power, are undermined."[19] In authoritarian regimes, instead of functioning as a constraint on political power, law and courts often become tools of the regime.[20]

Singapore and Malaysia's regimes have been described as practicing "rule by law"[21] and "authoritarian rule of law."[22] Others have labeled its system as adhering to "mere" rule-of-law constitutionalism,[23] or an exceedingly thin version of the rule of law.[24] The next section explores the rhetoric on the rule of law in the constitutional discourse of these Asian states.

B. Rule of Law Rhetoric in Practice

A thin, formalist understanding of the rule of law has traditionally dominated Malaysian jurisprudence. For instance, following the 1988 constitutional amendment to Article 121(1), which removed the reference to judicial power being vested in the courts,[25] the Malaysian Federal Court in *Public Prosecutor v. Kok Wah*

[16] Tom Bingham, The Rule of Law 67 (2010).

[17] *See* Brian Z. Tamanaha, On the Rule of Law: History, Politics, Theory 92 (2004).

[18] *See, e.g.*, Ratna Rueban Balasubramaniam, *Has Rule by Law Killed the Rule of Law in Malaysia?*, 8 Oxford Uni. Commonwealth L.J. 211, 225 (2008) ("[R]ule by law emerges as a contrast to rule of law because rule by law captures the idea that an exercise of political power is at odds with an overall aspiration towards the rule of law.").

[19] *See* Rajah, *supra* note 2, at 4.

[20] *See* Tom Ginsburg & Tamir Moustafa, Rule by Law: The Politics of Courts in Authoritarian Regimes (2008).

[21] *See, e.g.*, Balasubramaniam, *supra* note 18; Li-ann Thio, *Lex Rex or Rex Lex? Competing Conceptions of the Rule of Law in Singapore*, 20 UCLA Pac. Basin L.J. 1, 75 (2002) (arguing that the dominant approach in Singapore is "more accurately characterised as the rule of 'rules' or the rule *by* law," where law is viewed as an "instrument for social engineering"); Rajah, *supra* note 2, at 52 (noting that " 'rule by law' has had a long and powerful presence in Singapore").

[22] Rajah, *supra* note 2.

[23] Tushnet, *supra* note 3, at 416–18.

[24] Gordon Silverstein, *Singapore's Constitutionalism: A Model, But of What Sort?*, 100 Cornell L. Rev. Online 1, 8 (2015) (stating that "[w]hile Singapore has a written constitution, and adheres to a thin version of the Rule of Law, Singapore makes no claims to be a liberal, western democracy").

[25] Fed. Const. (Malay.), art. 121(1) ("There shall be two High Courts of co-ordinate jurisdiction ... and the High Courts and inferior courts shall have such jurisdiction and powers as may be conferred by or under federal law.") (as amended by the Constitutional (Amendment) Act 1988). Prior to the amendment, Article 121(1) provided that "the judicial power of the Federation shall be vested into High Courts of co-ordinate jurisdiction."

Kuan interpreted the courts' judicial power as under the legislature's control.[26] In a similar vein, in *Danaharta Urus v. Kekatong*, the Federal Court held that "the manner and the extent of the exercise of the right to access to justice is subject to and circumscribed by the jurisdiction and powers of the court as provided by federal law."[27]

Singapore's government has consistently claimed that the state is "committed to the rule of law" and that its "application must be adapted" to the country's specific context.[28] The state has long held up the Singapore legal system as an exemplar of certainty and efficiency, crediting Singapore's "rule of law" as key to the country's economic development and success as an international trade center.[29] What is clear is that the Singaporean state has employed legality with ruthless efficiency.[30] Jothie Rajah writes that "the Singapore state's account of the 'rule of law' as a corruption-free delivery of social order and efficiency is so entrenched, so taken for granted and so effective in securing continuing economic and political legitimacy" from its citizenry and Western states that it "continues to supply a legitimising basis for rights-violating legislation in Singapore."[31]

Consider, as an illustrative case study, the events following the infamous case of *Chng Suan Tze v. Minister of Home Affairs*.[32] In an unprecedented decision, the Singapore Court of Appeal struck down a preventive detention order made under Singapore's Internal Security Act, which authorizes preventive detention if the President is satisfied that the detainee posed a threat to national security.[33] The Court ruled that it was insufficient for the President to be subjectively satisfied; rather, the courts could review whether there was an "objective" basis for the executive's decision that the detention was reasonable. Declared the Singapore Court of Appeal, "the notion of a subjective or unfettered discretion is contrary to the rule of law."[34]

The Singapore government's response was swift and forceful. It employed its formal legal powers to pass constitutional and statutory amendments to override the court's decision. The legislature amended the Singapore Constitution to remove judicial review of the executive's decisions under the Internal Security Act and to prevent appeals against the government's actions in security cases.[35] It also

[26] [2008] 1 MALAYAN L.J. 1 (F.C.). The amendment and this case are discussed in more detail in Chapter 4, The Separation of Powers.

[27] [2004] 2 MALAYAN L.J. 257 (F.C.), at [27] [hereinafter *Kekatong* (F.C.)].

[28] Shanmugam, *supra* note 1, at 365.

[29] *See* Li-Ann Thio, *Between Apology and Apogee, Autochthony: The Rule of Law Beyond the Rules of Law in Singapore*, SING. J. LEGAL STUD. 269, 269–70 (2012); Eugene Tan, *Law and Values in Governance: The Singapore Way*, 30 HONG KONG L.J. 109–10 (2000).

[30] RAJAH, *supra* note 2, at 286.

[31] *Id.*

[32] [1988] 2 SING. L. REP. (R.) 525.

[33] *See* Internal Security Act, Cap. 143, 1985 Rev. Ed. Sing., § 8(1).

[34] *Chng Suan Tze*, [1988] 2 SING. L. REP. (R.) 525, at 553.

[35] Article 149(3) of Singapore's Constitution states that "any decision made or act done in pursuance of any power conferred upon the President or the Minister by any law referred to in this article,

restored the subjective standard of review by amending the Internal Security Act to roll back the law governing judicial review to the doctrine set by an earlier judicial precedent that had endorsed the subjective test.[36]

In strict compliance with the *Chng Suan Tze* decision, which had ordered the detainees released, the government let the prisoners go. They were driven through the gates of the jail. When the detainees stepped out of the car, they were promptly re-arrested under the new laws—and driven back into the prison.[37] The government had formally complied with the law, and was able to eliminate judicial review by "strictly and precisely following the provisions of Singapore's Constitution to the letter."[38]

The following year, the same detainees brought another case challenging the constitutional amendments and the modified Internal Security Act. The Singapore High Court in *Teo Soh Lung v. Minister of Home Affairs* rejected the detainees' challenge, concluding that there had been "no abrogation of judicial power."[39] Taking a highly formalistic approach to the rule of law, the High Court declared:

> It is erroneous to contend that the rule of law has been abolished by legislation and that Parliament has stated its absolute and conclusive judgment in applications for judicial review or other actions. Parliament has done no more than to enact the rule of law relating to the law applicable to judicial review.[40]

The Court of Appeal dismissed the applicants' appeal, holding that the applicants could not show that their re-detention had not been based on national security considerations.[41]

The Singapore High Court's incredibly thin formulation reduces the rule of law to the law formally enacted by Parliament,[42] which relies on "legal technicalities" to discount the need to hold accountable the exercise of government power.[43] As Gordon Silverstein observes, the Singapore example illustrates that "one *can* have a thin rule of law, build a stable and prosperous nation on a robust economy, and

such question shall be determined in accordance with the provisions of any law as may be enacted by Parliament for this purpose." Article 149(3) of the Constitution also states that "nothing in Article 93 shall invalidate any law enacted pursuant to this clause."

36 Internal Security Act, Cap. 143, 1985 Rev. Ed. Sing., § 8B(1). This amendment reinstated the subjective test of review established in *Lee Mau Seng v. Minister of Home Aff.* [1971] 2 MALAYAN L.J. 137.

37 *See* Silverstein, *supra* note 4, at 80.

38 *Id.* at 78–79.

39 [1989] 1 SING. L. REP. 461 (H.C.).

40 *Id.* at [48].

41 Teo Soh Lung v. Minister of Home Aff. [1990] 1 SING. L. REP. 347 (C.A.).

42 Jack Tsen-Ta Lee, *Shall the Twain Never Meet? Competing Narratives and Discourses of the Rule of Law in Singapore*, 2012 SING. J. LEGAL STUD. 298, 312 (2012) (describing the High Court's approach as "the thinnest form of the formal conception of the rule of law").

43 LI-ANN THIO, A TREATISE ON SINGAPORE CONSTITUTIONAL LAW ¶ 03.080 (2012).

never veer too close to a full-blown Lockean-liberal system with firm limits on government."[44]

C. Locating a Basis for the Rule of Law

These thin conceptions of the rule of law are sometimes assumed to be influenced by the inherited legal traditions in Malaysia and Singapore, like parliamentary sovereignty or the common law. But this misguided view stems from lack of clarity regarding the basis for the rule of law. In these modern democracies with written constitutions, the principle of the rule of law must be located in an explicitly constitutional basis.

Judges in Malaysia have sometimes tried to justify judicial review in line with the presumed intent of Parliament. Under traditional British legal doctrine on parliamentary sovereignty, courts exercise judicial review because Parliament intends, explicitly or implicitly, to legislate in accordance with principles of legality.[45] In that vein, Justice Gopal Sri Ram in *Marathei v. JG Containers* declared that the courts should "act upon the presumption that Parliament does not intend an unfair or unjust result" and "that it accords with the Rule of Law."[46] The problem with relying on presumed parliamentary intent is that it is often artificial. Especially in a dominant party state, the legislature may not be committed to act in line with principles of legality, as starkly illustrated at various points in Malaysian and Singaporean political history.[47]

Some courts have tried to ground the rule of law in common law principles of constitutionalism. Thus, the Malaysian Court of Appeal in *Kekatong v. Danaharta Urus*[48] reasoned that the expression "law" in the Constitution's equal protection clause refers to a system of law that "incorporates the fundamental principles of natural justice of the common law."[49] Justice Gopal Sri Ram drew on the common law as a "vehicle for protecting rights" by providing a "body of principles" that function as "a continuing framework for the legitimate exercise of government

[44] Silverstein, *supra* note 4, at 76.

[45] *See, e.g.*, H.W.R. Wade & C.F. Forsyth, Administrative Law 41, 44 (1994); Mark Elliot, *The Ultra Vires Doctrine in a Constitutional Setting: Still the Central Principle of Administrative Law*, 58 Cambridge L.J. 129 (1999); Christopher Forsyth, *Of Fig Leaves and Fairy Tales: The Ultra Vires Doctrine, the Sovereignty of Parliament and Judicial Review*, 55 Cambridge L.J. 122 (1996).

[46] [2003] 2 Malayan L.J. 337, at 343; *see also* Tan Boon Wah v. Datuk Seri Ahmad Said Hamdan [2010] 2 Malayan L.J. 411, at [21] (reasoning that "it cannot be the presumed intention of Parliament to enact a law that violates personal liberties").

[47] Prominent examples include the Malaysian government's 1988 constitutional amendments to Article 121(1) of the Malaysian Constitution to remove the reference to the judicial power being vested in the courts as well as the constitutional and statutory amendments passed by the Singapore government to oust judicial review of Internal Security Act detentions.

[48] [2003] 3 Malayan L.J. 1 (C.A.) [hereinafter *Kekatong* (C.A.)].

[49] *Id.* at [27].

power."[50] However, the Federal Court dismissed the Court of Appeal's common law approach as "simplistic,"[51] declaring it "abundantly clear" that "the reception of the common law" in Malaysia "may be lawfully modified at any time by any written law."[52] The Federal Court's understanding of common law constitutionalism may be flawed, but its reasoning highlights that the idea of a rule of law principle located in the common law appears easily trumped by the legislature.

More fundamentally, justifying judicial review on parliamentary intent or common law constitutionalism is simply unnecessary. Unlike the British legal system which is based on parliamentary sovereignty, the Malaysian and Singaporean legal systems are explicitly based on the supremacy of the constitution.[53]

Ultimately, the basis for the rule of law in these Asian democracies is properly located in their constitutions.[54] Courts in other post-colonial democracies have drawn on their written constitutions in this manner. The South African Constitutional Court, for example, made clear that the courts' power of judicial review "is now to be found in the first place not in the doctrine of ultra vires, nor in the doctrine of parliamentary sovereignty, nor in the common law itself, but in the principles of our Constitution."[55] So, too, in Malaysia and Singapore, judicial review derives from the rule of law as a fundamental feature of the constitutional framework.

III. Developing the Rule of Law

A. *Indira Gandhi*: Entrenching the Basic Structure Doctrine in Malaysia

The 2018 case of *Indira Gandhi* firmly entrenched the constitutional basic structure doctrine in Malaysian jurisprudence.[56] Consequentially, the Malaysian Federal

[50] Justice Gopal Sri Ram refers to a theory of common law constitutionalism, which seeks to *place* limits on Parliament's power through higher order rule of law principles. *See Kekatong* (C.A.), [2003] 3 MALAYAN L.J. 1, at [30] (citing T.R.S. Allan, *Constitutional Rights and Common Law*, 11 OXFORD J. LEG. STUD. 453 (1991)).

[51] *See Kekatong* (F.C.), [2004] 2 MALAYAN L.J. 257, at [23].

[52] *Id.* at [17]–[18].

[53] FED. CONST. (MALAY.), pt. I, art. 4(1) ("This Constitution is the supreme law of the Federation and any law passed after Merdeka Day which is inconsistent with this Constitution shall, to the extent of the inconsistency, be void."); CONST. OF THE REP. OF SING., pt. II, art. 4 ("This Constitution is the supreme law of the Republic of Singapore and any law enacted by the Legislature after the commencement of this Constitution which is inconsistent with this Constitution shall, to the extent of the inconsistency, be void.").

[54] *See* Jaclyn Neo, *Parsing Privity Clauses in Malaysia: Rights, Security and Judicial Review in Malaysia*, 1 PUB. L. 25, 30 (2010).

[55] Bato Star Fishing v. Ministry of Envtl. Aff. and Tourism, 2004 (4) SA 490 (C.C.), at [22] (S. Afr.).

[56] *Indira Gandhi* (F.C.), [2018] 1 MALAYAN L.J. 545.

Court established the rule of law and judicial review as fundamental features of the constitution's unamendable core.

When Indira Gandhi wed, she and her husband were both Hindus, and they were married under the general civil law governing marriage for non-Muslims.[57] Several years later, unbeknownst to Indira Gandhi, her husband converted to Islam. Without her knowledge, he then applied to the Sharia Court for certificates converting their three children to Islam and then obtained custody for all the children. After a heated argument, he left their home, forcibly taking their youngest daughter, barely a year old at the time, leaving the two older children with Indira Gandhi.

When India Gandhi found out about her husband and children's conversions, she was left in a dilemma. As a non-Muslim, she could not challenge the children's conversion and custody orders in the Sharia court, which has jurisdiction only over persons professing the Islamic faith. Indira Gandhi petitioned the civil courts to quash the children's conversion certificates and custody orders that had been unilaterally obtained by her husband. The High Court found in favor of Indira Gandhi, but its decision was overruled by the Court of Appeal. Indira Gandhi's legal battle, which drew wide press coverage, had lasted almost a decade by the time it reached the Malaysian Federal Court.

In January 2018, the Malaysian Federal Court unanimously overruled the Court of Appeal's decision. It held that both parents must consent to a child's religious conversion and voided the children's certificates of conversion. The apex court's decision marks a constitutional turning point of magnitude for a number of reasons. First, the Malaysian Court took a purposive and gender-equal approach to the constitutional right to equality by interpreting the right of a "parent" to determine a child's religious upbringing to mean that both parents have an equal say in deciding a child's conversion.[58]

Second, the Federal Court expressly asserted the civil courts' authority vis-à-vis the religious courts. Upending previous precedent,[59] the Court dismissed the notion that "since matters of conversion involves Islamic law and practice, it must follow that the Syariah Courts must have jurisdiction over such matters to the exclusion of the civil courts."[60] It affirmed that the civil courts retain jurisdiction over constitutional issues even when Islamic law matters are involved.[61]

That the Federal Court's clarified the jurisdictional boundaries between the civil and Sharia courts is particularly significant when viewed against the fraught

[57] Law Reform (Marriage and Divorce) Act of 1976.

[58] *Indira Gandhi* (F.C.), [2018] 1 MALAYAN L.J. 545, at [181].

[59] *See, e.g.*, Soon Singh a/l Bikar Singh v. Pertubuhan Kebajikan Islam Malaysia (Perkim) [1999] 1 MALAYAN L.J. 489; Lina Joy v. Majlis Agama Islam Wilayah Persekutuan [2007] 4 MALAYAN L.J. 585 (F.C.). For more detail, see Chapter 7, Judicializing Religion.

[60] *Indira Gandhi* (F.C.), [2018] 1 MALAYAN L.J. 545, at [104].

[61] *Id.*

context of religious authority in Malaysia. Over the past two decades, civil courts in Malaysia have extensively deferred jurisdiction to the religious Sharia courts.[62] Some civil court judges have justified this deference by dint of Article 121(1A) of the Constitution, which states that the civil courts "shall have no jurisdiction in respect of any matter within the jurisdiction of the Sharia courts."[63] It's salient to note that the Article 121(1A) clause was inserted along with the constitutional amendments passed in 1988 discussed in Chapter 4, which altered the Article 121(1) clause on judicial power.[64] Since then, debate had ensued over whether Article 121(1A) affects the civil courts' jurisdiction over constitutional matters involving Islamic issues.

The *Indira Gandhi* Court answered the question explicitly. It held: "Article 121(1A) does not constitute a blanket exclusion of the jurisdiction of the civil courts whenever a matter relating to Islamic law arises."[65] The Court emphasized that the 1988 constitutional amendment "does not oust the jurisdiction of the civil courts nor does it confer judicial power on the Syariah Courts."[66] "The inherent judicial power of civil courts in relation to judicial review and questions of constitutional and statutory interpretation," declared the Court, "is not and cannot be removed by the insertion of [Article 121(1A)]."[67]

Third, and of broad significance, the *Indira Gandhi* decision expressly cemented the basic structure doctrine in Malaysian jurisprudence. The Court declared that the fundamental principles of the Constitution "cannot be abrogated or altered by Parliament by way of constitutional amendment."[68] Articulating the scope of the doctrine in its fullest form so far, the Court said: "The Federal Constitution is premised on certain underlying principles. . . [T]hese principles include the separation of powers, the rule of law and the protection of minorities; these principles are part of the basic structure of the Constitution. Hence, they cannot be abrogated or removed."[69]

Central to the Court's understanding of the rule of law as one of the fundamental features of the Constitution's basic structure is that it is connected to the power of judicial review. Building on its decision the year before in *Semenyih Jaya*,[70] the *Indira Gandhi* Court declared: "The power of the courts is a natural and necessary corollary of the rule of law."[71] It viewed the judicial power inherent to the civil

[62] For more detail, see Chapter 7, Judicializing Religion, section IV(A).

[63] FED. CONST. (MALAY.), art. 121(1A) ("The courts referred to in Clause (1) shall have no jurisdiction in respect of any matter within the jurisdiction of the Syariah courts.").

[64] *See* Chapter 4, The Separation of Powers, section III.

[65] *Indira Gandhi* (F.C.), [2018] 1 MALAYAN L.J. 545, at [98].

[66] *Id.* at [92].

[67] *Id.* at [98].

[68] *Id.* at [48].

[69] *Id.* at [90].

[70] *Semenyih Jaya*, [2017] 3 MALAYAN L.J. 561 (stating that "judicial power, judicial independence and the separation of powers are as critical as they are sacrosanct in our constitutional framework").

[71] *Indira Gandhi* (F.C.), [2018] 1 MALAYAN L.J. 545, at [33].

courts as "inextricably intertwined with their constitutional role as a check and balance mechanism."[72]

What does it entail for judicial power to vest exclusively in the civil courts? The Court described the significance of the role of judicial review in the Constitution's basic structure as "two-fold."[73] So, "judicial power cannot be removed from the *civil* courts,"[74] and also the courts' power "cannot be conferred on any other body whose members do not enjoy the same level of constitutional protection as judges do to ensure their independence."[75] The Court emphasized that the civil courts are different constitutionally from the Sharia courts. While "the civil courts are ensconced within the constitutional framework," Sharia courts are "non-existent until such time when the State Legislature makes law to establish them."[76] The religious courts thus have "limited" jurisdiction, and any jurisdiction it has must be expressly conferred by state legislation.[77] "It is evident from the marked differences in the establishment and constitution of the civil and Syariah Courts," the Court concluded, "that the two courts operate on a different footing altogether."[78]

Taken together, the Court's declarations in *Indira Gandhi* reveal a view of the civil courts' place at the apex of the judicial hierarchy as well as a check on other branches of government. The Federal Court reaffirmed the horizontal separation of powers established in *Semenyih Jaya*, which locates judicial power in the courts as a check and balance mechanism vis-à-vis the political branches.[79]

And as a matter of vertical separation of powers, the Federal Court established the civil courts' status as the institution ultimately responsible for exercising judicial review.[80] The Court was unequivocal about its "firm stand" on how to interpret Article 121(1A) in relation to the jurisdiction of the Sharia courts: "If [the nature of the matter] involves constitutional issues, [the civil court] should not decline to hear merely on the basis of no jurisdiction."[81]

Remarkably, the Court in effect invalidated the amendment to the Article 121(1A) constitutional clause. According to the Court, Article 121(1A) "does not oust the jurisdiction of the civil courts nor does it confer judicial power on the Sharia courts" and "Parliament does not have the power to make any constitutional amendment to give such an effect." Such an amendment "would be invalid, if not

[72] *Id.* at [42].
[73] *Id.* at [51].
[74] *Id.* (emphasis added).
[75] *Id.* at [53].
[76] *Id.* at [59].
[77] *Id.* at [61].
[78] *Id.* at [70].
[79] *Id.* at [42] (quoting from *Semenyih Jaya*, [2017] 3 MALAYAN L.J. 561 that "the concept of the independence of Judiciary is the foundation of the principles of the separation of powers" and that "judicial power, judicial independence, and the separation of powers are as critical as they are sacrosanct in our constitutional framework").
[80] *Id.* at [49].
[81] *Id.* at [105].

downright repugnant to the notion of judicial power inherent in the basic structure of the constitution."[82]

The Court's judicial move in *Indira Gandhi* to nullify Article 121(1A) is in line with its earlier decision in *Semenyih Jaya*, where it had similarly immunized the 1988 constitutional amendment removing the judicial power from the courts. In *Indira Gandhi*, the Federal Court extended the approach it had taken in *Semenyih Jaya* to the other constitutional provision put in place by the 1988 amendment, expressly ruling that Article 121(1A) has no effect on the judicial review power of the civil courts over the Sharia courts.

Indira Gandhi marks a critical point for constitutional jurisprudence on the rule of law and judicial power. Of broad importance is that it affirmed the judicial review power of the courts as part of the Malaysian Constitution's basic structure,[83] building on its assertion of power in *Semenyih Jaya* where it established that the power of judicial review power lies solely with the civil courts.

Moreover, *Indira Gandhi* underscored the interpretive authority of the civil courts in determining constitutional meaning. Interpreting what the Constitution means is a matter for civil courts, not the Sharia courts.[84] As the Federal Court declared, "constitutional and statutory interpretation" are "pivotal constituents of the civil courts' judicial power" that is "fundamentally inherent in their constitutional role as the bulwark against unlawful legislation and executive action."[85]

B. Singapore: "All Power has Legal Limits"

In the 1988 case of *Chng Suan Tze v. Minister of Home Affairs*,[86] the Singapore Court of Appeal memorialized its understanding of the rule of law in a seminal passage:[87] "In our view, the notion of a subjective or unfettered discretion is contrary to the rule of law. All power has legal limits and the rule of law demands that the courts should be able to examine the exercise of discretionary power."[88]

Chng, along with three others, had been detained under Singapore's preventive detention law for allegedly being involved in what government officials called a "Marxist conspiracy" to destabilize the country. The detainees challenged their detentions which had been carried out under the Internal Security Act. The Singapore Court of Appeal held in favor of the detainees, ruling that it was not enough for the

82 *Id.* at [92].
83 *Id.* at [58].
84 *Id.* at [93] (quoting Latifah bte Mat Zin v. Rosmawati bte Sharibun & Anor. [2007] 5 MALAYAN L.J. 101, 123).
85 *Id.* at [104].
86 [1988] 2 SING. L. REP. (R.) 525.
87 *Id.*
88 *Id.* at [86].

President to be "satisfied" that the detainee posed a security threat; rather, there had to be some objective basis for that belief.[89]

What followed next is now infamous in the annals of Singapore's constitutional history. In an aggressive rebuke to the courts, the Singapore Parliament retaliated by amending the Constitution and passing statutes to overrule the Court's decision and remove judicial review over such preventive detentions.[90] *Chng Suan Tze* has come to be seen as a cautionary example of the Singapore government's ability to wield its formidable power to subdue the judiciary.[91]

But although the Singapore legislature did overrule the specific aspect on the standard of review in *Chng Suan Tze*, the broader principles declared in that case have endured.[92] To be sure, in the direct aftermath of *Chng Suan Tze*, the courts retreated in the cases that directly followed the government's aggressive response.[93] Nevertheless, recent decisions have revitalized the broad principles of legality articulated in *Chng Suan Tze*. Consider, for instance, the 2011 case of *Yong Vui Kong v. Attorney-General*.[94] Chief Justice Chan endorsed the "principle of legality laid down by this court in *Chng Suan Tze*," noting that "Parliament left untouched the full amplitude of the *Chng Suan Tze* principle, and thereby implicitly endorsed it."[95]

The 2016 case of *Tan Seet Eng v. Attorney-General* provides a key example of the Singapore courts' increasing willingness to draw on the principle of legality laid down in *Chng*.[96] Described as the "mirror image of *Chng*," this case involved a detainee who had been preventively detained under the Criminal Law (Temporary Provisions) Act.[97] The criminal statute allowed the Minister for Home Affairs to detain any person associated with criminal activities so long as the Minister was "satisfied" that the detention was necessary in the interests of "public safety, peace, and good order."[98] The Singapore Court of Appeal ordered the detainee released. It held that the Court had the power to review whether there was a reasonable basis for the Minister's actions and beliefs,[99] rejecting "a purely subjective analysis" because it "would result in the court being bound to accept whatever was put before it."[100] To reach this conclusion, the Court wriggled out of the precedent of *Chng Suan Tze* by finding that the constitutional amendments that overruled that

[89] *Id.* at [55].

[90] *See* Chapter 8, Balancing Security and Liberty, section III.

[91] *See* Po Jen Yap, Constitutional Dialogue in Common Law Asia 73–77 (2015) (describing the events following *Chng Suan Tze* as a judicial crisis in Singapore).

[92] Jaclyn Neo, *"All Power Has Legal Limits"—The Principle of Legality as a Constitutional Principle of Judicial Review*, 29 Sing. Acad. L.J. 667, 668 (2017).

[93] *See, e.g.*, Teo Soh Lung v. Minister of Home Aff. [1989] 1 Sing. L. Rep. 461 (H.C.); Teo Soh Lung v. Minister of Home Aff. [1990] 1 Sing. L. Rep. (R.) 347 (C.A.).

[94] [2011] 2 Sing. L. Rep. 1189, at [33].

[95] *Id.* at [79].

[96] [2016] 1 Sing. L. Rep. 779 [hereinafter *Tan Seet Eng*].

[97] Criminal Law (Temporary Provisions) Act, Cap. 67, 2000 Rev. Ed. Sing.

[98] *Id.* § 30.

[99] *Tan Seet Eng*, [2016] 1 Sing. L. Rep. 779, at [56].

[100] *Id.* at [61].

decision applied only to detentions made under the Internal Security Act—and not to other statutes authorizing preventive detentions.[101]

Strikingly, in reaching its decision in *Tan Seet Eng*, the Court of Appeal expressly affirmed that the broad principles that flow from the *Chng Suan Tze* decision "continue to be relevant."[102] It reiterated several of these principles, including: "Unfettered discretion is contrary to the rule of law."[103] Indeed, the Court notably opened its opinion by declaring: "The rule of law is the bedrock on which our society was founded ... [O]ne of its core ideas is the notion that the power of the State is vested in the various arms of government and that such power is subject to legal limits."[104]

The *Tan Seet Eng* decision's emphasis on the rule of law has noteworthy implications for Singapore's jurisprudence. For one, the Singapore court strongly endorsed the principle of legality set out in *Chng Suan Tze*, paving the way for greater judicial scrutiny of executive and legislative powers.[105] Although *Tan Seet Eng* dealt with the administrative review of executive power, as Neo points out, the presumption of reviewability articulated by the Singapore Court of Appeal could apply not only to statutory powers but also to constitutional powers.[106] In that way, the Court could elevate the principle of legality articulated in *Chng Suan Tze* and affirmed in *Tan Seet Eng* to constitutional status.

In addition, the Singapore Court of Appeal recognized that the judiciary's power over constitutional interpretation "carries with it the power to pronounce authoritatively and conclusively on the meaning of the Constitution and all other laws."[107] In marked contrast to the "prevailing constitutional orthodoxy" found in earlier Singaporean decisions, which generally accepted "the legislature has the *sole* and *final* say over constitutional matters,"[108] *Tan Seet Eng* represents a distinct turn toward recognizing the judiciary as the ultimate authority in interpreting the Constitution.

IV. Judicial Power and Judicial Strategy

The *Indira Gandhi* and *Tan Seet Eng* decisions reflect a shift away from "thin" notions of legality toward a more robust account of the rule of law. I highlight two aspects of

[101] *Id.* at [98].
[102] *Id.* at [98].
[103] *Id.*
[104] *Id.* at [1].
[105] For cases involving the judicial review of executive powers, see Law Soc'y of Singapore v. Tan Guat Neo Phyllis [2008] 2 Sing. L. Rep. (R.) 239; Ramalingam Ravinthran v. Att'y-Gen. [2012] 2 Sing. L. Rep. 49; Yong Vui Kong v. Public Prosecutor [2012] 2 Sing. L. Rep. 872; Vellama d/o Marie Muthu v. Att'y Gen. [2013] 4 Sing. L. Rep. 1.
[106] *See* Neo, *"All Power Has Legal Limits," supra* note 92, at [6].
[107] *Id.* at [90].
[108] Swati Jhaveri & Jaclyn Neo, *The Many Facets of Constitutional Dialogue: The Case of Singapore*, 18 Austl. J. Asian L. 1, 5 (2017).

these apex court decisions: the first relates to how the judicial role is connected to the rule of law and the other has to do with the judicial strategy involved in entrenching this principle in the constitution's basic structure.

In terms of judicial power, the rule of law account in the contemporary jurisprudence is intrinsically connected to the power of judicial review and constitutional interpretation. As the Malaysian Federal Court declared in *Indira Gandhi*, judicial review is "a natural and necessary corollary of the rule of law," grounded in the judiciary as "the ultimate arbiter of the lawfulness of state action."[109] Likewise, the principle of legality endorsed by the Singapore Court of Appeal in *Tan Seet Eng* is premised on judicial scrutiny functioning as a constitutional constraint on all state power.[110] A presumption of judicial review over the exercise of legislative or executive power tips the balance in favor of a constitutional rule of law.[111]

Courts are also acknowledged to have final authority on constitutional interpretation. Both apex courts emphasized the power of the courts "to pronounce authoritatively and conclusively on the meaning of the Constitution,"[112] echoing the U.S. Supreme Court's declaration in *Marbury v. Madison* that it is "emphatically the province and duty of the judicial department to say what the law is."[113] This position provides a long overdue corrective to the courts' longstanding deference to the political branches to determine what the constitution means. The courts are now more willing to assume their position as the primary authority on constitutional interpretation.[114]

This declaration of judicial power is particularly significant in the Malaysian system for clarifying the relationship between the civil courts and Sharia courts.[115] *Indira Gandhi* affirmed that the power of judicial review and constitutional interpretation lie solely with the *civil* courts, not the religious courts. The Court's declaration of the federal civil courts' position over the state Sharia courts in the Malaysian constitutional system[116] marks a "radical shift" in the hierarchy of the civil courts and religious courts in a context that has long been marked by jurisdictional deference to the religious courts.[117]

But expounding on the meaning of the rule of law is one thing; *how* a court is able to entrench its authority to enforce the rule of law principle is another, more difficult, question. The other striking aspect of these decisions is the judicial

[109] *Indira Gandhi* (F.C.), [2018] 1 MALAYAN L.J. 545, at [33].

[110] *Tan Seet Eng*, [2016] 1 SING. L. REP. 779, at [1].

[111] Neo, *"All Power Has Legal Limits," supra* note 92, at [42].

[112] *Tan Seet Eng*, [2016] 1 SING. L. REP. 779, at [90]; *see also Indira Gandhi* (F.C.), [2018] 1 MALAYAN L.J. 545, at [37] (citing *Tan Seet Eng*).

[113] Marbury v. Madison, 5 U.S. 137 (1803).

[114] *See* Jhaveri & Neo, *supra* note 108, at 5.

[115] *Indira Gandhi* (F.C.), [2018] 1 MALAYAN L.J. 545, at [51] (noting that "judicial power cannot be removed from the civil courts").

[116] *Id.* at [70]–[72].

[117] Jaclyn Neo, *Return of Judicial Power: Religious Freedom and the Tussle over Jurisdictional Boundaries in Malaysia*, INT'L J. CONST. L. BLOG (Mar. 15, 2018), https://perma.cc/4UWT-NCQ2.

strategy involved in entrenching the rule of law and judicial power as beyond the legislature's reach, even through constitutional amendment.

Judicial statecraft is critical for fragile courts in newer democracies. The Malaysian Federal Court in *Semenyih Jaya* and *Indira Gandhi* cemented its judicial power in two stages. It first established a foundation in *Semenyih Jaya* by identifying certain features as fundamental to the constitution and suggesting that these principles were beyond Parliament's amendment power.[118] Barely a year later, the Court in *Indira Gandhi* provided its "clearest endorsement of the basic structure doctrine so far,"[119] declaring that "the power of judicial review is essential to the constitutional role of the courts and inherent in the basic structure of the Constitution," which "cannot be abrogated or altered by Parliament by way of a constitutional amendment."[120] In addition to the separation of powers, the Court expressly specified the "rule of law" and "the protection of minorities" as fundamental principles impervious to legislative tempering.[121] That the Court in *Indira Gandhi* felt capable of delivering such a forceful affirmation of a doctrine of unamendable constitutional features is testament to the careful groundwork it laid earlier in *Semenyih Jaya*.

Indira Gandhi and *Semenyih Jaya* established a constitutional core of fundamental features like the rule of law and the separation of powers, which courts can build on to shape future adjudication. Indeed, in the 2019 case of *Alma Nudo v. Public Prosecutor*, the Federal Court referred to both those cases to reiterate: "As the bulwark of the Federal Constitution and the rule of law, it is the duty of the Courts to protect the Federal Constitution from being undermined by the whittling away of the principles upon which it is based."[122] In *Alma Nudo*, the Federal Court articulated a rule of law understanding expressly grounded in the Constitution. Drawing on the Article 5(1) guarantee against being deprived of "life and personal liberty save in accordance with law"—which it described as the "foundational fundamental right" from which other constitutional rights "draw their support"—the Court emphasized that the reference to "law" in Article 5(1) "does not mean just any law validly enacted by Parliament."[123]

The rule of law, said the Court, requires the law to be clear, sufficiently stable, generally prospective, of general application, administered by an independent judiciary, and contains principles of natural justice and the right to a fair trial.[124]

[118] *Semenyih Jaya*, [2017] 3 MALAYAN L.J. 561, at [76].

[119] Jaclyn Neo, *Beyond Mortals? Constitutional Identity, Judicial Power, and the Evolution of the Basic Structure Doctrine in Malaysia*, *in* CPG PUBLICATION: "IDENTITY AND CHANGE—THE BASIC STRUCTURE IN ASIAN CONSTITUTIONAL ORDERS" (2016).

[120] *Indira Gandhi* (F.C.), [2018] 1 MALAYAN L.J. 545, at [48].

[121] *Id.* at [90].

[122] [2019] CURRENT L.J. 780, at [91].

[123] *Id.* at [106].

[124] *Id.* at [104].

These "minimum requirements of the rule of law" are broadly accepted, but the Court emphasized they "are by no means exhaustive."[125] As Lord Bingham so "persuasively argued," wrote the Court, "the rule of law requires that fundamental rights be protected."[126] This reveals an account of the rule of law as a principle capable of being expanded to include the protection of fundamental rights.

V. Conclusion

Central to the rule of law principle reflected in the contemporary constitutional discourse of Malaysia and Singapore is the civil courts' power of judicial review and to interpret the constitution. The *Indira Gandhi* case illustrates not only judicial assertiveness, but also judicial strategy in entrenching this principle as an immutable feature of the constitution. As the Malaysian Court recognized, the judiciary's role in upholding the rule of law does not constitute judicial supremacy nor is it inimical to democratic governance. It is, simply, "an exercise of power in accordance with the judiciary's proper constitutional role."[127]

125 *Id.* [105].
126 *Id.* at [107].
127 *Id.* at [37]–[38].

6
Courts in Transition

I. Introduction

In a world in which most constitutions and constitutional courts were created after the end of the Second World War,[1] the judicial role in young democracies is an issue of global significance. Courts in evolving democracies like Malaysia and Singapore face particular constitutional challenges. These judiciaries function without the benefit of a developed rights culture and often also contend with the outsized power of dominant political branches.

This chapter, the final in Part II, draws the lens back to consider what role courts should play in developing democracies and then turns to how courts can carry out this task. It shows how courts employ strategies to establish their authority and then sets out the types of interventions courts can use to develop constitutional adjudication. It begins with the discourse on the judicial role in a democracy. Debates over judicial and legislative supremacy have long preoccupied constitutional scholars in the mature liberal democracies of the West, but many of these accounts do not apply to newer democracies controlled by a ruling party or negotiating a fragile political system. Some scholars have argued for courts in some Asian states to exercise weak judicial review to avoid confrontations with dominant state power. In the face of concentrated political power, however, judicial practices premised on deference or dialogue with the political branches can only go so far. This chapter makes the case for an empowered role for courts in emerging Asian democracies like Malaysia and Singapore. In these states with a history of control by a single political party or coalition, the judicial role in constraining political power is especially important. Courts in these contexts have a protective role to play as a constitutional check on governing power as well as a constructive role in developing the foundational principles of the constitutional order.

Next, I take up the question of how courts can establish their authority when confronted with consolidated political power. Courts can manifest judicial power through strategic assertiveness, most strikingly in the form of *Marbury*-style strategies in which they lay the foundation for asserting their power by anticipating future confrontation with the political branches. The key feature that these strategic

[1] Since the Second World War, more than 100 sovereign states have enacted codified constitutions. *See* Constitute Project, https://perma.cc/VUM7-ZWS7 (data on file with author).

Constitutional Statecraft in Asian Courts. Yvonne Tew, Oxford University Press (2020). © Yvonne Tew.
DOI:10.1093/oso/9780198716839.001.0001

approaches share is that they are aimed at strengthening, not restricting, judicial authority.

To illustrate this point, I draw on two landmark decisions issued by the Malaysian apex court. In 2017, the Malaysian Federal Court laid the groundwork for establishing judicial power in the case of *Semenyih Jaya*,[2] a decision that exhibited strategic self-empowerment. Having sown the seeds for a doctrine of broad judicial authority, the apex court consolidated its institutional position a year later in *Indira Gandhi*,[3] a case that involved a contentious issue of religious authority in which the Federal Court cemented its power to review unconstitutional constitutional amendments. These decisions reveal a burgeoning jurisprudence directed at empowering the court to act as a bulwark against threats to the constitution's core.

Understanding judicial empowerment as part of a broader endeavor to protect fundamental constitutional principles in these democracies is crucial for developing constitutional adjudication. This vision of the judicial role requires a corresponding constitutional jurisprudence in Malaysia and Singapore. Chapters 3, 4, and 5 each explored foundational elements of the constitution: the constitution's original framework, the separation of powers, and the rule of law.[4] Courts can draw on these core constitutional features to structure constitutional adjudication.

The chapter concludes by considering how they do this. I outline three types of judicial interventions for Malaysian and Singaporean courts to use in practice. Begin with the doctrine of an unalterable constitutional basic structure. Applied at its most robust, courts could apply a locally contextual version of the Indian basic structure doctrine to strike down constitutional amendments that violate the constitution's core. Courts can also draw on these basic structure principles as a powerful basis to interpret laws or constitutional amendments in line with core constitutional values.

A second mechanism calls on courts to use a generous, purposive approach to interpret rights guarantees in light of the constitution's overarching purposes. Finally, I examine how courts can apply a robust proportionality analysis in constitutional rights adjudication. Under a balancing frame, the suitability of the government's challenged actions is brought under judicial assessment, empowering courts to evaluate the justifications claimed by political institutions. Taken together, these judicial tools preserve structural protections against excessive majoritarian power and provide a rights-protective foundation for developing constitutional adjudication.

[2] Semenyih Jaya v. Pentadbir Tanah Daerah Hulu Langat [2017] 3 MALAYAN L.J. 561 [hereinafter *Semenyih Jaya*].

[3] Indira Gandhi a/p Mutho v. Pengarah Jabatan Agama Islam Perak & Ors. [2018] 1 MALAYAN L.J. 545 (F.C.) [hereinafter *Indira Gandhi* (F.C.)].

[4] *See* Chapter 3, Constitutional History; Chapter 4, The Separation of Powers; Chapter 5, The Rule of Law.

II. Courts and Judicial Review in Evolving Democracies

A. In Judges or Legislatures We Trust?

Much of the debate on the role of courts and the legitimacy of judicial review has largely developed in the mature democracies of North America and Europe. Scholars remain preoccupied with the "counter-majoritarian difficulty" identified by Alexander Bickel more than half a century ago: how can we justify unelected judges intervening in the face of electoral majorities?[5]

Critics of strong judicial review argue against courts overriding decisions of elected representatives. Jeremy Waldron, for example, argues that "judicial review of legislation is inappropriate as a mode of final decisionmaking in a free and democratic society."[6] For Waldron, majority decision-making through the legislature offers the most appropriate means of resolving contested outcomes by treating each of the participants equally in the process.[7] Another defender of political constitutionalism, Richard Bellamy in the United Kingdom, argues that only legislatures provide "an equitable process for deciding between individuals' often competing claims."[8]

But most of these arguments about the proper judicial role in a democracy are based on assumptions that apply primarily to mature liberal democracies. Waldron's core case against judicial review, for instance, explicitly assumes a society in which there are "democratic institutions in reasonably good working order."[9] In addition, his preconditions include judicial institutions "again in reasonably good working order," a general societal commitment "to the idea of individual and minority rights," and "persisting, substantial and good faith disagreement about rights."[10] Likewise, Bellamy advocates for majority rule in a setting where there is "competition between political parties in elections and parliament" as well as "citizens tolerant of each other and willing to reciprocate and collaborate."[11] And Mark Tushnet's argument for political constitutionalism expressly states as "cultural"

[5] Alexander Bickel, The Least Dangerous Branch 16–17 (1962) ("The root difficulty is that judifical review is a counter-majoritarian force in our system."); *see also* Barry Friedman, *The Birth of an Academic Obsession: The History of the Counter-Majoritarian Difficulty*, 112 Yale L.J. 153, 155 (2002) (noting that a "spate of articles decry[] the inconsistency of democracy with judicial review, and call[] for constitutional interpretation outside the courts"); Daniel A. Farber & Suzanna Sherry, Desperately Seeking Certainty: The Misguided Quest for Constitutional Foundations 145 (2002) (observing that "the countermajoritarian difficulty has . . . been blown out of proportion").

[6] Jeremy Waldron, *The Core of the Case Against Judicial Review*, 115 Yale L.J. 1341, 1346 (2006).

[7] *Id.* at 1388.

[8] Richard Bellamy, Political Constitutionalism: A Republican Defence of the Constitutionality of Democracy 261 (2007).

[9] Waldron, *supra* note 6, at 1360.

[10] *Id.*

[11] Bellamy, *supra* note 8, at 219.

conditions a "widespread commitment among the nation's citizens to constitutional values" and robust party competition.[12]

The premises underlying these judicial review accounts do not apply to many young democracies.[13] Across Asia, Africa, and Latin America, many developing regimes lack a strong constitutional culture and also often have to deal with a dominant political party or the threat of democratic backsliding. Singapore has been governed by the same political party since independence and operates a model of authoritarian constitutionalism.[14] And until 2018, Malaysia had never experienced a change of government since gaining independence in 1957. In newer democracies, as David Landau observes, courts and constitutional designers "often work off of the premise that democratic institutions should be distrusted, and not just to protect insular minorities but also to carry out majoritarian will."[15]

Emerging scholarship has begun to examine the judicial role in newer democracies. Scholarly attention has focused on the role of constitutional courts in South Africa, the Middle East, Latin America, Central and Eastern Europe, and parts of Asia.[16] A number of scholars have explored a strong role for courts in the constitution-building of these fragile democracies,[17] including in the Asian constitutional systems of Taiwan, Korea, and Indonesia.[18]

In the case of the Southeast Asian states of Malaysia and Singapore, however, scholars tend to view "judicially enforced constitutionalism" as "inapt."[19] In democracies with "relatively weak forms of constitutional review in the face of strong executive governments," courts are dismissed as playing a marginal role in shaping

[12] Mark Tushnet, *The Relation Between Political Constitutionalism and Weak-Form Judicial Review*, 14 German L.J. 2249, 2255–56 (2013).

[13] *See* Samuel Issacharoff, *Judicial Review in Troubled Times: Stabilizing Democracy in a Second-Best World*, 98 N.C. L. Rev. 1, 9–16 (2019); David Landau, *A Dynamic Theory of Judicial Role*, 55 B.C.L. Rev. 1501, 1502 (2014); Tom Daly, The Alchemists: Questioning our Faith in Courts as Democracy-Builders 250–51 (2017).

[14] Mark Tushnet, *Authoritarian Constitutionalism*, 100 Cornell L. Rev. 391 (2015).

[15] Landau, *supra* note 13, at 1502–03.

[16] *See, e.g.*, Samuel Issacharoff, *Constitutional Courts and Consolidated Power*, 62 Am. J. Comp. L. 585 (2014); Theunis Roux, The Politics of Principle: The First South African Constitutional Court, 1995–2005 (2013); Nathan J. Brown & Julian G. Waller, *Constitutional Courts and Political Uncertainty: Constitutional Ruptures and the Rule of Judges*, 14 Int. J. Const. L. 817 (2016); Daly, *supra* note 13; Wojciech Sadurski, Rights Before Courts: A Study of Constitutional Courts in Postcommunist States of Central and Eastern Europe (2008); Kim Lane Scheppele, *Guardians of the Constitution: Constitutional Court Presidents and the Struggle for the Rule of Law in Post-Soviet Europe*, 154 U. Pa. L. Rev. 1757 (2006) ; Andrew Harding & Penelope Nicholson, New Courts in Asia (2010); Tom Ginsburg, Judicial Review in New Democracies: Constitutional Courts in Asia (2003).

[17] *See* Samuel Issacharoff, Fragile Democracies: Contested Power in the Era of Constitutional Courts 158 (2015); Landau, *supra* note 13.

[18] Wen-Chen Chang, *Strategic Judicial Responses in Politically Charged Cases: East Asian Experiences*, 8 Int. J. Const. L. 885 (2010); Stefanus Hendrianto, Law and Politics of Constitutional Courts: Indonesia and the Search for Judicial Heroes (2018).

[19] Li-ann Thio, *Soft Constitutional Law in Nonliberal Asian Constitutional Democracies*, 8 Int. J. Const. L. 766, 767 (2010).

constitutional understandings.[20] At most, scholars have argued, these Asian courts should exercise no more than "weak" or "dialogic" forms of judicial review.[21]

B. Deconstructing Dialogue

Weak-form judicial review has emerged as a response to the counter-majoritarian dilemma, drawing much scholarly attention in recent decades.[22] Under this alternative model of constitutionalism, which is often described as "dialogic" in character, courts lack the final say over constitutional understandings. Unlike the "strong" version of judicial review familiar to American constitutionalism, "weak" or "dialogic" judicial review endows courts with the power of rights review but allows the legislature to limit or override judicial decisions. Because courts do not have the last word under this model, weak-form review is thought to provide an attractive middle ground between the "two polar opposites" of judicial supremacy and legislative supremacy.[23] Proponents of weak-form judicial review argue that it promotes constitutional "dialogue" by creating "the potential for a collaborative and continuing conversation" between the various branches of government about the optimal way to protect rights.[24]

Dialogic review is often associated with Commonwealth countries in which weak-form mechanisms are features of the constitution's design. In Canada, the United Kingdom, and New Zealand, for example, constitutional or statutory bills of rights expressly allow the legislature to override judicial decisions despite an adverse declaration by the courts.[25]

Unlike the Western jurisdictions in which the "Commonwealth" model has emerged, though, Asian constitutions do not have structural devices that enable the legislature to reverse a judicial decision with which it disagrees, except through constitutional amendment. Almost all constitutional courts in Asia have strong-form powers to review legislation incompatible with the constitution.[26] Like most of the constitutions created in the twentieth century, the Malaysian and

[20] *Id.* at 767, 769

[21] *See* Po Jen Yap, Constitutional Dialogue in Common Law Asia 8 (2015).

[22] *See* Mark Tushnet, *Alternative Forms of Judicial Review*, 101 Mich. L. Rev. 2781 (2003); Rosalind Dixon, *Weak-Form Judicial Review and American Exceptionalism*, 32 Oxford J. Legal Stud. 487 (2012).

[23] Stephen Gardbaum, *The New Commonwealth Model of Constitutionalism*, 49 Am. J. Comp. L. 707, 709 (2001).

[24] *See* Christine Bateup, *Reassessing the Dialogic Possibilities of Weak-Form Bills of Rights*, 32 Hastings Int'l & Comp. L. Rev. 529 (2009).

[25] *See* Canadian Charter of Rights and Freedoms, Part I of Constitution Act, 1982, *being* Schedule B to the Canada Act 1982, c. 11 (Can.), § 33; Human Rights Act 1998, c. 42, § 4(1) (U.K.); New Zealand Bill of Rights Act 1990, § 7.

[26] *See* Rosalind Dixon & Mark Tushnet, *Weak-Form Review and its Constitutional Relatives: An Asian Perspective*, *in* Comparative Constitutional Law in Asia 102, 103 (Rosalind Dixon & Tom Ginsburg eds., 2014).

Singaporean constitutions specifically empower courts to declare legislation unconstitutional and have no provision for the legislature to override a judicial decision except by amending the constitution.

Some scholars have argued for courts in new democracies to exercise "weak-form" judicial review.[27] Notably, Po Jen Yap advocates expanding dialogic review to the Asian common law jurisdictions of Malaysia, Singapore, and Hong Kong.[28] Yap advocates for courts in these contexts to employ what he calls "sub-constitutional" doctrines that preserve the right of the legislature to override judicial decisions, such as non-binding advisory opinions, administrative review, rational basis review of legislative action, and delayed declarations of incompatibility.[29] On Yap's account, dialogic review treats the courts and the political branches as "participants in an enduring constitutional colloquy" allowing "a constitutional dialogue between co-equal branches of government";[30] courts and political institutions act as "collaborators in a common enterprise to promote public welfare."[31]

This vision of dialogue appears undeniably appealing. But a dialogic relationship is possible only if each branch of government is mutually committed to such a collaborative discourse and to cooperate in a joint enterprise of governance. In a dominant party democracy—like Singapore and, until recently, Malaysia—the powerful political branches of government have little incentive, if any, to be committed to a mutually respectful "dialogue" with the courts. In these political contexts, judicial deference to the legislature is not likely to be perceived by the political branches as an endeavor by a co-equal branch to foster "an ongoing, iterative process where interlocutors advance their own points of view."[32] If anything, judicial acquiescence will likely be viewed simply as expected submission from the weakest branch. In polities where the balance of power is skewed overwhelmingly in favor of the political branches, a more robust judicial role does not detract from democracy. Rather, it presents a strong case for the judiciary to assert itself to protect democracy as a co-equal branch of government.[33]

Moreover, in these Asian democracies counter-majoritarian concerns connected to constitutional rigidity are misplaced. Dialogue proponents argue that judicial decisions that can be reversed only through constitutional amendment foreclose the democratic process from correcting judicial errors.[34] Yet in practice it is the government's aggressive alterations of these constitutions that is worrying.[35]

[27] *See* Stephen Gardbaum, *Are Strong Constitutional Courts Always a Good Thing for New Democracies?*, 53 COLUM. J. TRANSN'L L. 285 (2015).

[28] YAP, CONSTITUTIONAL DIALOGUE, *supra* note 21, at 8.

[29] *Id.* at 79.

[30] *Id.* at 105.

[31] *Id.* at 106.

[32] Aileen Kavanagh, *The Lure and the Limits of Dialogue*, 66 U. TORONTO. L.J. 83, 86 (2016).

[33] *See* ISSACHAROFF, FRAGILE DEMOCRACIES, *supra* note 17, at 13 (arguing that the court's role as a constraint on political power is particularly important in countries with a dominant political party).

[34] YAP, CONSTITUTIONAL DIALOGUE, *supra* note 21, at 224.

[35] *See* ANDREW HARDING, THE CONSTITUTION OF MALAYSIA: A CONTEXTUAL ANALYSIS 103 (2012).

Most constitutional provisions in Malaysia and Singapore can be amended by a two-thirds parliamentary majority.[36] Singapore's People's Action Party has always controlled well over the supermajority required to amend the constitution and has passed more than forty constitutional amendments since the nation's independence in 1962.[37] And while the Barisan Nasional ruling coalition was in power, it passed over fifty amendment acts amounting to approximately 700 individual amendments to the Malaysian Constitution.[38] The counter-majoritarian difficulty posed by rigid amendment rules is not typically an issue for many Asian democracies where amending the constitution is relatively easy.[39]

What this does illustrate, though, is that almost any institutional configuration gives the legislature or judiciary an opportunity to respond to each other could potentially be characterized as "dialogic." "The inherent elasticity of dialogue as a concept, and the resulting ubiquity of dialogue in practice," has led some to "raise questions about the value of dialogue as either an analytical concept or normative ideal."[40] When stretched to cover an increasing number of institutional interactions, including a range of sub-constitutional tools in Malaysia and Singapore, the notion of "dialogic" review may be reach a point where it means everything, and nothing.[41]

Ultimately, Yap's argument for courts in these dominant party systems to employ "dialogic tools" appears deeply driven by political pragmatism. For Yap, weak-form review is "politically more efficacious":

> If the judiciary consciously preserves the right of the legislature to disagree with the court's decision via the use of the ordinary political processes, such that an override via constitutional amendment can be avoided, any strain on the inter-branch relations and any potential backlash from the dominant ruling government could equally be minimized.[42]

But deliberately allowing the legislature to overrule courts through ordinary law cuts both ways. A dominant party government may wield this power easily

[36] Fed. Const. (Malay.), art. 159(3); Const. of the Rep. of Sing., art. 5(2).

[37] Li-ann Thio, A Treatise on Singapore Constitutional Law ¶ 04.052 (2012).

[38] Cindy Tham, *Major Changes to the Constitution*, The Sun (July 17, 2007), https://perma.cc/23UX-HEPS.

[39] *See* Dixon & Tushnet, *supra* note 26 at 108–13. In India, for example, Parliament can amend some constitutional provisions with a simple majority. Other amendments to the Indian Constitution require a special majority and, in certain specified cases, ratification by at least half of the State legislatures in addition to the special majority.

[40] David S. Law & Hsiang-Yang Hsieh, *Judicial Review of Constitutional Amendments: Taiwan, in* Constitutionalism in Context 1, 46 (David S. Law ed., forthcoming) (manuscript on file with author).

[41] *See* Swati Jhaveri & Jaclyn Neo, *The Many Facets of Constitutional Dialogue: The Case of Singapore*, 18 Austl. J. Asian L. 1, 2 (2017); Kavanagh, *supra* note 32, at 84–85.

[42] Yap, Constitutional Dialogue, *supra* note 21, at 57.

and with minimal political consequence precisely because, as Yap puts it, the political "stakes are so much lower." And they have. Governments in Malaysia and Singapore have passed laws to authorize preventive detention,[43] create a national security council,[44] and prohibit fake news;[45] these laws are all outputs of a majoritarian process harnessed by the ruling party. Rather than encouraging a culture of constitutionalism, weak-form review may simply cultivate a culture of judicial submissiveness. Nor is it apparent whether and when such judicial deference premised on avoiding political reprisals should end. The upshot of Yap's account seems to be that courts should avoid asserting strong judicial review indefinitely so long as they face significant constraints from political actors, with no end in sight for such judicial passivity.[46]

A related, and troubling, consequence is that a dialogic model allows a powerful government to claim a cloak of constitutional legitimacy for its actions if courts "are simply unable or unwilling to assert themselves, even when the need exists for them to do so."[47] As David Law and Hsiang-Yang Hsieh point out, applying the "dialogic" label indiscriminately "runs the risk of endorsing the capitulation of toothless courts under authoritarian rule . . . or of mistaking judicial passivity, cowardice, or self-preservation for a normative commitment to dialogue." Democratic legitimacy concerns in these young democracies do not typically arise from judges standing in opposition to the democratic will, a power which these courts have rarely exercised in practice;[48] rather, such threats are more likely to stem from political institutions seeking to consolidate political power. The dialogic case for not binding the political branches breaks down when those institutions are not playing at the same game.

By portraying the branches of government as engaged in a conversation where no institution can bind the other, a dialogic frame distorts the relationship between courts and legislatures.[49] Rather, as Aileen Kavanagh writes, each branch of government has "a distinct, though complementary, role to play in the joint enterprise

[43] Prevention of Terrorism Act 2015 (Malay.); *see* Thomas Fuller, *Malaysia Resurrects Detention Without Trial, Alarming Government Critics*, N.Y. TIMES (Apr. 7, 2015), https://perma.cc/7V6U-Q52G.

[44] National Security Council Act 2016 (Malay.); *see Malaysia Approves Security Law amid Warning It Could Lead to Dictatorship*, GUARDIAN (Dec. 3, 2015), https://perma.cc/WXR5-FYL5.

[45] *See* Jamie Fullerton, *Singapore to Introduce Anti-Fake News Law, Allowing Removal of Articles*, GUARDIAN (Apr. 1, 2019), https://perma.cc/74TH-DNGT.

[46] *Compare* YAP, CONSTITUTIONAL DIALOGUE, *supra* note 21, at 78 (arguing that courts in a dominant party state should avoid a 'robust judicial reading of the Constitution' that may provoke the government), *with* H.P. Lee, *Constitutionalized Emergency Powers*, *in* EMERGENCY POWERS IN ASIA: EXPLORING THE LIMITS OF LEGALITY 393, 410 (Victor Ramraj & Arun Thiruvengadam eds., 2010) (arguing that expecting courts to wait for a change of political climate before they act more robustly is "akin to asking judges to display courage when such a display is not necessary").

[47] Law & Hsieh, *supra* note 40, at 10.

[48] For example, Singapore's Court of Appeal, the apex court, has never declared a law unconstitutional. The High Court struck down a law as unconstitutional in Taw Cheng Kong v. Public Prosecutor [1998] 2 SING. L. REP. 410, but this was later overturned by the Court of Appeal.

[49] Kavanagh, *supra* note 32, at 119.

of governing." For the courts that role is to interpret constitutional rights and to issue authoritative and binding decisions on constitutionality.

C. Judicial Empowerment and Judicial Role

Courts have a constitutional role to protect and develop core constitutional principles in a democracy. In a fragile democracy with a history of dominant party rule, the judicial obligation to serve as a constraint on consolidated political power is of particular importance.[50] Courts in contexts like Malaysia and Singapore should not deliberately avoid exercising their power to invalidate acts by the political branches that violate constitutional guarantees—a power explicitly imparted to them by the constitution.

Sometimes it is necessary for the judiciary to assert power in the face of legislative or executive conduct inconsistent with constitutional fundamentals. Insofar as courts are able to develop greater constitutional engagement between the institutional branches through using "dialogic" or sub-constitutional tools, they may do so. But in certain situations, there is value in the judiciary asserting its authority to protect core structural principles or rights guarantees.

My aim in what follows is to argue for a more empowered judicial role in developing democracies like Malaysia and Singapore. My argument is not for either judicial supremacy or dialogic review. I do not suggest that the courts are the sole or most important actor in the constitutional order. Of course, the vision of constitutional governance as a shared endeavor between the various branches of government, and with the people,[51] is an attractive ideal. As far as possible, courts exercising review should try to assume that other institutional actors are committed to shared constitutional principles.

But this idealized vision is not always the constitutional reality in practice. When the balance of power is overwhelmingly tilted in favor of the political branches, they have little incentive to participate in a mutually collaborative "dialogic" relationship with the courts. Simply put, in some situations constitutional dialogue does not go far enough. A monopoly on political power too easily translates to a monopoly over constitutional power. Dominant party governments in Malaysia and Singapore in the past have had little trouble passing statutes and constitutional amendments to entrench their position.

Ultimately, particularly in the face of concentrated political power, judicial practices premised on deference or restraint can only go so far. Judicial passivity shields constitutional transgressions with a cloak of legal legitimacy. When political

[50] *See* ISSACHAROFF, FRAGILE DEMOCRACIES, *supra* note 17, at 13.

[51] *See* LARRY D. KRAMER, THE PEOPLE THEMSELVES: POPULAR CONSTITUTIONALISM AND JUDICIAL REVIEW (2004); MARK TUSHNET, TAKING THE CONSTITUTION AWAY FROM THE COURTS (1999).

institutions act in a manner that is manifestly unconstitutional, courts must be prepared to exercise their constitutional authority. One of the hallmarks of the constitutions of the twentieth and twenty-first centuries are judiciaries that are specifically tasked with the power to enforce the guarantees of these written constitutions.[52] Courts in these modern democracies have an express constitutional mandate to exercise strong judicial review in protecting the constitution.

On my account, courts in the developing democracies of Malaysia and Singapore have both a *protective* role and *constructive* role. In their protective capacity, courts exercise judicial review to safeguard core elements of the constitutional order from being altered or destroyed.[53] In states controlled by a dominant political party or coalition that can harness the political process to pass constitutional amendments, this protective role is particularly important. When political institutions cannot be relied on to defend the democratic process, there is a powerful argument that judicial review of legislation or even constitutional amendment is in the service of promoting democratic governance.[54] Judicial intervention in such situations can take the form of invalidating constitutional amendments that threaten fundamental constitutional principles, such as the separation of powers and the rule of law. It's worth highlighting that courts have usually sought to protect judicial power as a key element essential to the constitution's basic structure. When courts in various contexts have reached for the basic structure doctrine, it has typically been used, at first instance, to defend against constitutional amendments that threaten the judiciary's independence or authority.[55]

Courts also have a constructive role in building and developing the foundations of an emerging constitutional order. This aspect of the judicial role is less about protecting the existing structure of the constitutional order; rather, it envisages a transformative role for courts.[56] Facilitative judicial review is expressly forward looking: it is directed at constructing the fundamental principles that form a culture of constitutionalism. It calls on courts to be self-conscious about building a culture of rights constitutionalism. To that end, courts can develop doctrines like a purposive interpretive approach and a proportionality analysis in rights adjudication. These judicial tools can be developed incrementally and used flexibly at different stages of constitutional or political transition in an evolving democracy.

52 *See* ISSACHAROFF, FRAGILE DEMOCRACIES, *supra* note 17, at 9.

53 *See* Law & Hsieh, *supra* note 40, at 21–22 (describing the "[r]earguard or protective use of amendment-review" to "defend key elements of the existing constitutional order" from amendment).

54 *See* JOHN HART ELY, DEMOCRACY AND DISTRUST: A THEORY OF JUDICIAL REVIEW (1980) (arguing that judicial review that protects political processes is "representation-reinforcing" and promotes democratic governance).

55 *See* Issacharoff, *Judicial Review in Troubled Times*, *supra* note 13, at 24.

56 *See* Law & Hsieh, *supra* note 40, at 22–23 (noting that courts can use "transformative amendment-review" to "precipitate or facilitate regime transformation").

III. Strategic Assertions of Judicial Power

For courts to assume an empowered role in constraining political power and developing constitutionalism, a key question is how they are to do so. Courts in many fragile Asian democracies have historically adopted a posture of extensive deference to the governing powers. Malaysia and Singapore are prime illustrations: constitutional adjudication in both contexts has been traditionally dominated by insular, narrow, and formalistic review, resulting in a culture of *de facto* legislative supremacy.[57] This section explores how courts can expand judicial power in a careful and strategic manner to strengthen their institutional role.

Judicial assertions of authority can take several forms. Courts can assert constitutional authority by exercising strong-form judicial review to strike down executive or legislative acts. More radically, courts can assume the power to invalidate constitutional amendments on the basis that the amendment undermines the basic structure of the constitution, as the Indian Supreme Court did in *Kesavananda Bharati v. Kerala*.[58]

Courts can also establish institutional authority through strategic assertions of judicial power. The use of such *Marbury*-style tactics often involve what Rosalind Dixon and Samuel Issacharoff call "judicial deferral" strategies, which are "designed to temporize" by enabling courts "to assert themselves short of a frontal confrontation with the political branches."[59] At base, these strategies allow courts to lay the foundation for enforcing judicial authority against the political branches in the future. Striking signs of judicial assertiveness have emerged recently in Malaysia. Two landmark decisions by the Malaysian apex court provide illuminating examples of strategic judicial empowerment.

A. *Semenyih Jaya*: Malaysia's *Marbury* Moment?

The 2017 case of *Semenyih Jaya*[60] appeared to involve a mundane dispute over land acquisition compensation; more broadly at stake, though, was nothing less than the scope of judicial power.[61] Landowners dissatisfied with the compensation awarded for their land, which had been compulsorily acquired by the state for a highway project, brought a challenge to the Land Acquisition Act of 1960. The statute provided for lay assessors, sitting with a judge in the High Court, to determine how

[57] *See* Chapter 2, Constitutional Adjudication and Constitutional Politics.

[58] AIR 1973 SC 1461 (India); *see also* Madhav Khosla, *Constitutional Amendment*, *in* OXFORD HANDBOOK OF THE INDIAN CONSTITUTION 232 (Sujit Choudhry et al. eds., 2016).

[59] Rosalind Dixon & Samuel Issacharoff, *Living to Fight Another Day: Judicial Deferral in Defense of Democracy*, 2016 WIS. L. REV. 685, 687 (2016).

[60] *Semenyih Jaya*, [2017] 3 MALAYAN L.J. 561.

[61] The *Semenyih Jaya* case and its implications are discussed in depth in Chapter 4, The Separation of Powers.

much the state should compensate owners for land it acquired from them, and also prevented appeals against this decision.[62] The landowners argued that because the lay assessors were empowered to make a conclusive determination, this unconstitutionally infringed the judicial power of the courts.

The challenge brought to the fore the scope of judicial power under Article 121(1) of the Malaysian Constitution, long the site of struggle between the legislature and the courts. In its original form, Article 121(1) provided: "The judicial power of the Federation shall be vested in a Supreme Court and such inferior courts as may be provided by federal law." In 1988, the Malaysian Parliament amended Article 121 to read:

> Judicial power of the Federation
>
> 121(1) There shall be two High Courts of co-ordinate jurisdiction and status . . . and such inferior courts as may be provided by federal law; and the High Courts and inferior courts shall have such jurisdiction and powers as may be conferred by or under federal law.

Much debate has since ensued over whether this amendment, which removed the text vesting judicial power in the courts, meant that the judiciary's powers are effectively subject to the legislature. Initially, the Malaysian apex court appeared cowed into passivity. In *Kok Wah Kuan*,[63] in an opinion that has been called "a remarkable act of self-flagellation,"[64] the Malaysian Federal Court took a stunningly literalist view of the amended Article 121(1), resulting in an extremely narrow view of judicial power and the separation of powers. The Court's majority stated that "to what extent such 'judicial powers' are vested in the two High Courts depends on what federal law provides, not on the interpretation of 'judicial power' as prior to the amendment."[65] The paucity of the majority's formalistic approach had the effect of subjecting the judiciary's powers to the legislature: "If we want to know the jurisdiction and powers of the [courts] we will have to look at the federal law."[66]

In *Semenyih Jaya*, a unanimous Federal Court struck down the land acquisition statutory provision as unconstitutional—the first time in twenty years that it had invalidated a federal law—holding that "judicial power or the power to adjudicate in civil and criminal matters brought to the court is vested only in the court."[67] Repudiating the "narrow compass" within which the *Kok Wah Kuan* majority approached the amended Article 121(1), the *Semenyih Jaya* Court declared that the

[62] Land Acquisition Act of 1960.

[63] Public Prosecutor v. Kok Wah Kuan [2008] 5 Malayan L.J. 1 (F.C.).

[64] Shad Saleem Faruqui, Document of Destiny: The Constitution of the Federation of Malaysia 740 (2008).

[65] *Kok Wah Kuan* (F.C.), [2008] 5 Malayan L.J. 1, at [11].

[66] *Id.* at [86].

[67] *Semenyih Jaya*, [2017] 3 Malayan L.J. 561, at [67].

implication of Article 121(1) "extends well beyond" the powers conferred by federal law.[68] Textually, the Court noted that Article 121(1), in its shoulder note, still contained a reference to "judicial power."[69]

ButMalaysia's highest court made a broader, and important, structural argument that the vesting of the judicial power in the courts is "an important feature in a democratic system of Government."[70] Because the constitution manifested an aim to secure power in an independent judiciary,[71] the Federal Court concluded that "the judicial power of the court resides in the Judiciary and no other as is explicit in [Article] 121(1) of the Constitution."[72] The Malaysian court found that "the 1988 constitutional amendment had the effect of undermining the judicial power of the Judiciary"; it thus impinged on the separation of powers and the independence of the judiciary—features that it identified as fundamental to the Malaysian Constitution.[73] The amendment "effectively suborned [the judiciary] to Parliament, with the implication that Parliament became sovereign," a result which the Court held "manifestly inconsistent with the supremacy of the Federal Constitution enshrined in Article 4(1)."[74]

Critically, the Federal Court proceeded to lay a framework for courts to assert the power to protect the Constitution's basic features. It explicitly drew on the basic structure doctrine that certain constitutional features cannot be altered by the legislature even by constitutional amendment, referring to the Indian Supreme Court's precedent affirming "the sanctity of the doctrine of separation of powers and the exclusivity of judicial power."[75] Endorsing the basic structure doctrine in the Malaysian context, the Court declared that "Parliament does not have power to amend the Federal Constitution to the effect of undermining the features" of the doctrine of separation of powers and the independence of the judiciary.[76] The principles of "judicial power, judicial independence, and the separation of powers are as critical as they are sacrosanct" in Malaysia's constitutional framework.[77]

What is striking about the decision is that the Malaysian Federal Court did not expressly invalidate the constitutional amendment. Instead, it interpretively read down the 1988 constitutional amendment, depriving it of any effect on the judicial power of the courts. By holding that the judicial power resides in the judiciary as

[68] *Id.* at [69].
[69] *Id.* at [62], [66].
[70] *Id.* at [70].
[71] *Id.* at [82]–[83].
[72] *Id.* at [86].
[73] *Id.* at [74].
[74] *Id.* at [75]; Fed. Const. (Malay.), art. 4(1) ("The Constitution is the supreme law of the Federation and any law passed ... which is inconsistent with this Constitution shall, to the extent of the inconsistency, be void.").
[75] *Semenyih Jaya*, [2017] 3 Malayan L.J. 561, at [87] (citing Kesavananda Bharati v. Kerala, AIR 1973 SC 1461 (India)).
[76] *Id.* at [76].
[77] *Id.* at [90].

inherent to Article 121(1) of the Constitution,[78] the Court effectively nullified the 1988 amendment. Interpretively, it restored Article 121(1) to the meaning it had before 1988.

The *Semenyih Jaya* decision has been hailed by many as a seminal step for judicial power and the separation of powers in Malaysian jurisprudence.[79] For some, however, the Malaysian Court did not go far enough in *Semenyih Jaya.* For example, Wilson Tay criticizes the Malaysian court for not taking "a more resolute approach" by striking down the 1988 constitutional amendment definitively.[80] And Jaclyn Neo observes that the Court's "somewhat ambivalent engagement with the basic structure doctrine" did not "squarely address the core" of the question about whether the courts can draw on meta-constitutional norms to strike down constitutional amendments.[81]

But such critiques fail to appreciate the full significance of the Malaysian court's careful assertion of power and strategic maneuvering. In *Semenyih Jaya,* the Federal Court laid the groundwork for sculpting a powerful doctrine aimed at strengthening the judiciary's institutional position. It stopped short of invalidating the constitutional amendments, deliberately insulating the court from immediate political repercussions while establishing the framework to assert judicial authority in the future. By articulating a basic structure doctrine premised on the separation of powers and judicial power, the Court established a potent tool for resisting political incursions even when channeled through the formal constitutional amendment process.

Semenyih Jaya is a prime example of judicial strategy in self-empowerment. Several features of the decision are especially telling. To begin, as we have seen, the Court refrained from invalidating the constitutional amendment outright; yet, in an expansive opinion, it established the groundwork for a robust tool that empowers the judiciary to assert authority against the political branches.

What's more, the Court articulated this power in a seemingly mundane case, which, on its face, did not necessarily signal huge constitutional implications. The *Semenyih Jaya* dispute over land acquisition and property law did not immediately appear to be a constitutional blockbuster involving contentious issues relating to democratic protection or fundamental rights.[82]

[78] *Id.* at [86].

[79] *See, e.g.*, Press Release, George Varughese, President, Malaysian Bar, An Independent Judiciary is Indispensable to the Rule of Law (May 8, 2017), https://perma.cc/T3QT-Y5WF.

[80] *See* Wilson Tay, *Basic Structure Revisited: The Case of* Semenyih Jaya *and the Defence of Fundamental Constitutional Principles in Malaysia*, 14 ASIAN J. COMP. L. 113, 135 (2019).

[81] Jaclyn Neo, *Beyond Mortals? Constitutional Identity, Judicial Power, and the Evolution of the Basic Structure Doctrine in Malaysia*, *in* CPG PUBLICATION: "IDENTITY AND CHANGE—THE BASIC STRUCTURE IN ASIAN CONSTITUTIONAL ORDERS" 22–23 (2016).

[82] This bears resemblance to the origins of the Indian Supreme Court's basic structure doctrine in a case involving restrictions on the ownership of private property. *See* Landau, *supra* note 13, at 1557 ("The origins of the basic structure doctrine in India in fact focus on the protection of private property, rather than on democratic protection.").

Another curious feature of the Court's decision lies in the remedy it issued. The Court invalidated the statutory provision and replaced it with an immensely detailed set of procedural guidelines which leave final determination only to the judge—but ruled that its decision would only have purely prospective effect.[83] By applying prospective overruling, the Court mitigated the impact of its decision by insulating itself from any immediate legal or political backlash.[84]

Finally, it bears noting that the Malaysian apex court's decision was unanimous. From the U.S. Supreme Court in *Marbury v. Madison* and *Brown v. Board of Education* to more recent decisions by the constitutional courts of Taiwan and South Korea,[85] courts the world over have sought to issue single-voice decisions in politically contentious cases. The Malaysian Court was no exception: the unanimous decision in *Semenyih Jaya* was issued by a full bench of five judges in the Federal Court.

The Malaysian Federal Court's *Semenyih Jaya* decision appears *Marbury*-like in its strategic establishment of judicial authority. In this case involving an apparently prosaic matter of land acquisition compensation, the Court could have avoided addressing the broader implications of the constitutional amendment to Article 121(1) relating to judicial power. Yet even as it issued a holding that insulated the court from any immediate political ramifications, the Malaysian apex court managed to embed the seeds for a broad doctrine of judicial authority over the core structure of the Constitution.

B. Judicial Entrenchment of Power: *Indira Gandhi*

In January 2018, barely a year after *Semenyih Jaya*, the Malaysian Federal Court issued another remarkable decision in *Indira Gandhi*,[86] firmly entrenching the basic structure doctrine and its judicial power.[87] Indira Gandhi's ex-husband had converted from Hinduism to Islam and then officially converted all three of their children without her knowledge. He then obtained custody orders over the children in his favor from the Sharia Court. With no standing to access the religious courts as a non-Muslim, Indira Gandhi challenged the children's conversions and custody in the civil courts. The High Court held in Indira Gandhi's favor, quashing the children's religious conversion certificates and granting her custody of all three

[83] *Semenyih Jaya*, [2017] 3 Malayan L.J. 561, at [126].

[84] *See* Rosalind Dixon & Samuel Issacharoff, *Living to Fight Another Day: Judicial Deferral in Defense of Democracy*, 2016 Wis. L. Rev. 683, 685 (2016) (observing that courts use doctrines like prospective overruling as a judicial deferral mechanism to avoid provoking direct political confrontation).

[85] *See* Wen-Chen Chang, *Strategic Judicial Responses in Politically Charged Cases: East Asian Experiences*, 8 Int'l J. Const. L. 885, 900–901 (2010).

[86] *Indira Gandhi* (F.C.), [2018] 1 Malayan L.J. 545.

[87] The *Indira Gandhi* case is discussed in depth in Chapter 5, The Rule of Law, and Chapter 7, Judicializing Religion.

children. But the High Court's decision was then overruled by the Court of Appeal, which held that religious conversion was a matter exclusively for the Sharia courts to decide.[88]

The Malaysian Federal Court's decision in *Indira Gandhi* had been long awaited. Indira Gandhi's protracted legal battle, which had been in the public eye for a decade, was emblematic of a broader struggle over Islam's position in the public order and the scope of fundamental rights for Muslims and non-Muslims. Unanimously, the Court quashed the children's conversion certificates, ruling that the constitutional right to equal protection requires both parents to consent to change the religion of minor children.[89] In its most explicit declaration so far of the boundaries between the civil courts and religious courts, the Federal Court affirmed that civil courts have jurisdiction over all constitutional matters even when questions of Islamic law are involved.[90] Doing so, it sharply departed from earlier precedents that had established a pattern of civil courts deferring jurisdiction to the Sharia courts in matters implicating Islamic law even when they involved constitutional rights.

Crucially, in *Indira Gandhi*, the Federal Court expressly grounded the *civil* courts' judicial power in the basic structure of the constitution. In a sweeping opinion in which it referred to its own decision in *Semenyih Jaya*, as well as the Indian Supreme Court cases of *Kesavananda Bharati* and *Minerva Mills*,[91] the Malaysian Federal Court declared that "the power of judicial review is essential to the constitutional role of the courts, and inherent in the basic structure of the Constitution."[92] And so: "It cannot be amended or altered by Parliament by way of a constitutional amendment."[93]

After establishing that the Constitution has an immutable basic structure, the Federal Court applied that doctrine to interpret Article 121(1A) of the Malaysian Constitution. That provision states that the civil courts "shall have no jurisdiction in respect of any matter within the jurisdiction of the Sharia courts." The origin of Article 121(1A) stems from the aggressive constitutional amendments passed in 1988 to alter the constitutional provision on judicial power. When Parliament amended the Article 121(1) provision on judicial power in 1988, it also introduced Article 121(1A), which demarcated the jurisdiction of the civil and religious courts. After the 1988 amendment, the civil courts exhibited a pattern of extensively deferring matters to the Sharia courts. Just as the Federal Court in *Semenyih*

[88] Pathmanathan a/l Krishnan v. Indira Gandhi a/p Mutho [2016] 4 MALAYAN L.J. 455 (C.A.), at [33] [hereinafter *Indira Gandhi* (C.A.)].

[89] The Federal Court interpreted Article 12(4) of the Federal Constitution of Malaysia, which states that "the religion of a person under the age of eighteen years shall be decided by his parent or guardian," as requiring the consent of both parents.

[90] *Indira Gandhi* (F.C.), [2018] 1 MALAYAN L.J. 545, at [104].

[91] *Id.* at [42], [48], [49].

[92] *Id.* at [48].

[93] *Id.*

Jaya had dealt with the constitutional amendment to Article 121(1) on judicial power, the *Indira Gandhi* Court now took on the Article 121(1A) provision on the authority of the civil and religious courts.

With *Indira Gandhi*, the Federal Court made clear that "the effect of [Article] 121(1A) is not to oust the jurisdiction of the civil courts as soon as a subject matter relates to the Islamic religion."[94] Declared the Court:

> The powers of judicial review and of constitutional or statutory interpretation are pivotal constituents of the civil courts' judicial power under Article 121(1)... As part of the basic structure of the constitution, it cannot be abrogated from the civil courts or conferred upon the Syariah Courts, whether by constitutional amendment, Act of Parliament or state legislation.[95]

The Court in *Indira Gandhi* declared that the judicial power lies solely with the *civil* courts—not the Sharia courts, which "operate on a different footing altogether."[96]

The *Indira Gandhi* decision has been called the Malaysian Federal Court's "clearest endorsement of the basic structure doctrine so far."[97] More striking still is the Federal Court's willingness to entrench the notion of the constitution's basic structure in a case involving religious authority, one of the most fraught areas in Malaysian law and politics.

In its decisive decision in *Indira Gandhi*, the Malaysian Court built on the foundation it had carefully laid earlier in *Semenyih Jaya* to further assert its judicial power, this time with a highly charged issue at stake. In another unanimous decision, the Court expressly applied the basic structure doctrine to entrench an empowered role for the civil courts. If *Semenyih Jaya* represents Malaysia's *Marbury* moment, *Indira Gandhi* might well be its *Cooper v. Aaron*.[98]

* * *

The Malaysian Federal Court in *Semenyih Jaya* and *Indira Gandhi* invoked the basic structure of the constitution to nullify constitutional amendments that sought to strip the courts of their power to review certain matters. In invoking the basic structure doctrine in defense of judicial review, the Malaysian court's use of the doctrine is similar to the initial formulation used by the Indian Supreme Court and courts around the world.[99] The key feature that these judicial approaches

94 *Id.* at [104].
95 *Id.*
96 *Id.* at [70].
97 Neo, *supra* note 81, at 26.
98 358 U.S. 1 (1958). *Cooper v. Aaron* is widely regarded as a declaration of judicial supremacy by the U.S. Supreme Court, in which the Court asserted that *Marbury* "declared the basic principle that the federal judiciary is supreme in the exposition of the law of the Constitution." *Id.* at 18-19.
99 *See* Issacharoff, *Judicial Review in Troubled Times*, *supra* note 13, at 20.

share is that they are aimed at strengthening—not restraining—judicial authority. Unlike weak or dialogic forms of judicial review, which seek to promote dialogue with the political branches, the ultimate goal of judicial empowerment strategies is to expand judicial power.

IV. Forward: A Framework for Constitutional Adjudication

Courts seeking to assert their constitutional authority require a corresponding jurisprudence. This final section outlines a framework for constitutional adjudication for courts in emerging Asian democracies. In Part II of this book, I explored fundamental elements of the constitutions of Malaysia and Singapore: constitutional supremacy based on the framework set up by the constitution, the separation of powers, and the rule of law. I now draw these strands together to outline how these core constitutional features can help structure constitutional adjudication.

On a doctrinal plane, I explore three specific ways that such an adjudicative framework could guide judicial interventions in Malaysia and Singapore. First, courts could draw on the basic structure doctrine to assume a power to nullify or invalidate constitutional amendments as unconstitutional. Or judges can use the fundamental features of the constitution's basic structure interpretively in constitutional adjudication. The other two methods are oriented toward the adjudication of constitutional rights. Courts should use a generous, purposive approach in line with the broader purposes of the constitution to interpret constitutional rights. Another judicial intervention for courts to develop is the use of proportionality review to enforce constitutional rights against the government.

A. The Basic Structure of the Constitution

The idea of unconstitutional constitutional amendments has been enormously influential globally.[100] Since the Indian Supreme Court famously articulated the concept of a set of immutable constitutional principles to resist the broad use of emergency powers during Indira Gandhi's administration, judicial protection of a constitutional basic structure has been invoked by courts across the world from Africa and Eastern Europe to Latin America.[101] Among Asian courts, in addition to

[100] *See* Kesavananda Bharati v. Kerala, AIR 1973 SC 1461 (India); Minerva Mills Ltd. v. India, 1981 1 S.C.R. 206 (India); *see also* Sudhir Krishnaswamy, Democracy and Constitutionalism in India: A Study of the Basic structure Doctrine (2009).

[101] *See* Yaniv Roznai, Unconstitutional Constitutional Amendments: The Limits of Amendment Powers 47–69 (2017).

India, the basic structure doctrine has been adopted by Bangladesh,[102] Pakistan,[103] and Taiwan.[104] Yet the legal notion of judicially enforced limits on constitutional amendments has not been prevalent in the practice of courts in Southeast Asia, although some variants have been referred to by the high courts of Thailand and the Philippines.[105]

With *Semenyih Jaya* and *Indira Gandhi*,[106] the Malaysian Federal Court not only entrenched the constitutional basic structure doctrine in Malaysian jurisprudence but also carved out a firm foothold for it in Southeast Asia. The journey of the Malaysian courts toward endorsing the basic structure doctrine has been one of constitutional twists and turns.[107] In earlier cases in the 1970s and 1980s, the Federal Court dismissed the idea that there could be such a thing as implied limits on the legislature's power to amend the constitution.[108] Signs of judicial openness toward the idea emerged in the 2010 case of *Sivarasa Rasiah*,[109] when the Malaysian supreme court said in *dicta*, "it is clear from the way that the Federal Constitution is constructed that there are certain features that constitute its basic fabric."[110] In 2017, the Court endorsed the basic structure doctrine in *Semenyih Jaya*— departing from precedent in "the most surprising, and the most radical, aspect" of the decision[111]—to nullify the amendment passed in 1988 to modify the Article 121(1) constitutional provision on judicial power. Then in *Indira Gandhi*, the Federal Court applied the basic structure doctrine to negate Article 121(1A), the other article put in place by the 1988 amendment, affirming the authority of the civil courts over the religious courts.

Which features form part of a constitution's basic framework? Identifying the basic features of the constitution requires determining the core principles central to a particular constitution. This task requires interpreters to pay attention to the

[102] *See* Ridwanul Hoque, *Eternal Provisions in the Constitution of Bangladesh: A Constitution Once and for All?*, *in* AN UNAMENDABLE CONSTITUTION? UNAMENDABILITY IN CONSTITUTIONAL DEMOCRACIES 195, 195–229 (Richard Albert & Emrah Order eds., 2018).

[103] *See* Zeeshaan Zafar Hashmi, *Unconstitutional Constitutional Amendments or Amending the Unamendable: A Critique of* District Bar Association Rawalpindi v. Federation of Pakistan, PAKISTAN L. REV. IX (2018).

[104] *See* Law & Hsieh, *supra* note 40.

[105] *See* Khemthong Tonsakulrungruang, *Constitutional Amendment in Thailand: Amending in the Spectre of Parliamentary Dictatorship*, *in* CONSTITUTIONAL AMENDMENT IN SOUTHEAST ASIA, 14 J. COMP. L. 173 (2019) (citing Constitutional Court Decision 18-22/2555 (2012)); Dante Gatmaytan, *Constitutional Change as Suspect Projects: The Philippines*, *in* CONSTITUTIONAL AMENDMENT IN SOUTHEAST ASIA, 14 J. COMP. L. 139 (2019).

[106] *Semenyih Jaya*, [2017] 3 MALAYAN L.J. 561; *Indira Gandhi* (F.C.), [2018] 1 MALAYAN L.J. 545.

[107] For more detailed discussion of the evolution of the doctrine of basic structure in Malaysia, see Chapter 2, Constitutional Adjudication and Constitutional Politics, section IV(C).

[108] *See* Loh Kooi Choon v. Gov't of Malaysia [1977] 2 MALAYAN L.J. 187; Phang Chin Hock [1980] 1 MALAYAN L.J. 70.

[109] Sivarasa Rasiah v. Badan Peguam Malaysia & Anor [2010] 2 MALAYAN L.J. 333 [hereinafter *Sivarasa Rasiah*].

[110] *Id.* at 342.

[111] H.P Lee et al., *Constitutional Change in Malaysia*, *in* CONSTITUTIONAL AMENDMENT IN SOUTHEAST ASIA, 14 J. COMP. L. 119, 135 (2019).

constitution's "foundational structuralism," using what Yaniv Roznai describes as "a structural interpretation of the constitution as a coherent whole."[112] On this account, a holistic structural interpretation considers the constitution's overarching values and principles, basic framework, and constitutional history. In essence, it is an interpretive approach based on what I view as the constitutional core.

In *Indira Gandhi*, Malaysia's apex court identified the basic features of the Malaysian Constitution as "the separation of powers, the rule of law and the protection of minorities."[113] As the Court recognized, the Constitution is premised on these "underlying principles" that form "part of the basic structure of the Constitution" and "cannot be abrogated or removed."[114] The Court's declaration builds on its decision the year before in *Semenyih Jaya*, where it identified the "features of the Federal Constitution" as "the doctrine of separation of powers" and "the independence of the judiciary."[115] All these principles are in line with the fundamental features identified in the earlier chapters of this book as constituting the core of the Malaysian Constitution.

Consider first the separation of powers.[116] Invoked in both the Federal Court's decisions as a fundamental feature of the Malaysian Constitution, the separation of powers is inextricably connected to the independence of the judiciary and judicial power.[117] Especially in a political system where the ruling government has historically used the constitutional amendment process to undermine the courts' judicial power, central to an effective system of the separation of powers is the judiciary's ability to function as an independent constraint on the political branches.[118]

The rule of law is a related, but distinct, basic feature of the Malaysian Constitution.[119] The power of judicial review is fundamental to the rule of law inherent in the constitution's core structure.[120] As the Federal Court in *Indira Gandhi* expressly declared, the civil courts have the exclusive power of judicial review. Two significant implications flow from understanding judicial review as "a natural and necessary corollary of the rule of law."[121] For one, judicial review cannot be

[112] Roznai, *supra* note 101, at 215.

[113] *Indira Gandhi* (F.C.), [2018] 1 Malayan L.J. 545, at [90].

[114] *Id.*

[115] *Semenyih Jaya*, [2017] 3 Malayan L.J. 561, at [74] (observing that the 1988 constitutional amendment impinges on these features of the Malaysian Constitution).

[116] *See* Chapter 4, The Separation of Powers.

[117] *Semenyih Jaya*, [2017] 3 Malayan L.J. 561, at [90] (noting "the important concept of judicial power, judicial independence and the separation of powers are as critical as they are sacrosanct in our constitutional framework").

[118] *Id.* at [88] (noting that 'the concept of the independence of the Judiciary is the foundation of the principles of the separation of powers').

[119] *See* Chapter 5, The Rule of Law.

[120] *Indira Gandhi* (F.C.), [2018] 1 Malayan L.J. 545, at [48] ("[T]he power of judicial review is essential to the constitutional role of the courts, and inherent to the basic structure of the Constitution."); *id.* at [58] ("[J]udicial power in particular the power of judicial review, is an essential feature of the basic structure of the Constitution.").

[121] *Id.* at [33].

removed from the civil courts and courts may review any constitutional amendments that restrict this power.[122] Another implication is that the power of judicial review cannot be conferred on bodies other than the civil courts, such as the religious Sharia courts.[123] What seems clear is that the structural principles of the separation of powers and the rule of law, which together protect judicial independence and judicial review, are recognized as fundamental to the constitution's basic structure.

But it is also of great significance that the Federal Court in *Indira Gandhi* declared "the protection of minorities" as part of the basic structure of the Constitution.[124] Citing precedent from the Canadian Supreme Court,[125] the Malaysian court appeared to accept the idea that protection of minority rights is inherent to a pluralistic constitutional order like Malaysia. The constitutional vision offered by the Malaysian court recognizes that part of the Constitution's pluralistic identity represents a commitment to safeguard the rights of minorities and individuals.

That the separation of powers, the rule of law, and the protection of minorities are features that have been recognized foundational to the Constitution's structure is not to suggest that they are exhaustive of the Constitution's basic features. As the Federal Court in *Sivarasa* noted: "Whether a particular feature is part of the basic structure must be worked out on a case by case basis."[126] The potential for the basic structure doctrine to evolve in Malaysian jurisprudence mirrors how it has developed in India and elsewhere.[127] It's worth noting that even when the Malaysian Supreme Court refused to adopt the basic structure doctrine in the 1977 case of *Loh Kooi Choon*,[128] the Court nevertheless recognized the Constitution as "embodying three basic concepts";[129] in addition to the separation of powers, these core features included "the protection of individual fundamental rights and the principle of federalism."[130]

In identifying the Constitution's core, the Malaysian courts have rightly implied its basic features from its text and structure, at times using constitutional history and the original framework as a guide. At heart, the basic structure doctrine is rooted in a recognition of constitutional supremacy. The Court in *Indira Gandhi* locates the textual basis for the idea of "a political system based on constitutional

122 *Id.* at [51].

123 *Id.* at [51], [59].

124 *Id.* at [90] (stating that the principles of "the separation of powers, the rule of law, and the protection of minorities . . . are part of the basic structure of the Constitution"); *see also id.* at [31].

125 *Id.* at [31].

126 *Sivarasa Rasiah*, [2010] 2 MALAYAN L.J. 333, at [342].

127 ROZNAI, *supra* note 101, at 44 (observing that "[t]he *Kesavananda* case did not provide a precise list of unamendable features that made up the Constitution's basic structure; rather, it formed a sort of common law doctrine that developed on a case-by-case basis").

128 Loh Kooi Choon v. Gov't of Malaysia, [1977] 2 MALAYAN L.J. 187.

129 *Id.* at 188.

130 *Id.*

supremacy" in the Constitution's supremacy clause.[131] The Malaysian Federal Court's assertiveness in cases like *Indira Gandhi, Semenyih Jaya*, and *Sivarasa* reflects the idea that it is the Constitution—not Parliament—that is supreme. Judicial recognition of this framework of constitutional supremacy marks a significant shift from the courts' earlier position of *de facto* legislative supremacy.

The notion that there are limits on the government's formal amendment power is grounded in the notion there are certain fundamental constitutional values beyond the reach of the legislature. I highlight two concrete implications of a basic structure framework for constitutional adjudication using Malaysia and Singapore as case studies, although the analysis can be extended to other emerging democracies in Asia.

First, courts should assume the power to invalidate constitutional amendments as unconstitutional by deploying a locally contextual version of the basic structure doctrine.[132] Striking down constitutional amendments on the ground that they conflict with core constitutional principles may appear, at first blush, to be a judicial act of extreme counter-majoritarianism.[133] But in dominant party states—like Singapore and, for much of its history, Malaysia—the ruling government does not typically face procedural obstacles in passing formal amendments. In fragile democracies that risk sliding into authoritarian control, extending the power of constitutional review over constitutional amendments is sometimes necessary as a bulwark against excessive majoritarianism that threatens the state's democratic governance.[134]

Not all amendment powers are created equal. In considering the standard of judicial review over constitutional amendments that should apply, its relation to the formal amendment process matters.[135] In a context like Singapore or Malaysia, where a ruling party government has used its legislative supermajority aggressively to amend the constitution, courts have a role to play in annulling amendments that threaten core aspects of constitutional governance and judicial power. As Jaclyn Neo writes about Malaysia, "[w]here one political party is able to control a supermajority of seats in Parliament for an extended period of time, procedural limits provide no bar to constitutional amendments," the judiciary may need to invoke "meta-norms in the form of the basic structure doctrine … to preserve judicial power and independence."[136] Even Yap, a proponent of dialogic review, endorses

[131] Fed. Const. (Malay.), art. 4(1) ("This Constitution is the supreme law of the Federation."); *Indira Gandhi* (F.C.), [2018] 1 Malayan L.J. 545, at [40].

[132] *See* Kesavananda Bharati v. Kerala, AIR 1973 SC 1461 (India).

[133] *See* Gary Jacobsohn, *The Permeability of Constitutional Borders*, 82 Tex. L. Rev. 1763, 1799 (2003) (observing that the basic structure doctrine "[e]ssentially … says that there are features of constitutional governance so important that they preservation requires the maintaining the option of exercising the most extreme of countermajoritarian judicial acts: overturning a constitutional amendment").

[134] Issacharoff, Fragile Democracies, *supra* note 17, at 164.

[135] *See* Roznai, *supra* note 101, at 219.

[136] Neo, *supra* note 81.

judicial review of amendments passed by a dominant government if the amendments would substantially undermine the existing constitution.[137]

Protective judicial review of amendment can be justified on political process grounds.[138] The arguments John Hart Ely advanced in favor of judicial review to protect democratic processes and reinforce representation "applies with equal, if not greater, force to amendment-review."[139] As Yaniv Roznai argues, amendment powers that resemble ordinary legislative procedures, which do not carry strong democratic legitimacy, should be subject to review if a core constitutional principle has been disproportionately violated.[140] This defensive judicial role protects key elements of the existing constitutional order,[141] such as structural principles foundational to democratic governance.

The Malaysian Federal Court has already shown itself willing to venture into this territory. As we saw earlier in this chapter, it has declared judicial review and constitutional interpretation "part of the basic structure of the constitution" that "cannot be abrogated from the civil courts" whether "by constitutional amendment, Act of Parliament or state legislation."[142] The Federal Court, in effect, nullified constitutional amendments that impinge on core structural principles like the separation of powers and the rule of law. If a future situation warrants further protective review to invalidate an amendment, it should do so, and explicitly.

Courts can also use amendment review in a transformative or constructive manner.[143] Judges can draw on the basic structure to assert the values that they believe should form the foundation of the constitutional order. For instance, with its explicit recognition in *Indira Gandhi* that the protection of minorities is part of the basic structure, the Court created the potential to extend the review power to protect core fundamental rights. Now that it has established the basic structure doctrine as part of Malaysian constitutional jurisprudence, the Court could well draw on this doctrine to construct the foundational values of the constitutional order.

Singapore, too, appears to be on a similar trajectory toward embracing a constitutional basic structure doctrine.[144] Former Chief Justice Chan Sek Keong has argued, extra-judicially and in a High Court decision, that the doctrine of implied limits on the Parliament's power should be applied to Singapore's Constitution.[145]

137 Po Jen Yap, Courts and Democracies in Asia 194–95 (2017).

138 *See* Ely, *supra* note 54.

139 Law & Hsieh, *supra* note 40, at 48.

140 Roznai, *supra* note 101, at 220.

141 Law & Hsieh, *supra* note 40, at 22 (observing that the basic structure doctrine and its variants are "inherently well suited to defense of the status quo because they explicitly prohibit alteration of constitutional fundamentals").

142 *Indira Gandhi* (F.C.), [2018] 1 Malayan L.J. 545, at [104].

143 Law & Hsieh, *supra* note 40, at 22–23 (describing transformative amendment review as a means of facilitating regime transformation).

144 *See* Chapter 2, Constitutional Adjudication and Constitutional Politics, section IV(C).

145 *See* Chan Sek Keong, *The Courts and the "Rule of Law" in Singapore*, Sing. J. Legal Stud. 209, 223 (2012); Chan Sek Keong, *Basic Structure and Supremacy of the Singapore Constitution*, 29 Sing. Acad. L.J. 619 (2017); Mohammad Faizal bin Sabtu v. Public Prosecutor [2012] 4 Sing. L. Rep. 947.

In a 2015 decision, the Singapore Court of Appeal acknowledged that features "fundamental and essential to the political system that is established thereunder" may be part of the basic structure, although it declined in that case to decide the question of the doctrine's extent and effect in Singapore.[146] It's worth emphasizing that the Singaporean and Malaysian courts would not be global outliers in asserting the power to review unconstitutional constitutional amendments. The use of the basic structure doctrine in India, Taiwan, Bangladesh, and beyond Asia, underscores that governmental "misuse of the amendment power is not a theoretical supposition," but "built on historical evidence."[147]

Another way in which courts can invoke the basic structure doctrine is to use its principles as a powerful interpretive basis in constitutional adjudication. Under this framework, courts should seek to interpret legislation and executive actions in line with the core constitutional values identified as part of the basic structure. As the *Indira Gandhi* Court declared: "A constitution must be interpreted in light of its historical and philosophical context, as well as its fundamental underlying principles," like the separation of powers and the rule of law.[148] Courts could use such an interpretive approach in exercising their constructive capacity to develop foundational constitutional principles. The approach would also be in line with the principle of legality practiced in various common law systems, under which courts operate on the assumption that Parliament does not intend to infringe constitutional principles or fundamental rights in the absence of clear statutory words.[149] But even when the text of the legislation suggests a clear intent to undermine the separation of powers or rule of law, I argue that courts should still try to interpret the provision in line with the Constitution's fundamental principles, regardless of the intent of Parliament.

Of particular significance in this regard are ouster clauses in statutes that limit the courts' judicial review power. The legislative landscape of Malaysia and Singapore is littered with ouster clauses that remove various categories of legislation or executive decisions from the jurisdiction of the civil courts. Singapore's ouster clauses prominently include one in its Internal Security Act, which precludes the judiciary from reviewing preventive detentions, while Malaysia has more than forty statutes containing clauses barring judicial review of matters within the law.[150] Given that judicial review has been explicitly declared as an inherent part of the constitution's basic structure, courts should restrict such ouster

[146] Yong Vui Kong v. Public Prosecutor [2015] 2 Sing. L. Rep. 1129, at [71]–[72].

[147] Roznai, *supra* note 101, at 144.

[148] *Indira Gandhi* (F.C.), [2018] 1 Malayan L.J. 545, at [29], [30], [32].

[149] Jaclyn Neo, *All Power Has Legal Limits–The Principle of Legality as a Constitutional Principle of Judicial Review*, 29 Sing. Acad. L.J. 667, 668–69 (2017).

[150] *See* Shaila Koshy, *Time to Repeal Ouster Clauses*, Star Online (May 20, 2018), https://perma.cc/EPF4-NXWH.

clauses by reading down any legislative provision that attempts to strip the courts of their power of judicial review.[151]

When an interpretative approach will not go far enough, though, courts must be prepared to strike down laws or executive acts that are inconsistent with constitutional core principles. Strong-form judicial review is manifestly part of the judiciary's constitutional authority in Malaysia and Singapore. Courts should exercise this power when a law threatens fundamental separation of powers or rule of law principles, as it did in *Semenyih Jaya*. Judicial deference premised on *de facto* parliamentary supremacy is misguided in the context of polities with constitutions that establish the power of judicial review.

B. Purposive Interpretation of Constitutional Rights

Like most modern constitutions,[152] the constitutions of Malaysia and Singapore expressly protect certain fundamental rights. The fundamental liberties chapters contained in these constitutions enshrine various individual rights, including the right to life and liberty, equal protection, freedom of speech, freedom of association, and freedom of religion.[153] For a long time, as Chapter 2 described, Malaysian and Singaporean courts took a highly literalist, restrictive approach to their constitutions' rights guarantees. Such a narrow approach is a poor fit for how these constitutional rights provisions should be understood and applied.

In approaching rights adjudication, I argue that the courts should take a broader, purposive approach toward interpreting constitutional rights. Such a purposive interpretative approach would reflect the broader principles and values that underlie a particular rights provision in the Constitution.

In the 2010 case of *Sivarasa Rasiah*, the Malaysian Federal Court advocated a generous, "prismatic" methodology of interpreting the Constitution's rights guarantees.[154] According to the Court, the fundamental liberties guaranteed in the constitution "must be generously interpreted" and "a prismatic approach to interpretation must be adopted."[155] Moreover, "provisos or restrictions that limit or derogate from a guaranteed right must be read restrictively."[156] Based on this approach, the Court in *Sivarasa* held that the right not to be deprived of personal

[151] Press Release, George Varughese, An Independent Judiciary is Indispensable to the Rule of Law, *supra* note 79.

[152] *See* David S. Law & Mila Versteeg, *The Evolution and Ideology of Global Constitutionalism*, 99 CALIF. L. REV. 1163, 1194 (2011).

[153] FED. CONST. (MALAY.), arts. 5–13; CONST. OF THE REP. OF SING., arts. 9–16.

[154] *Sivarasa Rasiah*, [2010] 2 MALAYAN L.J. 333, at [3].

[155] *Id.*

[156] *Id.* at [5].

liberty "save in accordance with law" encompasses an implied right of access to justice.[157]

More recently, the 2018 case of *Indira Gandhi* displayed a purposive interpretive approach used to achieve a rights-protective outcome. Ruling that both parents must consent to a child's change of religious status, the Court used what it called a "purposive interpretation" of the constitutional text to interpret the word "parent" to mean "parents."[158] According to the Court, a "purposive reading" of the provision that "promotes the welfare of the child and is consistent with good sense" would require the consent of both parents for a child's religious conversion.[159] To endorse this "purposive approach," the Court drew from the Canadian Supreme Court's jurisprudence, citing with approval a recent decision stating that "constitutional documents be interpreted in a broad and purposive manner," informed by foundational constitutional principles like democracy, constitutionalism, and the rule of law.[160] The Malaysian Federal Court's endeavored to determine the underlying purpose of the rights provision and then to interpret the scope of protection for the right in light of that purpose.

The Court viewed such a purposive approach as going hand in hand with a "broad" or "generous" approach to constitutional interpretation; after all, "constitutional provisions are not to be interpreted literally or pedantically."[161] A purposive account of constitutional interpretation allows courts to take a holistic view of what a constitutional rights provision protects in light of the overarching purposes motivating the constitutional project.

In another 2018 decision, the Federal Court affirmed that "the courts must always be vigilant to any interpretation which may dilute the importance of any constitutional rights of this country."[162] Emphasizing that "in this country we practise constitutional supremacy as opposed to parliamentary supremacy," the Court declared that "it is incumbent on the Courts when interpreting any statutes, resort must be made to the Federal Constitution when appropriate to do so."

Approaching constitutional rights adjudication in a generous, purposive interpretive manner has another salutary implication. Unlike constitutional interpretation mired in an insular approach, a broader approach to rights interpretation looks beyond the confines of the "four walls" of the domestic constitution.[163] The Malaysian Federal Court's decision in *Indira Gandhi* is aligned with the lower High

[157] *Id.* at [4]; FED. CONST. (MALAY.), art. 5(1) ("No person shall be deprived of his life or personal liberty save in accordance with law.").

[158] *Indira Gandhi* (F.C.), [2018] 1 MALAYAN L.J. 545, at [181]; FED. CONST. (MALAY.), art. 12(4) ("[T]he religion of a person under the age of eighteen years shall be decided by his parent or guardian.").

[159] *Indira Gandhi* (F.C.), [2018] 1 MALAYAN L.J. 545, at [164].

[160] *Id.* at [29] (citing Reference re Senate Reform [2014] 1 SCR 704 (Canada)).

[161] *Id.* at [154].

[162] Tenaga Nasional Berhad v. Bukit Lenang Development Sdn Bhd [2018] M.Y.F.C. 26, at [28] (quoting the Federal Court's earlier decision in Datuk Seri Khalid Abu Bakar & Ors. v. N. Indra P Nallathamby & Anor Appeal [2014] 9 CURRENT L.J. 15).

[163] *See* Chapter 2, Constitutional Adjudication and Constitutional Politics, section IV(A).

Court's decision, which it found "consistent with other fundamental provisions in the Constitution" and "international norms and conventions vesting equal rights in both parents."[164] This is especially notable given that the Court of Appeal had rebuked the High Court on this precise point, declaring that paying close attention to international norms is "not in tandem" with "accepted principles of constitutional interpretation."[165] Not so according to the Federal Court, which overruled the Court of Appeal in a decision that endorsed a purposive and outward-looking approach to constitutional interpretation.

For rights to be effectively protected, they must be interpreted generously within the context of a constitutional framework that explicitly guarantees such rights. A purposive or prismatic interpretive approach orients courts toward considering the broader purposes underlying the constitution and also resists parochialism in constitutional practice.

C. Proportionality Analysis

Over the last half century proportionality has emerged as a key mechanism for courts throughout the world in adjudicating rights claims.[166] Long part of the standard practice of courts in Europe, as well as in common law systems like the United Kingdom and Canada, proportionality analysis has also spread to newer democracies, like Israel, South Africa, and the Latin American countries of Colombia, Mexico, and Brazil, where it has become a become a dominant judicial tool in rights review.

For courts in many of these contexts, proportionality has replaced doctrines of deference to legislatures and executives.[167] Judicial balancing instead "necessitates a judicial examination of the functioning of the political branches."[168] Such an approach requires courts to assess the suitability of the challenged law and the importance of the government's objective. Proportionality provides courts with a powerful instrument that enables them to adjudicate rights more effectively and to renegotiate their relationship with the political branches.

"Asia is proportionality's new frontier," as Alec Stone Sweet and Jud Mathews proclaim.[169] Yet, among Asian courts, only the judiciaries of Taiwan, South Korea,

[164] These international conventions include the Universal Declaration of Human Rights (UDHR), the Convention of the Rights of the Child, and the Convention on the Elimination of All Forms of Discrimination Against Women (CEDAW). *Indira Gandhi* (F.C.), [2018] 1 MALAYAN L.J. 545, at [144].

[165] *Indira Gandhi* (C.A.), [2016] 4 MALAYAN L.J. 455, at [66].

[166] *See* Alec Stone Sweet & Jud Mathews, *Proportionality Balancing and Global Constitutionalism*, 47 COLUM. J. TRANSNAT'L L. 72 (2008) (discussing the diffusion of proportionality globally); *see also* NIELS PETERSEN, PROPORTIONALITY AND JUDICIAL ACTIVISM 6 (2017) (noting that "some form of proportionality test is used by most courts exercising judicial review outside of the United States today").

[167] *See* Sweet & Mathews, *supra* note 166, at 79.

[168] Dixon & Issacharoff, *supra* note 59, at 709.

[169] Alec Stone Sweet & Jud Mathews, *Proportionality and Rights Protection in Asia: Hong Kong, Malaysia, South Korea, Taiwan—Whither Singapore?*, 29 SING. ACAD. L.J. 774, 775 (2017).

and Hong Kong have developed a structured form of proportionality that has been applied regularly against the government.[170] In other parts of Asia, notably Southeast Asia, judicial adoption of proportionality has been haphazard and weak. While the Indonesian Constitutional Court has accepted on occasion that laws derogating from constitutional rights must be proportionate, it has not applied proportionality robustly or routinely.[171] The Constitutional Court of Thailand has sometimes relied on a form of proportionality in its constitutional jurisprudence and has held in recent decisions that laws restricting rights must be "appropriate, necessary, and proportional." Nevertheless, the court has not often invalidated laws for failing proportionality and still defers substantially to lawmakers.[172] Singapore has stubbornly rejected any form of proportionality, with its courts remaining attached to formalized doctrines of deference to the political branches.[173]

Of particular significance, then, is how the Malaysian Federal Court managed to establish, apply, and deepen a proportionality doctrine in its constitutional jurisprudence. That doctrinal journey has taken various twists and turns. Judicial endorsement of proportionality initially emerged in the 2010 case of *Sivarasa Rasiah*,[174] which involved a challenge to a statute preventing a Bar Council member holding office in a political party, the same case in which the Court advocated a "prismatic," purposive approach toward interpreting fundamental liberties.[175] The Federal Court expressly adopted a proportionality framework in assessing whether the statute violated the right to equal protection:

> The test here is whether the legislative state action is disproportionate to the legislation it passes . . . whether: "(i) the legislative objective is sufficiently important to justify limiting a fundamental right; (ii) the measures designed to meet the legislative objective are rationally connected to it; and (iii) the means used to impair the right or freedom are no more than is necessary to accomplish the objective."[176]

In that case, the Court found the challenged provision to be proportionate after taking into account the public interest involved in insulating the Bar Council from

[170] *See* Po Jen Yap, *Introduction* to PROPORTIONALITY IN ASIA 1 (Po Jen Yap ed., forthcoming 2020) (manuscript on file with author).

[171] *See* Stefanus Hendrianto, *Against the Currents: The Indonesian Constitutional Court in an Age of Proportionality*, *in* PROPORTIONALITY IN ASIA 169 (Po Jen Yap ed., forthcoming 2020) (manuscript on file with author).

[172] *See* Narongdech Srukhosit, *Manifest Disproportionality and the Constitutional Court of Thailand*, *in* PROPORTIONALITY IN ASIA 192, 198–99 (Po Jen Yap ed., forthcoming 2020) (manuscript on file with author) (citing CCD No.8/B.E.2561 (2018), 26 December 2018 [Royal Gazette Vol.136, Part 9A, 23 January 2019]; CCD No.4/B.E.2561 (2018), 5 June 2018 [Royal Gazette Vol.135, Part 45A, 29 June 2018]).

[173] *See* Sweet & Mathews, *Proportionality and Rights Protection in Asia*, *supra* note 169, 795–98.

[174] *Sivarasa Rasiah*, [2010] 2 MALAYAN L.J. 333.

[175] *Id.* at [3].

[176] *Id.* at [29] (citing de Freitas v. Permanent Sec'y of Ministry of Ag., Fisheries, Lands and Housing [1998] UKPC 30).

political influence and that lawyer-politicians were not restricted from practicing law or speaking at Bar Council meetings.[177] Still, in a comparison-laden opinion which cited judicial decisions on proportionality from the United Kingdom, South Africa, Canada, and India,[178] the *Sivarasa* Court established legitimacy for a proportionality analysis in Malaysian constitutional rights adjudication.

Later cases endorsed this proportionality framework. In *Azmi Sharom*, the Federal Court cited the proportionality test in a freedom of expression challenge to the Sedition Act, although it ended up not striking down the law.[179] Shortly after, the Court of Appeal invalidated a part of the sedition law in *Mat Shuhaimi bin Shafiei*,[180] observing that Malaysian jurisprudence on fundamental liberties guarantees "had now evolved to a stage" that any valid legislation had to "meet the test of proportionality," which it declared "an entrenched part" of Malaysian law.[181] Still, the application of proportionality among various Malaysian courts remained sporadic at this stage.

Then the Malaysian Federal Court delivered its 2019 decision in *Alma Nudo v. Public Prosecutor.*[182] In this landmark ruling by a full nine-member bench of the Federal Court, the apex court struck down as unconstitutional a statutory provision that allowed a presumption of possession and knowledge to apply against accused drug traffickers. The Court explicitly endorsed a three-stage proportionality analysis: first, whether there is a sufficiently important objective to justify infringement of the right; second, whether the means designed by Parliament have a rational nexus with the objective they are intended to meet; and, third, whether the restriction on fundamental rights is proportionate to the importance of the right at stake.[183] In that case, the Federal Court found that "the unacceptably severe incursion into the right [to life and liberty] of the accused under Article 5(1) is disproportionate to the aim of curbing crime" and failed to satisfy "the requirement of proportionality housed under Article 8(1)."[184]

Strikingly, and importantly, the Court held that the Article 8(1) equal protection guarantee "imports the principle of substantive proportionality."[185] In so doing, the Court located a textual basis for proportionality in the Malaysian Constitution itself, which it underscored by stating that the doctrine of proportionality forms "part of Malaysian common law, developed by our Courts based on a prismatic interpretation of the FC without recourse to case law relating to the European

[177] *Id.* at [33].
[178] *Id.* at [28]–[31].
[179] Public Prosecutor v. Azmi Sharom [2015] M.L.J.U. 594.
[180] [2017] 1 MALAYAN L.J. 436. The Court of Appeal's decision was later overruled by the Federal Court on procedural grounds.
[181] *Id.* at [25].
[182] [2019] 5 CURRENT L.J. 780.
[183] *Id.* [143]–[145].
[184] *Id.* at [150].
[185] *Id.* at [118]; FED. CONST. (MALAY.), art. 8(1) ("All persons are equal before the law and entitled to equal protection of the law.").

Convention of Human Rights."[186] With the Malaysian Federal Court's explicit embrace of proportionality in *Alma Nudo*, the doctrine now appears to have a firmly entrenched basis in Malaysia's constitutional landscape.

In stark contrast, Singapore courts have staunchly resisted any form of proportionality analysis in their judicial decision-making. "Proportionality is a more exacting requirement than reasonableness," observed the Singapore High Court in *dicta* in 2006, before pointedly rejecting it. "[T]he notion of proportionality has never been part of the common law in relation to the judicial review of the exercise of a legislative and/or an administrative power or discretion. Nor has it ever been part of Singapore law."[187] Singapore is a outlier in this regard among the Asian courts of South Korea, Taiwan, Hong Kong, and now Malaysia.[188] Singaporean courts remain attached to "formalized deference doctrines," like *Wednesbury* reasonableness or manifest arbitrariness, which "deprives rights ... of their *juridical* existence."[189]

Proportionality provides a framework for adjudicating constitutional rights that is robust yet nuanced, a potent tool for courts in developing democracies in Asia and elsewhere. By subjecting both government interests and rights to balancing, it empowers courts to engage political institutions directly. Unlike a judicial deference frame, under which courts leave the scope of rights to be primarily determined by the political branches, a balancing frame requires courts to assess the government's justification for its action. Courts are tasked with scrutinizing the exercise of political power and the state's justifications for limiting rights. Proportionality analysis enables courts in Asian dominant party systems "to engage ruling parties directly, even when it comes to highly sensitive policy areas."[190]

At the same time, proportionality's balancing framework provides a nuanced instrument for rights adjudication. Compared to either a deferential posture to the political branches or a categorical approach to rights as trumps, proportionality allows judges greater flexibility in dealing with hard cases. But it also structures the process of judicial discretion, requiring judges to be more forthright about the steps in their decision-making.[191] What a proportionality frame takes seriously is that judges have a duty to provide reasoned arguments for their decisions; it promotes greater transparency about the basis of a judicial outcome.

Relatedly, a proportionality approach offers a response to the universalism and cultural relativism dichotomy perpetuated by the "Asian values" debate.[192] Under

[186] *Alma Nudo*, [2019] 5 Current L.J. 780, at [126].

[187] Chee Siok Chin v. Minister of Home Aff. [2006] 1 Sing. L. Rep. (R.) 582, at [88].

[188] Sweet & Mathews, *Proportionality and Rights Protection in Asia, supra* note 169, at 796.

[189] *Id.* at 798.

[190] *Id.* at 796.

[191] *See* Aharon Barak, *Proportionality: Sources, Nature, Function, in* The Oxford Handbook of Comparative Constitutional Law 129 (2012); David Beatty, The Ultimate Rule of Law 172 (2004).

[192] Sweet & Mathews, *Proportionality and Rights Protection in Asia, supra* note 169, at 798.

a balancing frame, rights are not universal absolutes that require a categorical approach of the sort favored by a Herculean judge that regards as rights as trumps.[193] Quite the opposite. Proportionality envisages that the way rights are applied will necessarily depend on the context, and may be limited when justified in the public interest. "Courts that enforce the proportionality principle," as Stone Sweet and Mathews put it, "are squarely in the business of adapting (abstract) rights to (concrete) circumstances."[194]

Judicial habits hardly die easily. Many Asian courts continue to operate under a mindset of substantially deferring to the political branches, as the Singaporean case illustrates, or even deferring jurisdiction to other bodies like the religious courts, as has often been the case with Malaysia's civil courts. But proportionality is a subtle instrument: it can be adapted to allow for deference to the state when necessary, and sometimes courts may well find that the governmental interest outweighs the individual right at stake. Crucially, though, a proportionality framework does not allow courts to abdicate from assessing whether the government's restrictions can be justified, and thus empowers courts to enforce constitutional rights against the state.

V. Conclusion

As a matter of design, the constitutions of the twentieth and twenty-first centuries, by and large, endow courts with the power of strong judicial review. Courts in these democracies, including Malaysia and Singapore, have a constitutional role to check majoritarian power and protect fundamental principles of the constitutional order. But constitutional realities do not necessarily reflect the constitutional text. Courts in evolving democracies have had to negotiate their position within cultures where, in the face of dominant political power, constitutional guardrails have not been entrenched. Against this backdrop, the Malaysian apex court's 2017 and 2018 decisions are striking examples of judicial assertiveness aimed strategically at strengthening the courts' position as a constitutional bulwark.

The Malaysian Federal Court's assertions of judicial power, which occurred even before the democratic transition in 2018, have become all the more relevant now.[195] The courts have to renegotiate the dynamics of their relationship with the political branches in Malaysia's fragile political order. With the judicial strategies that have begun to emerge in contemporary constitutional jurisprudence, courts are poised to entrench and develop core constitutional principles. Safeguarding

[193] Jamal Greene, *Foreword: Rights as Trumps?*, 132 Harv. L. Rev. 28 (2018).

[194] Sweet & Mathews, *Proportionality and Rights Protection in Asia*, *supra* note 169, at 798.

[195] *Malaysia Election: Opposition Scores Historic Victory*, BBC (May 10, 2018), https://perma.cc/LD7U-36BB; *but see Malaysia Gets New PM, Muhyiddin Yassin, After Week of Turmoil*, BBC (Mar. 1, 2020), https://perma.cc/TU7E-PYSB.

the basic structure of the constitution through judicial review of constitutional amendments, interpreting constitutional rights in light of the constitution's overarching purposes, and developing a robust, yet nuanced, proportionality analysis in rights adjudication offer important tools for the endeavor of constructing constitutionalism.

PART III
APPLYING CONSTITUTIONAL ADJUDICATION IN PRACTICE

7
Judicializing Religion

I. Introduction

On March 31, 2009, Indira Gandhi, a Hindu kindergarten teacher living in the Malaysian city of Ipoh, was in the midst of a heated argument with her husband.[1] Sixteen years earlier, Indira Gandhi and her husband, both Hindus at the time, had married under Malaysia's civil law governing non-Muslim marriages,[2] and they now had three children together. The argument escalated, and culminated abruptly when her husband forcibly snatched their eleven-month-old daughter away from her before speeding off on his motorbike.[3]

When Indira Gandhi reported her youngest child's abduction to the police, she found out that her husband had formally converted to Islam. She later learnt that he had also changed the religious status of their children to Islam without her knowledge. He had then obtained custody orders for all three children from the Sharia Court, which has jurisdiction over Muslim personal and family law. As a non-Muslim with no legal standing in the religious courts, Indira Gandhi turned to the civil courts, filing a petition challenging the legality of her children's religious conversions and seeking to obtain custody. And so began a protracted legal battle, spanning almost a decade and drawing nationwide attention, before being decided in 2018 by the Malaysian Federal Court.

Indira Gandhi's case foregrounds fundamental questions about religion, the Constitution, and the state in Malaysia. Indira Gandhi's dispute, along with many others, is fraught because of the complicated relationship between the civil courts and religious courts as well as between Islam's position and individual rights in the constitutional order. Courts and law are especially salient in matters of religion and the state because these legal disputes are central to the struggle over the Constitution's identity.[4] At stake is a broader contestation over the contemporary Malaysian state's secular or religious character.

[1] Indira Gandhi a/p Mutho v. Pengarah Jabatan Agama Islam Perak [2013] 5 Malayan L.J. 552 (H.C.) [hereinafter *Indira Gandhi* (H.C.)].

[2] Law Reform (Marriage and Divorce) Act 1976 (Act 164).

[3] *See* Eileen Ng, *Malaysia's Sharia Law Costs Non-Muslims Their Kids*, AP (Nov. 10, 2014), https://perma.cc/CN4J-CQU9.

[4] *See* Tamir Moustafa, Constituting Religion: Islam, Liberal Rights, and the Malaysian State (2018).

Constitutional Statecraft in Asian Courts. Yvonne Tew, Oxford University Press (2020). © Yvonne Tew.
DOI:10.1093/oso/9780198716839.001.0001

This chapter focuses on the judicialization of religion in Malaysia.[5] Malaysia regulates religion more extensively than most countries in the world. In 2017, the Pew Research Center ranked Malaysia third—after China and Iran—among 198 countries in an index of government restrictions on religion.[6] Religious identity in Malaysia is not merely a matter of personal conscience; it is regulated by comprehensive legal and religious codes that encompass criminal law, family law, and personal law. All of this regulation operates within a dual court system comprising civil courts and religious courts.

Religion has become one of the great fault lines of modern Malaysian politics and adjudication. Politicization of religion over the past quarter century, fueled by religion's intimate connection to race and ethnicity, has led to polarizing debate over the Malaysian state's identity. At the heart of this debate are Malaysia's constitutional arrangements on religion. Article 3(1) of the Constitution declares: "Islam is the religion of the Federation; but other religions may be practised in peace and harmony." The Constitution also contains a bill of rights, including the right in Article 11(1) "to profess and practice" one's religion.

This chapter examines the constitution-making process of these religion clauses to locate the role of Islam and the right to religious freedom within the Constitution's original framework. The Malaysian Constitution's recognition of a state religion was drafted as part of a social contract struck at the founding to accommodate the competing demands of various ethnic and religious communities. Malaysia's pluralistic society is made up of a Malay-Muslim majority group and non-Malay ethnic minorities who identify as Buddhists, Christians, Hindus, or others. According to a 2010 census, Malays constitute more than 60 percent of the country's population, while the Chinese and Indians constitute approximately 25 percent and 7.3 percent respectively.[7]

Over the past quarter of a century, the politicization and judicialization of religion has expanded the role of Islam and transformed the original constitutional arrangements on religion. Courts have played a key role in the expansion of religion in the Malaysian public order. As this chapter shows, courts have judicialized religion through jurisdictional deference to the religious courts and judicial

[5] This chapter focuses on the role of Islam and religion in the Malaysian constitutional order. Unlike Malaysia, the Constitution of Singapore does not establish any particular religion. Nevertheless, Singapore's constitution does authorize state intervention in religion, and the Singaporean state has regulated religion in various ways, usually by controlling religious activities in the name of public or social order. Singaporean courts have generally been willing to decide in favor of state limitations on individual religious liberty rights. *See generally* Jaclyn Neo, *Secular Constitutionalism in Singapore: Between Equality and Hierarchy*, 5 Oxford J. L. & Rel. 431 (2016) (arguing that while Singapore's political discourse has centered on claims of state neutrality and equal treatment of all religions, its legal jurisprudence displays a clear priority of secular over religious laws and authorities).

[6] *See* Pew Research Center, Government Restrictions on Religion in 2017, Appendix A: Government Restrictions Index, https://perma.cc/5G3K-VS5Q.

[7] *See* Population and Housing Census of Malaysia, Population Distribution and Basic Demographic Characteristic Report 2010, https://perma.cc/2LBT-VP64.

Islamization by expanding Islam's position through constitutional interpretation. Malaysia's bifurcated legal structure has resulted in tensions over jurisdictional authority between the secular federal courts and religious state courts. That fraught context between the civil and religious courts makes the Malaysian Federal Court's 2018 decision in *Indira Gandhi* especially significant.[8] The case marks a sea change in the civil courts' approach to religion and rights, and their judicial authority over the religious courts.[9]

The final part of this chapter turns from the descriptive to the prescriptive. It discusses how courts can draw on the constitutional basic structure doctrine to entrench the judicial power of the civil courts to reclaim jurisdictional areas involving constitutional rights that they have ceded to the religious courts in the past, such as apostasy and religious conversion. It also outlines a purposive interpretive approach in line with the Constitution's framework of protection for religious minorities and individual rights and shows how the court can operationalize a proportionality analysis in rights claims.

II. Constitutionalizing Religion

The Malayan Constitution was born when the Federation gained independence from the British in 1957.[10] Later, when Singapore, Sabah, and Sarawak merged with Malaya to create the Federation of Malaysia in 1963, that independence constitution became the Federal Constitution of Malaysia. The constitution that was drafted at the birth of the new nation was based on a constitutional bargain struck at the founding. As a result of negotiations between various religious and racial groups, the drafters eventually included the Article 3(1) constitutional declaration: "Islam is the religion of the Federation; but other religions may be practised in peace and harmony."[11] Understanding the Article 3(1) constitutional declaration requires locating it in historical and political context.

The 1957 constitution-making process was meant to establish a generally secular state; it was not aimed at creating a constitutional theocracy.[12] The constitutional commission chaired by Lord Reid initially rejected the suggestion that a provision establishing Islam as the religion of the Federation should be included

[8] Indira Gandhi a/p Mutho v. Pengarah Jabatan Agama Islam Perak & Ors. [2018] 1 MALAYAN L.J. 545 (F.C.) [hereinafter *Indira Gandhi* (F.C.)].

[9] Shanmuga Kanesalingam, *Judges, Lawyers, Politics: Religion Still Divides Malaysia*, IMMANENT FRAME (July 11, 2019), https://perma.cc/Z89G-3AZS.

[10] *See* Chapter 3, Constitutional History, section II(A).

[11] FED. CONST. (MALAY.), art. 3(1).

[12] *See* DIAN SHAH, CONSTITUTIONS, RELIGION, AND POLITICS IN ASIA: INDONESIA, MALAYSIA AND SRI LANKA 46 (2017).

in the new constitution.[13] The Reid Commission's decision not to include a state religion clause decision was supported by the Malay rulers of the individual states in the Federation, who were concerned that a clause establishing an official religion would encroach on their traditional positions as the head of Islam of their respective states.[14]

The main push for constitutionalizing Islam as the religion of the Federation came from the Alliance, the predecessor to the Barisan Nasional coalition that would dominate Malaysian politics for the next six decades.[15] The Alliance was composed of three parties, each representing the three major ethnic groups in Malaya: the United Malays National Organisation (UMNO), the Malayan Chinese Association (MCA), and the Malayan Indian Congress (MIC). Race and religion were thus structured into the heart of modern Malaysian politics. Anxious that the country's historical and cultural traditions would be threatened by the growing non-Malay population, comprising primarily Chinese and Indian immigrants,[16] UMNO sought to include a state religion clause in the new constitution. It did so not because it wanted an Islamic theocracy, but as part of a larger package of demands connected to Malay special privileges, language, and citizenship.[17]

Significantly, there was no suggestion that a declaration of a state religion would affect the new nation's status as a secular state—not even from those pushing for Islam as the state religion. The Alliance Party's own memorandum declared: "The religion of Malaysia shall be Islam. The observance of this principle shall not impose any disability on non-Muslim nationals professing and practicing their own religions, and shall not imply that the State is not a secular State."[18] And even as the Reid Commission rejected the Alliance's initial proposal, it nevertheless emphasized that if such a provision were to be inserted, there was "universal agreement" that "it would not in any way affect the civil rights of non-Muslims."[19]

Only one member of the Reid Constitutional Commission supported a constitutional clause declaring Islam as the state religion. Justice Abdul Hamid from

[13] For an examination of the historical sources on the drafting of the role of Islam in the Malaysian Constitution, see Joseph M. Fernando, *The Position of Islam in the Constitution of Malaysia*, 37 J. SE. ASIAN STUD. 249 (2006).

[14] *See* FEDERATION OF MALAY CONSTITUTIONAL COMMISSION, REPORT OF 1956-57 § COLONIAL NO. 330 [hereinafter REID REPORT].

[15] The Alliance and its successor, Barisan Nasional, governed the country for sixty-one years consecutively until the Barisan Nasional's upset in the 2018 Malaysian general elections when the Pakatan Harapan coalition took over the federal government.

[16] SHAH, *supra* note 12, at 28.

[17] *See* Kristen Stilt, *Contextualizing Constitutional Islam: The Malayan Experience*, 13 INT'L J. CONST. L. 407, 430 (2015).

[18] Alliance Memorandum to the Reid Constitutional Commission, Sept. 27, 1956, at 19.

[19] REID REPORT, *supra* note 14, at [169]. In a letter to the Reid Commission, the Secretary of State for the Colonies, Alan Lennox-Boyd, emphasized the need for freedom of religion to be guaranteed in the Constitution. The Straits Chinese British Association, among other non-Muslim organizations, likewise urged the Reid Commission to ensure that there was "no discrimination against any citizen on the grounds of religion, race, sex, place of birth, or any of them." Fernando, *supra* note 13, at 265.

Pakistan, in an about-turn from his earlier position during the constitution drafting process, wrote a separate dissenting note endorsing a state religion clause. Yet even he thought that such a provision would be "innocuous."[20] He maintained that such a clause would not "impose any disability on non-Muslim citizens" nor "prevent the State from being a secular State."[21] Similar establishment clauses existed in many constitutions around the world, he observed, including the "Christian countries" of Ireland, Norway, Denmark, Spain, Argentina, Bolivia, Panama, and Paraguay as well as the "Muslim countries" of Afghanistan, Iran, Iraq, Jordan, Saudi Arabia, and Syria.[22]

A constitutional working group was put together to review the Reid Commission's draft constitution. The Alliance argued for Islam as the state religion, but insisted that including such a provision would serve a symbolic purpose, rather than have any practical effect.[23] Tunku Abdul Rahman, the leader of the Alliance who would become Malaysia's first prime minister, declared that "the whole Constitution was framed on the basis that the Federation would be a secular state."[24]

Representatives from the non-Malay communities eventually agreed to the Islamic constitutional clause on the basis of explicit guarantees that the declaration was symbolic and would not compromise non-Muslim rights.[25] The political settlement was part of a larger compromise among the Malay and non-Malay groups; non-Malays were assured of citizenship and the right to be educated in their mother tongue. The Article 3(1) constitutional clause "was the result of a political act and a social compromise, motivated by the desire to minimize resistance from various sections of the community."[26]

The common understanding shared by all key stakeholders in the constitution-making process—that constitutionalizing Islam would not undermine the state's secular basis—is documented in numerous historical sources. The London Colonial Office eventually accepted the working party's recommendation to include a clause declaring Islam the state religion on the understanding that the declaration's effect was "more political than practical."[27] It noted that the Alliance delegation "stressed that they had no intention of creating a Muslim theocracy and that Malaya would be a secular State." Back in Malaya, the Alliance government

[20] Reid Report, *supra* note 14, at [12].
[21] *Id.* at [11].
[22] *Id.* at [12].
[23] Fernando, *supra* note 13, at 260.
[24] *Id.* at 258 (citing Minutes of the 19th Meeting of the Working Party, Apr. 17, 1957, CO 941/87). Historian Joseph Fernando calls Tunku's statement "the clearest indication of the intentions of the framers." *Id.* at 266.
[25] *Id.* at 258.
[26] Shah, *supra* note 12, at 46.
[27] Fernando, *supra* note 13, at 260 (citing Memorandum by Jackson, Colonial Office, May 23, 1957, CO 1030/494 (20)).

tabled a white paper in Parliament on the new draft constitutional document, which explained:

> There has been included in the proposed Federation Constitution a declaration that Islam is the religion of the Federation. This will in no way affect the present position of the Federation as a secular state, and every person will have the right to profess and practice his own religion and the right to propagate his religion[.][28]

Soon after, the British Parliament passed the Federation of Malaya Independence Bill, crystallizing the newly drafted Constitution into force and creating a sovereign state.

What seems clear is that all those involved in creating the Constitution—the Reid Commission, the working party, the Alliance Party, the Malay rulers, and the non-Muslim communities—intended to create a generally secular constitutional arrangement for the new state. The text of Article 3 reflects this basic understanding. Article 3(1) declares that "Islam is the religion of the Federation" along with a guarantee that "other religions may be practised in peace and harmony." What's more, Article 3(4) specifies that: "Nothing in this Article derogates from any other provision of this Constitution,"[29] which includes the constitutional guarantees of fundamental rights.

Under the Malaysian Constitution's bill of rights, Article 11(1) protects "the right to profess and practice" one's religion.[30] Individual states may regulate the propagation of religious doctrine among Muslims,[31] although there are no restrictions on proselytizing to non-Muslims. Religious freedom is also subject to limitations relating to public order, public health or morality.[32] The Article 8 equal protection guarantee prohibits discrimination based on religion, except for Islamic personal law matters.[33] Article 12 of the Malaysian Constitution allows religious communities to establish religious institutions for children's education.[34] It also guarantees that "[n]o person shall be required to receive instruction in or to take part in any

[28] *Id.* at 262 (citing White Paper on the Federation of Malaya Constitutional Proposals 1957, 18 (Kuala Lumpur: Government Printer, 1957), Legislative Council Paper No. 42 of 1957).

[29] *See, e.g.*, HARRY E. GROVES & L.A. SHERIDAN, THE CONSTITUTION OF MALAYSIA 31 (1987); Tommy Thomas, *Is Malaysia an Islamic State?*, 4 MALAYAN L.J. xv, xxix (2006); SHAD SALEEM FARUQI, DOCUMENT OF DESTINY: THE CONSTITUTION OF THE FEDERATION OF MALAYSIA 135 (2008).

[30] FED. CONST. (MALAY.), art. 11(1).

[31] *Id.* art. 11(4) ("State law and in respect of the Federal Territories of Kuala Lumpur, Labuan and Putrajaya, federal law may control or restrict the propagation of any religious doctrine or belief among persons professing the religion of Islam.").

[32] *Id.* art. 11(5) ("This Article does not authorize any act contrary to any general law relating to public order, public health or morality.").

[33] *Id.* art. 8(2) ("Except as expressly authorized by this Constitution, there shall be no discrimination against citizens on the ground only of religion, race, descent, place of birth or gender[.]"); *id.* art. 8(5) (specifying exception for any provision "regulating personal law" or any provision or restricting office or employment connected with the affairs of any religion or of an institution managed by a group professing any religion").

[34] *Id.* arts. 12(1)–(2).

ceremony or act of worship of a religion other than his own,"[35] and specifies that a minor's religion shall be determined by their parent.[36]

Civil courts and Sharia courts have separate jurisdictions under the constitutional framework. Unlike the federal civil courts, which have general jurisdiction over civil and criminal laws, state Sharia courts are limited to personal law and "offences against the precepts of Islam" and only over "persons professing the religion of Islam."[37] A constitutional amendment in 1988 inserted a provision specifying that the civil courts "shall have no jurisdiction in respect of any matter within the jurisdiction of the Sharia Courts."[38] Heated debate ensued over the impact of Article 121(1A). Many view Article 121(1A) as doing no more than preventing civil courts from interfering in matters spelled out in the Constitution as properly within the jurisdiction of the Islamic courts.[39] Others, however, argue that Article 121(1A) prevents review of Sharia court decisions and, in effect, elevated the Sharia courts to be equal in status to the civil courts.[40]

Finally, something must be said how identity based on religion and race appear inextricably connected in Malaysia. The Constitution defines "Malay" as "a person who *professes the religion of Islam*, habitually speaks the Malay language, conforms to Malay custom," and is domiciled in the country,[41] thus fusing ethnic and religious identity. Because the Constitution enshrines special privileges for the Malay (and Muslim) majority, debate over the place of religion are often closely tied to anxieties over race and the special position of the Malays. In Malaysian public discourse over religion, "race is never far behind."[42]

III. Politicizing Religion

Religion has become a fault line in contemporary Malaysia politics in recent decades. The politicization of Islam was at the forefront of the battleground between

[35] *Id.* art. 12(3).

[36] *Id.* art. 12(4) ("For the purposes of Clause (3) the religion of a person under the age of eighteen years shall be decided by his parent or guardian.").

[37] *Id.* art. 74(2), sched. 9, list II, item 1. Schedule II specifies that these matters include marriage, divorce, inheritance, custody, and offences against Islamic precepts.

[38] *Id.* art. 121(1A).

[39] *See, e.g.*, Li-ann Thio, *Jurisdictional Imbroglio: Civil and Religious Courts, Turf Wars and Article 121(1A) of the Federal Constitution*, *in* Constitutional Landmarks in Malaysia: The First 50 Years 202 (Andrew Harding & H.P. Lee eds., 2007);. Andrew Harding, Law, Government, and the Constitution in Malaysia 136–37 (1996); Shanmuga Kanesalingam, *Article 121(1A)—What Does It Really Mean?*, Loyar Burok (Dec. 11, 2006), https://perma.cc/G7WQ-V5PH.

[40] *See, e.g.*, Hassan Saeed, *Apostasy Laws in Malaysia: Jurisdiction and Constitutionality*, *in* Freedom of Religion, Apostasy and Islam 149, 150 (Abdullah Saeed & Hassan Saeed eds., 2004) ("The objective of the new clause, therefore, was to prevent the High Court from exercising its power of judicial review over decisions of the Syariah court.").

[41] Fed. Const. (Malay.), art. 160(2) (emphasis added).

[42] Jaclyn Neo, *Constituting Religion, Contesting Constitutional Identity*, Immanent Frame (July 18, 2019), https://perma.cc/J8LV-GQ9Z.

UMNO, the Malay party in the Barisan Nasional coalition, and the Malaysian Islamic Party, Parti Islam Se-Malaysia (PAS), an Islamist opposition party. Malaysia's Islamization phenomenon was initially spurred by the Islamic revival movements in the late 1970s and 1980s, following the Iranian revolution in the Middle East.[43] Amidst this growing Islamic consciousness, in 1990, PAS gained control of the state government of Kelantan. It would later also form the state government in Terengganu from 1999 to 2004. PAS's political platform was to project itself as the authentic Islamic party, and as more Islamic than the Barisan Nasional government. In response, UMNO sought to expand its own Islamic credentials by setting out a series of Islamic initiatives. This set the stage for an Islamization race between PAS and UMNO, beginning in the 1980s and intensifying throughout the 1990s, to secure the support of the Malay-Muslim electorate.[44]

Against this backdrop of political competition between UMNO and PAS, in a speech given on September 29, 2001, Prime Minister Mahathir Mohamad made an unprecedented declaration: "UMNO wishes to state clearly that Malaysia is an Islamic state."[45] In 2013, Najib Razak, Malaysia's sixth prime minister, affirmed UMNO's commitment to uphold Islam's position and Malaysia's position as an Islamic state; later, in 2017, Najib Razak's administration maintained that the Barisan Nasional government remained dedicated to an Islamic agenda.[46]

The growing Islamization in Malaysia's public discourse pushed Islam's constitutional position into the spotlight. The Article 3(1) clause declaring Islam as the religion of the state became a focal point of the debate. Supporters of an Islamic state argued that Article 3(1) justifies an elevated position for Islam vis-à-vis other religions.[47] Secularists defended the state's secular nature, arguing that an expanded role for Islam is inconsistent with the framers' vision.[48] Others have

[43] *See* HUSSIN MUTALIB, ISLAM IN MALAYSIA: FROM REVIVALISM TO ISLAMIC STATE? (1993); Jaclyn Neo, *Malay Nationalism, Islamic Supremacy and the Constitutional Bargain in the Multi-ethnic Composition of Malaysia*, 13 INT'L J. ON MINORITY & GROUP RTS. 95, 103–104 (2006).

[44] *See* JOSEPH LIOW, PIETY AND POLITICS: ISLAMISM IN CONTEMPORARY MALAYSIA 73-148 (2009).

[45] *See* Mahathir Mohamad, Prime Minister of Malaysia, Speech at the 30th Annual General Meeting of the Gerakan Party Malaysia (Sept. 29, 2001), at [18], https://perma.cc/DL8R-RQ2S (translated from Malay by the author); *see also Mahathir: Malaysia is "Fundamentalist State"*, CNN (June 18, 2002), https://perma.cc/KQE6-GZNU.

[46] *Full Text of UMNO Presidential Speech*, NEW STRAITS TIMES (Nov. 27, 2014), https://perma.cc/ZS4X-5J7C. *BN Government Committed to Make Malaysia an Islamic State*, MALAY MAIL (Oct. 14, 2017), https://perma.cc/2QLY-PSH8.

[47] *See, e.g.*, Mohamed Ismail Shariff, *The Legislative Jurisdiction of the Federal Parliament in Matters Involving Islamic Law*, 3 MALAYAN L.J. cv, cx (2005) ("[T[here is no reason to circumscribe [Article 3] meaning to rituals and ceremonies only . . . what the framers of the Constitution have in fact done is to resurrect the lost or hidden power relating to Islamic law, that which was taken away by the British, and entrenched it in Article 3.").

[48] *See, e.g.*, Benjamin Dawson & Steven Thiru, *The Lina Joy Case and the Future of Religious Freedom in Malaysia*, 2007 LAWASIA J. 151 (2007); Tommy Thomas, *The Social Contract: Malaysia's Constitutional Covenant*, 1 MALAYAN L.J. cxxxii (2008); Andrew Harding, *The Keris, the Crescent and the Blind Goddess: The State, Islam and the Constitution in Malaysia*, 6 SING. J. INT'L & COMP. L. 154 (2002); Jaclyn Neo, *Malay Nationalism, Islamic Supremacy and the Constitutional Bargain in the Multi-ethnic Composition of Malaysia*, 13 INT'L J. ON MINORITY & GROUP RTS. 95, 104 (2006).

described Malaysia's constitutional order as a hybrid state containing both secular and Islamic elements.[49]

Within Malaysia's broader social and political context, where religious and ethnic identities are seen as fused and fixed, things became more complicated. Claims of Islam's supremacy are viewed as connected to a rising ethno-nationalist movement seeking to protect the special position of the Malays.[50] Politicizing Islam fuels tensions between the Malay majority and non-Malay ethnic minorities, many of whom have long felt as if they are being treated as second-class citizens.

The Pakatan Harapan multi-ethnic coalition that came into power in 2018 promised policies based on an inclusive "multi-racial and multi-religious" agenda.[51] Seeking to recoup from its electoral defeat, in 2019, UMNO announced that it would ally itself with PAS, forming a pact uniting the country's two largest Malay-Muslim parties.[52] The Perikatan Nasional coalition that took over federal government power in March 2020 is a largely mono-ethnic alliance of Malay-Muslim parties—including UMNO and PAS—indicating that race and religion remain potent forces in Malaysian society.[53]

IV. Judicializing Religion

Courts play a crucial role in the constitutional contestations over religion that shape the Malaysian state's constitutional identity.[54] In the high stakes debate over the place of Islam in the public order, courts have become key players in

[49] *See, e.g.*, Shad Saleem Faruqi, *The Malaysian Constitution, The Islamic State and Hudud Laws*, *in* ISLAM IN SOUTHEAST ASIA: POLITICAL, SOCIAL AND STRATEGIC CHALLENGES FOR THE 21ST CENTURY 284 (K.S. Nathan & Mohamad Hashim Kamali, eds., 2005) (arguing that "the Malaysian legal system is neither fully secular not fully theocratic," rather "[i]t is a hybrid.")

[50] For example, Member of Parliament Badruddin bin Amiruldin's declared in a House of Representatives debate in 2005: "Malaysia is an Islamic state! You don't like it you get out of Malaysia!" (translated from Malay). Hansard of Malaysia's Parliament (July 11, 2005), at 34; *see also Parlimen Malaysia*, YOUTUBE (Apr. 25, 2006), https://perma.cc/2QM8-6YDT. For discussion on the interrelation between religion and ethno-nationalism in Malaysia, see JOSEPH LIOW, RELIGION AND NATIONALISM IN SOUTHEAST ASIA 135-74 (2016).

[51] PAKATAN HARAPAN MANIFESTO, REBUILDING OUR NATION, FULFILLING OUR HOPES 102, https://perma.cc/M8Z6-W6W4 ("[T]he Pakatan Harapan Government will implement policies and programmes that unite the nation and create an inclusive society and maintain the harmony of multi-racial and multi-religious Malaysia.").

[52] Tashny Sukumaran, *Malaysia's UMNO Confirms "Cooperation" with Islamist Party PAS after Weeks of Denials*, S. CHINA MORNING POST (Mar. 6, 2019), https://perma.cc/TB76-S6XF; *see also* Harris Zainul, *Commentary: Race, Religion and Rhetoric Ramp Up in New Malaysia*, CHANNEL NEWS ASIA (Apr. 4, 2019), https://perma.cc/YK3V-Y3B8.

[53] *See* Laignee Barron, *Malaysia's 94-Year-Old Prime Minister Is Out. The New Leader Is Likely to Inflame Racial Tensions*, TIME (Mar. 4, 2020), https://perma.cc/B3X5-W4V3.

[54] *See* GARY JACOBSOHN, CONSTITUTIONAL IDENTITY 4 (2010) (arguing that disharmonic constitutional contestations is a critical part of the development of constitutional identity).

constructing the constitutional narrative.[55] Malaysia's hybrid legal system, which consists of secular civil courts and religious courts, adds another dimension—jurisdictional battles—to conflicts over the interpretation of the constitution's religion clauses.

Initially, the Supreme Court affirmed the Malaysian Constitution's secular basis as settled jurisprudence.[56] In the 1988 decision of *Che Omar bin Che Soh v. Public Prosecutor*,[57] the Lord President of the Supreme Court, Mohamed Salleh Abas, concluded that Islam's position under Article 3 of the Constitution "means only such acts as relate to rituals and ceremonies," holding that it was in this sense that "the framers of the Constitution understood the meaning of the word 'Islam' in the context of Article 3."[58] The case involved appellants facing the mandatory death penalty who had challenged their sentence on the basis that crimes involving drugs and firearms did not require the death penalty under Islamic law. They argued that given the constitutional declaration that Islam is the religion of the Federation, Islamic precepts should be regarded as the source of all law and thus the death penalty could not be imposed for offenses not in line with Islamic law.

The Supreme Court unanimously rejected the idea that laws could be struck down as unconstitutional being incompatible with Islamic principles. After tracing the history of British colonial rule and the establishment of secular institutions, the Lord President held that "Islamic law was rendered isolated in a narrow confinement of the law of marriage, divorce, and inheritance only."[59] The Court dismissed the notion that "the law passed by Parliament must be imbued with Islamic and religious principles" as "contrary to the constitutional and legal history of the Federation."[60] Instead, the Court observed the opposite to be the case: the Federal Constitution "purposely preserves the continuity of secular law prior to the Constitution."[61] It concluded: "[T]he law in this country is still what it is today, secular law."[62]

In another case two years later, *Teoh Eng Huat v. Kadhi Pasir Mas*, the Supreme Court reaffirmed the secular understanding of the Constitution.[63] In this 1990 case, the Court relied on the Constitution's secular founding principles and the framers' intent to uphold the constitutionality of a statute that allowed a parent or guardian to decide a child's religious upbringing. In reaching this decision, the Supreme Court referred to historical documents written by the framers at the time

[55] *See* Carolyn Evans, *Constitutional Narratives: Constitutional Adjudication on the Religion Clauses in Australia and Malaysia*, 23 Emory Int'l L. Rev. 437 (2010).

[56] The Supreme Court (known as the Federal Court after 1994) is Malaysia's final appellate court.

[57] [1988] 2 Malayan L.J. 55.

[58] *Id.* at 56–57.

[59] *Id.* at 56.

[60] *Id.* at 57.

[61] *Id.* at 56.

[62] *Id.* at 57.

[63] Teoh Eng Huat v. Kadhi Pasir Mas (*Susie Teoh*) [1990] 2 Malayan L.J. 300.

of the Constitution's drafting, which made clear that the recognition of Islam as the state religion "would not in any way affect the civil rights of non-Muslims."[64] Lord President Abdul Hamid Omar emphasized that the Malaysian Constitution "was not the product of an overnight thought"; rather, it represented a settlement reached by "negotiations, discussions and consensus between the British government, the Malay rulers and the Alliance party representing various racial and religious groups."[65] The Supreme Court in these two early decisions established the Malaysian Constitution's secular foundations, viewing Islam's position as chiefly ceremonial.

That understanding would soon change. Over the years following these decisions, judicial discourse showed a distinct shift toward elevating the role of religion in the Malaysian public order. Courts in Malaysia have expanded Islam's position in two main ways. The first has been through *jurisdictional deference* by the civil courts to the authority of the Sharia courts, even on matters involving constitutional rights. A second means has been through the civil courts' expansive interpretation of the Article 3(1) declaration of Islam as state religion. This *judicial Islamization* has taken place through the civil courts prioritizing Islam's position over other constitutional norms.

A. Jurisdictional Deference and Religious Authority

Civil courts for many years have been reluctant to adjudicate any matters implicating Islam even when the case involved constitutional rights, such as religious liberty or equality. Civil court judges tended to justify their jurisdictional deference to the Sharia courts by relying on Article 121(1A), a provision inserted by a constitutional amendment in 1988, which provides that the civil courts "shall have no jurisdiction in respect of any matter within the jurisdiction of the Syariah courts."[66] As a result of the civil courts extensively deferring matters to the exclusive authority of the Sharia courts, the power and scope of authority of these religious courts were greatly expanded.

1. Apostasy Cases: Individuals Seeking to Leave Islam

Apostasy is a major area of jurisdictional contention. Consider the high-profile case of *Lina Joy v. Majlis Agama Islam*.[67] Lina Joy was born and raised in a Malay-Muslim family. She became Catholic as an adult and was baptized at age

[64] *Id.* at 301–02.
[65] *Id.* at 301.
[66] FED. CONST. (MALAY.), art. 121(1A).
[67] Lina Joy v. Majlis Agama Islam Wilayah Persekutuan [2007] 4 MALAYAN L.J. 585 (F.C.) [hereinafter *Lina Joy* (F.C.)].

thirty-six. She met and fell in love with a Catholic man, and they wanted to marry. But therein lay a complication: because of her official religious status as a Muslim, Lina Joy was unable to marry her non-Muslim fiancé under Malaysia's civil marriage statute.[68] She applied to the National Registration Department to change the name and religion on her national identity card, supplying a copy of her baptismal certificate. The government department issued Lina Joy a new identity card that reflected her change of name but stated her religious affiliation as "Islam." It refused to remove this religious status on her identity card without a certificate of apostasy from a Sharia court confirming that she was no longer a Muslim.

There's a problem with this requirement, though: obtaining an official declaration of apostasy from the Sharia courts for a Malay-Muslim is virtually impossible. Apostasy is regulated by individual state legislatures,[69] and is regarded in several states—for example, Pahang, Perak, Terengganu, and Malacca—as an offense punishable by fines, imprisonment, or whipping.[70] Other state legislatures require would-be apostates to undergo mandatory rehabilitation at Islamic faith centers.[71] In the Federal Territories, where Lina Joy's case took place, there appeared to be no formal legal procedure for obtaining an official declaration of apostasy from the Sharia court administration.[72] Indeed, Lina Joy's lawyers noted the

[68] The Law Reform (Marriage & Divorce) Act of 1976 governs civil marriages between non-Muslim couples. Muslims must contract their marriage under the Islamic Family Law (Federal Territories) Act of 1984, which prohibits marriage with non-Muslims. *See* Islamic Family Law (Federal Territories) Act of 1984 § 10(2) ("No woman shall marry a non-Muslim."); *see also* Brief of All Women's Action Society, Sisters in Islam, Women's Aid Organisation, Women's Centre for Change, and Women's Development Collective as Amici Curiae Supporting Apellant, at [3.2], Lina Joy v. Majlis Agama Islam Wilayah Persekutuan [2007] 4 MALAYAN L.J. 585 (F.C.).

[69] Federal statutory limits on the sentencing powers of state-level Sharia courts exist: up to three years' imprisonment, fines of no more than RM5000, and six lashes. *See* Syariah Courts (Criminal Jurisdiction) Act of 1965 (Act 355) (revised 1988) § 2.

[70] Administration of the Religion of Islam and the Malay Custom of Pahang Enactment of 1982 § 185 (amended 1989) ("Any Muslim who states that he has ceased to be a Muslim, whether orally, in writing or in any other manner whatsoever, commits an offence, and on conviction shall be liable to a fine not exceeding five thousand ringgit or to imprisonment for a term not exceeding three years or to both and to whipping of not more than six strokes."). *See* Jaclyn Neo, *Competing Imperatives: Conflicts and Convergences in State and Islam in Pluralist Malaysia*, 4 OXFORD J.L. & RELIGION 1, 16–17 (2015); Mohamed Azam Mohamed Adil, *Law of Apostasy and Freedom of Religion in Malaysia*, 2 ASIAN J. COMP. L. 29 (2007); *see also* Perak Islamic Criminal Law Enactment of 1992 § 13; Terengganu Administration of Islamic Law Enactment of 1996 § 29; Malacca Administration of Islamic Law Enactment 1991 § 209.

[71] One case illustrating this is that of Revathi, an Indian-Malaysian woman who converted to Hinduism. Following her application to renounce Islam, the Malacca Sharia Court ordered that she be detained for 100 days at an Islamic rehabilitation center. *See* Claudia Theophilus, *Malaysian Family Split by Faith*, AL-JAZEERA (May 7, 2007), https://perma.cc/8JXF-VB32. In Malacca, Sharia courts can order mandatory detention for rehabilitation as a precursor to conviction. *See* Melaka Sharia Offences Enactment 1991 § 66. In Negeri Sembilan, those who wish to leave the faith are not detained but are required to undergo a mandatory counseling session to urge the potential apostate to reconsider the change of religion. *See* Administration of the Religion of Islam (Negeri Sembilan) Enactment 2003 § 119(4)(b).

[72] MOUSTAFA, *supra* note 4, at 71.

lack of any empirical evidence about whether people had in fact been granted an apostasy order from the Sharia courts.[73]

Lina Joy brought a challenge before the civil courts, arguing that her constitutional right to religious freedom had been infringed. The High Court held that the constitutional right to "profess and practice" one's religion under Article 11 did not extend to individuals who wished to leave Islam without the Sharia court's permission.[74] The judge ruled that Lina Joy's conversion from Islam was a matter for the religious courts, holding the right to religious freedom "distinct" from the freedom to choose one's religion.[75] On full display in the High Court judge's opinion is how religion and race are conflated: "By Article 160 of the Federal Constitution, the plaintiff is a Malay and therefore as long as she is a Malay by that definition she cannot renounce her Islamic religion at all. As a Malay, the plaintiff remains in Islamic faith until her dying days."[76]

The Court of Appeal upheld the High Court's decision, finding it reasonable as a matter of administrative law for the National Registry Department to require that Lina Joy obtain a certificate of apostasy from a Sharia court.[77] In a two-to-one decision, the majority held that whether a person had renounced Islam is "a question of Islamic law" that was "not within the jurisdiction" of the National Registration Department and that the department was "not equipped or qualified to decide."

In 2007, the Malaysian Federal Court ruled against Lina Joy, agreeing that a Muslim cannot leave Islam without obtaining authorization from the Sharia Court.[78] According to the majority, "freedom of religion under Article 11 of the Federal Constitution requires [the individual] to comply with the practices or law of the Islamic religion in particular with regard to converting out of the religion."[79]

The Federal Court majority held that matters relating to apostasy are exclusively within the domain of the religious courts.[80] Since the Sharia court "had expressly been granted jurisdiction to adjudge matters pertaining to embracing Islam," by "necessary implication" it had "jurisdiction to adjudge on matters

[73] Dawson & Thiru, *supra* note 48, at 160. The High Court opinion in *Indira Gandhi* cites a statement made by the Islamic Affairs Minister in the Prime Minister's Department on June 14, 2011, that "from 2000–2010, there were 864 applications [to convert out of Islam] to the Syariah courts and out of that only 168 have been granted." *Indira Gandhi* (H.C.), [2013] 5 MALAYAN L.J. 552, at [83]. However, it is unclear how many, if any, of these were living Malay-Muslim applicants.

[74] Lina Joy v. Majlis Agama Islam Wilayah & Anor [2004] 2 MALAYAN L.J. 119, 142 (H.C.) [hereinafter *Lina Joy* (H.C.)].

[75] *Id.* at [7]. For critique of the High Court judgment, see Li-ann Thio, *Apostasy and Religious Freedom: Constitutional Issues Arising from the Lina Joy Litigation*, 2 MALAYAN L.J. i (2006).

[76] *Lina Joy* (H.C.), [2004] 2 MALAYAN L.J. 119, at [58]; *see also* FED. CONST. (MALAY.), art. 160(2) ("'Malay' means a person who professes the religion of Islam, habitually speaks the Malay language, conforms to Malay customs[.]").

[77] Lina Joy v. Majlis Agama Islam Wilayah Persekutuan [2005] 6 MALAYAN L.J. 193 (C.A.), at [34] [hereinafter *Lina Joy* (C.A.)].

[78] *Lina Joy* (F.C.), [2007] 4 MALAYAN L.J. 585.

[79] *Id.* at [14].

[80] *Id.* at [10]–[14].

pertaining to a Muslim converting out of Islam or being an apostate."[81] In doing so, the Court affirmed its earlier decision in *Soon Singh*, where it had held that since matters regarding converting *to* Islam are expressly within the jurisdiction of the Sharia courts, matters relating to converting *out* of Islam impliedly fell under the jurisdiction of the religious courts.[82] It was "evident" that "apostasy is a matter that relates to Islamic Law" and thus "lies within the jurisdiction of the Sharia Court," declared the *Lina Joy* majority, finding that "by reason of Article 121(1A) of the Federal Constitution, the civil courts cannot interfere in this matter."[83]

In a forceful dissent, Justice Richard Malanjum emphasized that when "constitutional issues are involved especially on questions of fundamental rights as enshrined in the Constitution it is of critical importance that the civil superior courts should not decline jurisdiction by merely citing Article 121(1A)."[84] Article 121(1A) "only protects the Syariah Court in matters within their jurisdiction, which does not include the interpretation of the provisions of the Constitution."[85] In contrast to the majority opinion, which entirely ignored that it was impracticable for Lina Joy to obtain permission to convert out of Islam from the religious courts, Justice Malanjum observed that it was unreasonable "to expect the appellant to apply for a certificate of apostasy when to do so would likely expose her to a range of offences under the Islamic law[.]"[86] He reminded the civil courts of their duty not to "abdicate their constitutional function" to adjudicate matters involving fundamental rights.[87] Laws "criminalizing apostasy or limiting the scope of the provisions of the fundamental liberties as enshrined in the Constitution are constitutional issues in nature which only the civil courts have jurisdiction to determine."[88]

In 2016, the High Court of Sabah and Sarawak appeared to signal willingness to move away from the *Lina Joy* majority approach in the case of Roneey Rebit.[89] Roneey Rebit had been raised a Christian in an indigenous Bidayuh community—worth noting because the applicant was not ethnically considered Malay. At some point in his childhood his parents had registered his religion as Islam, and he now wanted this religious status removed from his identity card. The High Court of Sabah and Sarawak held that the exercise of the constitutional religious freedom right is outside the Sharia Court's jurisdiction, declaring that the "right to choose

81 *Id.* at [15.5].

82 Soon Singh v. Pertubuhan Kebajikan Islam Malaysia Kedah [1999] 2 MALAYAN L.J. 489, at 501–02.

83 *Lina Joy* (F.C.), [2007] 4 MALAYAN L.J. 585, at [16].

84 *Id.* at [85] (Malanjum, J., dissenting).

85 *Id.*

86 *Id.* at [90].

87 *Id.* at [85].

88 *Id.*

89 Azmi Mohamad Azam v. Director of Jabatan Agama Islam Sarawak & Others [2016] 6 CURRENT L.J. 562.

his religion lies with the applicant himself and not the religious body."[90] The High Court's decision was lauded for its defense of an individual's freedom of conscience by rights advocates, including progressive Muslim organizations.[91]

But this notion of freedom of conscience in apostasy cases was not echoed by the other appellate courts. In 2017, the Federal Court unanimously deferred to the Sharia courts in an appeal brought by four applicants wishing to leave Islam, affirming that the religious courts have jurisdiction over matters of apostasy.[92] The Court of Appeal had also rejected the applicants' appeal; it explicitly followed the approach taken by the *Lina Joy* majority, stating that precedent "had consistently held matters of apostasy are within the jurisdiction of the Sharia Courts and not the civil courts."[93]

By deferring apostasy matters to the Sharia Court's exclusive jurisdiction, the civil courts effectively enabled the Islamic authorities to act as sole gatekeepers over an individual's exit from the religious community. For those seeking to leave Islam, the stark conclusion articulated by the Malaysian Federal Court's majority in *Lina Joy* remains the reality: "One cannot renounce or embrace a religion at one's own whims and fancies."[94]

2. Child Conversion and Custody Cases

Another major area of tension between the authority of the civil courts and Sharia courts involves disputes over religious conversion and custody of children.[95] A typical scenario occurs when one parent (usually the father) converts to Islam and applies to the Sharia courts to convert the children as well, then obtains custody without the knowledge of the other parent. The non-Muslim parent is left unable to apply to the Sharia courts to contest the conversion or custody orders of the children.

This was the situation for Indira Gandhi, whose story began this chapter. Seeking redress in the civil courts, she challenged the legality of her husband's unilateral conversion of their children. In a separate suit, also in a civil court, she obtained a custody order for the three children. Her ex-husband, however, refused to abide by the civil court's custody order because he had a competing custody order from a Sharia court. Thus began Indira Gandhi's lengthy constitutional litigation through

[90] *Id.* at [38]. The National Registration Department later withdrew its appeal against the High Court's decision. *See Najib Gave his Word to Drop Apostasy Case against S'wakian, says Adenan*, MALAYSIAKINI (May 2, 2016), https://perma.cc/N3U3-YYTA.

[91] *See, e.g.*, Press Release, Sisters in Islam, Sarawak High Court Judgment Defends Freedom of Religion in Malaysia (Mar. 28, 2016), https://perma.cc/CMU5-CDL4.

[92] Sulok Tawie, *Federal Court Defers to Shariah Courts in Sarawak Apostasy Cases*, MALAY MAIL (Feb. 27, 2018), https://perma.cc/2FVM-U9LS.

[93] Jenny bt Peter @ Nur Muzdhalifah Abdullah v. Director of Jabatan Agama Islam Sarawak & Ors [2017] 1 MALAYAN L.J. 340, at [24].

[94] *Lina Joy* (F.C.), [2007] 4 MALAYAN L.J. 585, at [14].

[95] *See, e.g.*, Subashini Rajasingam v. Saravanan Thangathoray [2008] 2 MALAYAN L.J. 147 (F.C.); Shamala Sathiyaseelan v. Jeyaganesh Mogarajah & Anor [2011] 2 MALAYAN L.J. 281.

the civil court system from the High Court to the Court of Appeal and finally to the Federal Court.

In 2013, the High Court quashed the certificates of conversion issued by the Sharia registrar for the three children, holding that their unilateral conversion unconstitutionally infringed Indira Gandhi's right to life and religious freedom.[96] In a separate decision, the High Court judge also granted Indira Gandhi custody of the children.[97]

But the Court of Appeal overruled the High Court's decision. It held that the civil courts had no jurisdiction over the matter of the children's conversion to Islam.[98] "It is beyond the shadow of a doubt," wrote the Court of Appeal, that "the issue of whether a person is a Muslim or not is a matter falling under the exclusive jurisdiction of the Syariah Court."[99]

In 2018, the Federal Court issued a unanimous decision of immense significance for judicial authority over religion in Malaysian constitutional jurisprudence.[100] Of immediate relevance for Indira Gandhi, it quashed her children's unilateral conversions to Islam, holding that the constitutional right of equality requires that both parents consent to change the religion of minor children.[101] Notably, the Court took a purposive and gender-equal approach to interpreting the right of a "parent" to determine a child's religious upbringing under Article 12(4), holding that both parents have an equal say in a child's religious conversion.[102]

Second, and particularly germane for our analysis here, the Federal Court clarified the jurisdictions of the civil and religious courts, declaring that the civil courts have jurisdiction over matters relating to the Islamic law that involve constitutional issues.[103] Taking on the Article 121(1A) provision directly, the Court declared that "the effect of Article 121(1A) is not to oust the jurisdiction of civil courts as soon as a subject matter relates to the Islamic religion."[104] Markedly departing from earlier precedent,[105] it declared it "unduly simplistic" to say that "since matters of conversion involve Islamic law and practice" the Sharia Courts "must have jurisdiction over such matters to the exclusion of the civil courts."[106] It unequivocally declared

96 *Indira Gandhi* (H.C.), [2013] 5 MALAYAN L.J. 552.

97 Indira Gandhi v. Patmanathan a/l Krishnan [2015] 7 MALAYAN L.J. 153 (H.C.) [hereinafter *Indira Gandhi* (H.C.) (No. 2)].

98 Pathmanathan a/l Krishnan v. Indira Gandhi a/p Mutho [2016] 4 MALAYAN L.J. 455 (C.A.) [hereinafter *Indira Gandhi* (C.A.)].

99 *Id.* at [33].

100 *Indira Gandhi* (F.C.), [2018] 1 MALAYAN L.J. 545.

101 *Id.* at [150]–[181].

102 *See* FED. CONST. (MALAY.), art. 12(4) ("[T]he religion of a person under the age of eighteen years shall be decided by his parent or guardian.").

103 *Id.* at [92]–[98].

104 *Id.* at [104].

105 *See, e.g.*, Soon Singh Soon Singh a/l Bikar Singh v. Pertubuhan Kebajikan Islam Malaysia (Perkim) [1999] 1 MALAYAN L.J. 489; *Lina Joy* (F.C.), [2007] 4 MALAYAN L.J. 585.

106 *Indira Gandhi* (F.C.), [2018] 1 MALAYAN L.J. 545, at [104].

that the amended Article 121(1A) does not impact the civil court's power of judicial review and constitutional interpretation.[107]

The *Indira Gandhi* case is a prime example of judicial empowerment, as discussed in Chapters 5 and 6, in which the Federal Court cemented the power to nullify constitutional amendments as unconstitutional. It declared that judicial review is a "natural and necessary corollary of the rule of law" and "inherent in the basic structure of the Constitution."[108] That the Court was willing to assert judicial power in such a manner in the highly fraught area of religious authority makes the decision all the more remarkable.

Still, it is worth noting that the Federal Court's opinion cautiously steered clear of the contentious issue of apostasy. It distinguished *Lina Joy* by emphasizing that *Indira Gandhi* did not involve determining the status of Muslim converts or questions of Islamic personal law. Instead it framed its decision as about "the more prosaic questions" of the "legality and constitutionality of administrative action" taken by the registrar of Muslim converts in issuing conversion certificates for the children when only one parent had consented.[109] So, although *Indira Gandhi* is a significant step in establishing the civil court's jurisdiction over Islamic issues involving constitutional matters, the Court stopped short of explicitly asserting authority over apostasy. And so, the "jurisdictional imbroglio continues."[110]

B. Judicial Islamization of the Article 3(1) Constitutional Clause

Civil courts have also expansively interpreted the Article 3(1) Islamic clause, which has led to judicial Islamization of the constitutional order. The most marked effect has been to elevate Islam's position under Article 3(1), using it as an interpretive lens through which to view other constitutional guarantees. Islam's prioritized role has been used to justify limiting the scope of constitutional rights like religious freedom. Reinterpreting Article 3(1) of the Federal Constitution in this way in effect advances what Tamir Moustafa calls "a new *grundnorm* for the Malaysian legal system."[111]

Consider the litigation over what has come to be known as the "Allah" case.[112] In 2009, the Ministry of Home Affairs issued an order to the Titular Roman Catholic Archbishop of Kuala Lumpur prohibiting the Malay language edition of the *Herald*, the Catholic Church's weekly newspaper, from using the word "Allah."

[107] *Id.* at [92]–[93].

[108] *Id.* at [33], [48].

[109] *Id.* at [108]

[110] Jaclyn Neo, *Return of Judicial Power: Religious Freedom and the Tussle Over Jurisdictional Boundaries in Malaysia*, Int'l J. Const. L. Blog (Mar. 15, 2018), https://perma.cc/G5NH-QETQ.

[111] Moustafa, *supra* note 4, at 138.

[112] Menteri Dalam Negeri & Ors. v. Titular Roman Catholic Archbishop of Kuala Lumpur [2013] Malayan L.J. 468 (C.A.) [hereinafter *Allah* Case (C.A.)].

The term "Allah" has long been used by Christians in Malaysia to refer to God in Malay-language Bibles, publications, sermons, and hymns.[113] The Catholic Church brought a constitutional challenge arguing that the government prohibition violated the church's religious liberty and freedom of speech.[114]

In 2013, the Malaysian Court of Appeal unanimously upheld the government ban on the use of "Allah" in non-Muslim publications.[115] It found that the Catholic Church's right to religious liberty had not been infringed because the use of "the word or name 'Allah' is not an integral part of the faith and practice of Christianity."[116] Non-Muslim publications using "Allah" would "cause unnecessary confusion within the Islamic community" and not be "conducive to the peaceful and harmonious tempo of life in the country."[117]

What is striking about the Court of Appeal's highly expansive interpretation of Islam's position under Article 3(1) is its insistence that the "purpose and intention" of the words "in peace and harmony" in the article is "to protect the sanctity of Islam as the religion of the country and also to insulate against any threat faced or any possible and probable threat to the religion of Islam."[118] That "most probable threat to Islam, in the context of this country," said Justice Apandi Ali, "is the propagation of other religions to the followers of Islam."[119] Holding that "Article 3(1) is to be read with the freedom of religion in Article 11(1),"[120] the Court of Appeal used Article 3(1) as an interpretive lens through which to limit the Constitution's rights guarantees. In his opinion, Justice Abdul Aziz Ab Rahim emphasized that: "The position of Islam as the religion of the Federation ... imposes certain obligations on the powers that be to promote and defend Islam as well [as] to protect its sanctity."[121]

[113] *See* Jaclyn Neo, *What's in a Name? Malaysia's "Allah" Controversy and the Judicial Intertwining of Islam with Ethnic Identity*, 12 INT'L J. CONST. L. 751 (2014).

[114] FED. CONST. (MALAY.), art. 11(1) ("Every person has the right to profess and practise [*sic*] his religion, and, subject to Clause (4), to propagate it."); FED. CONST. (MALAY.), art. 11(3) ("Every religious group has the right—to manage its own religious affairs; to establish and maintain institutions for religious or charitable purposes; and to acquire and own property and hold and administer it in accordance with law.").

[115] *Allah* Case (C.A.), [2013] MALAYAN L.J. 468, *overruling* Titular Roman Catholic Archbishop of Kuala Lumpur v. Menteri Dalam Negeri & Anor [2010] 2 MALAYAN L.J. 78 (H.C.).

[116] *Id.* at [51] (Mohamed Apandi Ali, J.); *see also id.* at [107]–[108] (Abdul Aziz Ab Rahim, J.); *id.* at [140] (Mohd Zawawi, J.).

[117] *Id.* at [53].

[118] *Allah* Case (C.A.), [2013] MALAYAN L.J. 468, at [33]; *see also* FED. CONST. (MALAY.), art. 3(1) ("Islam is the religion of the Federation; but other religions may be practised in peace and harmony in any part of the Federation.").

[119] *Allah* Case (C.A.), [2013] MALAYAN L.J. 468, at [33].

[120] *Id.* at [48].

[121] *Id.* at [104]. In 2014, the Federal Court rejected the Catholic Church's application for leave to appeal. *See* Titular Roman Catholic Archbishop of Kuala Lumpur v. Menteri Dalam Negeri & Ors. [2014] 4 MALAYAN L.J. 765. The Federal Court later also dismissed an application to review its decision. *See* Ida Lim & Shaun Tan, *Last Nail in Catholic Church's "Allah" Case as Federal Court Again Says No*, MALAY MAIL (Jan. 21, 2015), https://perma.cc/66PB-BGE8.

The "Allah" case is emblematic of an expansionist interpretation of the Article 3(1) Islamic constitutional clause. A few other examples illustrate this phenomenon. Take, for instance, the High Court's opinion in *Meor Atiqulrahman bin Ishak v. Fatimah bte Sihi.*[122] Three Muslim schoolboys were expelled for wearing turbans (*serban*) to school, which was against a state regulation that prohibited certain religious dress in schools. The High Court found the prohibition on the wearing of turbans unconstitutional because it infringed the right to religious freedom under Article 11(1). But the High Court's decision was not based on a robust protection of religious freedom—instead, it stemmed from an expansive interpretation of Article 3(1).[123] According to the High Court judge, Article 3(1) gives primacy to Islam over other religions:

> "Islam is the religion of the Federation, but other religions can be practised in peace and harmony," means that Islam is the dominant religion among the other religions that are professed in this country like Christianity, Buddhism, Hinduism and others. Islam is not of the same status as other religions; it does not sit shoulder to shoulder or stand at the same height. Islam sits at the top, it walks first... If this were not the case, Islam would not be the religion of the Federation but just one of the several religions practiced in the country and every person would be equally free to practice any religion he or she professes, no one better than the other.[124]

Other cases have also relied on broad readings of Article 3(1) to restrict the religious freedom guaranteed by Article 11(1). Returning to *Lina Joy*, the High Court in that case declared: "Freedom of religion under art 11(1) must be read with art 3(1) which places Islam in a special position as the main and dominant religion" of the Malaysian Federation.[125] For High Court Judge Faiza Thamby Chik, Article 3(1) has "a far wider and meaningful purpose than a mere fixation of the official religion."[126] He rejected the idea that the right to religious freedom meant that Muslims were free to convert out of Islam insisting that such an interpretation "would result in absurdities not intended by the framers" of the Malaysian Constitution.[127] Religious liberty is necessarily restricted, he wrote, because of the "clear nexus" between the Article 3(1) Islamic constitutional clause and the Article 11(1) religious freedom guarantee.[128]

[122] [2000] 5 MALAYAN L.J. 375.

[123] *See* Neo, *Competing Imperatives, supra* note 70, at 21 (observing that "[w]hile the result vindicates the applicants' religious freedom, this was not based on a liberal interpretation of the right to freedom of religion, but based on a reading of the constitution as giving primacy to Islam").

[124] *Fatimah bte Sihi*, [2000] 5 MALAYAN L.J. 375, at 377 (translated from Malay by the author).

[125] *Lina Joy* (H.C.), [2004] 2 MALAYAN L.J. 119, at 142.

[126] *Id.* at 127.

[127] *Id.* at [18].

[128] *Id.*

Echoes of this strand of reasoning are also evident in an earlier decision by the same High Court Judge. In *Daud Mamat v. Majlis Agama Islam*,[129] Justice Faiza Thamby Chik rejected the idea that Article 11(1) included the right to profess and practise the religion of one's *choice* as absurd—such an interpretation "would stretch the scope of [Article 11(1)] to ridiculous heights, and rebel against the canon of construction."[130]

The Federal Court majority in *Lina Joy* agreed with this expansive understanding of Islam's constitutional position. Writing for the majority, the Chief Justice said:

> [W]ith regards to Islam ... Article 11 cannot be construed or defined with such a wide meaning to the extent it annuls all laws that require a Muslim to perform an Islamic obligation or that restricts them from performing a matter that is prohibited by Islam or which prescribe the method of conducting a matter in relation to Islam. This is because the position of Islam in the Federal Constitution differs from the position of other religions ... [O]nly Islam as a religion is mentioned by its name in the Federal Constitution i.e. "*as the religion of the Federation*"—Article 3(1).[131]

And so the majority concluded: "If a person professes and practices Islam, it would definitely mean that he must comply with the Islamic law which has prescribed the way to embrace Islam and convert[] out of Islam."[132]

Overall, the tenor of these decisions has been to endorse Islam's supremacy over other constitutional guarantees, including fundamental rights. Put another way, Article 3(1) is treated as an interpretive lens through which to read the rest of the Constitution; viewed in this manner, judges justify curtailing constitutional rights to accommodate Islam's position.

Expansive interpretation of the Article 3(1) constitutional clause is one thing, civil court judges referring to Islamic texts and materials in judicial rhetoric is another.[133] Consider, for example, the High Court's opinion in the 2004 case of *Shamala*.[134] In a decision interpreting a *civil* statute allowing the spouse of someone who converts to Islam to elect for divorce, the High Court judge cited a verse from the Qur'an on polygamy:

> [T]he defendant husband, now a Muslim though [he] cannot file a petition for divorce against his plaintiff Hindu wife, can take another wife—a Muslim wife

[129] [2001] CURRENT L.J. 161.
[130] *Id.* at [172].
[131] *Lina Joy* (F.C.), [2007] 4 MALAYAN L.J. 585, at [17.4].
[132] *Id.* at [17.2].
[133] *See* Amanda Whiting, *Desecularising Malaysian Law?*, *in* EXAMINING PRACTICE, INTERROGATING THEORY: COMPARATIVE LEGAL STUDIES IN ASIA 223, 229, 249–52 (Sarah Biddulph et al. eds., 2008).
[134] Shamala Sathiyaseelan v. Jeyaganesh Mogarajah [2004] 2 MALAYAN L.J. 241 (H.C.).

> because the defendant husband being a Muslim is now practising a polygamous marriage... The word used in the Section is "may", i.e. to maintain the status of the civil marriage (Hindu marriage) if the unconverted wife wishes to remain the wife of her converted husband although the converted husband can take another wife if he can do justice as the Holy Quran *Al-Nisa* (IV) Ayat 3 states and which reads, "if ye fear that ye shall not Be able to deal justly With the orphans, Marry women of your choice, Two, Three, or Four; But if ye fear that ye shall not Be able to deal justly (with them), Then only one or two (a captive)."[135]

Such references to Islamic sources were also on rhetorical display in *Subashini*.[136] Like *Indira Gandhi*, this case involved the unilateral conversion of children by a spouse who had himself officially converted to Islam. Subashini sought an injunction to restrain her husband from applying to the religious courts to convert their children and dissolve the marriage. Court of Appeal Justice Suriyadi rebuked Subashini as "brazen" for attempting to use an injunction to "shackle" the Sharia Court:

> Surely that Syariah judge must be more than equipped to be given the confidence to deal with subject matters promulgated by Parliament. [The Sharia Court judge's] position would squarely fall under these Quranic revelations: "And We have set you on a road of Our Commandment (a Syariah, or a Sacred Law of Our Commandment, *Syaria'tin min al-amr*); so follow it, and follow not the whims of those who know not (45:18)."[137]

It is noteworthy that these religious sources are being used in the opinions of *civil* court judges. While Islamic sources may well be regarded as properly within the domain of Sharia court judges who are tasked with administering Islamic law, that is not the role of civil courts judges who deal with secular legislation and common law. Civil courts are meant to apply the general law of the land. For judges in the federal civil courts to refer to Islamic sources is troubling "both in terms of their objective place in the Malaysian legal-political system, and in terms of judicial self-perception."[138]

All of this is additionally fraught because of the perceived fusion between religious and ethnic identity. Within a socio-political context in which Islam's position is viewed as connected to the Malays' special position, apostasy and religious conversion bring to the fore tensions that resonate with those threatened by the loss of the Malay-Muslim majority's dominance. Recall the High Court judge in *Lina*

[135] *Id.* at [13].
[136] *Subashini*, [2008] 2 Malayan L.J. 147.
[137] *Id.* at [57], [59].
[138] Neo, *Competing Imperatives, supra* note 70, at 14.

Joy declaring that a Malay "remains in Islamic faith until his or her dying days,"[139] while the Court of Appeal majority asserted that "[r]enunciation of Islam is generally regarded by the Muslim community as a very grave matter."[140] The dissenting judges in the Court of Appeal and Federal Court of *Lina Joy*, both non-Muslims, were the only judges who ruled in favor of allowing Lina Joy to convert away from Islam. Decisions like these deepen divisions in a society already polarized along religious and ethnic lines.

Another striking feature of the judicial Islamization phenomenon is that it has not been limited to the regulation of Muslims by Islamic personal law. The civil courts' expansive interpretation of Article 3(1) impacts the rights of religious liberty and free speech not only for Muslims but also for non-Muslims.

Consider the 2015 case of *ZI Publications v. Kerajaan Negeri Selangor*, which involved a freedom of speech challenge.[141] In 2012, the Islamic Religious Department of Selangor raided a publishing company, ZI Publications, and confiscated 180 copies of the book *Allah, Love, and Liberty* by Canadian author Irshad Manji. Ezra Zaid, the director of ZI Publications, was charged under the Selangor state's Sharia legislation, which criminalized publishing, distributing, or possessing books that the state religious authority deemed "contrary to Islamic law."[142] He argued that his constitutional right to free speech had been infringed by the state's Sharia legislation.

The Federal Court unanimously dismissed the challenge, declaring that the constitutional freedom of expression guarantee "must be read in particular" with Article 3 since "Article 3(1) declares Islam as the religion of the Federation."[143] In the Court's view, this meant that Ezra Zaid's freedom of expression right had not been infringed because "a Muslim in Malaysia is not only subjected to the general laws enacted by Parliament, but also to the state laws of religious nature enacted by the Legislature of a state."[144]

Bans on religious books have also been issued under the Printing Presses and Publications Act of 1984, which grants the Home Minister the "absolute discretion" to order a ban on publications that he finds likely to be prejudicial to public order or public interest.[145] Recent High Court decisions have displayed inconsistent approaches to various book bans issued. In 2017, the then Home Minister, under the Barisan Nasional government, banned a compilation of writings by a group of prominent Malay-Muslims, *Breaking the Silence: Voices of Moderation—Islam in a*

[139] *Lina Joy* (H.C.), [2004] 2 MALAYAN L.J. 119, at [58]; *see also* FED. CONST. (MALAY.), art. 160(2) ("'Malay' means a person who professes the religion of Islam, habitually speaks the Malay language, conforms to Malay customs[.]").

[140] *Lina Joy* (C.A.), [2005] 6 MALAYAN L.J. 193, at 208.

[141] [2016] 1 MALAYAN L.J. 153 [hereinafter *ZI Publications*].

[142] Syariah Criminal Offences (Selangor) Enactment 1995 § 16.

[143] *ZI Publications*, [2016] 1 MALAYAN L.J. 153, at [17].

[144] *Id.* at [31].

[145] Printing Presses and Publications Act of 1984 § 7(1).

Constitutional Democracy; the ban was quashed in April 2019 by the High Court.[146] Yet in another case decided later that same month, the High Court upheld a ban on books issued by the think tank Islamic Renaissance Front.[147]

* * *

Apostasy and the unilateral conversion of children have been divisive battle lines in jurisdictional tussles between civil and religious courts. Individuals caught in these jurisdictional gaps are often left unable to access a legal forum to adjudicate their issues. These jurisdictional lacunae are a product of the civil courts' willingness for many years to cede wide authority to the Sharia courts.[148] Cases like *Lina Joy* and *Indira Gandhi* have become focal points in an ideologically polarized debate over the place of religion in Malaysia's public order. The Federal Court's *Indira Gandhi* decision is a welcome affirmation that Article 121(1A) does not constitute a "blanket exclusion" of the civil courts' jurisdiction whenever a matter relates to Islam, particularly when constitutional rights are involved.[149] Still, by distinguishing *Indira Gandhi* from *Lina Joy*, the Federal Court avoided directly addressing the religious freedom claim, leaving unresolved the question of judicial authority over apostasy.

Another strand that emerges from the religion cases is the interpretation of Islam's constitutional role under Article 3(1). Expansive interpretations of Article 3(1) have led to an adjudication approach that prioritizes Islam over other constitutional norms. This approach rejects the idea that secular constitutional norms control religious laws and, in effect, results in a "priority reversal" of religious norms over constitutional authority.[150] As the "Allah" case and the book ban decisions illustrate, such an expansive interpretation of Islam's position has consequences for the constitutional rights to religious liberty and freedom of speech of both Muslims and non-Muslims.

V. Application: Adjudicating Religion and Rights

This section explores the way forward in adjudicating religion and rights in Malaysia's pluralistic constitutional order. It examines foundational elements of the constitutional core that can structure constitutional adjudication on religion.

[146] *See* Ida Lim, *Court Quashes Zahid's Ban on G25's Book on Islam*, MALAY MAIL (Apr. 9, 2019), https://perma.cc/BA69-YGU8.

[147] *See* Terence Tang, *Judge Upholds Zahid's Ban on Three Islamic Renaissance Front Berhad Books*, MALAY MAIL (Apr. 22, 2019), https://perma.cc/6THV-MQZR.

[148] FED. CONST. (MALAY.), art. 121(1A) (stating that the civil courts "shall have no jurisdiction in respect of any matter within the jurisdiction of the Syariah courts").

[149] *Indira Gandhi* (F.C.), [2018] 1 MALAYAN L.J. 545, at [98].

[150] Neo, *Competing Imperatives*, *supra* note 70, at 7.

The original framework and constitutional bargain negotiated at the Malaysian Constitution's founding provides us with an important contextual understanding of the role of religion in the Malaysian state. And the constitutional features of the separation of powers and the rule of law are intimately linked to the judicial power of the civil courts. Courts can draw on these principles to use specific approaches in constitutional decision-making on religion.

A. Judicial Power of the Civil Courts Inherent to Constitution's Basic Structure

At base, protecting the core structure of the constitutional order provides courts with a doctrine to assert their authority even against procedurally proper constitutional amendments. We see this strikingly illustrated in the 2018 case of *Indira Gandhi*. The Malaysian Federal Court expressly established that judicial review and constitutional interpretation are "pivotal constituents of the civil courts' judicial power" and that "[a]s part of the basic structure of the constitution, it cannot be abrogated from the civil courts or conferred upon the Syariah Courts, whether by constitutional amendment, Act of Parliament, or state legislation."[151] *Indira Gandhi* further entrenched the Court's earlier decision in *Semenyih Jaya*,[152] cementing the notion that the Constitution's basic features cannot be altered or removed by constitutional amendment.[153]

What is particularly remarkable about the establishment of the basic structure doctrine in Malaysia is that the Federal Court explicitly invoked the doctrine in the context of asserting the judicial power of the civil courts vis-à-vis the Sharia courts. Religious authority is a fraught area and, as discussed earlier in this chapter, one in which the civil courts have long deferred matters relating to religion to the exclusive jurisdiction of the Sharia courts. The Malaysian Federal Court's decision in *Indira Gandhi* marked a significant reversal of this trend by declaring that authority over constitutional issues lies solely with the civil courts.

The judicial power of the civil courts is now recognized as part of a domain of principles so fundamental to the constitution that it cannot be altered. Courts can draw on the constitutional basic structure doctrine in several ways. Begin with judicial power. Courts should build on this basic structure protection to establish the civil courts' authority by reclaiming jurisdiction over certain areas from the religious courts.

[151] *Indira Gandhi* (F.C.), [2018] 1 Malayan L.J. 545, at [98].

[152] Semenyih Jaya v. Pentadbir Tanah Daerah Hulu Langat [2017] 3 Malayan L.J. 561 [hereinafter *Semenyih Jaya*].

[153] *Indira Gandhi* (F.C.), [2018] 1 Malayan L.J. 545, at [39] (citing Kesavananda Bharati v. State of Kerala, AIR 1973 SC 1461 (India)).

Returning to apostasy, for years, this area has been emblematic of jurisdictional fissures; civil courts have avoided the contentious issue of people seeking to leave Islam by claiming that such matters are solely for the Sharia courts to determine. Even in Indira Gandhi's case, a challenge to her ex-husband converting their children's religious status to Islam, the Malaysian Federal Court shied away from explicitly making its decision about religious freedom. It took pains to say that it did not think the case involved religious status or Islamic personal law. Rather, the Court framed the "pith of the question at hand" as a "prosaic" issue of administrative action: an administrative authority had incorrectly granted the conversion certificates without obtaining the consent of both parents.[154] Whereas in apostasy cases involving individuals seeking to leave Islam, the Malaysian courts have generally continued to affirm the *Lina Joy* orthodoxy that civil courts should leave matters relating to such converts to the sole jurisdiction of the Sharia courts.[155]

But the *Lina Joy* majority's approach of deferring apostasy to the Sharia courts is deeply problematic. Individuals caught in this jurisdictional lacuna between the civil and Islamic courts are left with no alternative if the Sharia Court refuses to recognize their conversion out of Islam—to say nothing of the criminal penalties that many states impose on apostates.[156] And state Islamic administrative authorities and courts have no incentive to reassess their position on apostasy when the civil courts completely relinquish authority over the matter to state Sharia courts.

Some have suggested merging the civil and Sharia legal systems as an alternative jurisdictional model. Former Chief Justice Abdul Hamid Mohamad, for example, has proposed having civil and religious court judges jointly decide cases that involve common law and Islamic law.[157] But this approach does not address the prior, more complex, question of which issues are considered Islamic. Nor does it give any clarity on how to resolve conflicts between Islamic norms and constitutional principles. Would apostasy be considered an Islamic matter or a religious liberty constitutional issue? If the case is heard by both civil and Sharia court judges, which judge would have the final say? In operational terms, the "harmonization" of civil and Sharia law appears directed at furthering the Islamization of the Malaysian legal system by expanding the powers of the Sharia court judges.[158]

Others have suggested that the civil courts should seek to engage with individual state legislatures over religious matters through a dialogic approach.[159] Po Jen Yap suggests that civil courts adopt a jurisdictional clear-statement rule, which would require individual state legislatures to confer adjudicatory jurisdiction on

[154] *Id.* at [108].

[155] *See* Sulok Tawie, *Federal Court defers to Shariah courts in Sarawak apostasy cases*, Malay Mail (Feb. 27, 2018), https://perma.cc/2FVM-U9LS.

[156] *See supra* note 70.

[157] *See* Abdul Hamid Mohamad, *Harmonisation of Common Law and Shariah in Malaysia: A Practical Approach*, 2 Malayan L.J. ix (2009).

[158] Moustafa, *supra* note 4, at 144.

[159] *See* Po Jen Yap, Constitutional Dialogue in Common Law Asia 153–56 (2015).

the Sharia courts expressly by legislation.[160] As Yap puts it, this approach "does not permanently foreclose the legislature from conferring adjudicatory jurisdiction on religious matters such as apostasy on the Syariah courts if it so chooses."[161] But the upshot of such a dialogic approach is that state legislatures need merely make clear their intended intrusion on an individual's rights to religious freedom or equality. Rights infringements would be permissible so long as "the government speaks clearly before it intrudes upon an individual's constitutional right to religious liberty."[162] Such judicial deference to state legislatures provides little protection against a state government willing to stretch the Sharia courts' jurisdiction as far as possible. To point to but one example, in 2015, state legislators in Kelantan unanimously passed amendments to the state's criminal code to implement a range of Islamic criminal law punishments (*hudud*), which would impose harsh penalties against Muslims contrary to the Constitution and common law tradition.[163] If matters like apostasy can be expressly removed from the civil courts' purview by state laws, this could shut out the federal courts and effectively leave individuals who wish to leave Islam with no constitutional recourse at all.

Jurisdictional authority between the civil courts and Sharia courts should be delineated based on a model of constitutional authority. I use the term "constitutional authority" to underscore that jurisdiction be determined along expressly constitutional lines. This jurisdictional demarcation is in line with the Federal Court's decision in *Indira Gandhi*, which made clear that the authority of the civil courts over judicial review and constitutional interpretation is not ousted "whenever a matter relating to Islamic law arises."[164] In short, when constitutional rights are implicated, civil courts should not sidestep judicial review by declining jurisdiction; they should engage directly with the constitutional issue. A constitutional authority approach clarifies the lines of jurisdictional authority between civil courts and religious courts. Matters fall within the authority of the civil courts precisely because they involve issues that are constitutional in nature—as the Federal Court did in taking seriously Indira Gandhi's right to equality. Courts have a duty to engage when constitutional rights are involved.

To wit, when it comes to apostasy, the civil courts should engage directly with the constitutional religious freedom right at stake. Scholars have noted that "one of the most common frustrations" with Malaysian rights jurisprudence "lies in the degree to which Malaysia's courts have sidestepped substantive reviews focusing on the constitutionality of decisions restricting fundamental rights."[165] Courts have used an

160 *Id.* at 155.
161 *Id.* at 156.
162 *Id.*
163 Jaclyn Neo & Dian Shah, *Hudud and the Struggle for Malaysia's Constitutional Soul*, ConstitutionNet (June 25, 2015), https://perma.cc/R8DT-N2DW.
164 *Indira Gandhi* (F.C.), [2018] 1 Malayan L.J. 545, at [72], [98].
165 Matthew J. Nelson & Dian Shah, *Operationalizing and Regulating Religious Freedom: Apostasy and Administrative "Reasonableness" in Malaysia and Beyond*, 16 Int'l J. Const. L. 1293, 1310 (2019).

administrative "reasonableness" test in such cases, "reinforcing a pattern of judicial deference to the executive."[166] As Justice Malanjum argued in his dissent, the *Lina Joy* majority missed a "cardinal principle" in not recognizing that the government's policy implicated Lina Joy's fundamental right to freedom of religion.[167] The constitutional issue must be given priority over any "reasonableness" determination. Courts should stop avoiding the substantive right at the heart of these disputes; they should extend their authority over matters that engage constitutional religious freedom—like apostasy—beyond an administrative level into a constitutional register.

The *Indira Gandhi* affirmation of the judicial power of the federal civil courts also has implications for how courts interact with religious bodies besides Sharia courts, like Islamic fatwa councils and Sharia advisory bodies. Recent developments illustrate the various religious authorities with which courts have to interact.

Consider, for example, the fatwa on naming children born out of wedlock. In 2013, the National Fatwa Council issued an edict forbidding children born outside a marriage from carrying their father's name. On their birth certificates, the last names of such children are recorded as "Abdullah"—a generic surname that exposes the child as illegitimate. A Malay-Muslim couple applied to the National Registration Department to change their child's surname from "Abdullah" to the father's name under a federal law that allows the father to request that his name be registered as the child's surname.[168] But because the child had been born within six months of the parents' marriage, the government department refused to remove the name "Abdullah" from the child's birth certificate, claiming that it was bound by the National Fatwa Council's edict. In 2017, the Court of Appeal unanimously ruled against the National Registration Department.[169] As the Court said, a fatwa issued by a religious body "if at all it has any force of law in syariah jurisprudence, relates purely to the administration of the Islamic law and has nothing to do with the [NRD's] statutory duty" to register births in Malaysia.[170]

Civil courts have been irresolute, however, in how they treat the authority of various religious bodies. In February 2020, the Malaysian Federal Court overruled the Court of Appeal in a four to three decision, holding that a Muslim child born out of wedlock cannot bear the father's name.[171] Another case involved a decree passed by the Selangor state fatwa committee in 2014 that declared Sisters in Islam, a Muslim women's rights organization, as "deviant" from Islamic teaching for subscribing to "religious liberalism and pluralism." In 2019, the High Court dismissed the Sisters in Islam's challenge to this fatwa, ruling that it did not have jurisdiction

[166] *Id.*

[167] *Lina Joy* (F.C.), [2007] 4 MALAYAN L.J. 585, at [84].

[168] *See* A Child & Ors. v. Jabatan Pendaftaran Negara [2017] 4 MALAYAN L.J. 440; *see also* Births and Deaths Registration Act 1957 § 13A(2).

[169] *A Child & Ors.*, [2017] 4 MALAYAN L.J. 440.

[170] *Id.* at [45].

[171] *See 'bin Abdullah' Case: Federal Court Says Illegitimate Muslim Child Cannot Bear Father's Name*, THE STAR (Feb. 13, 2020), https://perma.cc/CE9V-88NA.

to rule on the case because the fatwa was an Islamic matter within the exclusive jurisdiction of the Sharia Court.[172]

In another 2019 decision, *JRI Resources v. Kuwait Finance House Berhad*, the Federal Court split five to four over whether the Sharia Advisory Council's authority to issue rulings on Islamic banking and finance infringed the courts' judicial power.[173] The majority held that it did not.[174] Emphasizing that "Shariah compliance is the backbone of Islamic banking and industry and Shariah principles are the *raison d'être* of all Islamic financial contracts,"[175] it stated that the Sharia Advisory Council's rulings are "solely confined" to the Sharia issue, thus leaving the court with the authority to "decide the case based on the evidence submitted."[176] In a dissenting opinion, Chief Justice Richard Malanjum noted that the federal statute provides that rulings made by the Sharia Advisory Council are final on the issue of Sharia compliance;[177] since the Council's ruling binds the civil court, its function "falls clearly within what may be termed the core area of judicial power."[178]

Still, the Federal Court's decision in *Indira Gandhi* embeds in Malaysian constitutional jurisprudence that judicial power lies solely in the civil courts, and that it forms an unassailable part of the constitution's basic structure. Courts should build on this foundation and lean into their judicial role with greater assurance to assert jurisdiction over all constitutional matters as the final constitutional interpreter vis-à-vis any religious authority.

B. Interpreting Religion and Rights Purposively

A broad question central to debates over the role of religion within the state is how to interpret the Article 3(1) constitutional declaration: "Islam is the religion of the Federation; but other religions may be practised in peace and harmony."[179] On top of jurisdictional conflicts over religious authority, much constitutional litigation has focused on Islam's position under Article 3(1) and how it relates to the constitution's rights guarantees of religious freedom and equality. As we have seen, judicial Islamization by the civil courts has led to Article 3(1) being expansively interpreted to mean that Islam is the "main and dominant religion" of the state.[180]

[172] *See In Sisters in Islam case, High Court says fatwa is Syariah Court's jurisdiction*, NEW STRAITS TIMES (Aug. 27, 2019), https://perma.cc/BZC2-6ZXS.
[173] [2019] 5 CURRENT L.J. 569.
[174] *Id.* at [108].
[175] *Id.* at [56].
[176] *Id.* at [108].
[177] *Id.* at [49] (Richard Malanjum, J., dissenting).
[178] *Id.* at [59].
[179] FED. CONST. (MALAY.), art. 3(1) ("Islam is the religion of the Federation; but other religions may be practised in peace and harmony in any part of the Federation.").
[180] *See, e.g., Lina Joy* (H.C.), [2004] 2 MALAYAN L.J. 119, at 142.

This jurisprudential move away from constitutional history and established precedent has reversed the priority of general constitutional norms over Islamic ones, resulting in an elevated role for Islam.[181]

Recall the case in which the Court of Appeal upheld the government ban on a Catholic publication's use of the word "Allah."[182] The Court of Appeal interpreted Article 3(1) as a constitutional exhortation to "protect the sanctity of Islam as the religion of the country."[183] It zeroed in on the second clause in Article 3(1)—"other religions may be practiced in peace and harmony"—to conclude that this provision meant that "the welfare of an individual or group must yield to that of the community."

In my view, the Court of Appeal, in interpreting the Article 3(1) constitutional provision, got it exactly backward. As we saw in Chapter 3, the constitutional history surrounding the constitutionalization of Islam's position makes it abundantly clear that it was not meant to affect the rights of non-Muslims or any of the other constitutional guarantees. That understanding is borne out in the constitutional text. The first clause of Article 3(1), "Islam is the religion of the Federation," is fused with its second clause—"other religions may be practised in peace and harmony"—precisely because that clause makes explicit a guarantee of protection for other minority religions. The second clause *constitutes* the constitutional compromise embodied by the text. Not only that, Article 3(4) of the same article underscores this point: "Nothing in this Article derogates from any other provision of the Constitution." Interpreting the Constitution holistically reveals a framework designed to declare Islam's position as the state religion while simultaneously guaranteeing protection for religious minorities and individuals.[184]

This broader understanding of the Article 3 constitutional provision puts into perspective the Federal Court's declaration in *Indira Gandhi*: "The Federal Constitution is premised on certain underlying principles… [T]hese principles include the separation of powers, the rule of law, and *the protection of minorities*; these principles are part of the basic structure of the Constitution. Hence, they cannot be abrogated or removed." Recognizing that the protection of minorities is part of the basic structure makes sense within a constitutional scheme that guarantees liberties for religious minorities as part of its Article 3(1) clause constitutionalizing an official religion.

How can courts build on these core features of the constitution in developing constitutional adjudication? As we have seen, a basic structure doctrine can be used

[181] Neo, *Competing Imperatives, supra* note 70, at 18.
[182] *Allah* Case (C.A.), [2013] Malayan L.J. 468.
[183] *Id.* at [33].
[184] This argument is made in greater detail in Chapter 3, Constitutional History, section IV(A).

to invalidate constitutional amendments that undermine fundamental principles of the separation of powers and rule of law—most obviously, those that undermine the courts' judicial power as we saw in *Indira Gandhi*. But striking down amendments is not the only way to use a constitutional basic structure doctrine. Courts can also draw on the constitution's basic features as an interpretive basis for constitutional adjudication. The protection of minorities identified in *Indira Gandhi* as part of the Constitution's basic structure can be relied on as a core constitutional principle to guide a purposive interpretation of both Article 3(1) and the fundamental liberties guarantees.

A purposive interpretive approach in line with the broad principles that underlie the constitution's core would go a significant way to reprioritize constitutional principles over religious norms. Consider in this light the "Allah" case. The Court of Appeal dismissed the Catholic Church's religious freedom claim claiming that "the word or name 'Allah' is not an integral part of the faith and practice of Christianity."[185] But the court seems primarily worried about "the protection and sanctity of Islam."[186] Purposivism would consider Article 3(1) and the right to religious freedom in light of the constitution's broader principle of protection of minorities. A purposive interpretive approach would foreground the constitutional right at stake and reverse the priority given to Islam's role vis-à-vis the constitutional right to religious freedom. It would enable us to see that the church's use of "Allah" in its religious practice is in line with a broader constitutional principle—one that safeguards the right of minority groups and individuals to "profess and practice" their religion.

The 2018 case of *Indira Gandhi* itself demonstrates a generous, purposive approach to interpreting constitutional rights. In ruling that Indira Gandhi had an equal right in the religious conversion of her children,[187] the Federal Court rejected "a literal construction" of the word "parent" for an interpretation that recognized "parents" in the plural, thus granting equal rights to both parents based on a "purposive reading" of the constitutional provision on a child's religious upbringing.[188] The provisions of the Constitution, especially its fundamental liberties guarantees, "are not to be interpreted literally or pedantically,"[189] declared the Court. Just so. Rather, as the Court affirmed, "constitutional documents [are to] be interpreted in a broad and purposive manner."[190]

[185] *Allah* Case (C.A.), [2013] MALAYAN L.J. 468, at [51]. It is worth noting that judicial assessment into what is essential to religious practice is considered by courts in the United States, Canada, and the United Kingdom to be an inherently problematic exercise. *See* Anna Su, *Judging Religious Sincerity*, 5 OXFORD J.L. AND RELIGION 28, 30–38 (2016).

[186] *Allah* Case (C.A.), [2013] MALAYAN L.J. 468, at [50].

[187] *Indira Gandhi* (F.C.), [2018] 1 MALAYAN L.J. 545, at [163].

[188] *Id.* at [164].

[189] *Id.* at [154].

[190] *Id.* at [29] (citing with approval the Reference re Senate Reform [2014] 1 SCR 704, at [25]–[26])).

C. Operationalizing Proportionality

Proportionality offers a judicial tool to operationalize the protection of constitutional rights by enabling courts to develop more a structured approach toward reviewing governmental rights restrictions. That has not traditionally been the approach of Malaysian courts in religion cases. Judges have tended to adopt a highly deferential doctrine of "reasonableness" in reviewing government restrictions on religious freedom.[191]

Courts using a proportionality analysis could more effectively scrutinize government actions that restrict religious liberty or equality. Take, for example, the government prohibition on a non-Muslim publication using the word "Allah." To begin, as discussed earlier, the court should explicitly recognize that the constitutional right to religious freedom has been impacted by the government ban. Once it is established that a religious liberty right is at stake, a proportionality assessment would consider whether the limitation can be justified as legitimate and proportionate. What that means is that a court should carefully assess the government's claim that the prohibition is justified because the Catholic newspaper's use of "Allah" would in fact cause "confusion among Muslims" and "threaten public order and security."[192] Instead of simply granting "great weight to the view of the executive" regarding concerns of public order and national security,[193] as it did in that case, the court should scrutinize whether there is any actual evidence of a credible threat to public order.

Government restrictions on freedom of speech—for example, bans on books on religion deemed against the public interest—should be subject to scrutiny along similar lines.[194] Courts should be less deferential about accepting at face value the government's public order claims and pay more attention to questions like whether such books had already been available to the public before the ban was imposed or whether they had already been published in English. Under a proportionality framework, courts are empowered to assess the government's public interest justifications for restricting rights like free speech; they should insist on doing so.

VI. Conclusion

In March 2018, shortly after the Federal Court delivered its decision in her case, Indira Gandhi was nominated for an International Women of Courage Award by

[191] Nelson & Shah, *supra* note 165, at 1296; *see also* Associated Provincial Picture Houses Ltd. v. Wednesbury Corp., 1 K.B. 223, 234 (1948) (UK) (stating that an administrative act is respected unless it becomes so capricious, perverse, or absurd that "no reasonable authority could have . . . come to it").

[192] *Allah* Case (C.A.), [2013] MALAYAN L.J. 468, at [38].

[193] *Id.* at [44].

[194] *See supra* notes 141–47 and accompanying text.

the U.S. State Department in recognition of her nine-year legal battle over the unilateral conversion of her children.[195] Still, the moment was bittersweet. Although the Federal Court had issued a unanimous decision in her favor and had ordered the police to locate her youngest daughter and ex-husband, at the time of the award, Gandhi had received no news about her daughter, whom she has not seen since her ex-husband took the child away almost a decade ago.

Conflicts over religion continue to populate Malaysia's legal landscape. The *Indira Gandhi* decision was a landmark assertion of constitutional supremacy and judicial power, but jurisprudence on religion is still developing. Malaysian courts should build on the constitution's basic structure foundation to affirm the civil courts' authority over all constitutional matters to resolve tangled areas of jurisdictional authority. Adopting an interpretive approach in light of the constitution's overarching purposes and operationalizing rights protection using a proportionality analysis would help reorient adjudication in religion cases toward reprioritizing constitutional supremacy.

[195] Victoria Brown, *Indira Gandhi Dedicates International Women of Courage Recognition to All Single Parents in Malaysia*, Star Online (Mar. 28, 2018), https://perma.cc/HJP7-NGJT.

8
Balancing Security and Liberty

I. Introduction

On September 15, 2011, in a Malaysia Day speech broadcast on prime-time television, Najib Razak, then the Malaysian Prime Minister, announced that his administration would abolish Malaysia's preventive detention law and all emergency proclamations.[1] The Prime Minister's declaration was momentous. Since the end of the Second World War, Malaysia had formally been under a continued state of emergency, one of the longest-running in the world. Now, the three emergency proclamations that had remained in force for more than forty years were about to be revoked along with the controversial Internal Security Act.

Optimism over the Prime Minister's announced reforms, however, would be short-lived. Soon after, the Barisan Nasional government passed a slew of new national security laws. It replaced the Internal Security Act with a security offense law and revived preventive detention under an anti-terrorism statute. In 2016, the ruling coalition passed a law creating national security council with extensive security powers. It also strengthened an existing sedition law and created an anti-fake news law, both fast-tracked through Parliament just before the 2018 elections, further restricting freedom of expression and assembly.[2]

Emergency powers and laws regulating security and public order have long formed a comprehensive network of state control in Malaysia and Singapore. Officials frequently invoke national security and public interest to justify using state authority to restrict individual rights to life and liberty as well as freedom of expression and assembly. Although the Pakatan Harapan coalition promised to repeal many security laws during its tenure in government, most of these statutes remain in force.[3] Across the causeway, Singapore's Internal Security

[1] *See* Najib Razak, Prime Minister of Malaysia, Malaysia Day Address (Sept. 15, 2011), https://perma.cc/CD57-JLRR; *see also PM Announces Repeal of ISA, Three Emergency Proclamations*, Star Online (Sept. 15, 2011), https://perma.cc/S6BP-HCXL; *Emergency Laws Lifted, EO Void*, Malaysia Today (Nov. 24, 2011), https://perma.cc/K27J-D85C.

[2] *See* Amanda Whiting, *Strengthening Sedition: Part II*, New Mandala (Apr. 21, 2015), https://perma.cc/BFX6-PYE2; *Malaysia's Anti-Fake News Legislation Becomes Law, Is Now Enforceable*, Straits Times (Apr. 11, 2018), https://perma.cc/883R-QCBP.

[3] Tharanya Arumugam & Norrasyidah Arshad, *PM: Laws which Repress the People to be Repealed*, New Straits Times (July 22, 2018), https://perma.cc/P4MN-SWKV; R. Loheswar, *Fulfill Promise to Repeal Draconian Laws, Human Rights Defenders Tell Pakatan*, Malay Mail (Jan. 2, 2019), https://

Constitutional Statecraft in Asian Courts. Yvonne Tew, Oxford University Press (2020). © Yvonne Tew.
DOI:10.1093/oso/9780198716839.001.0001

Act continues to exist and the state recently passed a statute to police fake news.[4]

Navigating the competing concerns of national security and individual liberty raises tensions familiar to democracies across the world. These challenges are particularly fraught in regimes controlled by dominant state power. This chapter explores the complex interaction between individual freedom and national security in the Asian states of Malaysia and Singapore. It outlines each regime's framework of emergency powers and extensive security and public order laws. It then tells the story of confrontations between the courts and the political branches in response to the government's use of emergency powers and security laws. Chastened by forceful political backlash, courts in Malaysia and Singapore retreated. For much of the late twentieth century, they adopted a highly deferential stance toward executive and legislative actions taken in the name of national security. Since the turn of the twenty-first century, though, signs of a revived judiciary have emerged, with recent cases revealing a more critical approach toward the exercise of government discretion.

How should courts approach the constitutionality of government actions justified on grounds of national security or public order? This chapter makes the case for more robust judicial review when the government restricts individual liberty or free expression and assembly. Judicial balancing based on proportionality offers a rigorous, yet flexible, analytical framework that courts can use to directly engage with government justifications of national security. And in the face of legislative efforts to oust judicial review, courts could use a constitutional basic structure doctrine to secure judicial power. These judicial tools would better equip courts in the complex, yet crucial, exercise of balancing security and liberty.

II. Emergency Powers and Security Laws

A. Constitutional Emergency Powers

When it comes to emergency powers and special powers to deal with security threats, Malaysia and Singapore operate constitutional regimes of exception. Constitutional provisions allow the government to use emergency powers (Article 150) and special powers to deal with subversion and threats to public order (Article 149).

perma.cc/6E8T-S278; *Revision of Harsh Laws among Ministry's Agenda—Muhyiddin*, EDGE MKTS. (May 7, 2019), https://perma.cc/J7J3-DZK3.

[4] Tom Benner, *Singapore Passes New Law to Police Fake News Despite Concerns*, AL-JAZERRA (May 8, 2019), https://perma.cc/X89J-22W5.

Article 150 empowers the head of state—the *Yang di-Pertuan Agong* in Malaysia and the President in Singapore—to declare an emergency if he is satisfied that a threat endangers "the security, or the economic life" of the state.[5] During a state of emergency, the head of state may make promulgations that have the force of law,[6] while Parliament can pass laws restricting fundamental rights in the interest of security and public order.[7] Moreover, in 1981, the Malaysian legislature passed an amendment inserting a new clause into the Constitution that excludes the courts from determining any question relating to an emergency proclamation or its continued operation.[8]

Historical context provides some explanation for these constitutional emergency and security regimes. In the aftermath of the Second World War, Malaya was a fragile state. It had just emerged from Japanese occupation, and the British had retaken control facing a Communist insurrection on the rise. In 1948, an armed insurgency by the Malayan Communist Party led the pre-independence government to proclaim the country's first state of emergency. That emergency proclamation was still in force when Malaya became independent in August 1957, and officially ended in 1960.

Negotiations for Malayan independence and the drafting of its new constitution thus took place in the midst a state of emergency—that constitutional history puts in context the constitutionalization of Articles 150 and 149. Writing in its report that it "must first take note of the existing emergency," the Reid Constitutional Commission recommended including constitutional emergency and special powers, observing that the state must have adequate power to protect state safety and to preserve a democratic way of life.[9] Significantly, though, the drafters emphasized that the use of such powers "should be limited and defined," recognizing that the infringement of fundamental rights "is only justified to such an extent as may be necessary to meet any particular danger which threatens the nation."[10] What seems clear is that these emergency and special powers were meant to be temporary and limited in scope.

And yet, the Malayan Emergency from 1948 to 1960 would not be the end of Malaysia's state of emergency. For most of its history since independence, Malaysia has been under a virtually uninterrupted state of emergency. Four other emergencies were proclaimed in 1964, 1966, 1969, and 1977, and three of them remained in

[5] Fed. Const. (Malay.), art. 150(1); Const. of the Rep. of Sing., art. 150(1). In addition to threats to the security and economic life of the state, the Malaysian Constitution lists threats to the "public order" as an additional ground under which a proclamation of emergency may be issued.

[6] Fed. Const. (Malay.), arts. 150(2B)–(2C); Const. of the Rep. of Sing., art. 150(2).

[7] Fed. Const. (Malay.), art. 150(6); Const. of the Rep. of Sing., art. 150(5).

[8] Fed. Const. (Malay.), art. 150(8)(b) (as amended by the Constitution (Amendment) Act (A514), 1981, § 15(d)).

[9] Federation of Malay Constitutional Commission, Report of 1956-57 § Colonial No. 330 [hereinafter Reid Report], at [172]–[173].

[10] *Id.* at [172].

force until the government finally revoked them in 2012. Paradoxically, for almost half a century, what was meant to be a constitutional regime of exception had become the norm.[11]

On top of emergency powers, the constitutions of Malaysia and Singapore include special powers under Article 149 that allow Parliament to enact laws against subversion and actions prejudicial to public order. Article 149 is a wide-ranging provision. It covers situations involving actions by a substantial body of persons to cause fear of organized violence against persons or property, to excite disaffection against the government, to promote hostility between racial groups likely to cause violence, to procure the unlawful alteration of anything established by law, and actions prejudicial to the security of the state.[12] Under Article 149, Parliament can pass laws to restrict constitutional rights to life and liberty, freedom of movement, and freedom of speech and assembly. And Singapore has amended its constitution to exempt the laws passed under Article 149 from judicial review and the constitutional equal protection guarantee.[13]

B. Preventive Detention

The Internal Security Act—perhaps the most prominent law passed under the Article 149 constitutional powers against subversion in post-colonial Malaysia and Singapore—authorizes the indefinite detention without trial of those believed to pose a security threat.[14] It originated in the 1947 emergency regulations used by the British authorities to combat rising communist insurrection.[15] In 1960, when Deputy Prime Minister Tun Abdul Razak presented the Internal Security Act to Parliament, he explained that the law was needed to deal with the threat of communist insurgencies in northern Peninsular Malaysia.[16] Singapore imported the preventive detention law when it joined Malaysia in 1963, and the law remained in force after Singapore left the federation.

In Malaysia, authorities used the Internal Security Act in 1987 in a large-scale operation known as *Operasi Lalang*, carried out under Mahathir Mohamad's administration, in which more than 100 opposition politicians, rights activists, and lawyers were detained without trial.[17] In 1998, the government used the preventive

[11] ANDREW HARDING, THE CONSTITUTION OF MALAYSIA: A CONTEXTUAL ANALYSIS 170 (2012).

[12] FED. CONST. (MALAY.), art. 149.

[13] CONST. OF THE REP. OF SING., arts. 149(1), 149(3).

[14] Internal Security Act, 1960, Act 82, § 8(1) (Malay.) [hereinafter ISA (Malay.)]; Internal Security Act, Cap. 143, 1985 Rev. Ed. Sing., § 8(1) (Sing.) [hereinafter ISA (Sing.)].

[15] *See generally* T.N. HARPER, THE END OF EMPIRE AND THE MAKING OF MALAYA (1999).

[16] *See* Therese Lee, *Malaysia and the Internal Security Act: The Insecurity of Human Rights After September 11*, SING. J. LEGAL STUD. 56, 58 (2002) (citing Parliamentary Debates: Dewan Rakyat (House of Representatives), June 21, 1960).

[17] *Id.* at 58–59.

detention law to detain Anwar Ibrahim after he was removed as deputy prime minister and arrested on what has been regarded as trumped-up charges of corruption and sodomy.[18] Singapore notably employed its Internal Security Act in 1987 to detain a group of Catholic social workers that the authorities alleged were part of a "Marxist conspiracy," even though the group's welfare work did not involve any illegal activity.[19]

In line with the Asian values ideology prominent through the 1990s, the governments of Malaysia and Singapore typically asserted that it was necessary to prioritize community interests and public order over individual rights in justifying expansive security laws. After September 11, 2011, terror-related security threats were also used as justifications for using these powers. From 2001 to 2003, authorities in both countries detained hundreds of people in connection with the *Jemaah Islamiyah* militant Islamist group.[20] Even so, the use of these security laws has not been confined to dealing with terror-related attacks. In 2008, for example, Malaysia detained an opposition member of parliament, a newspaper journalist, and an online blogger under the Internal Security Act despite the lack of any real or perceived national security threat.[21]

The precise scope of the Internal Security Act is difficult to gauge, but it is significant. And although official numbers of preventive detentions made are hard to come by,[22] the law's impact reaches beyond the actual detentions. As Mark Tushnet observes, the Internal Security Act "is the classic sword of Damocles, which is effective in deterring dissent even when it merely hangs suspended over their heads."[23]

In 2012, after the Malaysian government announced it would abolish the preventive detention law, the Singapore government released a statement insisting

[18] *See* Jesse Min Aun Wu, *The Saga of Anwar Ibrahim*, *in* CONSTITUTIONAL LANDMARKS IN MALAYSIA: THE FIRST 50 YEARS 1957–2007 1 (Andrew Harding & H.P. Lee eds., 2007).

[19] *See 16 held in security swoop*, STRAITS TIMES, May 22, 1987, at 1; Michael Hor, *Constitutionalism and Subversion: An Exploration*, *in* EVOLUTION OF A REVOLUTION: FORTY YEARS OF THE SINGAPORE CONSTITUTION 260, 267 (Kevin Tan & Li-ann Thio eds., 2009).

[20] *See* HUMAN RIGHTS WATCH, IN THE NAME OF SECURITY: COUNTERTERRORISM AND HUMAN RIGHTS ABUSES UNDER MALAYSIA'S INTERNAL SECURITY ACT 3 (2004), https://perma.cc/2VYA-5ZSU (noting that "more than one hundred individuals have been detained on terror-related grounds under the ISA" in Malaysia); *see also* Richard Borsuk, *The Secure Aura of Singapore Dims With Terror Plots*, WALL ST. J., Jan. 30, 2002; *Sweeping Asian Terror Alliance Uncovered*, CNN (Sept. 19, 2002), https://perma.cc/V2MX-Q7MB; Raymond Bonner, *Singapore Announces Arrest of 21 Terror Suspects*, N.Y. TIMES (Sept. 16, 2002), https://perma.cc/GR4T-VCAY.

[21] *See Raja Petra, Teresa Kok, and Sin Chew, Reporter Arrested under ISA*, STAR ONLINE (Sept. 13, 2008), https://perma.cc/S5UW-43X7. The Home Minister claimed that the journalist had been detained for "her safety." *See Opposition Slams "Ridiculous" Reason for Using ISA*, STAR ONLINE (Sept. 14, 2008), https://perma.cc/EFZ5-F6KW.

[22] In relation to Singapore's use of the Internal Security Act, see HUMAN RIGHTS WATCH, "KILL THE CHICKEN TO SCARE THE MONKEYS": SUPPRESSION OF FREE EXPRESSION AND ASSEMBLY IN SINGAPORE 14 (2017), https://perma.cc/X3CN-4JFT (stating that "[t]he government conducted a wave of arrests of people for alleged communist subversion through the 1970s and 1980s, with at least 690 people detained without trial under the ISA").

[23] Mark Tushnet, *Authoritarian Constitutionalism*, 100 CORNELL L. REV. 391, 400 (2015).

that its Internal Security Act remained necessary for national security reasons.[24] Singapore has continued to use the law in practice; recently, in 2019, the state detained and issued restriction orders against several Singaporeans it believed to be in danger of being radicalized by the Islamic State in Iraq and Syria (ISIS).

C. National Security and Public Order Laws

For those who viewed Malaysia's repeal of the Internal Security Act and existing emergency declarations as a promising sign of Prime Minister Najib Razak's declared commitment to an agenda of liberalization, the next few years would prove spectacularly disappointing. In the years following the Prime Minister's 2011 speech, the Malaysian government passed several new security and public order laws.

Immediately after the Internal Security Act's repeal, the Barisan Nasional government passed the Security Offences (Special Measures) Act in 2012.[25] This security law authorizes the police to detain any person believed to be involved in security offenses for up to twenty-eight days.[26] These security offenses include espionage, sabotage, and the vaguely defined offense of "activity detrimental to parliamentary democracy."[27] In 2016, authorities used the new security law to arrest fifteen rights activists following the *Bersih Five* rally for clean and fair elections, including rally organizer Maria Chin Abdullah.[28]

In 2015, the Barisan Nasional government reinstated preventive detention under the Prevention of Terrorism Act,[29] which the ruling coalition pushed through in a parliamentary late-night sitting.[30] A Prevention of Terrorism Board can order suspects of terrorism-related activity to be detained for up to two years, renewable for

[24] *Singapore Ministry of Home Affairs will not follow Malaysia to abolish the ISA*, YouTube (Sept. 16, 2011), https://perma.cc/RT9C-FFFQ.

[25] Sumisha Naidu, *Malaysia's Controversial National Security Council Act Kicks In*, Channel News Asia (Aug. 1, 2016), https://perma.cc/VFM5-DRB8; Security Offences (Special Measures) Act, Act 747, 2012, https://perma.cc/SC7E-USMY.

[26] Security Offences (Special Measures) Act, Act 747, 2012 §§ 4(1), 4(5).

[27] Penal Code, Act 574, § 124B-N.

[28] *See* Rozanna Latiff & Praveen Menon, *Malaysian Protesters March Against Prime Minister Najib*, Reuters (Nov. 18, 2016), https://perma.cc/Y9RK-BS9T; Joon Ian Wong, *Malaysia is Responding to a Peaceful Protest by Locking up its Organizer in Solitary Confinement Without Trial*, Quartz (Nov. 21, 2016), https://perma.cc/3VLH-2FC5.

[29] Prevention of Terrorism Act, 2015, § 3(1) [hereinafter POTA], https://perma.cc/FY3H-FUTS. *See* Thomas Fuller, *Malaysia Revives Detention Without Trial With New Law*, N.Y. Times (Apr. 7, 2015), https://perma.cc/M789-UG8B.

[30] *See Parliament Passes Controversial Anti-Terrorism Law by 79 to 60 Votes*, Malaysian Insider (Apr. 7, 2015), https://perma.cc/3PJL-47VC; Jason Ng, *Malaysian Parliament Passes Anti-Terrorism Bill*, Wall St. J. (Apr. 7, 2015), https://perma.cc/JH7D-99GN; *see also* Steven Thiru, Press Release, Malaysian Bar, Prevention of Terrorism Bill 2015 Violates Malaysia's Domestic and International Commitments, is an Affront to the Rule of Law and is Abhorrent to Natural Justice (Apr. 5, 2015), https://perma.cc/XDF9-CGZ9.

an indefinite period of time.[31] The anti-terrorism law also curtails judicial review of any of the Board's decisions.[32]

The following year—in another late-night parliamentary sitting that ended in the early hours of the morning—the Barisan Nasional government passed the National Security Council Act.[33] That law allows the prime minister, on advice of a security council, to declare security areas over which security forces would then have broad powers to arrest, search and seize without warrant.[34] Alarmed by the expansive powers afforded to the executive, opposition members of parliament pointed out that the prime minister had the power to declare what in effect amounted to a state of emergency, bypassing the constitution's emergency provisions.[35]

Public order laws restricting freedom of assembly and expression were also passed by the Najib Razak administration. It passed the Peaceful Assembly Act 2012, which requires police authorization of all assemblies,[36] and strengthened an existing colonial-era sedition law.[37] Amendments passed in 2015 to the Sedition Act created harsher penalties, introducing a minimum three-year jail term and increasing the maximum jail term to up to twenty years.[38] In addition to creating a new seditious offense—the promotion of ill will, hostility, or hatred "on the grounds of religion"[39]—the new law extended the courts' power to prohibit the circulation of seditious material to include online media.[40] Sedition investigations and prosecutions increased sharply in practice following the repeal of the Internal Security Act.[41]

On top of all that, in the months leading up to the national elections in 2018, the Barisan Nasional government passed the Anti-Fake News Act.[42] Widely seen

[31] POTA §§ 8(1), 13(1), 17(1).

[32] *Id.* § 19.

[33] *See* National Security Council Act, Act 776, 2016 [hereinafter NSCA], https://perma.cc/CE2R-ABJN; *see also* Leslie Shaffer, *Malaysia's New National Security Law Gives Najib, Army, Police New Powers, amid 1MDB Probe*, CNBC (July 31, 2016), https://perma.cc/7MKN-LYF3; Austin Ramzy, *Malaysian Security Law Invites Government Abuses, Rights Groups Say*, N.Y. TIMES (Dec. 3, 2015), https://perma.cc/MW7B-D72Z.

[34] NSCA §§ 18, 25, 26.

[35] *Malaysia Approves Security Law Slammed by Critics*, AP (Dec. 3, 2015), https://perma.cc/D3ZP-AC4T.

[36] Peaceful Assembly Act 2012, Act 736, §§ 9–15.

[37] *See* Amanda Whiting, *Strengthened Sedition: Part III*, NEW MANDALA (Apr. 22, 2015), https://perma.cc/B9E4-2QJ4; *see also Malaysia's Deplorable Sedition Act*, N.Y. TIMES (Oct. 6, 2014), https://perma.cc/E8FC-ZUCE; *Malaysia Approves Security Law Amid Warning It Could Lead to Dictatorship*, GUARDIAN (Dec. 3, 2015), https://perma.cc/VYB2-7N9G.

[38] Sedition (Amendment) Act, 2015, § 4(a) (amending § 4 of the Sedition Act); *id.* § 4(b) (inserting § 4(1)(a) into the Sedition Act), https://perma.cc/MZ2V-ACDS.

[39] *Id.* §§ 3(a)(iv)–(v) (amending § 3(1)(e) of the Sedition Act and inserting a new § 3(1)(ea)).

[40] *Id.* § 9 (inserting § 10(a) into the Sedition Act).

[41] *See* Whiting, *supra* note 2; *see also* Hew Lee Yee, *Sedition Act 2015: Who Have Been Arrested, Investigated, and Charged So Far?* (May 6, 2015), SAYS, https://perma.cc/Q582-LCUK. The list includes several opposition politicians, journalists, an academic, and a human rights activist.

[42] *See* Anti-Fake News Act, 2018, https://perma.cc/N34T-MBYD; *see also Malaysia Opposition Blocks Repeal of "Fake News" Law in Challenge to Mahathir*, REUTERS (Sept. 12, 2018), https://perma.cc/R6F2-Z7PD; Gulizar Haciyakupoglu, *Malaysia's Elections and the Anti-Fake News Act*, DIPLOMAT (Apr. 26, 2018), https://perma.cc/GZW3-X74C.

as a means to control the public's use of social media to criticize the government, the new law made it an offense punishable by hefty fines and a jail term of up to ten years to publish what the government deemed to be "fake news."[43]

Altogether, the legal reforms enacted during Najib Razak's Barisan Nasional government from 2012 to 2018 demonstrate the sweeping breadth of government powers justified in the name of national security and public order. The Pakatan Harapan government that came into power in 2018 promised in its election manifesto that it would repeal these repressive laws. But in practice, that did not fully materialize. The Harapan government voted to repeal the anti-fake news law and said several security and public order laws were under review. It had initially imposed a moratorium on several security laws,[44] although there were times it lifted the moratorium to deal with threats to the public order and race relations.[45] The new Perikatan Nasional government has not indicated that it plans to repeal any existing security laws.

Singapore, too, has a panoply of national security and public order laws that restrict individual liberty and freedom of expression. In addition to its Internal Security Act, which remains in force, the Criminal Law (Temporary Provisions) Act authorizes the Home Affairs Minister to detain without trial a person who has been associated with activities of a criminal nature if the Minister believes it "necessary in the interests of public safety, peace, and good order."[46]

Like Malaysia, Singapore also has a colonial-style sedition law, which it has used on a number of occasions, typically to restrain speech deemed to promote hostility based on race and religion.[47] Examples include sedition charges brought against a couple for distributing evangelical Christian tracts deemed offensive to Muslims. The state also charged another couple for running a website that allegedly promoted racial hostility and anti-foreigner rhetoric,[48] and investigated an imam for allegedly making insensitive comments about other religious communities in a prayer at a mosque.[49] The Singapore government has also frequently used libel laws to bring defamation suits, including against the media. Defamation suits

[43] Anti-Fake News Act § 4(1).

[44] *See* Tarrence Tan, *Dr M: Pakatan to Repeal Controversial Laws, Including Fake News Act*, Star Online (Apr. 3, 2018), https://perma.cc/E75H-KKZ3; *Repeal Sedition Act at coming Parliament Sitting, Urges Gobind*, New Straits Times (Oct. 8, 2018), https://perma.cc/BBH5-U845; *Kit Siang Joins Calls for a Moratorium on Repressive Laws*, Malaysiakini (Oct. 10, 2018), https://perma.cc/A6ZY-JH78.

[45] Danial Dzulkifly, *Sedition Act, Security Laws Open to Abuse, Activists Tell Putrajaya*, Malay Mail (Dec. 4, 2018), https://perma.cc/7VGC-BQ3P.

[46] Criminal Law (Temporary Provisions) Act, Cap. 67, 2000 Rev. Ed. Sing., § 30, https://perma.cc/8NTK-MGTW.

[47] Jaclyn Neo, *Seditious in Singapore! Free Speech and the Offence of Promoting Ill-Will and Hostility Between Different Racial Groups*, 2011 Sing. J. Legal Stud. 351, 353 (2011).

[48] *See, e.g.*, Public Prosecutor v. Ong Kian Cheong [2009] SGDC 163; *Australian behind Singapore Anti-Foreigner Website The Real Singapore Convicted of Sedition*, ABC (Mar. 8, 2016), https://perma.cc/R7M6-QJRJ.

[49] *See* Yuen Sin, *Imam Being Probed over Comments on Christians and Jews*, Straits Times (Mar. 2, 2017), https://perma.cc/M97M-JZ5G.

that have resulted in substantial monetary damage awards have sometimes bankrupted opposition politicians, leaving them ineligible to run for public office under Singapore's electoral rules.[50]

In 2019, while the Malaysian houses of parliament were battling over the repeal of the Anti-Fake News Act, Singapore passed its own law against false news. Under the Protection from Online Falsehoods and Manipulation Act, authorities may order online platforms to remove content deemed false or block websites deemed to be propagating false statements against the public interest.[51] The new law prohibits false factual statements that are likely to be prejudicial to national security or public safety, to incite enmity between different groups of persons, or diminish public confidence in the government.[52] As with many of its laws regulating speech and expression, the Singapore government defended these restrictions on online social and news media as in the interest of public order.

III. Judicial Review and State Power

When confronted with consolidated power between the legislative and executive branches, courts appear to face a Sisyphean task in seeking to force governing powers to comply with legal constraints. Judicial assertiveness in fragile democracies is especially perilous when exercised over state power wielded in the name of national security. To set this in context, I trace the arc of the struggle between the courts and political branches in the constitutional histories of Malaysia and Singapore.

A. Confrontation

The story of the institutional contest between the political branches and the judiciary cannot properly be told without an account of the clashes over preventive detentions under the Internal Security Act in Malaysia and Singapore, which has continued to figure in the collective memory of citizens in these states.[53] Central to the Internal Security Act is the provision authorizing the Home Affairs Minister to detain individuals without trial if the executive is "satisfied" that the detention

[50] Const. of the Rep. of Sing., art. 45(1)(b); *see also* Cameron Sim, *The Singapore Chill: Political Defamation and the Normalization of a Statist Rule of Law*, 20 Pac. Rim L. & Pol'y J. 319, 331–45 (2011).

[51] *See* Tom Benner, *Singapore Passes New Law to Police Fake News Despite Concerns*, Al-Jazeera (May 8, 2019), https://perma.cc/X89J-22W5; Tessa Wong, *Singapore Fake News Law Polices Chats and Online Platforms*, BBC (May 9, 2019), https://perma.cc/38NM-GMTA.

[52] Protection from Online Falsehoods and Manipulation Bill, No. 10/2019, 2019, § 7(1), https://perma.cc/V5XS-ZHHW.

[53] *See, e.g.*, Andrew Jacobs, *As Singapore Loosens Its Grip, Residents Lose Fear to Challenge Authority*, N.Y. Times (June 16, 2012), https://perma.cc/PU3W-MX6X.

is necessary to prevent the person from disrupting national security.[54] This provision has been the main site for challenges to authoritarian state power. Courts in Malaysia and Singapore initially held that it was sufficient that the executive believed that the detainee posed a national security threat, without requiring a reasonable basis for such belief. In line with the "subjective" approach advocated in the British case of *Liversidge v. Anderson*,[55] the Malaysian Supreme Court said that the executive had "complete discretion" over detention decisions, declaring "it is not for a court of law to question the sufficiency or relevancy of those allegations of fact."[56] A similar formulation was applied by the Singapore High Court in the 1971 case of *Lee Mau Seng v. Minister for Home Affairs*.[57]

Yet even as the Malaysian and Singaporean courts affirmed this subjective approach in 1969 and 1971, the legacy of *Liversidge v. Anderson* had already begun to wane in Britain and elsewhere. Over the second half of the twentieth century, courts in the United Kingdom and across the Commonwealth began to adopt the approach advocated by Lord Atkin's famous dissent in *Liversidge*,[58] where he argued that the executive's exercise of discretion should be determined on an objective basis.[59] By the late 1980s, some Malaysian judicial decisions, too, began to reflect a move toward an objective test of the minister's satisfaction.[60]

Against this backdrop, the Singapore Court of Appeal delivered its decision in *Chng Suan Tze v. Minister of Home Affairs*.[61] Recall from Chapter 5 that this 1987 case involved the Singapore government's detention of Catholic social workers for being involved in what government officials called a "Marxist conspiracy" to subvert the Singapore government.[62] In a landmark decision, the Court of Appeal unanimously decided that it was not enough for the President to be subjectively satisfied that the detention was necessary. Rather, it held that there must be some objective basis for the executive's belief that the detainee posed a threat,[63] noting that "the court can examine whether the executive's decision was in fact based on national security considerations."[64] Chief Justice

54 ISA (Malay.) § 8(1); ISA (Sing.) § 8(1).

55 [1942] A.C. 206.

56 Karam Singh v. Menteri Hal Ehwal Dalam Negeri [1969] 2 MALAYAN L.J. 129, 151.

57 [1971] 2 MALAYAN L.J. 137.

58 *Liversidge*, [1942] A.C. 206, at 244.

59 *See, e.g.*, A-G of St. Christopher, Nevis and Anguilla v. Reynolds [1980] A.C. 637 (P.C) (citing Nakkuda Ali v. Jayaratne [1951] A.C. 66 (P.C.)); *see also* R. v. IRC *ex parte* Rossminster [1980] A.C. 952, 1011 (H.L.) (Lord Diplock) ("[T]he time has come to acknowledge openly that the majority of this House in *Liversidge v. Anderson* were expediently . . . wrong and the dissenting speech of Lord Atkin was right.").

60 *See* Re Tan Sri Raja Khalid bin Raja Harun [1988] 3 MALAYAN L.J. 89 (observing, in granting a *habeas corpus* application, that it would be "naïve to preclude the judge from making his own evaluation and assessment from an obvious statement of fact").

61 [1988] 2 SING. L. REP. (R.) 525.

62 *See* Chapter 5, The Rule of Law, section III(B).

63 *Chng Suan Tze*, [1988] 2 SING. L. REP. (R.) 525, at [55].

64 *Id.* at [139].

Wee Chong Jin's opinion recognized that: "[T]he notion of a subjective or unfettered discretion is contrary to the rule of law. All power has legal limits and the rule of law demands that the courts should be able to examine the exercise of a discretionary power."[65]

The Singapore government's reaction was swift and forceful. In 1988, immediately after the decision in *Chng Suan Tze*, the government pushed through amendments to both the Constitution and the Internal Security Act. The constitutional amendments allowed the government to derogate from the constitutional equal protection guarantee and the provision vesting judicial power in the courts. The legislature also inserted two clauses into Singapore's Internal Security Act to curtail judicial review. The first statutory clause provided that the law governing judicial review of any decision under the statute "shall be the same as was applicable and declared in Singapore on the 13th day of July 1971."[66] This peculiar clause was meant to reinstate the subjective test for the President's discretion over preventive detention that had been the Singapore Court's earlier position—laid out in a case decided on July 13, 1971.[67] Remarkably, the Singapore legislature's move was meant to freeze the common law at the point in time when judicial precedent had held the test to be a purely subjective one.[68] In addition, the Parliament amended the statute to prohibit any judicial review, except on procedural grounds, of "any act done or decision made by the President or the Minister" under the Internal Security Act.[69]

Meanwhile, Malaysia's Mahathir Mohamad had become increasingly frustrated with the Malaysian judiciary. As we saw in Chapter 4, following several judicial rulings against the government,[70] the Malaysian legislature amended Article 121 of the Malaysian Constitution in 1988 to remove the reference to the judicial power vesting in the courts and to provide instead that the courts "shall have such jurisdiction and powers as may be conferred by or under federal law."[71] And six months after the Singapore Parliament passed its constitutional and legislative amendments relating to its Internal Security Act, the Malaysian government likewise amended its own preventive detention law to preclude any judicial review except on purely procedural grounds.[72]

[65] *Id.* at [86].

[66] ISA (Sing.) § 8B(1).

[67] *Lee Mau Seng*, [1971] 2 MALAYAN L.J. 137.

[68] Kevin Tan, *Recent Developments in the Law and Practice of Preventive Detention*, *in* PUBLIC LAW IN CONTEMPORARY MALAYSIA 293, 307 (Min Aun Wu ed. 1999) (arguing that amending the statute in this way was "tantamount to directing the court to decide cases in a certain way").

[69] ISA (Sing.) § 8B(2).

[70] *See* Chapter 4, The Separation of Powers, section III; *see, e.g.*, Karpal Singh v. Minister for Home Aff. [1988] 1 MALAYAN L.J. 468; Inspector-Gen. of Police v. Tan Sri Raja Khalid [1988] 1 MALAYAN L.J. 182; Lim Kit Siang v. Dr. Mahathir Mohamed [1987] 1 MALAYAN L.J. 383.

[71] FED. CONST. (MALAY.), art. 121(1).

[72] ISA (Malay.) § 8B(1).

B. Retreat

Chastened, the courts retreated to a more cautious position. In the 1989 case of *Teo Soh Lung v. Minister for Home Affairs*,[73] the Singapore High Court ruled against the detainees—the same ones in *Chng Suan Tze*, whom the state had released and immediately re-arrested under the amended internal security statute. The High Court's decision appeared to affirm that the legislature had succeeded in turning back the judicial clock to the prior position of non-justiciability. In contrast to the robust principle of legality laid out in *Chng Suan Tze*, the High Court's decision was rigidly formalist: "Parliament has done no more than to enact the rule of law relating to the law applicable to judicial review."[74] The detainees appealed, and the case ended up back before the same Court of Appeal bench that had decided *Chng Suan Tze*.

This time, the Singapore Court of Appeal's judgment was more enigmatic.[75] Singapore's apex appellate court studiously focused its decision on the facts of the case before it, upholding the detentions on the basis that they could not be shown to be unrelated to national security considerations. But the Court avoided resolving broader questions about whether the courts could review detentions made for a purpose other than national security or whether the post-*Chng Suan Tze* constitutional amendments were unconstitutional. The Singapore Court's judicial maneuvering—in what has been described "an elegant piece of judicial 'kung fu' "[76]—leaves open the opportunity for the judiciary to revisit these issues in the future, potentially from a position of greater institutional strength.

C. Resurgence

For many years courts in Malaysia and Singapore adopted a highly deferential approach to the executive's decisions about what was necessary in the interest of national security. Judges avoided review of executive decisions on internal security matters or, even when they didn't, exercised judicial review narrowly on purely procedural grounds.[77]

In recent years, there have been occasional signs of greater judicial willingness to scrutinize the constitutionality of government actions justified in the name of

[73] [1989] SING. L. REP. 108.

[74] *Id.* at [48].

[75] Teo Soh Lung v. Minister for Home Aff. [1990] 2 MALAYAN L.J. 129 (C.A.).

[76] Hor, *supra* note 19, at 287.

[77] The Malaysian courts in the past have found several detentions invalid for procedural breaches. *See, e.g.*, Puvaneswaran v. Menteri Hal Ehwal Dalam Negeri Malaysia [1991] 3 MALAYAN L.J. 28 (finding procedural defect in failure to serve two copies of the detention order to the detainee); Lee Swee Fei v. Menteri Hal Ehwal Dalam Negeri Malaysia [1994] 2 MALAYAN L.J. 468 (finding procedural defect in delay between the alleged facts and the issuing of the detention order).

national security.[78] Even before the repeal of the Internal Security Act in Malaysia, the Malaysian Federal Court rejected a subjective test for a police officer's belief that a suspect posed a security threat, ruling that the police must have an objectively reasonable basis for that suspicion before arresting someone.[79] And in a 2008 case involving detention of Malaysian blogger Raja Petra Kamaruddin, the High Court dismissed the notion that the Internal Security Act's ouster clause excluded judicial review of ministerial decisions made outside of the statute's fundamental objectives.[80] With the demise of the internal security law in 2011, much of the constitutional review discourse has centered on government regulations on expression and assembly.

The Malaysian courts' approach to reviewing public order laws restricting free expression or assembly has been highly inconsistent. In 2014, the Malaysian Court of Appeal in *Nik Nazmi v. Public Prosecutor* considered a freedom of assembly challenge to the Peaceful Assembly Act.[81] Under the Act, section 9(1) requires organizers of an assembly to provide the police with ten days of advance notice and section 9(5) criminalizes a failure to provide the notice.[82] The Court of Appeal unanimously struck down section 9(5) of the Public Assembly Act as unconstitutional and acquitted the appellant, an organizer of a peaceful assembly calling for electoral reform. Justice Hamid Sultan held that criminalizing the failure to provide notice "has no nexus to 'public order' or 'interest of the security of the federation' unless the assembly was not peaceful."[83] Thus, the restriction on the constitutional right to freedom of assembly failed both a reasonableness and proportionality test.[84] Justice Mah Weng Kwai went further; he found both sections 9(1) and 9(5) unconstitutional because the government "has not produced any evidence to show how failure to give the ten days' notice will necessarily result in a threat to national security or public order."[85]

In stark contrast, barely a year later, in the case of *Public Prosecutor v. Yuneswaran*,[86] a differently constituted Court of Appeal bench departed from its previous decision, upholding the Peaceful Assembly Act as constitutionally valid. In a complete about turn from *Nik Nazmi*, the Court of Appeal held that restrictions on freedom of expression and assembly had to be neither reasonable nor proportionate.[87]

78 *See* Jaclyn Neo, *Parsing Privity Clauses in Malaysia: Rights, Security and Judicial Review in Malaysia*, 1 PUB. L. 25 (2010).
79 Mohamad Ezam Noor v. Ketua Polis Negara [2002] 4 MALAYAN L.J. 449.
80 Raja Petra Kamaruddin v. Menteri Hal Ehwal Dalam Negeri [2008] M.L.J.U. 1095 (H.C.).
81 [2014] 4 MALAYAN L.J. 157 [hereinafter *Nik Nazmi*]
82 Peaceful Assembly Act, 2012, §§ 9(1), 9(5).
83 *Nik Nazmi*, [2014] 4 MALAYAN L.J. 157, at [141].
84 *Id.*
85 *Id.* at [111].
86 [2015] 9 CURRENT L.J. 873 [hereinafter *Yuneswaran*].
87 *Id.* at [58].

Several days later, the Federal Court in *Public Prosecutor v. Azmi Sharom* unanimously upheld the Sedition Act against a freedom of expression challenge.[88] Although the Federal Court accepted that a proportionality analysis should be used to determine the statute's constitutionality, its application of the proportionality test was far from rigorous.[89] Offering little analysis for its conclusion, the Court held that the restrictions imposed by the sedition law were not "too remote or not sufficiently connected" to the constitutional limits on the right to freedom of assembly, which allows Parliament to impose such restrictions "as it deems necessary or expedient" in the interest of national security.[90] Without considering whether the statute's broad definition of "seditious tendency" was no more restrictive than necessary, beyond observing that the law was subject to a number of exceptions, the Court found the Sedition Act's provisions to be proportionate. Applied in such a perfunctory manner, the adoption of a supposed proportionality analysis is unlikely to exercise any meaningful review over government intrusions on constitutional rights.[91]

The case of *Mat Shuhaimi bin Shafiei v. Government of Malaysia* illustrates similar battle lines. The Court of Appeal struck down a provision of the Sedition Act criminalizing sedition on a strict liability basis, ruling that the law disproportionately infringed the right to freedom of expression.[92] Declaring that the Federal Court in *Azmi Sharom* had "expressly endorsed" the proportionality test as "an entrenched part" of Malaysian law, the court held that the jurisprudence relating to guarantees of fundamental liberties "had now evolved to a stage" that any valid legislation had to "meet the test of proportionality."[93] But when the case reached the Federal Court in 2018, the apex court set aside the Court of Appeal's decision on procedural grounds.[94] Ruling that the appeal was an abuse of process because the issue was *res judicata* for having been raised in earlier criminal proceedings, the Federal Court's decision effectively revived the strict liability provision of the sedition law.

88 [2015] M.L.J.U. 594 [hereinafter *Azmi Sharom*].

89 *Id.* at [41]–[43]. The Court refers to the proportionality analysis adopted by the United Kingdom Privy Council in *de Freitas v. Permanent Secretary of Ministry of Agriculture, Fisheries, Lands and Housing* [1998] UKPC 30 ("In determining whether a limitation is arbitrary or excessive … the court would ask itself: whether: (i) the legislative objective is sufficiently important to justify limiting a fundamental right; (ii) the measures designed to meet the legislative objective are rationally connected to it; and (iii) the means used to impair the right or freedom are no more than is necessary to accomplish the objective.").

90 *Azmi Sharom*, [2015] M.L.J.U. 594, at [43]; *see also* FED. CONST. (MALAY.), art. 10(2).

91 *See* Yvonne Tew, *On the Uneven Journey to Constitutional Redemption: The Malaysian Judiciary And Constitutional Politics*, 25 WASH. INT'L L. J. 673, 689–90 (2016).

92 Mat Shuhaimi v. Gov't of Malaysia [2017] 1 MALAYAN L.J. 436 (C.A.) [hereinafter *Mat Shuhaimi* (C.A.)].

93 *Id.* at [25].

94 Gov't of Malaysia v. Mat Shuhaimi [2018] 2 MALAYAN L.J. 133 (F.C.) [hereinafter *Mat Shuhaimi* (F.C.)], at [19]–[41]. For discussion, see Shukri Ahmad Shahizam, *One Step Forward, Two Steps Back? Constructive res judicata in Malaysian Constitutional Cases*, INT'L J. CONST. L. BLOG (Feb. 3, 2018), https://perma.cc/3A64-7GXN.

After the 2018 transition of government in Malaysia, several security laws came under review by the Pakatan Harapan government.[95] The future of these security statutes is uncertain, especially now that the federal government has been taken over by the Peikatan Nasional coalition, which includes parties from the Barisan Nasional coalition that had previously implemented many of these statutes. It's worth noting that a number of constitutional challenges have been brought against these laws. For example, in 2016, Anwar Ibrahim began a lawsuit challenging the constitutionality of the National Security Council Act.[96] The lawsuit sought to invalidate both the statute and the constitutional amendment under which it was passed for infringing the Constitution's basic structure.

What of the Singaporean courts? For many years after *Chng Suan Tze* and political backlash against the Court of Appeal, the Singaporean judiciary approached constitutional interpretation in a highly literalist manner and avoided scrutinizing the reasonableness of government actions.[97] But more recently the Singapore judiciary has shown signs of emerging from the long shadow of political retaliation to *Chng Suan Tze*.

In 2015, the Singapore Court of Appeal revisited the standard of review in preventive detention cases in *Tan Seet Eng v. Attorney General*,[98] described as "one of the most significant decisions affirming the principle of legality,"[99] as we discussed in Chapter 5.[100] *Tan Seet Eng*, a case that presented the "mirror image of *Chng*," involved a preventive detention order under the Criminal Law (Temporary Provisions) Act.[101] Like the Internal Security Act, this statute empowers the Minister for Home Affairs to detain an individual indefinitely—in this case, if the person is associated with activities of a criminal nature and the Minister believes it "necessary in the interests of public safety, peace, and good order."[102] Ordering that the detainee be released, the Court rejected a subjective analysis of ministerial discretion in favor of an objective inquiry into whether there is reasonable basis for the Minister's belief.[103] The Court recognized that "a court may and indeed should examine whether the power that is vested in the Minister is being properly invoked."[104]

[95] *See* Siti Fatimah Zainal, *Home Ministry denies Pakatan Backtracking Repeal of Draconian Laws*, STAR ONLINE (Apr. 20, 2019), https://perma.cc/Z85U-YMHR.

[96] *See* Khairah N. Karim, *Anwar seeks Apex Court rule on validity of National Security Council Act*, NEW STRAITS TIMES (Feb. 27, 2019), https://perma.cc/Q5L9-9G2J.

[97] *See* Chapter 2, Constitutional Adjudication and Constitutional Politics, section IV. *See, e.g.*, Chee Siok Chin v. Minister for Home Aff. [2006] 1 SING. L. REP. (R.) 582; Lim Meng Suang v. Att'y Gen. [2015] 1 SING. L. REP. 26.

[98] [2016] 1 SING. L. REP. 779.

[99] Jaclyn Neo, *"All Power Has Legal Limits"–The Principle of Legality as a Constitutional Principle of Judicial Review*, 29 SING. ACAD. L.J. 667, 681 (2017).

[100] *See* Chapter 5, The Rule of Law, section III(B).

[101] *See* Neo, *supra* note 99, at 681.

[102] Criminal Law (Temporary Provisions) Act, Cap. 67, 2000 Rev. Ed. Sing., § 30, https://perma.cc/3NTK-MGTW.

[103] *Tan Seet Eng*, [2016] 1 SING. L. REP. 779, at [56].

[104] *Id.* at [97].

Of particular import in *Tan Seet Eng* is that the Singapore Court of Appeal deliberately revived the principles articulated in *Chng Suan Tze*. While it acknowledged that *Chng* was legislatively overruled by amendments to the Constitution and the Internal Security Act, it made clear that the propositions laid down in *Chng* "continue to be relevant" today.[105] Repeatedly referring to the rule of law propositions set forth in *Chng Suan Tze*, the Court explicitly concluded that the exercise of discretion by the executive and legislative branch "remains a matter for the courts to decide."[106] In ruling that the amendments did not affect the position before it in *Tan Seet Eng*, the Court seized on the fact that this case is not concerned with the Internal Security Act. But that distinction is merely a technicality. Crucially, the Court in *Tan Seet Eng* endorsed the notion in *Chng* that "[a]ll power has legal limits," with the corollary that it is the role of the courts "to determine whether those limits have been exceeded."[107] Through its phoenix-like maneuver in *Tan Seet Eng*, the Singapore Court of Appeal manage to resurrect an account of judicial power to rise from the constitutional ashes left in the wake of *Chng Suan Tze*.

IV. Application: Judicial Balancing of Security and Liberty

Constitutional rights are not absolute; they can be overridden when the government deems it justified in the interests of national security and public order. So goes the dominant narrative that has traditionally dominated the constitutional discourse on state interests and individual liberties. Courts in Malaysia and Singapore have tended to defer extensively to the government's prioritization of state or public interests over constitutional rights. Instead of reflexive judicial deference to the executive or legislature, I argue in this section that courts should seek to engage directly with the rights and interests at stake.

Judicial balancing through proportionality has become prevalent as the dominant legal device used by courts across the world to review rights claims.[108] A proportionality approach reflects an endeavor to balance competing interests and to weigh the government's claims against the rights of the individual. A proportionality analysis offers a structured device well-suited for the judicial balancing of individual liberty and security interests that these Asian courts can use to adjudicate rights more effectively.

105 *Id.*

106 *Id.* at [98].

107 *Id.*

108 *See* Alec Stone Sweet & Jud Mathews, *Proportionality Balancing and Global Constitutionalism*, 47 COLUM. J. TRANSNAT'L L. 72 (2008).

A. From Deference to Proportionality

For decades, judiciaries in Malaysia and Singapore have adopted a posture of submissively deferring to the political branches. Many have questioned whether Asian courts are able and willing to take on effective rights protection. To be sure, the challenges of having to coexist with a dominant ruling regime play some part in the lack of judicial willingness to exercise constitutional review.[109] But political dynamics shift, and even dominant political parties do not remain invulnerable.[110]

The traditional framework of strong judicial deference to the political branches is out of place in contemporary Malaysia and Singapore. Formal deference doctrines result in courts simply accepting the government's prioritization of collective interests over individual rights.[111] Modern rights claims, like those challenging governmental regulations on public assemblies or prohibiting speech, call for more robust scrutiny of the government's reasons for its actions in light of the rights impacted.

Proportionality analysis provides courts with a sensitive yet potentially robust tool to weigh the government's justification for its liberty-impairing actions. In few other contexts is the endeavor of balancing competing interests as crucial, and as complex, as when assessing state actions defended in terms of national security or public order. Unlike uncritical judicial deference, a proportionality analysis does not allow courts reflexively to accept the government's rationale, even when stated in terms of national security or public interest. Proportionality requires the government to justify its objective and the methods it uses to achieve those ends; it is meant to constrain government actions taken unwarrantedly, or carelessly, in the name of security.

As a matter of constitutional design, like many twentieth century post-colonial constitutions,[112] the rights provisions in the Malaysian and Singaporean constitutions contain limitations. So, for example, Article 10 of the Malaysian Constitution,

[109] *See* Alec Stone Sweet & Jud Mathews, *Proportionality and Rights Protection in Asia: Hong Kong, Malaysia, South Korea, Taiwan—Whither Singapore?*, 29 SING. ACAD. L.J. 774, 782 (2017); Jack Tsen-Ta Lee, *According to the Spirit and not to the Letter: Proportionality and the Singapore Constitution*, 8 VIENNA J. ON INT'L CONST. L. 276, 281 (2014).

[110] The defeat of the Barisan Nasional ruling party in Malaysia's 2018 elections is the most obvious example, but even Singapore's ruling party, the People's Action Party, stated that it would have to undergo some "soul searching" after losing 39.9 per cent of the popular vote after its narrowest election victory since independence in Singapore's 2011 national elections. *See* Shamim Adam, *Lee Kuan Yew Ends Five-Decade Role in Singapore Cabinet After Poll Setback*, BLOOMBERG (May 16, 2011), https://perma.cc/7D2J-72LE.

[111] *See* Jaclyn Neo, *Balancing Act: The Balancing Metaphor as Deference and Dialogue in Constitutional Adjudication*, *in* CONSTITUTIONAL INTERPRETATION IN SINGAPORE: THEORY AND PRACTICE 159, 160 (Jaclyn Neo ed., 2017).

[112] Sweet & Mathews, *supra* note 109, at 779.

which guarantees the right to freedom of expression and speech, authorizes Parliament to impose:

> [S]uch restrictions as it deems necessary or expedient in the interest of the security of the Federation or any part thereof, friendly relations with other countries, public order or morality and restrictions designed to protect the privileges of Parliament or of any Legislative Assembly or to provide against contempt of court, defamation, or incitement to any offence.[113]

The Singapore Constitution contains a virtually identical clause to the Malaysian Constitution's freedom of expression provision.[114] The right to life and personal liberty in both constitutions is set out in the following terms: "No person shall be deprived of his life or personal liberty save in accordance with law."[115]

While the textual formulation of a constitutional clause does not mandate a specific judicial approach, proportionality analysis is particularly well-suited—some say "tailor-made"[116]—for analyzing whether government restrictions exceed the authority permitted by these sorts of limitation clauses. Courts adjudicating other constitutional documents containing limitation clauses, like the European Convention of Human Rights and the Canadian Charter of Rights and Freedoms, use proportionality as the standard tool in assessing whether the government's rights-impinging action is constitutionally permissible. Likewise, courts in Malaysia and Singapore can interpret their constitutional rights provisions in line with subjecting the government's justifications to a proportionality inquiry.

The judicial turn toward proportionality has already taken place in Malaysia. Judicial embrace of proportionality has come after an inconsistent approach in the Malaysian courts, marked by a series of judicial overtures and retreat. In the 2010 case of *Sivarasa Rasiah v. Badan Peguam Negara*, the Federal Court endorsed a structured proportionality analysis to evaluate an individual liberty and equal protection challenge to a statute prohibiting politicians from membership in the Bar Council.[117] And in *Nik Nazmi*,[118] the Court of Appeal applied a proportionality analysis to strike down a provision in the Peaceful Assembly Act, only for the decision to be overruled a year later by a differently constituted Court of Appeal in *Yuneswaran*.[119] And then in *Azmi Sharom*,[120] the Federal Court formally endorsed the doctrine of proportionality as part of Malaysian jurisprudence, although its

[113] FED. CONST. (MALAY.), art. 10(2)(a).
[114] CONST. OF THE REP. OF SING., art. 14(1).
[115] FED. CONST. (MALAY.), art. 5(1); CONST. OF THE REP. OF SING., art. 9(1).
[116] Sweet & Mathews, *supra* note 109, at 779.
[117] [2010] 3 CURRENT L.J. 507, at [29] (citing de Freitas v. Permanent Secretary of Ministry of Agriculture, Fisheries, Lands and Housing [1998] UKPC 30).
[118] *Nik Nazmi*, [2014] 4 MALAYAN L.J. 157.
[119] *Yuneswaran*, [2015] 9 CURRENT L.J. 873.
[120] *Azmi Sharom*, [2015] M.L.J.U. 594.

feeble application of the doctrine left the challenged Sedition Act provision as constitutionally valid.

After these fits and starts,[121] the Malaysian Federal Court fully embraced proportionality as part of Malaysia's constitutional jurisprudence in 2019. The Federal Court in *Alma Nudo v. Public Prosecutor* expressly employed a proportionality analysis to unanimously strike down a legislative provision allowing a double presumption to apply against accused drug traffickers. The Court laid out a proportionality formulation in three stages: (i) a determination of "whether there is a sufficiently important [legislative] objective to justify the infringement of the right"; (ii) an assessment of "whether the means designed by Parliament has a rational nexus with the objective it is intended to meet"; and (iii) "an assessment of proportionality," a balancing exercise to determine whether the restrictive measure is "proportionate to the importance of the right at stake."[122]

Significantly, the Federal Court in *Alma Nudo* derived the principle of proportionality from the Article 8(1) constitutional equal protection provision.[123] "[W]hen any State action is challenged as violating a fundamental right," declared the Court, "Article 8(1) will at once be engaged such that the action must meet the test of proportionality."[124] By locating the basis for a substantive principle of proportionality in the constitutional equal protection guarantee, the Court established that the proportionality analysis extends to all claims involving fundamental liberties, rather than being confined to a particular constitutional right. *Alma Nudo* itself involved a statute infringing the right to personal liberty under Article 5(1) of the Constitution. But the Court's formulation of the proportionality analysis broadens its reach to other individual liberties, such as the right to freedom of expression and assembly.[125]

Let's return to the constitutional challenges to Malaysia's sedition law, which the Federal Court has so far upheld against various freedom of expression claims. As we saw earlier in this chapter, the Court of Appeal in *Mat Shuhaimi* attempted a different path when it invalidated the provision in the Sedition Act criminalizing any act having a "seditious tendency" on a strict liability basis.[126] This decision would later be overruled by the Federal Court in a formalistic decision made on procedural grounds.[127] In contrast to the Federal Court's anemic decision, the Court of Appeal held that any valid legislation had to "meet the test of proportionality,"[128] and ruled that the statute's strict liability provision disproportionately infringed the right to freedom of expression. The law's "total displacement of any intent," the

[121] *See supra* Section III(C).
[122] Alma Nudo Atenza v. Public Prosecutor [2019] 5 Current L.J. 780, at [143]–[145].
[123] *Id.* at [118].
[124] *Id.* at [119].
[125] *See* Fed. Const. (Malay.), art. 10(1).
[126] *Mat Shuhaimi* (C.A.), [2017] 1 Malayan L.J. 436.
[127] *Mat Shuhaimi* (F.C.), [2018] 2 Malayan L.J. 133.
[128] *Mat Shuhaimi* (C.A.), [2017] 1 Malayan L.J. 436, at [25].

Court of Appeal declared, is like "using a hammer to confront the menace of a mosquito."[129] It's not wrong.

Sedition law is but one example of a myriad of national security and public order laws which restrict personal liberty, expression, and assembly with hammer-like bluntness. Think, for example, of the Peaceful Assembly Act and Security Offences (Special Measures) Act in Malaysia, or Singapore's Criminal Law (Temporary) Provisions Act, and the new law against fake online news. Courts would be better equipped to scrutinize the rights restrictions imposed by these laws using a proportionality analysis. Under a proportionality frame, the government must do more than merely defend such laws in broad security and public interest terms. Proportionality requires the government not only to justify its objectives but to tailor its legislative and executive actions narrowly to those necessary to achieve its objectives. The government must show that the actions it employs are sensitive and proportionate to the actual security risk, particularly if the claimed threat appears "mosquito-sized."

Singapore has so far to been a stubborn holdout against the move toward proportionality.[130] Yet the legal footholds for the Singapore courts to move toward proportionality are already embedded in Singapore's existing constitutional jurisprudence. While proportionality analysis as such has not been explicitly endorsed by Singaporean courts, Jaclyn Neo observes, that "there appears to be an increasing openness to the idea that judicial balancing is a legitimate mode of constitutional adjudication and within the proper scope of the judicial role."[131] That move is particularly significant in light of the emerging growth of litigation by citizens seeking to vindicate their constitutional rights in Singapore.[132]

Proportionality analysis is in line with the principle of legality, the notion that "a subjective or unfettered discretion is contrary to the rule of law,"[133] recognized as a "basic principle in constitutional and administrative judicial review" in Singapore.[134] As Singapore Court of Appeal declared in *Chng Suan Tze*, and affirmed recently in *Tan Seet Eng*: "All power has legal limits and the rule of law demands that the courts should be able to examine the exercise of discretionary power."[135] As Jaclyn Neo argues, that reference to legal limits on discretionary power "suggests that balancing rights/interests is an *aspect* of ensuring legality of legislative and executive action according to the Constitution."[136] Viewed thus,

[129] *Id.* at [35].

[130] *See* Sweet & Mathews, *supra* note 109 (observing that "the turn to proportionality shows that Asian courts are, indeed, willing to engage ruling parties directly," whereas "these developments" show Singapore "to be a laggard state").

[131] Neo, *Balancing Act, supra* note 111, at 168.

[132] *See* V.K. Rajah, Attorney General, Speech at the Opening of the Legal Year 2015, The Rule of Law (Jan. 5, 2015), at [16], https://perma.cc/HQ7Q-D2QE.

[133] *Chng Suan Tze*, [1988] 2 SING. L. REP. 132, at [88].

[134] Chan Sek Keong, *Judicial Review—From Angst to Empathy*, 22 SING. ACAD. L.J. 469, at [8] (2010).

[135] *Tan Seet Eng*, [2016] 1 SING. L. REP. 779.

[136] Neo, *Balancing Act, supra* note 111, at 176.

the principle of legality, "as an aspect of the rule of law, provides the courts with a strong basis for a more robust approach towards judicial review."[137] Judicial balancing is justified as part of the courts' constitutional judicial review task.[138] The presumption that courts can and should review the exercise of discretionary government decisions fits comfortably with a proportionality framework.

Consider, for example, judicial review of preventive detention under the Internal Security Act and the Criminal Law (Temporary) Provisions in Singapore. Proportionality would provide the doctrinal legs for an objective test for the executive's belief that the detention is necessary to prevent the detainee from disrupting national security or public order. A proportionality analysis is structured to weigh rights against state interests, empowering courts to scrutinize whether a decision to detain has a reasonable connection to security or public interests. Judges could also evaluate whether the terms of the detention—such as its duration and scope—is no more than necessary and proportionate to achieve the government's objective. This approach reflects the principle laid out in the *Chng Suan Tze* decision that restrictions on constitutional rights "be construed so as to derogate as little as possible from such fundamental liberties."[139] Proportionality enables courts to determine, in a structured manner, whether the government's restriction of a constitutional right can be reasonably justified.[140]

Judicial balancing through proportionality offers an effective doctrinal tool for adjudicating constitutional rights claims in these Asian democracies. Some might argue that a more categorical approach would afford rights greater protection. Ronald Dworkin famously conceived of rights as "trumps,"[141] which cannot be outweighed by other interests because to subject rights to balancing against the public interest is to deny them altogether.[142] There are compelling normative arguments to be made more generally against an approach that views rights as trumps,[143] but my argument is focused on emerging constitutional democracies. In fragile states habituated to operating under dominant political power, like Malaysia and Singapore, a categorical approach to rights is unlikely to gain much legal or political traction.[144] An approach that acknowledges rights must be balanced against other interests, rather than treating rights as absolute, offers a more feasible judicial frame.

And apart from pragmatic concerns, a balancing frame is a better fit for contemporary constitutional adjudication compared to a rigid categorical approach.

[137] *Id.*

[138] *See* Lee, *supra* note 109, at 291.

[139] *Chng Suan Tze*, [1988] 2 Sing. L. Rep. 132, at [79].

[140] *See* Lee, *supra* note 109, at 302.

[141] Ronald Dworkin, Taking Rights Seriously xi (1977).

[142] *Id.* at 192.

[143] *See* Jamal Greene, *Foreword: Rights as Trumps?*, 132 Harv. L. Rev. 28 (2018).

[144] Neo, *Balancing Act, supra* note 111, at 175 (observing that "Singapore's political context, where there appears to be a preference for a dominant party and an efficient state, suggests that a rights as trumps approach is unlikely to be accepted as legal doctrine or have much traction in society").

Rights claims are not usually all or nothing propositions. Courts the world over are coming to see that the paradigmatic rights conflicts in modern democracies often require the weighing of multiple principles and competing interests.[145] Proportionality equips constitutional decisionmakers with a balancing frame that is flexible and powerful enough to address the nuances in rights conflicts, and which can also evolve over time to suit the needs of a particular constitutional culture.

B. Protecting the Constitution's Basic Structure

Sometimes certain conditions warrant a bolder judicial response. When political institutions fundamentally undermine the constitution's basic features, courts have a role in defending the constitution's core structure from being altered or destroyed through formal amendment. Legislative intrusions have particular relevance in the context of emergency and national security powers where the institutional safeguards on these powers have been systematically weakened through constitutional amendment.

Constitutional amendments passed over decades by the Malaysian government have enlarged executive power and eroded institutional constraints on the exercise of emergency and security powers.[146] In 1960, the government amended the Constitution to remove the temporal limits on the executive's emergency powers and preventive detention under its anti-subversion powers, limits which had provided for these powers to lapse automatically.[147] In 1981, the Malaysian state extensively amended the Article 150 emergency powers constitutional framework to expand the powers of the executive to proclaim a state of emergency and promulgate emergency ordinances.[148] A new provision—Article 150(8)—was inserted expressly to prevent judicial review over the validity of any emergency proclamation or ordinance.

Another constitutional amendment passed in 1984 removed the requirement for royal assent to a legislative bill.[149] The Malaysian Constitution now provides that the *Yang di-Pertuan Agong* may return a bill presented to him to the House of Representatives, but once the bill is approved by a legislative majority and again presented to the King, it will become law after thirty days even if he fails to assent.[150]

[145] Greene, *supra* note 143, at 34.

[146] H.P. Lee et al., *Constitutional Change in Malaysia*, *in* CONSTITUTIONAL AMENDMENT IN SOUTHEAST ASIA, 14 J. COMP. L. 119, 127–132 (2019).

[147] Constitution (Amendment) Act 1960 (Act 10 of 1960) (amending FED. CONST. (MALAY.), arts. 150(3), 149(2)).

[148] Constitution (Amendment) Act 1981 (Act 514) (amending FED. CONST. (MALAY.), art. 150(2) and inserting art. 150(8)).

[149] Constitution (Amendment) Act 1984 (amending FED. CONST. (MALAY.), art. 66)

[150] FED. CONST. (MALAY.), art. 66(4B).

The amendment also created a role for the prime minister to "advise" the *Yang di-Pertuan Agong* to make an emergency proclamation when the prime minister is "satisfied" that a grave emergency exists.[151] These amendments limit checks on the legislature's power while expanding the executive's role in emergency powers.

In 1988, the Barisan Nasional-controlled Parliament amended Article 121(1) of the Federal Constitution to strip the courts of its constitutional judicial power. As detailed in earlier chapters, the Malaysian Federal Court nullified that amendment in decisions in 2017 and 2018 that endorsed and entrenched a basic structure doctrine.[152] The central principle that has emerged from the Federal Court's recent, and radical, jurisprudential shift is that the courts' judicial power is a basic feature of the constitution that the legislature cannot alter or undermine.[153]

Confronting government attempts to remove judicial review over national security and public order decisions is where the basic structure doctrine would have concrete bite. Now that the Malaysian court has acknowledged that the courts' judicial power is a fundamental constitutional feature, constitutional amendments and security laws seeking to limit judicial review may well come under scrutiny. Take, for example, Article 150(8), the provision inserted by the 1981 amendment to declare that "no court shall have jurisdiction to entertain or determine any application, question or proceeding, in whatever form, on any ground" regarding the validity of an emergency proclamation or ordinance.[154] In light of the Malaysian decisions entrenching judicial power as part of the basic structure, as scholars like H.P. Lee have noted, "a strong case can be made out for the invalidation of Article 150(8)."[155]

Ouster clauses removing judicial review over government decisions in security and public order laws are ubiquitous across Malaysia and Singapore's statutory landscape. For example, Singapore's Internal Security Act prohibits the review of any act or decision of the President or Minister relating to preventive detentions,[156] inserted when amendments to the constitution and statute were passed in 1988 to curtail judicial review.[157] In Malaysia, ouster clauses are part of many security laws, such as the Prevention of Terrorism Act and the National Security Council Act,[158] to say nothing of the numerous other laws that have nothing to do with security or public order.[159] Such ouster clauses strike at the heart of the courts' power of

151 Fed. Const. (Malay.), art. 150(1).

152 *See* Semenyih Jaya v. Pentadbir Tanah Daerah Hulu Langat [2017] 3 Malayan L.J. 561; Indira Gandhi a/p Mutho v. Pengarah Jabatan Agama Islam Perak & Ors. [2018] 1 Malayan L.J. 545 (F.C.).

153 *See* Chapter 6, Courts in Transition, section III.

154 Fed. Const. (Malay.), art. 150(8).

155 Lee et al., *supra* note 146, at 131.

156 ISA (Sing.) §8(B)(2).

157 *See supra* notes 61–69 and accompanying text.

158 Prevention of Terrorism Act, 2015, § 19(1); National Security Council Act, 2016, §38.

159 More than forty Malaysian statutes have clauses ousting judicial review. *See* Shaila Koshy, *Time to Repeal Ouster Clauses*, Star Online (May 20, 2018), https://perma.cc/X4KJ-7FTP for list of statutes with ouster clauses.

judicial review. Less radical than invalidating a constitutional amendment, courts should draw on the basic structure doctrine to strike down or interpretively nullify such statutory attempts to remove judicial scrutiny.

Other constitutional challenges to amendments based on the basic structure doctrine are already on the horizon. Take, for example, the lawsuit brought by Anwar Ibrahim to strike down the National Security Council Act and to invalidate the constitutional amendment passed in 1984.[160] When the Barisan Nasional government sought to pass the National Security Council Bill in 2016, the *Yang di-Pertuan Agong* did not give his assent to the contentious security bill. Nevertheless, the national security law came into force because of the legislative procedure put in place by the 1984 constitutional amendment. Anwar, who was released from prison shortly after Pakatan Harapan's electoral victory in 2018, sought to invalidate the amendment removing the requirement for royal assent to a legislative bill, arguing that the 1984 amendment infringes the Malaysian Constitution's basic structure. In 2020, the Malaysian Federal Court, in a majority decision, declined to answer the question on the constitutionality of the National Security Council statute and the 1984 constitutional amendment, finding the broad question in this case abstract and purely academic.[161]

Although it remains to be seen how far the Malaysian apex court will extend the basic structure doctrine in future cases, what seems clear is that the notion of an implied domain of immutable values now occupies a solid place in Malaysia's contemporary jurisprudence and that the doctrine will increasingly be invoked in future constitutional litigation. If so, some of the amendments passed by the ruling government that eroded institutional safeguards on the executive's exercise of emergency and security power may well come under increasing judicial scrutiny. With the basic structure doctrine, courts have a significant doctrinal tool to review the constitutionality of legislative efforts that have substantially altered the constitution's institutional distribution of power.

V. Conclusion

The constitutions of Malaysia and Singapore were created at a time when these newly independent democracies faced existential challenges in the unstable period after the Second World War. During this period of crisis in the mid-twentieth century, a range of emergency and special powers were crafted into the constitutions

[160] *See* Khairah N. Karim, *Anwar Seeks Apex Court Rule on Validity of National Security Council Act*, New Straits Times (Feb. 27, 2019), https://perma.cc/Q5L9-9G2J; Datuk Seri Anwar Ibrahim v. Kerajaan Malaysia & Anor [2018] M.L.J.U. 289 (C.A.); Datuk Seri Anwar Ibrahim v. Kerajaan Malaysia & Anor [2017] M.L.J.U. 338 (H.C.).

[161] *See* Nurbaiti Hamdan, *Anwar Seeks to Set Aside Federal Court's Decision on NSCA's Constitutionality*, The Star (Apr. 7, 2020), https://perma.cc/ER55-5R6C.

of these fragile states to enable them to counter forces, like armed communist insurgencies, that jeopardized their survival. Viewed against this backdrop, the constitutional schemes under Articles 149 and 150 are limited regimes of exceptions located within a broader arrangement of constitutional rights protection.

The story that emerges from the Malaysian and Singaporean states illustrates the danger when constitutional exceptions become normalized. Their experiences are also a warning for democracies globally. Decades after the initial threats to these nations' security have collapsed, emergency powers and security laws became endemic to the legal and political landscape. Dominant party governments exerted these powers through a plethora of laws—authorizing preventive detention, enlarging executive power, and restricting expression and assembly—all justified in the name of national security and public order. Courts found themselves sidelined, with the legislature often taking measures to remove judicial review over governmental actions that they defended in security terms. For some time, courts retreated to a position of extensive deference to the political branches on security issues. But the lesson those years have shown us is that such judicial acquiescence only allows the government's liberty infringements to be cloaked in purported legal legitimacy.

Courts have a constitutional responsibility to articulate and uphold the principles fundamental to the constitution's architecture even, indeed especially, when the political branches of government depart from those core principles.[162] In recent years, there have been indications in Malaysia and Singapore of the judiciary's willingness to step up to this constitutional role. Shifts in the political and legal culture have also created greater space for the courts to enforce the constitutional balance of power in these Asian democracies.

Challenges to constitutional amendments and laws defended in terms of national security and public order are on the constitutional horizon. Courts can draw on various constitutional mechanisms to address these structural or rights claims. The constitutional basic structure doctrine provides a powerful tool for courts to defend the judicial role against legislative efforts to exclude judicial review or as a potential means to restore the constitution's institutional balance of power. Yet as these contemporary Asian states move into the future, most cases involving individual liberty restrictions are likely to require a nuanced evaluation of the competing rights and interests at stake. Once the judicial role is secured as part of the constitution's basic core, proportionality equips courts with a sensitive, yet robust, tool in rights adjudication to balance the interests of security and liberty.[163]

[162] *See* David Dyzenhaus, The Constitution of Law: Legality in a Time of Emergency 4 (2006).

[163] Sweet & Mathews, *supra* note 109, at 775.

Conclusion

Beyond Sisyphus and Hercules

The constitutional transitions of contemporary Malaysia and Singapore tell a story of the legacies of colonialism, of politics rooted in race and religion, and of state hegemony fortified by emergency and security regimes. This story would be immediately recognizable outside Malaysia and Singapore, too.

Across many other fledgling democracies in Asia, the same core issues of democratic constitutionalism are playing out. Many Asian states have a history of authoritarian control; some continue to be under single party or military rule, while others are only now transitioning from a dominant party regime. Race, religion, and identity remain potent and often divisive forces in the religiously or ethnically pluralistic societies of Indonesia, Myanmar, Sri Lanka, India, and Pakistan. Vestiges of Western colonialism are evident in most Asian democracies; like Malaysia and Singapore, the jurisdictions of Myanmar, Hong Kong, Sri Lanka, India, Bangladesh, and Pakistan inherited common law legal systems from Britain, along with colonial-era emergency powers, sedition laws, and penal codes. Evolving democracies in Asia do not have robust constitutional cultures, yet rising political participation and civil society engagement—from Thailand and Indonesia to Malaysia and Hong Kong—reflect sustained efforts among the nation's citizens toward developing constitutional democracy. Still, these aspiring democracies remain deeply fragile, at risk of veering back into authoritarianism.

These developing post-colonial Asian states are finding new paths to constitutional democratization. Their experience is fundamentally different from the constitutional transitions in Eastern Europe, Latin America, and South Africa at the end of the twentieth century, where highly active courts were instrumental to the democratization process.[1] It is also different from the East Asian states of South Korea, Taiwan, and Japan, all of which have developed stable cultures of constitutionalism on the back of ethnically homogenous societies, strong economies, and successful democratization.[2]

[1] *See, e.g.*, Samuel Issacharoff, Fragile Democracies: Contested Power in the Era of Constitutional Courts (2015); Tom Daly, The Alchemists: Questioning our Faith in Courts as Democracy-Builders (2017); Theunis Roux, The Politics of Principle: The First South African Constitutional Court, 1995–2005 (2013).

[2] *See* Jiunn-rong Yeh & Wen-Chen Chang, *The Emergence of East Asian Constitutionalism: Features in Comparison*, 59 Am. J. Comp. L. 805 (2011) ; *see also* Po Jen Yap, Courts and Democracies in Asia

Constitutional Statecraft in Asian Courts. Yvonne Tew, Oxford University Press (2020). © Yvonne Tew.
DOI:10.1093/oso/9780198716839.001.0001

Courts in nascent Asian democracies face special challenges. In countries where consolidated political power has been the norm, courts must delicately balance the demands of powerful political institutions and actors.[3] That task becomes all the more challenging in times of political transition, especially when states emerge from dominant party rule, and courts seek to renegotiate their position as institutional stakeholders. Religious and ethnic divisions further complicate judicial dynamics in pluralistic legal systems that accommodate religious courts and personal law, like those in Indonesia, Brunei, the Philippines, Bangladesh, and India, where constitutional disputes often reflect deep conflict over the state's secular or religious character.

Asian courts in aspiring democracies can play a crucial part in constitutional state-building. This book has explored the strategic and dynamic ways in which courts can strengthen the legal and institutional underpinnings of effective constitutional governance. Drawing on the case studies of Malaysia and Singapore to situate and sharpen our understanding, a picture emerges of how courts can develop and refine the judicial tools needed to reshape institutions and craft constitutionalism.

Different judicial strategies may be suited for different political or constitutional stages. One potent judicial mechanism for emerging democracies, for instance, is the doctrine that protects an implied constitutional core of basic principles so that it cannot be altered by an overreaching legislature through amendment. With the Malaysian Federal Court's landmark decisions in 2017 and 2018, which expressly entrenched the notion that parliament does not have the power to amend the constitution's basic structure,[4] the doctrine of unconstitutional constitutional amendments now has a concrete foothold in Southeast Asia. The scope and limits of a basic structure doctrine are ultimately connected to democratic legitimacy,[5] as the Malaysian case study illustrates. When the power to amend the constitution is concentrated in a dominant governing power, which might abuse constitutional amendment for authoritarian purposes,[6] sometimes it is necessary for courts to enforce the constitution's basic structure against the majoritarian branches of government.[7] Remarkably, the Malaysian court accomplished this step in a fraught area involving civil courts and religious courts, explicitly safeguarding the protection of minorities as part of the pluralistic constitution's fundamental core.

7–10 (2017) (characterizing South Korea and Taiwan as dynamic democracies with multi-party political competition).

[3] *See* Jiunn-rong Yeh & Wen-Chen Chang, *Introduction* to Asian Courts in Context (Jiunn-rong Yeh & Wen-Chen Chang eds., 2015).

[4] Semenyih Jaya v. Pentadbir Tanah Daerah Hulu Langat [2017] 3 Malayan L.J. 561[hereinafter *Semenyih Jaya*]; Indira Gandhi a/p Mutho v. Pengarah Jabatan Agama Islam Perak & Ors. [2018] 1 Malayan L.J. 545 (F.C.) [hereinafter *Indira Gandhi* (F.C.)].

[5] *See* Yaniv Roznai, *Constitutional Amendability and Unamendability in South-East Asia, in* Constitutional Amendment in Southeast Asia, 14 J. Comp. L. 188, 194–95 (2019).

[6] *See* David Landau, *Abusive Constitutionalism*, 47 U.C.D. L. Rev. 189 (2014).

[7] *See* Roznai, *supra* note 5, at 194–95; *see also* Jaclyn Neo, *Beyond Mortals? Constitutional Identity, Judicial Power, and the Evolution of the Basic Structure Doctrine in Malaysia, in* CPG Publication: "Identity and Change—The Basic Structure in Asian Constitutional Orders" (2016).

While the idea of limits on formal constitutional amendment was famously introduced by the Indian Supreme Court,[8] and has since migrated to courts in Bangladesh,[9] Pakistan,[10] and Taiwan,[11] few courts in Southeast Asia have caught on. Some variants of the basic structure doctrine have registered in fits and starts in the practice of the Thai Constitutional Court,[12] the Supreme Court of the Phillippines,[13] and attracted extra-judicial support in Singapore.[14] In general, though, it has not thrived in the region's jurisprudence, as yet remaining a constitutional novelty with an uncertain future.

Many of Southeast Asia's emerging democracies are important democratic battlegrounds of constitutional change. Amendment has been the primary mode of changing the constitution for many countries in the region,[15] which, by and large, have easily amendable constitutions and powerful governing elites. Cambodia, Indonesia, and Thailand—like Malaysia and Singapore—have all experienced major constitutional revision at the hands of the governing powers. The Malaysian example illustrates the careful use of the doctrine to protect judicial power, and the conditions under which judicial scrutiny of constitutional amendments are democratically justified. Significantly, too, Malaysia has revealed a vision of the Constitution's basic structure that recognizes its pluralistic character and embeds within it protection for minorities and individuals.

Proportionality analysis has emerged as another judicial tool that can be used to great effect in rights adjudication at particular stages of a constitutional democracy's development. Despite its prevalence elsewhere in the world, in Asia, only the courts of Taiwan, South Korea, and Hong Kong apply a structured form of proportionality analysis to scrutinize government restrictions on rights.[16] Among other Asian courts, the invocation of proportionality has been sporadic and anemic.[17] Of especial significance, therefore, is the Malaysian apex court's decision in 2019, which

[8] Kesavananda Bharati v. State of Kerala, AIR 1973 SC 1461 (India).

[9] *See* Ridwanul Hoque, *Eternal Provisions in the Constitution of Bangladesh: A Constitution Once and for All?, in* AN UNAMENDABLE CONSTITUTION? UNAMENDABILITY IN CONSTITUTIONAL DEMOCRACIES 195, 195–229 (Richard Albert & Emrah Oder eds., 2018).

[10] *See* Zeeshaan Zafar Hashmi, *Unconstitutional Constitutional Amendments or Amending the Unamendable: A Critique of* District Bar Association Rawalpindi v. Federation of Pakistan, PAKISTAN L. REV. IX (2018).

[11] *See* David S. Law & Hsiang-Yang Hsieh, *Judicial Review of Constitutional Amendments: Taiwan, in* CONSTITUTIONALISM IN CONTEXT 1 (David S. Law ed., forthcoming) (manuscript on file with author).

[12] *See* Khemthong Tonsakulrungruang, *Constitutional Amendment in Thailand: Amending in the Spectre of Parliamentary Dictatorship, in* CONSTITUTIONAL AMENDMENT IN SOUTHEAST ASIA, 14 J. COMP. L. 173 (2019) (citing Constitutional Court Decision 18-22/2555 (2012)).

[13] *See* Dante Gatmaytan, *Constitutional Change as Suspect Projects: The Philippines, in* CONSTITUTIONAL AMENDMENT IN SOUTHEAST ASIA, 14 J. COMP. L. 139 (2019).

[14] *See* Chapter 2, Constitutional Adjudication and Constitutional Politics, section IV(C).

[15] *See* Jaclyn Neo & Bui Ngoc Son, *Expanding the Universe of Comparative Constitutional Amendments in Southeast Asia, in* CONSTITUTIONAL AMENDMENT IN SOUTHEAST ASIA, 14 J. COMP. L. 46, 49 (2019).

[16] *See* Po Jen Yap, *Introduction* to PROPORTIONALITY IN ASIA 1 (Po Jen Yap ed., forthcoming 2020) (manuscript on file with author).

[17] *Id.*

used a robust, multi-stage proportionality analysis to strike down a federal law.[18] The Malaysian Federal Court's embrace of proportionality marks not merely a shift in legal doctrine but, more broadly, a shift in the judiciary's perception of its own institutional position.

This story has important resonance for courts in other emerging Asian democracies that operate in systems with dominant political parties or military regimes. While the journey may be long, and uneven, the Malaysian experience shows that it is nevertheless possible for courts in challenging political circumstances to embed, develop, and eventually fully wield a doctrine that empowers courts to enforce constitutional rights against the government. These Asian courts sit at different points on that uneven path. In Indonesia and Thailand, although proportionality has not generally been applied in a robust fashion to invalidate legislation, constitutional courts have endorsed the notion that rights derogations must be proportionate.[19] At the other end of the spectrum stands Singapore, whose courts have so far stubbornly refused to adopt any form of proportionality, instead granting substantial deference to the political branches.[20] Proportionality offers a path between a position of reflexive deference to the political powers and a Herculean model of categorical rights reasoning.[21] As the Malaysian case study illustrates, the adaptability of rights balancing as a doctrinal device allows it to be used in a context-sensitive manner by courts negotiating different stages of political and constitutional transition.

This book advances neither an ideal of Herculean judges forcing the governing powers into legal compliance nor a view of a futile judiciary cowed into passivity seeking to avoid political confrontation. More broadly, beyond specific judicial strategies, it is an account of the careful and strategic expansion of judicial power in an emerging democracy, as illustrated by the Malaysian judiciary's deliberate two-stage process to entrench judicial authority and expand constitutional review.[22] At its core, the story that this book tells is one of judicial statecraft and constitutional vision.

* * *

Malaysia's astonishing government transition in 2018 appeared to be a democratic breakthrough, a turning point of political and constitutional magnitude. And in many ways, it was. The Pakatan Harapan government—the Alliance of Hope—took

[18] Alma Nudo v. Public Prosecutor [2019] 5 CURRENT L.J. 780

[19] *See* Stefanus Hendrianto, *Against the Currents: The Indonesian Constitutional Court in an Age of Proportionality*, *in* PROPORTIONALITY IN ASIA 169 (Po Jen Yap ed., forthcoming 2020) ; Narongdech Srukhosit, *Manifest Disproportionality and the Constitutional Court of Thailand*, *in* PROPORTIONALITY IN ASIA 192 (Po Jen Yap ed., forthcoming 2020).

[20] *See* Alec Stone Sweet & Jud Mathews, *Proportionality and Rights Protection in Asia: Hong Kong, Malaysia, South Korea, Taiwan—Whither Singapore?*, 29 SING. ACAD. L.J. 774 (2017).

[21] *See* RONALD DWORKIN, TAKING RIGHTS SERIOUSLY (1977).

[22] *See Semenyih Jaya*, [2017] 3 MALAYAN L.J. 561; *Indira Gandhi* (F.C.), [2018] 1 MALAYAN L.J. 545.

power, fresh from its electoral victory, with an agenda of governance reforms. It repealed an anti-fake news law and promised to abolish several oppressive security laws. At the U.N. General Assembly, Prime Minister Mahathir Mohamad pledged to ratify all core U.N. human rights conventions.[23] Government officials swiftly arrested former premier Najib Razak and filed criminal charges against Wall Street bank Goldman Sachs for allegedly being embroiled in the billion-dollar 1Malaysia Development Berhad state fund corruption scandal[24]—a tale of such spectacular financial fraud that it has become the subject of a global bestseller.[25] Over the next year, the new government would appoint two new chief justices, putting in place the first non-Muslim and then the first female head of the Malaysian judiciary.[26]

Yet challenges quickly became apparent. A swath of national security and public order laws, including a colonial-era sedition law, remained on the books. Deeper issues around race and religion resurfaced. Tens of thousands of Malay-Muslims gathered in a mass protest against the International Convention on the Elimination of All Forms of Racial Discrimination. Later, the Pakatan Harapan government backtracked from ratifying the U.N. Convention and withdrew from joining the International Criminal Court.[27]

And then, in 2020, the Alliance of Hope collapsed. After a government crisis in February 2020, spurred by a series of political defections and alliance realignments that resulted in three leading contenders competing for premiership, a new governing coalition and prime minister ascended to power.[28] The Perikatan Nasional alliance consists predominantly of Malay-Muslim parties, including the United Malays National Organisation—a constituent party of the Barisan Nasional coalition voted out two years earlier—as well as the Malaysian United Indigenous Party and the Malaysian Islamic Party. The political developments culminating in the

[23] Yushaimi Yahaya, *Dr M Pledges to Uphold UN Principles in New Malaysia*, New Straits Times (Sept. 28, 2018), https://perma.cc/K2Q4-CLWJ.

[24] Jamie Fullerton, *Malaysia's ex-PM Najib Razak Goes on Trial over 1MDB Scandal*, Guardian (Apr. 3, 2019), https://perma.cc/8E48-J6HD; Liz Hoffman & Aruna Viswanatha, *Goldman Sachs in Talks to Admit Guilt, Pay $2 Billion Fine to Settle 1MDB Probe*, Wall St. J. (Dec. 19, 2019), https://perma.cc/2E5A-239H.

[25] *See* Bradley Hope & Tom Wright, Billion Dollar Whale: The Man Who Fooled Wall Street, Hollywood, and the World (2018).

[26] In July 2018, Justice Richard Malanjum was appointed as the Chief Justice of Malaysia. Malanjum, who became Malaysia's first non-Muslim Chief Justice, authored the landmark dissents in the Federal Court's decisions in *Lina Joy v. Majlis Agama Islam Wilayah Persekutuan* [2007] 4 Malayan L.J. 585 (F.C.), and *Public Prosecutor v. Kok Wah Kuan* [2008] 1 Malayan L.J. 1. After Malanjum retired in 2019, when he reached the mandatory retirement age, he was succeeded by Tengku Maimun Tuan Mat, who became the first woman to head the Malaysian judiciary. *See Richard Malanjum is New Chief Justice*, New Straits Times (July 11, 2018), https://perma.cc/S6XZ-RDQ6; *Malaysia Appoints Its First Woman Chief Justice*, Straits Times (May 3, 2019), https://perma.cc/9YJN-FRW3.

[27] *See* Yantoultra Ngui & James Hookway, *Thousands of Malaysians Rally to Defend Race-Based Policies*, Wall St. J. (Dec. 8, 2018), https://perma.cc/NBN4-AEGS; Joseph Sipalan, *Malaysia Backpedals on U.N. Race Measure in Face of Protests*, Reuters (Nov. 23, 2018), https://perma.cc/5WAA-KNB8; *Malaysia Withdraws from the Rome Statute*, The Star (Apr. 5, 2019), https://perma.cc/9A9M-28F6.

[28] *See* Hannah Beech, *Malaysia's Premier, Mahathir Mohamad, Is Ousted in a Surprising Turn*, N.Y. Times (Feb. 29, 2020), https://perma.cc/98KE-6YSH; Laignee Barron, *Malaysia's 94-Year-Old Prime*

2020 regime change appeared to underscore that identity politics driven by race and religion have not disappeared from the heart of Malaysian society.

For decades, democratic change in Malaysian politics primarily meant breaking the hegemony of the dominant ruling party. The 2018 political transition was the first change of government achieved through a democratic election. But as has quickly become apparent, political regime change alone is not sufficient. An illiberal constitutionalism rooted in ethno-nationalism and authoritarianism is not easily eradicated.

And yet, from the immediacy of history, more than one story can emerge. Glimmers of a new constitutional vision are now visible, too.

To build a stable constitutional democracy requires strengthening the institutions that sustain its endurance. Courts and constitutional mechanisms are central to that endeavor. And while, like Sisyphus's rock, the burdens of an authoritarian past may sometimes set back the enterprise, the judicial strategies this book has explored provide the constitutional footholds needed to prevent the tragedy of democratic backsliding. Courts can use particular strategies to entrench basic constitutional structures and to protect rights proportionately in line with the constitution's overarching purposes. This book shows how judicial institution-building can be undertaken in service of crafting a culture of constitutionalism.

Courts in developing Asian democracies have lain passive for too long, regarding the task before them as formidable as the mountain that Sisyphus is condemned to confront endlessly. Still, there is another narrative: one that speaks to a new project of constitutional imagination. Courts are now realizing their role as partners in the enterprise of constitutional statecraft. Where once the climb to democratic constitutionalism appeared impossibly steep, the task no longer seems to be without hope.

Minister Is Out. The New Leader Is Likely to Inflame Racial Tensions, TIME (Mar. 4, 2020), https://perma.cc/B3X5-W4V3.

The February 2020 regime change was not generated through a democratic national election, but came about after a battle among political elites for the country's leadership, precipitated by a faction of defectors, and eventually resolved through royal appointment.

Bibliography

Books and Articles

Abdul Aziz Bari, *Islam in the Federal Constitution: A Commentary on the Decision of* Meor Atiqulrahman, 2 Malayan L.J. cxxix (2000).

Abdul Hamid Mohamad, *Harmonisation of Common Law and Shariah in Malaysia: A Practical Approach*, 2 Malayan L.J. ix (2009).

Allan, T.R.S., Law, Liberty, and Justice: The Legal Foundations of British Constitutionalism (1993).

Amar, Akhil Reed, *Philadelphia Revisited: Amending the Constitution Outside Article V*, 55 U. Chi. L. Rev. 1043 (1988).

Anwar Ibrahim, Speech from The International Conference on Rethinking Human Rights (Dec. 7, 1994), https://perma.cc/E843-42LF.

Balasubramaniam, Ratna Rueban, *Has Rule by Law Killed the Rule of Law in Malaysia?*, 8 Oxford Uni. Commonwealth L.J. 211 (2008).

Balkin, Jack, *Framework Originalism and the Living Constitution*, 103 Nw. U. L. Rev. 549 (2009).

Balkin, Jack, Living Originalism (2011).

Barak, Aharon, *Proportionality: Sources, Nature, Function*, *in* The Oxford Handbook of Comparative Constitutional Law 129 (2012).

Barendt, E., *Separation of Powers and Constitutional Government*, Pub. L. 599 (1995).

Bari, Abdul Aziz, *Islam in the Federal Constitution: A Commentary on the Decision of* Meor Atiqulrahman, 2 Malayan L.J. cxxix (2000).

Barnett, Randy E., Restoring the Lost Constitution: The Presumption of Liberty (2004).

Bateup, Christine, *Reassessing the Dialogic Possibilities of Weak-Form Bills of Rights*, 32 Hastings Int'l & Comp. L. Rev. 529 (2009).

Beatty, David, The Ultimate Rule of Law (2004).

Bellamy, Richard, Political Constitutionalism: A Republican Defence of the Constitutionality of Democracy (2007).

Bickel, Alexander, The Least Dangerous Branch (1962).

Bilchitz, David & Landau, David, *Introduction* to The Evolution of the Separation of Powers: Between the Global North and the Global South 1 (David Bilchitz & David Landau eds., 2018).

Bingham, Tom, The Rule of Law (2010).

Bogdanor, Vernon, The New British Constitution (2009).

Brown, Nathan J. & Waller, Julian G., *Constitutional Courts and Political Uncertainty: Constitutional Ruptures and the Rule of Judges*, 14 Int. J. Const. L. 817 (2016).

Campbell, Tom, Rights: A Critical Introduction (2006).

Chan, Sek Keong, *Basic Structure and Supremacy of the Singapore Constitution*, 29 Sing. Acad. L.J. 619 (2017).

Chan, Sek Keong, *Judicial Review—From Angst to Empathy*, 22 Sing. Acad. L.J. 469 (2010).

Chan, Sek Keong, *The Courts and the "Rule of Law" in Singapore*, SING. J. LEGAL STUD. 209 (2012).

Chan, Tsu Chong, *Democratic Breakthrough in Malaysia—Political Opportunities and the Role of Bersih*, 37 J. CURRENT SE. ASIAN AFF. 109 (2018).

Chang, Wen-Chen, *Strategic Judicial Responses in Politically Charged Cases: East Asian Experiences*, 8 INT. J. CONST. L. 885 (2010).

Chen, Albert, *Pathways of Western Liberal Constitutional Development in Asia: A Comparative Study of Five Major Nations*, 8 INT'L J. CONST. L. 849 (2010).

Chew, Ernest C.T. & Lee, Edwin (eds.), A HISTORY OF SINGAPORE (1991).

Choudhry, Sujit, *Living Originalism in India: Our Law and Comparative Constitutional Law*, 25 YALE J.L. & HUMAN. 1 (2013).

Colby, Thomas B., *The Sacrifice of the New Originalism*, 99 GEO. L.J. 713 (2011).

CONSTITUTION WRITING, RELIGION AND DEMOCRACY (Aslı Ü Bâli & Hanna Lerner eds., 2017).

DALY, TOM, THE ALCHEMISTS: QUESTIONING OUR FAITH IN COURTS AS DEMOCRACY-BUILDERS (2017).

Dawson, Benjamin & Thiru, Steven, *The Lina Joy Case and the Future of Religious Freedom in Malaysia*, 2007 LAWASIA J. 151 (2007).

DIAN SHAH, CONSTITUTIONS, RELIGION, AND POLITICS IN ASIA: INDONESIA, MALAYSIA AND SRI LANKA (2017).

DICEY, ALBERT VENN, INTRODUCTION TO THE STUDY OF THE LAW OF THE CONSTITUTION (1959).

Diplock, William John Kenneth, *Judicial Control of the Government*, MALAYAN L.J. cxl (1979).

Dixon, Rosalind & Tushnet, Mark, *Weak-Form Review and its Constitutional Relatives: An Asian Perspective*, *in* COMPARATIVE CONSTITUTIONAL LAW IN ASIA 102 (Rosalind Dixon & Tom Ginsburg eds., 2014).

Dixon, Rosalind & Issacharoff, Samuel, *Living to Fight Another Day: Judicial Deferral in Defense of Democracy*, 2016 WIS. L. REV. 683 (2016).

Dixon, Rosalind, *Weak-Form Judicial Review and American Exceptionalism*, 32 OXFORD J. LEGAL STUD. 487 (2012).

DONNELLY, JACK, UNIVERSAL HUMAN RIGHTS IN THEORY AND PRACTICE (2013).

DWORKIN, RONALD, FREEDOM'S LAW: THE MORAL READING OF THE AMERICAN CONSTITUTION (1996).

Dworkin, Ronald, *Hard Cases*, 88 HARV. L. REV. 1057 (1975).

DWORKIN, RONALD, LAW'S EMPIRE (1986).

DWORKIN, RONALD, TAKING RIGHTS SERIOUSLY (1977).

DYZENHAUS, DAVID, THE CONSTITUTION OF LAW: LEGALITY IN A TIME OF EMERGENCY (2006).

ELDRIDGE, PHILIP J., POLITICS OF HUMAN RIGHTS IN SOUTHEAST ASIA (2001).

Elliot, Mark, *The Ultra Vires Doctrine in a Constitutional Setting: Still the Central Principle of Administrative Law*, 58 CAMBRIDGE L.J. 129 (1999).

ELY, JOHN HART, DEMOCRACY AND DISTRUST: A THEORY OF JUDICIAL REVIEW (1980).

Engle, Karen, *Culture and Human Rights: The Asian Values Debate in Context*, 32 N.Y.U. INT'L L. & POL. 291 (2000).

EPP, CHARLES R., THE RIGHTS REVOLUTION: LAWYERS, ACTIVISTS, AND SUPREME COURTS IN COMPARATIVE PERSPECTIVE (1ST ED. 1998).

Evans, Carolyn, *Constitutional Narratives: Constitutional Adjudication on the Religion Clauses in Australia and Malaysia*, 23 EMORY INT'L L. REV. 437 (2010).

Executive Board, *Am. Anthropological Ass'n, Statement on Human Rights*, 49 AM. ANTHROPOLOGIST 539 (1947).

FARBER, DANIEL A. & SHERRY, SUZANNA, DESPERATELY SEEKING CERTAINTY: THE MISGUIDED QUEST FOR CONSTITUTIONAL FOUNDATIONS (2002).

Feldman, David, *'Which in Your Case You Have Not Got': Constitutionalism at Home and Abroad*, 64 CURRENT LEGAL PROBS. 117 (2011).

Fernando, Joseph M., *A Playmaker and Moderator: Lord Reid and the Framing of the Malayan Federal Constitution*, 50 J. SE. ASIAN STUD. 431 (2019).

FERNANDO, JOSEPH M., FEDERAL CONSTITUTIONS: A COMPARATIVE STUDY OF MALAYSIA AND THE UNITED STATES (Univ. Malaya Press 2007).

FERNANDO, JOSEPH M., THE MAKING OF THE MALAYAN CONSTITUTION (2002).

Fernando, Joseph M., *The Position of Islam in the Constitution of Malaysia*, 37 J. SE. ASIAN STUD. 249 (2006).

Foo, Richard, *Malaysia—The Death of a Separate Constitutional Judicial Power*, SING. J. LEGAL STUD. 227 (2010).

Forsyth, Christopher, *Of Fig Leaves and Fairy Tales: The Ultra Vires Doctrine, the Sovereignty of Parliament and Judicial Review*, 55 CAMBRIDGE L.J. 122 (1996).

FRANKENBERG, GÜNTER, COMPARATIVE CONSTITUTIONAL STUDIES: BETWEEN MAGIC AND DECEIT (2018).

FRANKFURTER, FELIX, THE COMMERCE CLAUSE UNDER MARSHALL, TANEY, AND WAITE (1937).

Freeman, Michael, *Human Rights, Democracy and "Asian Values"*, 9 PAC. REV. 352 (1996).

Friedman, Barry, *The Birth of an Academic Obsession: The History of the Counter-Majoritarian Difficulty*, 112 YALE L.J. 153 (2002).

Fukuyama, Francis, *Asian Values in the Wake of the Asian Crisis*, *in* DEMOCRACY, MARKET ECONOMICS & DEVELOPMENT: AN ASIAN PERSPECTIVE 151 (Farrukh Iqbal & Jong-Il You eds., 2001).

FULLER, LON L., THE MORALITY OF LAW (1964).

Gardbaum, Stephen, *Are Strong Constitutional Courts Always a Good Thing for New Democracies?*, 53 COLUM. J. TRANSN'L L. 285 (2015).

Gardbaum, Stephen, *The New Commonwealth Model of Constitutionalism*, 49 AM. J. COMP. L. 707 (2001).

Gardbaum, Stephen, *What is Judicial Supremacy?*, *in* COMPARATIVE CONSTITUTIONAL THEORY 21 (Gary Jacobsohn & Miguel Schor eds., 2018).

Gatmaytan, Dante, *Constitutional Change as Suspect Projects: The Philippines*, *in* CONSTITUTIONAL AMENDMENT IN SOUTHEAST ASIA, 14 J. COMP. L. 139 (2019).

Ghai, Yash, *Yash Ghai*, *in* HUMAN RIGHTS, SOUTHERN VOICES (William Twining ed., 2009).

Ginsburg, Tom & Simpser, Alberto, *Introduction* to CONSTITUTIONS IN AUTHORITARIAN REGIMES 1 (Tom Ginsburg & Alberto Simpser eds., 2015).

GINSBURG, TOM & HUQ, AZIZ Z., HOW TO SAVE A CONSTITUTIONAL DEMOCRACY (2018).

Ginsburg, Tom & Moustafa, Tamir, *Introduction* to RULE BY LAW: THE POLITICS OF COURTS IN AUTHORITARIAN REGIMES 1 (Tom Ginsburg & Tamir Moustafa eds., 2008).

GINSBURG, TOM, JUDICIAL REVIEW IN NEW DEMOCRACIES: CONSTITUTIONAL COURTS IN ASIA (2003).

Greene, Jamal & Tew, Yvonne, *Comparative Approaches to Constitutional History*, *in* COMPARATIVE JUDICIAL REVIEW 379 (Erin Delaney & Rosalind Dixon eds., 2018).

Greene, Jamal, *Foreword: Rights as Trumps?*, 132 HARV. L. REV. 28 (2018).

Greene, Jamal, *Rule Originalism*, 116 COLUM. L. REV. 1639 (2016).

GROVES, HARRY E. & SHERIDAN, L.A., THE CONSTITUTION OF MALAYSIA (1987).

Lord Hailsham of St. Marylebone, Richard Dimbleby Lecture, *Elective Dictatorship*, 96 THE LISTENER 496 (1976).

Harding, A.J., *The 1988 Constitutional Crisis in Malaysia*, 39 INT'L COMP. LAW Q. 57 (1990).

Harding, Andrew & Whiting, Amanda, *Custodian of Civil Liberties and Justice in Malaysia: The Malaysian Bar and the Moderate State*, *in* FORTUNES AND MISFORTUNES OF POLITICAL LIBERALISM: THE LEGAL COMPLEX IN THE BRITISH POST-COLONY (T.C. Halliday et al. eds., 2011).

HARDING, ANDREW & NICHOLSON, PENELOPE, NEW COURTS IN ASIA (2010).

Harding, Andrew, et al., *Malaysia: The State of Liberal Democracy*, 16 INT'L J. CONST. L. 625 (2018).

Harding, Andrew, *Does the "Basic Structure" Doctrine Apply in Singapore's Constitution? An Inquiry into Some Fundamental Constitutional Premises*, *in* CONSTITUTIONAL INTERPRETATION IN SINGAPORE 32 (Jaclyn Neo ed., 2016).

HARDING, ANDREW, LAW, GOVERNMENT, AND THE CONSTITUTION IN MALAYSIA (1996).

HARDING, ANDREW, THE CONSTITUTION OF MALAYSIA: A CONTEXTUAL ANALYSIS (2012).

Harding, Andrew, *The Death of a Doctrine? Phang Chin Hock v. Public Prosecutor*, 21 MALAYAN L.J. 365 (1979).

Harding, Andrew, *The Keris, the Crescent and the Blind Goddess: The State, Islam and the Constitution in Malaysia*, 6 SING. J. INT'L & COMP. L. 154 (2002).

Harding, Andrew, *The "Westminster Model" Constitution Overseas: Transplantation, Adaptation and Development in Commonwealth States*, 4 OXFORD U. COMMW. L.J. 143 (2004).

Harper, T.N., THE END OF EMPIRE AND THE MAKING OF MALAYA (1999).

Hashmi, Zeeshaan Zafar, *Unconstitutional Constitutional Amendments or Amending the Unamendable: A Critique of* District Bar Association Rawalpindi v. Federation of Pakistan, PAKISTAN L. REV. IX (2018).

Hendrianto, Stefanus, *Against the Currents: The Indonesian Constitutional Court in an Age of Proportionality*, *in* PROPORTIONALITY IN ASIA 169 (Po Jen Yap ed., forthcoming 2020).

HENDRIANTO, STEFANUS, LAW AND POLITICS OF CONSTITUTIONAL COURTS: INDONESIA AND THE SEARCH FOR JUDICIAL HEROES (2018).

HIRSCHL, RAN, COMPARATIVE MATTERS: THE RENAISSANCE OF COMPARATIVE CONSTITUTIONAL LAW (2014).

HIRSCHL, RAN, CONSTITUTIONAL THEOCRACY (2010).

HIRSCHL, RAN, TOWARDS JURISTOCRACY (2004).

HOPE, BRADLEY & WRIGHT, TOM, BILLION DOLLAR WHALE: THE MAN WHO FOOLED WALL STREET, HOLLYWOOD, AND THE WORLD (2018).

Hoque, Ridwanul, *Eternal Provisions in the Constitution of Bangladesh: A Constitution Once and for All?*, *in* AN UNAMENDABLE CONSTITUTION? UNAMENDABILITY IN CONSTITUTIONAL DEMOCRACIES 195 (Richard Albert & Emrah Order eds., 2018).

Hor, Michael, *Constitutionalism and Subversion: An Exploration*, *in* EVOLUTION OF A REVOLUTION: FORTY YEARS OF THE SINGAPORE CONSTITUTION 260 (Kevin Tan & Li-ann Thio eds., 2009).

HUSSIN MUTALIB, ISLAM IN MALAYSIA: FROM REVIVALISM TO ISLAMIC STATE? (1993).

IGNATIEFF, MICHAEL, HUMAN RIGHTS AS POLITICS AND IDOLATRY (2003).

Issacharoff, Samuel, *Comparative Constitutional Law as a Window on Democratic Institutions*, *in* COMPARATIVE JUDICIAL REVIEW 60 (Erin F. Delaney & Rosalind Dixon eds., 2018).

Issacharoff, Samuel, *Constitutional Courts and Consolidated Power*, 62 AM. J. COMP. L. 585 (2014).

ISSACHAROFF, SAMUEL, FRAGILE DEMOCRACIES: CONTESTED POWER IN THE ERA OF CONSTITUTIONAL COURTS (2015).

Issacharoff, Samuel, *Judicial Review in Troubled Times: Stabilizing Democracy in a Second-Best World*, 98 N.C. L. Rev. 1 (2019).
Jackson, Vicki, Constitutional Engagement in a Transnational Era (2010).
Jacobsohn, Gary, Constitutional Identity (2010).
Jacobsohn, Gary, *The Permeability of Constitutional Borders*, 82 Tex. L. Rev. 1763 (2003).
Jennings, Ivor, The Law and the Constitution (5th ed. 1967).
Jeshurun, Chandran, *Tunku Abdul Rahman Putra and His Links with the Universities of Cambridge and Malaya, 1960–1962*, 82 J. Malaysian Branch Royal Asiatic Soc'y 1 (2009).
Jhaveri, Swati & Neo, Jaclyn, *The Many Facets of Constitutional Dialogue: The Case of Singapore*, 18 Austl. J. Asian L. 1 (2017).
Jhaveri, Swati, *Recent Judicial Comments on the Basic Structure of the Constitution*, Sing. Pub. L. Blog (Apr. 20, 2016), https://perma.cc/U8YZ-TXN2.
Kanesalingam, Shanmuga, *Monkey in a Wig: Loyarburok, Undimsia!, Public Interest Litigation and Beyond*, 31 Wis. Int'l L.J. 586 (2013).
Karl, Terry Lynn, *The Hybrid Regimes of Central America*, 6 J. Democracy 72 (1995).
Kausikan, Bilahari, *Asia's Different Standard*, 92 Foreign Pol'y 24 (1993).
Kavanagh, Aileen, *The Lure and the Limits of Dialogue*, 66 U. Toronto. L.J. 83 (2016).
Kellogg, Thomas, *Rule of Law in Asia: The Case of China*, *in* Handbook on the Rule of Law 490 (Christopher May & Adam Winchester eds., 2018).
Khosla, Madhav, *Constitutional Amendment*, *in* Oxford Handbook of the Indian Constitution 232 (Sujit Choudhry et al. eds., 2016).
Kingsbury, Damien, *Universalism and Exceptionalism in "Asia"*, *in* Human Rights in Asia: A Reassessment of the Asian Values Debate 33 (Leena Avonius & Damien Kingsbury eds., 2008).
Kipling, Rudyard, From Sea to Sea: Letters of Travel (1913).
Kramer, Larry D., The People themselves: Popular Constitutionalism and Judicial Review (2004).
Krishnaswamy, Sudhir, Democracy and Constitutionalism in India: A Study of the Basic Structure Doctrine (2009).
Kumarasingham, H., *A Foreign Commission for Domestic Needs: The Constitutional Founding of Malaysia*, *in* Constitutional Founding in Southeast Asia 139 (Kevin Tan & Bui Ngoc Sun eds., 2017).
Landau, David, *A Dynamic Theory of Judicial Role*, 55 B.C.L. Rev. 1501 (2014).
Landau, David, *Abusive Constitutionalism*, 47 U.C.D. L. Rev. 189 (2014).
Law, David S. & Hsieh, Hsiang-Yang, *Judicial Review of Constitutional Amendments: Taiwan*, *in* Constitutionalism in Context 1 (David S. Law ed., forthcoming).
Law, David S. & Versteeg, Mila, *The Evolution and Ideology of Global Constitutionalism*, 99 Calif. L. Rev. 1163 (2011).
Lawson, Stephanie, *Culture, Relativism and Democracy: Political Myths about "Asia" and the "West"*, *in* Pathways to Asia: The Politics of Engagement 108 (Richard Robison ed., 1995).
Lee, H.P., Foo, Richard, & Tan, Amber, *Constitutional Change in Malaysia*, *in* Constitutional Amendment in Southeast Asia, 14 J. Comp. L. 119 (2019).
Lee, H.P. & Foo, Richard, *The Malaysian Judiciary: A Sisyphean Quest for Redemption?*, *in* Asia-Pacific Judiciaries: Independence, Impartiality and Integrity 231 (H.P. Lee & Marilyn Pittard eds., 2018).
Lee, H.P., Constitutional Conflicts in Contemporary Malaysia (2017).
Lee, H.P., *Constitutionalized Emergency Powers*, *in* Emergency Powers in Asia: Exploring the Limits of Legality 393 (Victor Ramraj & Arun Thiruvengadam eds., 2010).

Lee, Jack Tsen-Ta, *According to the Spirit and not to the Letter: Proportionality and the Singapore Constitution*, 8 VIENNA J. ON INT'L CONST. L. 276 (2014).

Lee, Jack Tsen-Ta, *Shall the Twain Never Meet? Competing Narratives and Discourses of the Rule of Law in Singapore*, 2012 SING. J. LEGAL STUD. 298 (2012).

Lee, Jack Tsen-Ta, *The Mandatory Death Penalty and A Sparsely Worded Constitution*, 127 LAW Q. REV. 192 (2011).

Lee, Therese, *Malaysia and the Internal Security Act: The Insecurity of Human Rights After September 11*, SING. J. LEGAL STUD. 56 (2002).

Leong, Laurence Wai-Teng, *From "Asian Values" to Singapore Exceptionalism*, *in* HUMAN RIGHTS IN ASIA: A REASSESSMENT OF THE ASIAN VALUES DEBATE 121 (Damien Kingsbury & Leena Avonius eds., 2008).

Leong, Pauline, *Political Communication in Malaysia: A Study on the Use of New Media in Politics*, 7 JEDEM 46 (2015).

LEVINSON, SANFORD, CONSTITUTIONAL FAITH (2011).

LEVITSKY, STEVEN & WAY, LUCAN A., COMPETITIVE AUTHORITARIANISM: HYBRID REGIMES AFTER THE COLD WAR (2010).

Liang, Calvin & Shi, Sarah, *The Constitution of Our Constitution: A Vindication of the Basic Structure Doctrine*, SING. L. GAZETTE 12 (Aug. 2014).

Linehan, W., *The Identifications of Some of Ptolemy's Place Names in the Golden Khersonese*, 24 J. MALAYAN BRANCH OF ROYAL ASIATIC SOC'Y, pt. 3 (1951), https://perma.cc/F9JA-L6PQ.

LIOW, JOSEPH, PIETY AND POLITICS: ISLAMISM IN CONTEMPORARY MALAYSIA (2009).

LIOW, JOSEPH, RELIGION AND NATIONALISM IN SOUTHEAST ASIA (2016).

Madison, James to William Eustis, July 6, 1819, *in* LETTERS AND OTHER WRITINGS OF JAMES MADISON, VOL. III (Philadelphia, 1865).

Mahathir Mohamad, Prime Minister of Malaysia, Speech on the Management of an Economy in Crisis, 6th Prime Ministerial Lecture of the Harvard Club (Oct. 5, 1998).

Menon, Sundaresh, Lecture, *The Rule of Law: The Path to Exceptionalism*, 28 SING. ACAD. L.J. 413 (2016).

Mohamed Azam Mohamed Adil, *Law of Apostasy and Freedom of Religion in Malaysia*, 2 ASIAN J. COMP. L. 29 (2007)

Mohamed Ismail Shariff, *The Legislative Jurisdiction of the Federal Parliament in Matters Involving Islamic Law*, 3 MALAYAN L.J. cv (2005).

Monaghan, Henry Paul, *Doing Originalism*, 104 COLUM. L. REV. 32 (2004).

MONTESQUIEU, CHARLES LOUIS DE SECONDAT, BARON DE, THE SPIRIT OF THE LAWS (BOOK XI) (1748), *in* THE COMPLETE WORKS OF M. DE MONTESQUIEU (1777).

Moustafa, Tamir & Ginsburg, Tom, *Introduction: The Functions of Courts in Authoritarian Politics*, *in* RULE BY LAW: THE POLITICS OF COURTS IN AUTHORITARIAN REGIMES (Tom Ginsburg & Tamir Moustafa eds., 2008).

MOUSTAFA, TAMIR, CONSTITUTING RELIGION: ISLAM, LIBERAL RIGHTS, AND THE MALAYSIAN STATE (2018).

MyConstitution Campaign: How the Constitution Affects Us, MALAYSIAN BAR, https://perma.cc/4KR6-JYCR.

Nelson, Matthew J. & Dian Shah, *Operationalizing and Regulating Religious Freedom: Apostasy and Administrative "Reasonableness" in Malaysia and Beyond*, 16 INT'L J. CONST. L. 1293 (2019).

Neo, Jaclyn & Son, Bui Ngoc, *Expanding the Universe of Comparative Constitutional Amendments in Southeast Asia*, *in* CONSTITUTIONAL AMENDMENT IN SOUTHEAST ASIA, 14 J. COMP. L. 46 (2019).

Neo, Jaclyn & Dian Shah, *Hudud and the Struggle for Malaysia's Constitutional Soul*, CONSTITUTIONNET (June 25, 2015), https://perma.cc/R8DT-N2DW.

Neo, Jaclyn & Lee, Yvonne, *Constitutional Supremacy: Still a Little Dicey?*, *in* EVOLUTION OF A REVOLUTION: FORTY YEARS OF THE SINGAPORE CONSTITUTION 153 (Li-ann Thio & Kevin Tan eds., 2009).

Neo, Jaclyn, *"All Power Has Legal Limits"—The Principle of Legality as a Constitutional Principle of Judicial Review*, 29 SING. ACAD. L.J. 667 (2017).

Neo, Jaclyn, *Balancing Act: The Balancing Metaphor as Deference and Dialogue in Constitutional Adjudication*, *in* CONSTITUTIONAL INTERPRETATION IN SINGAPORE: THEORY AND PRACTICE 159 (Jaclyn Neo ed., 2017).

Neo, Jaclyn, *Beyond Mortals? Constitutional Identity, Judicial Power, and the Evolution of the Basic Structure Doctrine in Malaysia*, *in* CPG PUBLICATION: "IDENTITY AND CHANGE—THE BASIC STRUCTURE IN ASIAN CONSTITUTIONAL ORDERS" (2016).

Neo, Jaclyn, *Competing Imperatives: Conflicts and Convergences in State and Islam in Pluralist Malaysia*, 4 OXFORD J.L. & RELIGION 1 (2015).

Neo, Jaclyn, *Constituting religion, contesting constitutional identity*, IMMANENT FRAME (July 18, 2019), https://perma.cc/J8LV-GQ9Z.

Neo, Jaclyn, *Constitutional Change in Singapore's Elected Presidency: Navigating Questions of Ethnic Identity and Representation*, IACL-AIDC BLOG (Dec. 1, 2017), https://perma.cc/DWB7-TEUC.

Neo, Jaclyn, *Introduction* to CONSTITUTIONAL INTERPRETATION IN SINGAPORE: THEORY AND PRACTICE 8 (Jaclyn Neo ed., 2016).

Neo, Jaclyn, *Malay Nationalism, Islamic Supremacy and the Constitutional Bargain in the Multi-ethnic Composition of Malaysia*, 13 INT'L J. ON MINORITY & GROUP RTS. 95 (2006).

Neo, Jaclyn, *Parsing Privity Clauses in Malaysia: Rights, Security and Judicial Review in Malaysia*, 1 PUB. L. 25 (2010).

Neo, Jaclyn, *Return of Judicial Power: Religious Freedom and the Tussle over Jurisdictional Boundaries in Malaysia*, INT'L J. CONST. L. BLOG (Mar. 15, 2018), https://perma.cc/6XUW-CWAK.

Neo, Jaclyn, *Secular Constitutionalism in Singapore: Between Equality and Hierarchy*, 5 OXFORD J.L. & REL. 431 (2016).

Neo, Jaclyn, *Secularism without Liberalism: Religious Freedom in a non-Secular State*, 2017 MICH. ST. L. REV. 333 (2017).

Neo, Jaclyn, *Seditious in Singapore! Free Speech and the Offence of Promoting Ill-Will and Hostility Between Different Racial Groups*, 2011 SING. J. LEGAL STUD. 351 (2011).

Neo, Jaclyn, *Towards a "Thin" Basic Structure Doctrine in Singapore*, INT'L J. CONST. L. BLOG (Jan. 17, 2018), https://perma.cc/BQL3-YXSP.

Neo, Jaclyn, *What's in a Name? Malaysia's "Allah" Controversy and the Judicial Intertwining of Islam with Ethnic Identity*, 12 INT'L J. CONST. L. 751 (2014).

Okoth-Ogendo, H.W.O., *Constitutions Without Constitutionalism: Reflections on an African Political Paradox*, *in* CONSTITUTIONALISM AND DEMOCRACY: TRANSITIONS IN THE CONTEMPORARY WORLD 67 (Douglas Greenberg et al. eds., 1993).

PARKINSON, CHARLES, BILLS OF RIGHTS AND DECOLONIZATION: THE EMERGENCE OF DOMESTIC HUMAN RIGHTS INSTRUMENTS IN BRITAIN'S OVERSEAS TERRITORIES (2007).

Peerenboom, Randall, *Beyond Universalism and Relativism: The Evolving Debates about "Values in Asia"*, 14 IND. INT'L & COMP. L. REV. 1 (2003)

PETERSEN, NIELS, PROPORTIONALITY AND JUDICIAL ACTIVISM (2017).

Rais Yatim, *The Road to Merdeka*, *in* CONSTITUTIONAL LANDMARKS IN MALAYSIA: THE FIRST 50 YEARS, 1957–2007 (Andrew Harding & H.P. Lee eds., 2007).

Rajah, Jothie & Thiruvengadam, Arun, *Of Masks, Absences and Exceptions: Cause Lawyering in Singapore*, 30 Wis. Int'l L.J. 646 (2013).

Rajah, Jothie, Authoritarian Rule of Law: Legislation, Discourse and Legitimacy in Singapore (2012).

Rajah, V.K., Attorney General, Speech at the Opening of the Legal Year 2015, The Rule of Law (Jan. 5, 2015), https://perma.cc/HQ7Q-D2QE.

Rajah, V.K., *Interpreting the Singapore Constitution*, *in* Constitutional Interpretation in Singapore: Theory and Practice 23 (Jaclyn Neo ed., 2016).

Ram, Gopal Sri, *The Dynamics of Constitutional Interpretation*, 4 Malayan L.J. i (2017).

Raz, Joseph, *The Rule of Law and its Virtue*, 93 Law Q. Rev. 195 (1977).

Roux, Theunis, The Politics of Principle: The First South African Constitutional Court, 1995-2005 (2013).

Roznai, Yaniv, *Constitutional Amendability and Unamendability in South-East Asia*, *in* Constitutional Amendment in Southeast Asia, 14 J. Comp. L. 188 (2019).

Roznai, Yaniv, *Unconstitutional Constitutional Amendments—The Migration and Success of a Constitutional Idea*, 61 Am. J. Comp. L. 657 (2013).

Roznai, Yaniv, Unconstitutional Constitutional Amendments: The Limits of Amendment Powers (2017).

Sadurski, Wojciech, Rights Before Courts: A Study of Constitutional Courts in Postcommunist States of Central and Eastern Europe (2008).

Saeed, Hassan, *Apostasy Laws in Malaysia: Jurisdiction and Constitutionality*, *in* Freedom of Religion, Apostasy and Islam 149 (Abdullah Saeed & Hassan Saeed eds., 2004).

Saunders, Cheryl, *Judicial Engagement*, *in* Comparative Constitutional Law in Asia 80 (Rosalind Dixon & Tom Ginsburg, eds., 2014).

Scalia, Antonin, A Matter of Interpretation: Federal Courts and the Law (1997).

Scheppele, Kim Lane, *Guardians of the Constitution: Constitutional Court Presidents and the Struggle for the Rule of Law in Post-Soviet Europe*, 154 U. Pa. L. Rev. 1757 (2006).

Scheppele, Kim Lane, *Jack Balkin Is an American*, 25 Yale J.L. & Human. 23 (2013).

Sen, Amartya, Development as Freedom (1999).

Sen, Amartya, *Human Rights and Asian Values*, Sixteenth Morgenthau Memorial Lecture on Ethics & Foreign Pol'y (1997), https://perma.cc/M2RV-QMRU.

Shanmugam, K., Minister for Law, Speech at the New York State Bar Association (NYSBA) Rule of Law Plenary Session (Oct. 27, 2009), https://perma.cc/V2VG-JXBQ.

Shanmugam, K., *The Rule of Law in Singapore*, Sing. J. Legal Stud. 357 (2012).

Shad Saleem Faruqi, Document of Destiny: The Constitution of the Federation of Malaysia (2008).

Shad Saleem Faruqi, *The Malaysian Constitution, The Islamic State and Hudud Laws*, *in* Islam in Southeast Asia: Political, Social and Strategic Challenges for the 21st Century 284 (K.S. Nathan & Mohamad Hashim Kamali, eds., 2005).

Shapiro, Martin & Stone Sweet, Alec, On Law, Politics and Judicialization (2002).

Shukri Ahmad Shahizam, *One Step Forward, Two Steps Back? Constructive Res Judicata in Malaysian Constitutional Cases*, Int'l J. Const. L. Blog (Feb. 3, 2018), https://perma.cc/5R9D-XU9Y.

Silverstein, Gordon, *Singapore: The Exception That Proves Rules Matter*, *in* Rule by Law: The Politics of Courts in Authoritarian Regimes 73 (Tom Ginsburg & Tamir Moustafa eds., 2008).

Silverstein, Gordon, *Singapore's Constitutionalism: A Model, But of What Sort?*, 100 Cornell L. Rev. Online 1 (2015).

Sim, Cameron, *The Singapore Chill: Political Defamation and the Normalization of a Statist Rule of Law*, 20 PAC. RIM L. & POL'Y J. 319 (2011).

Sinnadurai, Visu, *The 1988 Judiciary Crisis and its Aftermath, in* CONSTITUTIONAL LANDMARKS IN MALAYSIA 173 (Andrew Harding & H.P. Lee eds., 2007).

Srukhosit, Narongdech, *Manifest Disproportionality and the Constitutional Court of Thailand, in* PROPORTIONALITY IN ASIA 192 (Po Jen Yap ed., forthcoming 2020).

Stilt, Kristen, *Contextualizing Constitutional Islam: The Malayan Experience*, 13 INT'L J. CONST. L. 407 (2015).

Strauss, David A., *Common Law, Common Ground, and Jefferson's Principle*, 112 YALE L.J. 1717 (2003).

Su, Anna, *Judging Religious Sincerity*, 5 OXFORD J.L. AND RELIGION 28 (2016).

Subramaniam, Surain, *The Asian Values Debate: Implications for the Spread of Liberal Democracy*, 27 ASIAN AFF. 19 (2000).

Sweet, Alec Stone & Mathews, Jud, *Proportionality Balancing and Global Constitutionalism*, 47 COLUM. J. TRANSNAT'L L. 72 (2008).

Sweet, Alec Stone & Mathews, Jud, *Proportionality and Rights Protection in Asia: Hong Kong, Malaysia, South Korea, Taiwan—Whither Singapore?*, 29 SING. ACAD. L.J. 774 (2017).

TAMANAHA, BRIAN Z., ON THE RULE OF LAW: HISTORY, POLITICS, THEORY (2004).

Tan, David, *Whither the Autochthonous Narrative of Freedom of Speech in Singapore?: A Guide to Defaming Politicians and Scandalising Judges, in* CONSTITUTIONAL INTERPRETATION IN SINGAPORE: THEORY AND PRACTICE 210 (Jaclyn Neo ed., 2016).

Tan, Eugene, *Law and Values in Governance: The Singapore Way*, 30 HONG KONG L.J. 109 (2000).

Tan, Eugene, *Much Ado About Nothing? The Enigma of Engagement of Foreign Constitutional Law in Singapore, in* CONSTITUTIONAL INTERPRETATION IN SINGAPORE: THEORY AND PRACTICE 289 (Jaclyn Neo ed., 2016).

Tan, Kevin & Thio, Li-ann, *Introduction* to EVOLUTION OF A REVOLUTION: FORTY YEARS OF THE SINGAPORE CONSTITUTION 2 (Kevin Tan & Li-ann Thio eds., 2009).

Tan, Kevin, *A Short Legal and Constitutional History of Singapore, in* THE SINGAPORE LEGAL SYSTEM 1 (Walter Woon ed., 1989).

Tan, Kevin, *Foundational Moments: The "Singapore Constitution", in* CONSTITUTIONAL FOUNDING IN SOUTHEAST ASIA 182 (Kevin Tan & Bui Ngoc Sun eds., 2017).

Tan, Kevin, *Into the Matrix: Interpreting the Westminster Model Constitution, in* CONSTITUTIONAL INTERPRETATION IN SINGAPORE: THEORY AND PRACTICE 50 (Jaclyn Neo ed., 2016).

Tan, Kevin, *Recent Developments in the Law and Practice of Preventive Detention, in* PUBLIC LAW IN CONTEMPORARY MALAYSIA 293 (Min Aun Wu ed. 1999).

Tan, Kevin, *Singapore: In and Out of the Federation, in* CONSTITUTIONAL LANDMARKS IN MALAYSIA: THE FIRST 50 YEARS 1957-2007 (Andrew Harding & H.P. Lee eds., 2007).

TAN, KEVIN, THE CONSTITUTION OF SINGAPORE: A CONTEXTUAL ANALYSIS (2015).

Tan, Kevin, *The Evolution of Singapore's Modern Constitution: Developments from 1945 to the Present Day*, 1 SING. ACAD. L.J. 17 (1989).

Tashima, A. Wallace, *The War on Terror and the Rule of Law*, 15 ASIAN AM. L.J. 245 (2008).

Tay, Wilson, *Basic Structure Revisited: The Case of* Semenyih Jaya *and the Defence of Fundamental Constitutional Principles in Malaysia*, 14 ASIAN J. COMP. L. 113 (2019).

Tew, Yvonne, *On the Uneven Journey to Constitutional Redemption: The Malaysian Judiciary And Constitutional Politics*, 25 WASH. INT'L L. J. 673 (2016).

Tew, Yvonne, *Stealth Theocracy*, 58 VA. J. INT'L L. 31 (2018).

THE FEDERALIST NO. 51 (James Madison).

Thio, Li-ann & Chong, David, *The Chan Court and Constitutional Adjudication: "A Sea Change into Something Rich and Strange?"*, *in* THE LAW IN HIS HANDS: A TRIBUTE TO CHIEF JUSTICE CHAN SEK KEONG 87 (Chao Hick Tin et al., 2012).

THIO, LI-ANN, A TREATISE ON SINGAPORE CONSTITUTIONAL LAW (2012).

Thio, Li-ann, *Apostasy and Religious Freedom: Constitutional Issues Arising from the Lina Joy Litigation*, 2 MALAYAN L.J. i (2006).

Thio, Li-Ann, *Between Apology and Apogee, Autochthony: The Rule of Law Beyond the Rules of Law in Singapore*, SING. J. LEGAL STUD. 269 (2012).

Thio, Li-ann, *Beyond the Four Walls in an Age of Transnational Judicial Conversations Civil Liberties, Rights Theories, and Constitutional Adjudication in Malaysia and Singapore*, 19 COLUM. J. ASIAN L. 428 (2006).

Thio, Li-ann, *Constitutionalism in Illiberal Polities*, *in* THE OXFORD HANDBOOK OF COMPARATIVE CONSTITUTIONAL LAW 133 (Michel Rosenfeld & András Sajó eds., 1st ed. 2012).

Thio, Li-ann, *Implementing Human Rights in ASEAN Countries: "Promises to Keep and Miles to Go Before I Sleep"*, 2 YALE HUM. RTS. AND DEV. L.J. 1 (1999).

Thio, Li-ann, *"It Is A Little Known Legal Fact": Originalism, Customary Human Rights Law, and Constitutional Interpretation*, SING. J. LEGAL STUD. 558 (2010).

Thio, Li-ann, *Jurisdictional Imbroglio: Civil and Religious Courts, Turf Wars and Article 121(1A) of the Federal Constitution*, *in* CONSTITUTIONAL LANDMARKS IN MALAYSIA: THE FIRST 50 YEARS 202 (Andrew Harding & H.P. Lee eds., 2007).

Thio, Li-Ann, *Lex Rex or Rex Lex? Competing Conceptions of the Rule of Law in Singapore*, 20 UCLA PAC. BASIN L.J. 1 (2002).

Thio, Li-ann, *Principled Pragmatism and the "Third Wave" of Communitarian Judicial Review in Singapore*, *in* CONSTITUTIONAL INTERPRETATION IN SINGAPORE: THEORY AND PRACTICE 75 (Jaclyn Neo ed., 2016).

Thio, Li-ann, *Soft Constitutional Law in Nonliberal Asian Constitutional Democracies*, 8 INT'L J. CONST. L. 766 (2010).

Thio, Li-ann, *The Passage of a Generation: Revisiting the Report of the 1966 Constitutional Commission*, *in* EVOLUTION OF A REVOLUTION: FORTY YEARS OF THE SINGAPORE CONSTITUTION 16 (Kevin Tan & Li-ann Thio eds., 2009).

Thiruvengadam, Arun, *The Continuing Resistance to Foreign Law in Constitutional Adjudication in Singapore*, *in* CONSTITUTIONAL INTERPRETATION IN SINGAPORE: THEORY AND PRACTICE 318 (Jaclyn Neo ed., 2016).

Thomas, Tommy, *Is Malaysia an Islamic State?*, 4 MALAYAN L.J. xv (2006).

Thomas, Tommy, *The Social Contract: Malaysia's Constitutional Covenant*, 1 MALAYAN L.J. cxxxii (2008).

Thompson, Mark, *Whatever Happened to "Asian Values"?*, 12 J. DEMOCRACY 154 (2001).

Tonsakulrungruang, Khemthong, *Constitutional Amendment in Thailand: Amending in the Spectre of Parliamentary Dictatorship*, *in* CONSTITUTIONAL AMENDMENT IN SOUTHEAST ASIA, 14 J. COMP. L. 173 (2019).

TROLLOPE, ANTHONY, AN AUTOBIOGRAPHY (Vol. 1) (1883).

Tushnet, Mark, *Alternative Forms of Judicial Review*, 101 MICH. L. REV. 2781 (2003).

Tushnet, Mark, *Authoritarian Constitutionalism*, 100 CORNELL L. REV. 391 (2015).

Tushnet, Mark, Editorial, *Varieties of Constitutionalism*, 14:1 INT'L J. CONST. L., https://perma.cc/J7TZ-B4QV.

TUSHNET, MARK, TAKING THE CONSTITUTION AWAY FROM THE COURTS (1999).

Tushnet, Mark, *The Relation Between Political Constitutionalism and Weak-Form Judicial Review*, 14 GERMAN L.J. 2249 (2013).

Ullah, Aman & Uzair, Samee, *Basic Structure of Constitution: Impact of* Kesavananda Bharati *on Constitutional Status of Fundamental Rights*, 26 S. ASIAN STUD. 299 (2011).
Varughese, George, President, Malaysian Bar, Press Release, An Independent Judiciary is Indispensable to the Rule of Law (May 8, 2017), https://perma.cc/T3QT-Y5WF.
VILE, M.J.C., CONSTITUTIONALISM AND THE SEPARATION OF POWERS (Liberty Fund, Inc., 2d ed. 1998).
WADE, H.W.R. & FORSYTH, C.F., ADMINISTRATIVE LAW (1994).
Waldron, Jeremy, *The Core of the Case Against Judicial Review*, 115 YALE L.J. 1341 (2006).
Waldron, Jeremy, *The Rule of Law and the Importance of Procedure*, *in* GETTING TO THE RULE OF LAW 3 (James E. Fleming ed., 2011).
WALLACE, ALFRED RUSSEL, THE MALAY ARCHIPELAGO 26 (London, 1872).
Weiss, Meredith L., *Parsing the Power of "New Media" in Malaysia*, 43 J. CONTEMP. ASIA 591 (2013).
Welsh, Bridget, *"Saviour" Politics and Malaysia's 2018 Electoral Democratic Breakthrough: Rethinking Explanatory Narratives and Implications*, 37 J. CURRENT SE. ASIAN AFF. 85 (2018).
Whiting, Amanda, *Desecularising Malaysian Law?*, *in* EXAMINING PRACTICE, INTERROGATING THEORY: COMPARATIVE LEGAL STUDIES IN ASIA 229 (Sarah Biddulph et al. eds., 2008).
WHITTINGTON, KEITH E., CONSTITUTIONAL INTERPRETATION: TEXTUAL MEANING, ORIGINAL INTENT, AND JUDICIAL REVIEW (1999).
Whittington, Keith E., *The New Originalism*, 2 GEO. J.L. & PUB. POL'Y 599 (2004).
Wu, Jesse Min Aun, *The Saga of Anwar Ibrahim*, *in* CONSTITUTIONAL LANDMARKS IN MALAYSIA: THE FIRST 50 YEARS 1957-2007 1 (Andrew Harding & H.P. Lee eds., 2007).
YAP, PO JEN, CONSTITUTIONAL DIALOGUE IN COMMON LAW ASIA (2015).
Yap, Po Jen, *Constitutional Fig Leaves in Asia*, 24 WASH. INT. L.J. 421 (2016).
Yap, Po Jen, *Constitutionalising Capital Crimes: Judicial Virtue or "Originalism" Sin?*, SING. J. LEGAL STUD. 281 (2011).
YAP, PO JEN, COURTS AND DEMOCRACIES IN ASIA (2017).
Yap, Po Jen, *Introduction* to PROPORTIONALITY IN ASIA 1 (Po Jen Yap ed., forthcoming 2020).
Yap, Po Jen, *Uncovering Originalism and Textualism in Singapore*, *in* CONSTITUTIONAL INTERPRETATION IN SINGAPORE: THEORY AND PRACTICE 117 (Jaclyn Neo ed., 2017).
Yeh, Jiunn-rong & Chang, Wen-Chen, *Introduction* to ASIAN COURTS IN CONTEXT (Jiunn-rong Yeh & Wen-Chen Chang eds., 2015).
Yeh, Jiunn-rong & Chang, Wen-Chen, *The Emergence of East Asian Constitutionalism: Features in Comparison*, 59 AM. J. COMP. L. 805 (2011).
Zakaria, Fareed, *Culture is Destiny: A Conversation with Lee Kuan Yew*, FOREIGN AFF., March/April 1994.
Zakaria, Fareed, *The Rise of Illiberal Democracy*, 76 FOREIGN AFF. 22 (1997).

Government Publications

Alliance Memorandum to the Reid Constitutional Commission, Sept. 27, 1956.
FEDERATION OF MALAYA CONSTITUTIONAL COMMISSION, REPORT OF 1956-57 § COLONIAL NO. 330.
Constitutional Commission, Report of 1966 (Singapore Government Printer, 1966).
House of Representatives Malaysia, Parliamentary Debates, Seventh Parliament, Session 2, Vol. 2 (Mar. 17, 1988).
POPULATION AND HOUSING CENSUS OF MALAYSIA, POPULATION DISTRIBUTION AND BASIC DEMOGRAPHIC CHARACTERISTIC REPORT 2010, https://perma.cc/2LBT-VP64.

Report of the Panel of Eminent Persons to Review the 1988 Judicial Crisis in Malaysia (Kuala Lumpur, Bar Council, 2008).

Report of the Tribunal Established under Article 125(3) and (4) of the Federal Constitution, Re: YAA Tun Dato Haji Mohamed Salleh Abas, Lord President, Malaysia (Kuala Lumpur, Government Printer, 1988)

Report of the Tribunal Established under Article 125(3) and (4) of the Federal Constitution, Re: YA Tan Sri Wan Suleiman bin Pawan Teh, Supreme Court Judge, etc., (Kuala Lumpur, Government Printer, 1988).

Reports

Document of the Copenhagen Meeting of the Conference on the Human Dimension of the CSCE, June 5-29, 1990, https://perma.cc/E2VC-GU4J.

Human Rights Resource Center, Keeping the Faith: A Study of Freedom of Thought, Conscience, and Religion in ASEAN (2015).

Human Rights Watch, "Kill the Chicken to Scare the Monkeys": Suppression of Free Expression and Assembly in Singapore (2017), https://perma.cc/X3CN-4JFT.

Human Rights Watch, In the Name of Security: Counterterrorism and Human Rights Abuses Under Malaysia's Internal Security Act (2004), https://perma.cc/2VYA-5ZSU.

Pakatan Harapan Manifesto, Rebuilding Our Nation, Fulfilling our Hopes, https://perma.cc/M8Z6-W6W4.

Pew Research Center, Government Restrictions on Religion in 2017, Appendix A: Government Restrictions Index, https://perma.cc/5G3K-VS5Q.

World Conference on Human Rights, Mar. 29–Apr. 2, 1993, *Report of the Regional Meeting for Asia of the World Conference on Human Rights*, U.N. Doc. A/Conf.157/ASRM/8 (Apr. 7, 1993).

Index

Note: *For the benefit of digital users, indexed terms that span two pages (e.g., 52–53) may, on occasion, appear on only one of those pages.*

Malay names are entered under first name element (the given name) and not the second name element (the patronymic). Footnotes are indicated by n after the page number.

Abdul Aziz Bari 81–82n77
Abdul Hamid Mohamad 102–3, 181
access to justice right, Malaysia 50, 109–10, 147–48
'Allah' case (CA Mal) 25, 173–75, 179, 185, 186, 187
Allan, T.R.S. 108–9n14
Alliance coalition, Malaysia 5–6n22, 36, 71, 74, 82–83, 160, 161–62
Alliance of Hope, *see* Pakatan Harapan coalition, Malaysia
Alma Nudo v. Public Prosecutor (FC Mal) 66
  rule of law conception 121–22
  three-stage proportionality analysis 64, 151–52, 207, 216–17
anti-sedition laws:
  in Malaysia 61, 190, 192, 195
    Azmi Sharom case, see *Azmi Sharom* case (FC Mal)
    Mat Shuhaimi bin Shafiei case (FC Mal) 50–51, 151, 202, 207–8
  in Singapore 61, 190, 192, 196–97, 202
anti-terrorism laws 189, 193–94
Anwar Ibrahim 1–2, 29, 192–93, 203, 212
apostasy cases in Malaysia 167–71, 173, 175–76, 177–78, 179, 181–83
ASEAN (Association of Southeast Asian Nations) 22–23, 26
Asia, post-colonial, *see* post-colonial Asia
Asian courts:
  in aspiring democracies, *see* aspiring democracies, courts in
  in authoritarian regimes 5
  constitutional statecraft by, *see* constitutional statecraft by Asian courts
  Federal Court of Malaysia 38
  judicial independence, *see* judicial independence
  Sharia courts in Malaysia, *see* Sharia (Syariah) courts in Malaysia
  in Singapore 41
  see also judicial review
Asian financial crisis (1997) 26
Asian values discourse, *see* rights discourse in post-colonial Asia
aspiring democracies:
  courts in 215
    constitutional statecraft by, *see* constitutional statecraft by Asian courts
    constructive constitutional role 4, 123, 132
    protective constitutional role 3–4, 123, 132
  judicial review in 11, 15, 42–43, 123–24, 126–27
    Malaysia, *see* judicial review in Malaysia
    Singapore, *see* judicial review in Singapore
    strong-form review advocated 42–44, 128–32, 147
  Malaysia 12
    authoritarian constitutionalism (pre-2018), *see* Malaysia, authoritarian constitutionalism (pre-2018)
    democratic transition (2018-) 1–3, 5–6, 17, 30, 33, 65–66, 153–54, 217–19
    government crisis (2020) 2–3n10, 5–6, 30, 33, 65–66, 219
    Pakatan Harapan coalition, *see* Pakatan Harapan coalition, Malaysia
  post-colonial Asia, democratization experiences 214–15, 216–17
  rights discourse in, *see* rights discourse in post-colonial Asia
  rule of law in 107, 113
  security-based restrictions of rights, *see* security-based restrictions of rights
  Singapore 12
    authoritarian constitutionalism, *see* Singapore, authoritarian constitutionalism
    democratic transition, early signs of 31, 66n250, 205n110
Association of Southeast Asian Nations (ASEAN) 22–23, 26

authoritarian constitutionalism:
  and Asian values discourse 23–24, 26, 27–28
  judicial review in authoritarian regimes 5
  of Malaysia (pre-2018) 32, 33
    rights discourse, *see* rights discourse in post-colonial Asia, in Malaysia
    single party dominance, *see* Barisan Nasional coalition, Malaysia
  in post-colonial states 7
  rule *by* law 109
  separation of powers in authoritarian regimes 94
  of Singapore 5, 12, 32, 107
    rights discourse 26–27, 28, 30–31
    single party dominance, *see* People's Action Party, Singapore
Azmi Sharom case (FC Mal) 50, 52–53, 62–63
  proportionality analysis endorsed 151, 202, 206–7

Badruddin bin Amiruldin 165n50
Balasubramaniam, Ratna Rueban 109n18
Bangkok Declaration on Human Rights 1993 (ASEAN) 22–23, 26
Barisan Nasional coalition, Malaysia 5–6, 8n29, 33, 34, 65–66, 94
  constitutional amendments 128–29
    to restrict judicial review, *see* constitutional amendment to restrict judicial review, Malaysia (1988)
  corruption allegations 1–2, 29, 217–18
  deferential judicial review under regime 7–8, 28, 41–42, 96–98, 200
    civil courts' deference to Sharia courts, *see* Sharia (Syariah) courts in Malaysia
  demonstrations against 27–28, 29–30
  electoral defeat (May 2018) 1, 30, 65
  politicization of religion, *see* Islam in Malaysia, as ethno-political issue
  rights discourse 27–28
  security protection laws 189–90, 192–96
  see also Mahathir Mohamad
Barnett, Randy E. 44n69
basic structure doctrine 53–57, 124, 140–44
  as constitutional statecraft mechanism 144–47, 215–16
    religious freedom cases in Malaysia 180–84
    security cases 210–12
  in India 53, 55, 80–81, 101, 103–4, 124, 133, 139–40, 143
  judicial endorsements
    Indira Gandhi case (FC Mal) 9, 55, 56–57, 63, 85, 107–8, 115–16, 117, 121, 138–40, 142, 146, 180, 185
    Semenyih Jaya case (FC Mal) 9, 54, 56–57, 63, 92–93, 101, 103–4, 121, 135, 139–40
    Singaporean jurisprudence 105–6
    Sivarasa Rasiah case *(obiter dicta)* (FC Mal) 54, 62, 141
    Yong Vui Kong case (CA Sing) 55–56, 88–89, 105–6, 145–46
  see also constitutional amendments; constitutional interpretation
Bateup, Christine 127
Bellamy, Richard 125–26
Bickel, Alexander 125
Bilchitz, David 94
Bingham, Lord Tom 108–9, 121–22
Bogdanor, Vernon 42n50
book bans, Malaysia 178–79, 187

Canada:
  Charter of Rights and Freedoms 1982 24, 206
  constitutional interpretation 43, 148
  religious freedom in 85–86
  weak-form (dialogic) judicial review 127
capital punishment in Singapore 51
  Yong Vui Kong case, see *Yong Vui Kong v. Public Prosecutor* (CA Sing)
Chan, Sek Keong 55, 145–46
Chang, Wen-Chen 33n78
Chen, Albert 33n78
children:
  illegitimate children, Islamic naming rules 183
  religious upbringing and custody 162–63, 166–67, 171, 172, 177
    equal rights of both parents (*Indira Gandhi* ruling) 47, 63, 114, 138, 148–49, 172, 186
Chng Suan Tze v. Minister of Home Affairs (CA Sing):
  decision reversed by constitutional amendment (1988) 8, 60, 61, 110–11, 118–19, 199
  principle of legality endorsed 9, 59–60, 64–65, 110, 117–18, 119, 198–99, 208–9
  second CA ruling *(Teo Soh Lung v. Minister of Home Affairs)* 60, 111–12, 200
  Tan Seet Eng case (HC Sing), ruling applied in 204
Chong, David 48n96
Choudhry, Sujit 81–82n79
civil courts' relations with Sharia courts, *see* Sharia (Syariah) courts in Malaysia
civil society in Malaysia 29–30
Colby, Thomas B. 81–82n78
colonial history of Malaysia and Singapore 6, 35–37, 39

common law legal systems 6–7, 112–13
communitarian rights discourse 24–25, 42, 193
constitutional adjudication, *see* judicial review
constitutional amendments:
amendment powers
Malaysian Constitution 8, 38, 59, 80–81, 128–29
Singapore Constitution 8, 41, 59, 77, 78, 80–81, 105, 128–29
basic structure doctrine, *see* basic structure doctrine
versus 'dead hand' critique 80–81
in India (basic structure doctrine) 53, 55, 80–81, 101, 103–4, 124, 133, 139–40, 143
unconstitutional amendments, *see* unconstitutional constitutional amendments
in United States 80–81
constitutional amendment to restrict judicial review, Malaysia (1988) 8, 60–61, 92, 95–96, 134, 199, 211
judicial response (pre-2017) 49–50, 96–98
Kok Wah Kuan case (FC Mal) 46–47, 49–50, 96–98, 99, 100, 102, 109–10, 134
Semenyih Jaya case, see *Semenyih Jaya v. Pentadbir Tanah Daerah Hulu Langat* (FC Mal)
Sharia courts, judicial review immunity 114–15, 138–39
Indira Gandhi case invalidating, see *Indira Gandhi a/p Mutho v. Pengarah Jabatan Agama Islam Perak & Ors.* (FC Mal)
see also judicial review in Malaysia; separation of powers
constitutional history 69–70
colonial history of Malaysia and Singapore 6, 35–37, 39
Constitutions as 'frameworks' for governance 78–80, 91
foundation of Malaysia as sovereign state 6–7, 14
constitutional narrative 7, 31, 79
drafting of Constitution 36–37, 70–75, 82–83, 87, 158, 159–63, 191
Malayan Emergency (1948-60) 191–92
foundation of Singapore as sovereign state 6–7, 14, 39, 75–76
constitutional narrative 7, 39–40
drafting of Constitution 76–78, 87–88, 89
originalist constitutional interpretation, *see* originalist constitutional interpretation
constitutional interpretation:
in Canada 43
in Malaysia and Singapore 42–44, 120
basic structure doctrine, *see* basic structure doctrine
'four walls' approach 46–49
'judicial Islamization' in Malaysia 173–79, 184–85
originalist approach, *see* originalist constitutional interpretation
purposive approach, *see* purposive constitutional interpretation
strict formalism and literalism 49–53
in United States 52, 81–82
see also judicial review
constitutional Islam, *see* Islam in Malaysia
constitutionalism 31–33
authoritarian, *see* authoritarian constitutionalism
Constitutions as 'frameworks' for governance 78–80, 91
courts' role 4
constitutional statecraft, *see* constitutional statecraft by Asian courts
judicial review, *see* judicial review
liberal constitutionalism 32
rights protection, *see* rights protection
rule of law, *see* rule of law
separation of powers, *see* separation of powers
constitutional politics in Malaysia:
constitutional amendment to restrict judicial review, *see* constitutional amendment to restrict judicial review, Malaysia (1988)
judicial crisis (1988) 57–58, 95
rights discourse, *see* rights discourse in post-colonial Asia, in Malaysia
security-based laws to restrict judicial review 146–47, 194–95, 199, 200–1, 211–12
see also separation of powers
constitutional politics in Singapore:
constitutional amendment to restrict judicial review (1988) 8, 59–60, 110–11, 118–19
rights discourse 26–27, 28, 30–31
security-based laws to restrict judicial review 60, 110–11, 118, 146–47, 199, 211–12
see also separation of powers
constitutional rights protection, *see* rights protection
constitutional statecraft by Asian courts 9–12, 17, 123–24, 133–40, 153–54
development of 15–17, 120–21, 219
judicial perspectives on 45
mechanisms 140–53
basic structure doctrine, *see* basic structure doctrine

constitutional statecraft by Asian courts (*cont.*)
proportionality analysis, *see* proportionality analysis
purposive constitutional interpretation, *see* purposive constitutional interpretation
religious freedom cases in Malaysia, *see* religious freedom in Malaysia
rights discourse, *see* rights discourse in post-colonial Asia
security cases, *see* security-based restrictions of rights, constitutional statecraft to remedy
Semenyih Jaya case (FC Mal), statecraft of ruling 121
Marbury tactics 103, 133–37
prospective overruling remedy 103
strong-form judicial review advocated 42–44, 128–32, 147
see also judicial review in Malaysia; judicial review in Singapore
Constitution of Malaysia, *see* Federal Constitution of Malaysia (1957)
Constitution of Singapore, *see* Singapore Constitution (1965)
constructive constitutional role of Asian courts 4, 123, 132
conversion from Islam (apostasy) in Malaysia 167–71, 173, 175–76, 177–78, 179, 181–83
corporal punishment in Singapore 48–49, 88–89
courts, Asian, *see* Asian courts
cultural relativism 22–23
Asian values discourse, *see* rights discourse in post-colonial Asia

'dead hand' critique of originalist constitutional interpretation 80–81
death penalty in Singapore 51
Yong Vui Kong case, see *Yong Vui Kong v. Public Prosecutor* (CA Sing)
democracy:
aspiring democracies, *see* aspiring democracies
as rule of law component 108–9
detention without trial, *see* preventive detention
dialogic (weak-form) judicial review 42, 45, 127, 128, 129–31, 181–82
Diplock, Lord Kenneth 45n76
discretionary powers:
justiciability, Singaporean rulings 59–60, 64–65, 118
Chng Suan Tze case, see *Chng Suan Tze v. Minister of Home Affairs* (CA Sing)
Tan Seet Eng case, see *Tan Seet Eng v. Attorney General* (HC Sing)
of Singaporean Parliament 51
of Singaporean President 40, 41n46, 88, 191
divorce in Malaysia, *see* religious freedom in Malaysia, marriage and divorce
Dixon, Rosalind 103, 133, 137n84
Dworkin, Ronald 4, 209

Ely, John Hart 3–4n13, 145
emergency powers 16–17, 61, 189, 190–92, 210–11
emerging democracies, *see* aspiring democracies
Epps, Charles 29–30
equal protection clause, Malaysian Constitution 44, 50, 112–13, 114, 162–63
establishment clause, Malaysian Constitution, *see* Islam in Malaysia
European Convention on Human Rights 1950 23, 24, 51–52, 87, 206

fair trial rights, *see* right to life and liberty
fake news prohibitions:
Malaysia 189, 195–96, 217–18
Singapore 129–30, 189–90, 197
Farber, Daniel A. 125n5
fatwa councils and Sharia advisory bodies in Malaysia 183–84
Federal Constitution of Malaysia (1957) 6
amendment powers 8, 38, 59, 80–81, 128–29
drafting history 36–37, 70–75, 82–83, 87, 158, 159–63, 191
emergency powers 16–17, 61, 189, 190–92, 210–11
establishment clause, *see* Islam in Malaysia
interpretation of, *see* constitutional interpretation, in Malaysia and Singapore
post-colonial narrative of 7, 31, 79
rights protection 37–38, 45
equal protection clause 44, 50, 112–13, 114, 162–63
supremacy clause 37–38, 42, 44–45, 113
Federal Court of Malaysia 38
Fernando, Joseph 69, 74, 83–84n85, 83–84n88, 161n24
foreign law applicability 46–49
formalist and literalist constitutional interpretation 49–53
'four walls' approach to constitutional interpretation 46–49
fragile democracies, *see* aspiring democracies
Frankenberg, Günter 23
Frankfurter, Felix 91n146
freedom of association and assembly:
political demonstrations, Malaysia 27–28, 29–30, 62–63, 218

security-based restrictions, *see* security-based restrictions of rights
Sivarasa Rasiah case, see *Sivarasa Rasiah v. Badan Peguam Malaysia & Anor.* (FC Mal)
freedom of expression:
constitutional restrictions 205–6
media restrictions, *see* media restrictions
religious expression, Malaysia 25, 173–75, 178–79, 185, 186, 187
security-based restrictions, *see* security based restrictions of rights
freedom of religion:
in Malaysia, *see* religious freedom in Malaysia
in Singapore 77–78, 158n5
Fukuyama, Francis 26n35
Fuller, Lon 108

Ghai, Yash 23–24
Ginsburg, Tom 17n68, 32, 48n77
Gopal Sri Ram 102
Greene, Jamal 152–53n193, 209n143

Hailsham, Lord Quintin 94
Hamid, Abdul 71–72, 82, 160–61
Harding, Andrew 56–57n176, 58, 72, 74n25
heads of state:
Malaysian King, see *Yang di-Pertuan Agong* (Malaysian King)
Singapore President 40, 41n46, 88, 89, 191
Hirschl, Ran 10n45, 12n56
history, constitutional, *see* constitutional history
Hsieh, Hsiang-Yang 3–4n11, 9n44, 130, 132n53, 132n56, 145n141, 145n143
human rights protection, *see* rights protection

illiberal democracies, *see* authoritarian constitutionalism
India:
basic structure doctrine 53, 55, 80–81, 101, 103–4, 124, 133, 139–40, 143
mandatory death penalty 90
Indira Gandhi a/p Mutho v. Pengarah Jabatan Agama Islam Perak & Ors. (FC Mal) 30, 66, 113–14, 124, 137–38, 157, 187–88
basic structure doctrine endorsed 9, 55, 56–57, 63, 85, 107–8, 115–16, 117, 121, 138–40, 142, 146, 180, 185
civil courts' jurisdiction over Sharia courts affirmed 16, 114–15, 116–17, 120, 138–39, 171–73, 180
constitutional statecraft of ruling 121
Lina Joy case (FC Mal) distinguished 173, 179, 181
purposive constitutional interpretation endorsed 63, 114, 148–49, 186
religious freedom declared foundational principle 85–86, 143, 145
religious upbringing of children, equal rights of both parents 47, 63, 114, 138, 148–49, 172, 186
rule of law conception 15, 108, 115–16, 120, 122, 142–43
transnational norms, applicability 47, 85–86, 148
individualist rights discourse 24–25, 42
inhuman or degrading treatment or punishment:
capital punishment, Singapore 51
Yong Vui Kong case, see *Yong Vui Kong v. Public Prosecutor* (CA Sing)
corporal punishment, Singapore 48–49, 88–89
Islamic criminal punishments *(hudud)* in Kelantin state, Malaysia 181–82
internal security protection, *see* security-based restrictions of rights
international norms applicability 46–49
Islam in Malaysia:
Egypt and Iraq distinguished 84n91
as ethno-political issue 158–59, 160, 163–65, 218
Malay people defined as Muslims 163, 169, 177–78
Islamic banking 184
Islamic criminal punishments *(hudud)* in Kelantan state, Malaysia 181–82
as official state religion 7, 14, 44, 70, 158
drafting of establishment clause 73, 82–83, 158, 159–63
'judicial Islamization' of establishment clause 173–79, 184–85
originalist interpretation of establishment clause 81–86, 160–62, 164–65, 185
purposive interpretation of establishment clause 184–86
religious freedom cases, *see* religious freedom in Malaysia
Sharia courts, *see* Sharia (Syariah) courts in Malaysia
Sharia fatwa councils and advisory bodies 183–84
Issacharoff, Samuel 103, 133, 137n84

Jackson, Vicki 49
Jacobsohn, Gary 165–66n54
Jennings, Sir Ivor 71–72, 78–79, 91
judicial independence 45
as basic structure element of constitutions, *see* basic structure doctrine
judicial appointments, Malaysia 59
judicial crisis, Malaysia (1988) 57–58, 95

judicialization of religion, *see* religious freedom in Malaysia
judicial power:
  in Malaysia, *see* judicial review in Malaysia
  in Singapore, *see* judicial review in Singapore
  strategic use of, *see* constitutional statecraft by Asian courts
judicial review:
  in aspiring democracies, *see* aspiring democracies, judicial review in
  in authoritarian regimes 5
  constitutional interpretation, *see* constitutional interpretation
  judicial role
    constitutional statecraft, *see* constitutional statecraft by Asian courts
    different scholarly perspectives 4–5, 8
  in Malaysia, *see* judicial review in Malaysia
  in Singapore, *see* judicial review in Singapore
  strong-form, *see* strong-form judicial review
  weak-form (dialogic) 42, 45, 127, 128, 129–31, 181–82
judicial review in Malaysia 13, 34, 38, 65–66
  assertive approach
    civil courts' authority over Sharia institutions advocated 182–84
    emerging assertiveness 62–64, 105–6
    Indira Gandhi case, see *Indira Gandhi a/p Mutho v. Pengarah Jabatan Agama Islam Perak & Ors.* (FC Mal)
    security cases 200–3
    Semenyih Jaya case, see *Semenyih Jaya v. Pentadbir Tanah Daerah Hulu Langat* (FC Mal)
    strong-form review advocated 42–44, 128–32, 147
  basis, judicial pronouncements on 112–13
  civil courts' relations with Sharia courts, *see* Sharia (Syariah) courts in Malaysia
  constitutional amendment to restrict (1988), *see* constitutional amendment to restrict judicial review, Malaysia (1988)
  constitutional interpretation, *see* constitutional interpretation, in Malaysia and Singapore
  deferential approach (pre-2017) 7–8, 28, 41–42, 96–98, 200
    civil courts' deference to Sharia courts, *see* Sharia (Syariah) courts in Malaysia
  legislative review 44–45
  public interest litigation 30
  religious freedom cases, *see* religious freedom in Malaysia
  rule of law, connection with 15, 108, 113, 115–16, 120, 122, 142–43
  security-based laws to restrict 146–47, 194–95, 199, 200–1, 211–12
  separation of powers, connection with 100, 101, 104, 116, 135, 142
  see also constitutional statecraft by Asian courts
judicial review in Singapore 13, 34, 65
  assertive approach
    emerging assertiveness 9, 105–6
    strong-form review advocated 42–44, 128–32, 147
  constitutional amendment to restrict (1988) 8, 59–60, 110–11, 118–19
  constitutional interpretation, *see* constitutional interpretation, in Malaysia and Singapore
  deferential approach 7–8, 28, 41–42, 65
  discretionary powers, justiciability rulings 59–60, 64–65
    Chng Suan Tze case, see *Chng Suan Tze v. Minister of Home Affairs* (CA Sing)
    Tan Seet Eng case, see *Tan Seet Eng v. Attorney General* (HC Sing)
  legislative review 44–45
  public interest litigation 10–11n48, 30–31
  rule of law, connection with 113
  security-based laws to restrict 60, 110–11, 118, 146–47, 199, 211–12
  see also constitutional statecraft by Asian courts
judicial supremacy 46, 131, 139n98

Kavanagh, Aileen 128, 130–31
Kellogg, Thomas 32n72
Kesavananda Bharati v. State of Kerala (SC, India) 53, 55, 80–81, 101, 103–4, 133, 143n127
King of Malaysia, see *Yang di-Pertuan Agong* (Malaysian King)
Kok Wah Kuan case (FC Mal) 46–47, 49–50, 96–98, 99, 100, 102, 109–10, 134
Kumarasingham, Harshan 70–71

Landau, David 59, 94, 126, 136n82
Law, David S. 3–4n11, 9n44, 130, 132n53, 132n56, 145n141, 145n143
Lee, H.P. 129–30n46, 141
Lee, Jack Tsen-Ta 111–12n42
Lee Hsien Loong 31, 66n250
Lee Kuan Yew 22–23, 24, 26, 39, 75, 88
legality principle, *see* principle of legality
Levinson, Sanford 79
liberal constitutionalism 32
Lina Joy v. Majlis Agama Islam (FC Mal) 28n48, 167–70, 175, 176, 177–78, 182–83

distinguished in *Indira Gandhi* case (FC Mal) 173, 179, 181
literalist and formalist constitutional interpretation 49–53
Locke, John 93
LoyarBurok (Malaysian Centre for Constitutionalism and Human Rights) 30

MacGillivray, Sir Donald 71–72, 73
McKell, Sir William 71–72
Madison, James 69, 93–94
Mahathir Mohamad 1–2, 92, 217–18
Asian values discourse 22–23, 24, 26
declaration that Malaysia is an Islamic state (2001) 164
judicial crisis (1988), role in 57–59, 95
judicial review restriction (1988), statement justifying 96
see also Barisan Nasional coalition, Malaysia
Malanjum, Richard 97–98, 170, 182–83, 184, 217–18n26
Malayan Emergency (1948-60) 191–92
Malay people, special position protection:
in Malaysia 36–37, 38, 73
Malay people defined as Muslims 163, 169, 177–78
in Singapore 77–78
see also Islam in Malaysia
Malaysia:
authoritarian constitutionalism (pre-2018) 32, 33
rights discourse, *see* rights discourse in post-colonial Asia, in Malaysia
single party dominance, *see* Barisan Nasional coalition, Malaysia
civil society in 29–30
colonial history 6, 35–37
common law legal system 6–7, 112–13
Constitution, *see* Federal Constitution of Malaysia (1957)
constitutional system
federal structure 37n6, 37
Islam, status of, *see* Islam in Malaysia
King, see *Yang di-Pertuan Agong* (Malaysian King)
Westminster parliamentary system 6–7, 37, 94
courts 8, 38
democratic transition (2018-) 1–3, 5–6, 17, 30, 33, 65–66, 153–54, 217–19
Pakatan Harapan coalition, *see* Pakatan Harapan coalition, Malaysia
foundation as sovereign state 6–7, 14
constitutional narrative 7, 31, 79
drafting of Constitution 36–37, 70–75, 82–83, 87, 158, 159–63, 191
Malayan Emergency (1948-60) 191–92
judicial review, *see* judicial review in Malaysia
rights protection, *see* rights protection
rule of law, *see* rule of law, in Malaysia
Malaysiakini (online news service, Malaysia) 29
Malaysian Bar Association 29–30
Malaysian Centre for Constitutionalism and Human Rights (LoyarBurok) 30
Malik, Bidhubhushan 71–72
mandatory death penalty in Singapore 51
Yong Vui Kong case, see *Yong Vui Kong v. Public Prosecutor* (CA Sing)
Marbury v. Madison (SC United States) 44–45, 103, 104, 120, 123–24, 133
Semenyih Jaya case (FC Mal), *Marbury* tactics 103, 133–37
marriage in Malaysia, *see* religious freedom in Malaysia, marriage and divorce
Marshall, David 76
Mathews, Jud 149–50, 152–53, 206
Mat Shuhaimi bin Shafiei case (FC Mal) 50–51, 151, 202, 207–8
media restrictions:
book bans, Malaysia 178–79, 187
fake news prohibitions
Malaysia 189, 195–96, 217–18
Singapore 129–30, 189–90, 197
journalists placed in preventive detention, Malaysia (2008) 193
libel suits against political opponents, Singapore 196–97
online news media, Malaysia 29
Menon, Sundaresh 27
Menteri Dalam Negeri & Ors. v. Titular Roman Catholic Archbishop of Kuala Lumpur ('Allah' case) (CA Mal) 25, 173–75, 179, 185, 186, 187
Merdeka Constitution of Malaysia, *see* Federal Constitution of Malaysia (1957)
Montesquieu 92, 93
Moustafa, Tamir 10–11n46, 173

Najib Razak 1–2, 27–28, 29, 164, 189, 194, 217–18
National Security Council, Malaysia 129–30, 189
national security protection, *see* security-based restrictions of rights
Nelson, Matthew J. 182–83
Neo, Jaclyn 31, 119, 144–45
on basic structure doctrine in Singapore 56, 136, 139
on proportionality analysis in Singapore 9n40, 208–9, 209n144

Nik Nazmi bin Nik Ahmad v. Public Prosecutor (CA Mal) 62–63, 98, 201, 206–7

Okoth-Ogendo, H.W.O. 7n26
originalist constitutional interpretation 70
  Constitutions as original 'frameworks' 78–80, 91
  'dead hand' critique 80–81
  establishment clause of Malaysian Constitution, originalist interpretation 81–86, 160–62, 164–65, 185
  in United States 81–82
  in *Yong Vui Kong* case (CA Sing) 51–52, 86–91

Pakatan Harapan coalition, Malaysia:
  electoral victory (May 2018) 1, 30, 65
  religious pluralism promise 165
  security laws relaxation promise 189–90, 196, 203, 217–18
parliamentary supremacy principle (Diceyan model) 42, 44–45, 94, 112
Parti Islam Se-Malaysia (Malaysian Islamic Party) 218
People's Action Party, Singapore 5, 8n29, 33, 34, 39, 59, 75, 94
  constitutional amendments 128–29
  democratic transition by regime, early signs 31, 66n250, 205n110
  rule of law and rights protection, perspective on 27
Perikatan Nasional coalition, Malaysia 33, 219
Petersen, Niels 149n166
political demonstrations in Malaysia 27–28, 29–30, 62–63
politicization of religion in Malaysia, *see* Islam in Malaysia, as ethno-political issue
populism 17
post-colonial Asia:
  constitutional narratives
    Malaysian Constitution 7, 31, 79
    Singapore Constitution 7, 39–40
  courts in, *see* Asian courts
  democratization experiences 214–15, 216–17
  judicial review 11
    Malaysia, *see* judicial review in Malaysia
    Singapore, *see* judicial review in Singapore
  rights discourse, *see* rights discourse in post-colonial Asia
  see also aspiring democracies
President of Singapore 40, 41n46, 88, 89, 191
preventive detention:
  in Malaysia 61, 129–30, 189, 192–95, 210
    anti-terrorist purposes 189, 193, 194–95
    judicial review of detentions ousted 146–47, 194–95, 199, 200–1, 211–12
  in Singapore 192–93, 196
    anti-terrorist purposes 193–94
    Chng Suan Tze case, see *Chng Suan Tze v. Minister of Home Affairs* (CA Sing)
    judicial review of detentions ousted 60, 110–11, 118, 146–47, 199, 211–12
    Tan Seet Eng case, see *Tan Seet Eng v. Attorney General* (HC Sing)
  see also security-based restrictions of rights
principle of legality:
  constitutional interpretation in line with 146
  judicial endorsements
    Chng Suan Tze case (CA Sing) 9, 59–60, 64–65, 110, 117–18, 119, 198–99, 208–9
    Tan Seet Eng case (CA Sing) 9, 15, 107–8, 118–19, 120, 203–4, 208–9
  other Singaporean rulings 59–60, 64–65, 118
  proportionality analysis, connection with 208–9
  see also rule of law
proportionality analysis 4, 23, 124, 149–53, 216–17
  judicial endorsements
    Alma Nudo case (FC Mal), three-stage test 64, 151–52, 207, 216–17
    Azmi Sharom case (FC Mal) 151, 202, 206–7
    Sivarasa Rasiah case (FC Mal) 62, 150–51, 206–7
  principle of legality, connection with 208–9
  religious freedom cases in Malaysia 187
  'rights as trumps' approach compared 209
  security cases 16–17, 151, 190, 202, 204–10
  Singaporean resistance to 149–50, 152, 208, 217
protective constitutional role of Asian courts 3–4, 123, 132
Ptolemy, Claudius 35
public interest litigation:
  in Malaysia 30
  in Singapore 10–11n48, 30–31
public order protection, *see* security-based restrictions of rights
Public Prosecutor v. Azmi Sharom (FC Mal), see *Azmi Sharom* case (FC Mal)
Public Prosecutor v. Kok Wah Kuan (FC Mal) 46–47, 49–50, 96–98, 99, 100, 102, 109–10, 134
purposive constitutional interpretation 4, 124, 147–49
  judicial endorsements
    Indira Gandhi case (FC Mal) 63, 114, 148–49, 186
    Sivarasa Rasiah case (FC Mal) 50, 62, 147–48
  religious freedom cases in Malaysia 184–86
  strict formalism and literalism distinguished 49–53

Raffles, Sir Stamford 39
Raja Azlan Shah 81
Rajah, Jothie 109, 109n21
Rajah, V.K. 30–31
Raz, Joseph 108–9
Reid Commission 36–37, 51–52, 71–73, 74–75, 87, 191
  role in drafting religious establishment clause 82–83, 159–61, 162
relativism 22–23
  Asian values discourse, *see* rights discourse in post-colonial Asia
religious freedom in Malaysia 10–11, 12, 16, 25, 158–59, 162–63
  apostasy cases 167–71, 173, 175–76, 177–78, 179, 181–83
  children, religious upbringing and custody 162–63, 166–67, 171, 172, 177
    equal rights of both parents (*Indira Gandhi* ruling) 47, 63, 114, 138, 148–49, 172, 186
  civil courts' relations with Sharia courts, *see* Sharia (Syariah) courts in Malaysia
  constitutional establishment clause, originalist interpretation 81–86, 160–62, 164–65, 185
  constitutional statecraft in religious freedom cases 179–80, 188
    basic structure doctrine 180–84
    proportionality analysis 187
    purposive constitutional interpretation 184–86
  as foundational principle (*Indira Gandhi* ruling) 85–86, 143, 145
  freedom of religious expression 25, 173–75, 178–79, 185, 186, 187
  'judicial Islamization' of establishment clause 173–79, 184–85
  marriage and divorce
    Islamic law applied by civil courts 176–77
    Lina Joy case, see *Lina Joy v. Majlis Agama Islam* (FC Mal)
  proportionality analysis 16
  state secularism, early cases endorsing 165–79
  see also Islam in Malaysia
religious freedom in Singapore 77–78, 158n5
rights discourse in post-colonial Asia 13, 21–22, 33
  constitutional narratives
    Malaysian Constitution 7, 31, 79
    Singapore Constitution 7, 39–40
  false dichotomies
    civil-political rights and economic development 25–26
    individualism and communitarianism 24–25, 42, 193
    universalism and relativism 22–24
  in Malaysia
    under Barisan Nasional regime 27–28
    emerging rights consciousness 28–30
    'judicial Islamization' 173–79, 184–85
  in Singapore 26–27, 28, 30–31
rights protection:
  discourse on, *see* rights discourse in post-colonial Asia
  under Federal Constitution of Malaysia 37–38, 45
    equal protection clause 44, 50, 112–13, 114, 162–63
  freedom of association and assembly, *see* freedom of association and assembly
  freedom of expression, *see* freedom of expression
  inhuman treatment, *see* inhuman or degrading treatment or punishment
  Malay people, special position, *see* Malay people, special position protection
  mechanisms
    proportionality analysis, *see* proportionality analysis
    purposive constitutional interpretation, *see* purposive constitutional interpretation
  religious freedom
    in Malaysia, *see* religious freedom in Malaysia
    in Singapore 77–78, 158n5
  'rights as trumps' approach 209
  right to life and liberty, *see* right to life and liberty
  rule of law, connection with 108–9, 121–22
  security-based rights restrictions, *see* security-based restrictions of rights
  under Singapore Constitution 39–40, 41, 45, 77–78
right to life and liberty 206
  access to justice right, Malaysia 50, 109–10, 147–48
  capital punishment, Singapore 51
    Yong Vui Kong case, see *Yong Vui Kong v. Public Prosecutor* (CA Sing)
  double presumption against accused drug traffickers, Malaysia, see *Alma Nudo v. Public Prosecutor* (FC Mal)
  legal counsel right, Singapore 51
  preventive detention, *see* preventive detention; *Tan Seet Eng v. Attorney General* (HC Sing)
  same-sex relationships, Singapore 48
  security-based restrictions of rights, *see* security-based restrictions of rights
Roznai, Yaniv 141–42, 143n127, 145–46

rule of law 15, 107–8
authoritarian model, *see* authoritarian constitutionalism
as basic structure element of constitutions, *see* basic structure doctrine
components, scholarly views 108–9
in Malaysia 109–10
basis of doctrine, judicial pronouncements 112–13
judicial review, connection with 15, 108, 113, 115–16, 120, 122, 142–43; see also *Indira Gandhi a/p Mutho v. Pengarah Jabatan Agama Islam Perak & Ors.* (FC Mal)
rights protection, connection with 121–22
principle of legality, *see* principle of legality
rule *by* law distinguished 109
in Singapore 15, 32, 107, 109, 110
Chng Suan Tze case, see *Chng Suan Tze v. Minister of Home Affairs* (CA Sing)
discretionary powers, rulings on justiciability 59–60, 64–65, 118
Tan Seet case, see *Tan Seet Eng v. Attorney General* (HC Sing)
unconstitutional constitutional amendments, *see* unconstitutional constitutional amendments

same-sex relationships, Singapore 48
Saunders, Cheryl 49
Scalia, Antonin 52
secularism:
in Malaysia
early cases endorsing 165–79
as original intention of Constitution (disputed) 81–84, 160–62, 164–65, 185
in Singapore 77–78, 158n5
see also Islam in Malaysia
security-based restrictions of rights 16–17, 51, 52–53, 61, 189–90, 212–13
anti-sedition laws, *see* anti-sedition laws
communitarian rights discourse 24–25, 42, 193
constitutional restrictions of freedom of expression right 205–6
constitutional statecraft to remedy
basic structure doctrine 210–12
proportionality analysis 16–17, 151, 190, 202, 204–10
emergency powers 16–17, 61, 189, 190–92, 210–11
judicial review, security laws to restrict
in Malaysia 146–47, 194–95, 199, 200–1, 211–12
in Singapore 60, 110–11, 118, 146–47, 199, 211–12
judicial review of rights restrictions 197–98
Chng Suan Tze case, see *Chng Suan Tze v. Minister of Home Affairs* (CA Sing)
in Malaysia 200–3
Tan Seet Eng case, see *Tan Seet Eng v. Attorney General* (HC Sing)
media restrictions, *see* media restrictions
National Security Council, Malaysia 129–30, 189
under Pakatan Harapan coalition regime, Malaysia 189–90, 196, 203, 217–18
preventive detention, *see* preventive detention
sedition laws, *see* anti-sedition laws
Semenyih Jaya v. Pentadbir Tanah Daerah Hulu Langat (FC Mal) 41n49, 66, 98–104, 124
background (1988 constitutional amendment to restrict judicial review) 8, 60–61, 92, 95–96, 134
basic structure doctrine endorsed 9, 54, 56–57, 63, 92–93, 101, 103–4, 121, 135, 139–40
constitutional statecraft of ruling 121
Marbury tactics 103, 133–37
prospective overruling remedy 103, 137
critical responses 102–4, 136
separation of powers conception 100, 101, 104, 116, 135
significance of ruling 14, 54, 56–57, 93, 106, 136
Sen, Amartya 26
separation of powers 14, 46, 92–93, 142
in authoritarian regimes 94
as basic structure element of constitutions, *see* basic structure doctrine
judicial independence, *see* judicial independence
judicial review restricted, Malaysia (1988), *see* constitutional amendment to restrict judicial review, Malaysia (1988)
judicial review restricted, Singapore (1988) 8, 59–60, 110–11, 118–19
parliamentary supremacy principle (Diceyan model) 42, 44–45, 94, 112
Semenyih Jaya case (FC Mal), separation of powers conception 100, 101, 104, 116, 135
strong-form judicial review, *see* strong-form judicial review
in United States 93–94
Shad Saleem Faruqi 134, 164–65n49
Shah, Dian 79, 159–60n12, 182–83
Shanmugam, K. 27, 107

Sharia (Syariah) courts in Malaysia 38, 84, 163
civil courts' deference to 167, 182–83
Islamic law applied by civil courts 176–77
Lina Joy case, see *Lina Joy v. Majlis Agama Islam* (FC Mal)
civil courts' jurisdiction over
advocated 182–84
Indira Gandhi ruling on 16, 114–15, 116–17, 120, 138–39, 171–73, 180
dialogic approach by civil courts
proposal 181–82
judicial review immunity (1988 constitutional amendment) 114–15, 138–39
Indira Gandhi case invalidating, see *Indira Gandhi a/p Mutho v. Pengarah Jabatan Agama Islam Perak & Ors.* (FC Mal)
shared jurisdiction with civil courts
proposal 181
see also Islam in Malaysia
Sharia (Syariah) fatwa councils and advisory bodies in Malaysia 183–84
Shariff, Mohamed Ismail 164–65n47
Sherry, Suzanna 125n5
Silverstein, Gordon 109n24, 111–12
Simpser, Alberto 32
Singapore:
authoritarian constitutionalism 5, 12, 32, 107
rights discourse 26–27, 28, 30–31
single party dominance, *see* People's Action Party, Singapore
colonial history 6, 35–37, 39
common law legal system 6–7
Constitution, *see* Singapore Constitution (1965)
constitutional system
President 40, 41n46, 88, 89, 191
secularism 77–78, 158n5
Westminster parliamentary system 6–7, 40, 94
courts 41
foundation as sovereign state 6–7, 14, 39, 75–76
constitutional narrative 7, 39–40
drafting of Constitution 76–78, 87–88, 89
judicial review, *see* judicial review in Singapore
rights discourse 26–27, 28, 30–31
rights protection, *see* rights protection
rule of law, *see* rule of law, in Singapore
Singapore Constitution (1965) 7
amendment powers 8, 41, 59, 77, 78, 80–81, 105, 128–29
drafting history 76–78, 87–88, 89
emergency powers 16–17, 61, 190–92
interpretation of, *see* constitutional interpretation, in Malaysia and Singapore
post-colonial narrative of 7, 39–40
rights protection 39–40, 41, 45, 77–78
supremacy clause 41, 42, 44–45, 77, 106, 113
Sivarasa Rasiah v. Badan Peguam Malaysia & Anor. (FC Mal):
basic structure doctrine endorsed *(obiter dicta)* 54, 62, 141
'prismatic' purposive constitutional interpretation advocated 50, 62, 147–48
proportionality analysis 62, 150–51, 206–7
social media 29
fake news prohibitions
Malaysia 189, 195–96, 217–18
Singapore 129–30, 189–90, 197
South Africa 11, 50, 62, 113, 149, 214
southeast Asia, *see* Malaysia; post-colonial Asia; Singapore
statecraft by Asian courts, *see* constitutional statecraft by Asian courts
Stone Sweet, Alec 149–50, 152–53, 206
strict formalist and literalist constitutional interpretation 49–53
strong-form judicial review 3–4, 8, 11
arguments for 42–44, 128–31, 147
judicial supremacy distinguished 46, 131
in Malaysia and Singapore 120
Indira Gandhi case, see *Indira Gandhi a/p Mutho v. Pengarah Jabatan Agama Islam Perak & Ors.* (FC Mal)
rejected in favour of deferential approach 28, 41–42, 96–98
Semenyih Jaya case, see *Semenyih Jaya v. Pentadbir Tanah Daerah Hulu Langat* (FC Mal)
uneven path towards 62–65, 105–6
Marbury v. Madison (SC United States) 44–45, 103, 104, 120, 123–24, 133
Semenyih Jaya case (FC Mal), *Marbury* tactics 103, 133–37
scholarly debate on 45–46, 125–26
aspiring democracies considered 126–27, 128–30
see also constitutional statecraft by Asian courts; separation of powers
Subramaniam, Surain 27
subversion laws, *see* anti-sedition laws
supremacy clauses:
Malaysian Constitution 37–38, 42, 44–45, 113
Singapore Constitution 41, 42, 44–45, 77, 106, 113
Syariah (Sharia) courts in Malaysia, *see* Sharia (Syariah) courts in Malaysia
Syariah (Sharia) fatwa councils and advisory bodies in Malaysia 183–84

Tan, Kevin 56, 76–77, 199n68
Tan Seet Eng v. Attorney General (HC Sing) 64, 107–8
  Chng Suan Tze ruling (CA Sing) applied 204
  principle of legality endorsed 9, 15, 107–8, 118–19, 120, 203–4, 208–9
Tay, Wilson 102, 103–4, 136
Tengku Maimun Tuan Mat 217–18n26
Teo Soh Lung v. Minister of Home Affairs (CA Sing) 60, 111–12, 200; see also *Chng Suan Tze v. Minister of Home Affairs* (CA Sing)
terrorist suspects, preventive detention 189, 193–95
Tham, Cindy 8n31
Thio, Li-ann 32, 41n47, 48n96, 75, 76–77, 91, 109n21
Thiruvengadam, Arun 48
Thomas, Tommy 74n25
torture prohibition, *see* inhuman or degrading treatment or punishment
transitional democracies, *see* aspiring democracies
transnational norms applicability 46–49
Tunku Abdul Rahman 36, 71–72, 73–74, 82–83, 161, 192
Tun Salleh Abas 58
Tushnet, Mark 32, 125–26, 193

unconstitutional constitutional amendments 3–4, 15, 128–29
  basic structure doctrine use to strike down, *see* basic structure doctrine
  judicial review restricted by, Malaysia (1988), *see* constitutional amendment to restrict judicial review, Malaysia (1988)
  judicial review restricted by, Singapore (1988) 8, 59–60, 110–11, 118–19, 199, 211–12
  Royal Assent power removed, Malaysia 210–11, 212
  security cases 16–17
  to Singapore President's powers 41n46
  see also rule of law
United Kingdom:
  colonial history of Malaysia and Singapore 6, 35–37, 39
  parliamentary supremacy principle (Diceyan model) 42, 44–45, 94, 112
  weak-form (dialogic) judicial review 42, 45, 127, 128, 129–31
United States:
  constitutional amendment powers 80–81
  constitutional interpretation 52, 81–82
  judicial review *(Marbury v. Madison)* 44–45, 103, 104, 120, 123–24, 133
  separation of powers 93–94
universal rights discourse 22
  in post-colonial Asia, *see* rights discourse in post-colonial Asia

Varughese, George 136
Vile, M.J.C. 94n14

Waldron, Jeremy 46n79, 108, 125–26
Wallace, Alfred Russel 6
weak-form (dialogic) judicial review 42, 45, 127, 128, 129–31, 181–82
Wee Chong Jin Commission 76–77, 87–88, 89
Welsh, Bridget 2–3n9
Westminster parliamentary systems:
  in Malaysia and Singapore 6–7, 37, 40, 94
  parliamentary supremacy principle (Diceyan model) 42, 44–45, 94, 112
Whittington, Keith E. 81–82n78

Yang di-Pertuan Agong (Malaysian King) 37, 38n24, 43–44, 83–84, 191
  Royal Assent power, constitutional amendment to remove 210–11, 212
Yap, Po Jen 52–53, 91, 128–30, 144–45, 181–82
Yeh, Jiunn-rong 33n78
Yong Vui Kong v. Public Prosecutor (CA Sing) 78
  basic structure doctrine endorsed 55–56, 88–89, 105–6, 145–46
  originalist constitutional interpretation in 51–52, 86–91
  Presidential power of clemency 88
  transnational norms, applicability 48–49

Zakaria, Fareed 24, 32